# DATA PRIVACY LAW

# Data Privacy Law

*An International Perspective*

LEE A. BYGRAVE

OXFORD
UNIVERSITY PRESS

# OXFORD
UNIVERSITY PRESS

Great Clarendon Street, Oxford, OX2 6DP,
United Kingdom

Oxford University Press is a department of the University of Oxford.
It furthers the University's objective of excellence in research, scholarship,
and education by publishing worldwide. Oxford is a registered trade mark of
Oxford University Press in the UK and in certain other countries

Published in the United States of America by Oxford University Press
198 Madison Avenue, New York, NY 10016, United States of America

British Library Cataloguing in Publication Data
Data available

Library of Congress Control Number: 2013946837

ISBN 978-0-19-967555-5

Printed in Great Britain by
CPI Group (UK) Ltd, Croydon, CR0 4YY

# Preface

Almost 25 years have passed since I began conducting research in the field of data privacy law. During that period, the field has burgeoned in multiple respects—the number of regulatory instruments embraced by it, their global spread, level of density, normative status, and practical impact on organizational processes. Data privacy law is no longer a niche subject attracting the interest of a small number of scholars, policy entrepreneurs, and legal practitioners. It now boasts a large amount of jurisprudence and scholarship, and forms a staple of many practitioners' professed competence. These developments reflect the continuing maturation of our 'information society' in which personal data is increasingly regarded as a valuable resource in itself and exploited accordingly.

The field's growth has been especially pronounced over the last ten years. My earlier monograph in the field—*Data Protection Law: Approaching Its Rationale, Logic and Limits*—was published in 2002. While its depiction of the origins, purposes, and mechanics of data privacy law is still fairly accurate, it fails to take adequate account of the numerous developments in the field during the last decade. Surprisingly, no other book has been published—at least in English—taking account of those developments and offering the same transnational overview of the field as offered by my earlier book. I hope that this new book will go a substantial way towards filling this gap.

The book is primarily intended for legal practitioners and scholars who wish to acquire understanding of the core principles and mechanics of data privacy law from a cross-jurisdictional perspective. It is not intended to be a handbook for practitioners. Thus, it does not provide, for instance, detailed advice on compliance strategies. It tackles, nonetheless, many points of law that trouble practitioners as much as legal scholars. An example is the meaning of 'personal data'—a festering issue that is crucial for determining the application of most data privacy law.

The book is also intended to be suitable as a textbook for teaching university students. It ought to function more suitably as a general introduction to the field than my 2002 book does. The latter bears the bane of having been closely based on a doctoral thesis and devoting a large number of pages to the issue of whether or not data privacy law ought to cover data on collective entities. Although far from trivial in principle, that issue is usually of marginal interest to newcomers to the field and, indeed, to those already working in it.

In this book, I have tried to keep the presentation succinct yet sensitive to the intricacies of the field. Thus, the text presents the basic bones of the regulatory framework supplemented by references to more elaborate analyses of, say, fissures in those bones. At the same time, the book does not have any large 'bone to pick'. In other words, it does not have the advancement of a particular argument as its basic remit. Its broad thrust is descriptive. This does not mean that it steers clear of controversy or that its descriptive endeavour is free of bias. I am sympathetic to the primary aims of data privacy law. I believe that the privacy-related interests it is intended to protect are far from being anachronisms. Yet I am critical of its potential for regulatory overreaching—that is, its potential for being applied so broadly that it stands scant chance of being enforced. My stance on these matters colours the book's presentation of the field.

Revised editions of the book are planned for publication at regular intervals. The intention is to establish an international standard text that remains reasonably current. The currency of this edition is likely to be short-lived. Significant changes to the legal landscape are afoot, particularly with the European Union in the throes of revising its regulatory framework for data privacy. As this book is being finalized, some of the general contours of the Union's revised framework have become visible but consensus has yet to be reached on many of the details. I have tried to take some account of the revision by referring where appropriate to the proposal for a new Regulation on data privacy issued by the European Commission in 2012. Yet the legislative process is highly contentious and likely to be protracted, as has frequently been the case with other data privacy legislation. Once the dust is settled, this book will be issued in a fresh edition that pays due consideration to the changed landscape.

In writing the book, I have benefited from the wonderful working environment of the Norwegian Research Centre for Computers and Law (NRCCL) and the Department of Private Law at the University of Oslo. The camaraderie of my colleagues there is deeply appreciated. I commend too Samson Yoseph Esayas and Francis Medeiros for diligent research assistance. Colleagues from elsewhere, particularly Graham Greenleaf and Chris Kuner, have also provided valuable input for which I am grateful. At Oxford University Press, thanks go to Ruth Anderson for sparking work on the book, and to Catherine Cotter and Emma Hawes for congenial assistance in finalizing it. Last but not least, I thank Toril, Sondre, and Tuva for their support and patience, especially during the last stage of the writing process.

References to legal instruments are to their amended state as of 15 September, 2013. Websites were last accessed on that same date.

Lee A. Bygrave
Oslo, 15 September, 2013

# Contents

| | |
|---|---|
| *List of Abbreviations* | ix |
| *Table of Cases* | xi |
| *Table of Legislation* | xv |
| *Introduction* | xxv |

| | |
|---|---|
| 1. Data Privacy Law in Context | 1 |
| A. Definition of Field | 1 |
| B. Significance of Field | 4 |
| C. Catalysts and Origins | 8 |
| D. Regulatory Cross-Fertilization and Colonization | 15 |
| E. Actors in the Field | 17 |
| F. Issues of Nomenclature and Conceptualization | 23 |
| 2. International Data Privacy Codes | 31 |
| A. Introduction | 31 |
| B. Council of Europe Initiatives | 31 |
| C. OECD Initiatives | 43 |
| D. UN Initiatives | 51 |
| E. EU Initiatives | 53 |
| F. APEC Initiatives | 75 |
| G. ASEAN Initiatives | 79 |
| H. African Initiatives | 80 |
| I. Special Role of Human Rights Treaties | 82 |
| 3. National Data Privacy Laws | 99 |
| A. Introduction | 99 |
| B. Europe | 100 |
| C. The Americas | 102 |
| D. Asia and Oceania | 103 |
| E. Africa and the Middle East | 105 |
| F. The USA and the Transatlantic Data Privacy Divide | 107 |
| 4. Aims and Scope of Data Privacy Law | 117 |
| A. Introduction | 117 |
| B. Aims | 117 |
| C. Scope | 126 |

5. Core Principles of Data Privacy Law                          145
    A.  Definition and Role of Principles                       145
    B.  Fair and Lawful Processing                              146
    C.  Proportionality                                         147
    D.  Minimality                                              151
    E.  Purpose Limitation                                      153
    F.  Data Subject Influence                                  158
    G.  Data Quality                                            163
    H.  Data Security                                           164
    I.  Sensitivity                                             165

6. Oversight and Enforcement of Data Privacy Law                169
    A.  Data Privacy Agencies                                   169
    B.  Other Regulatory Bodies                                 175
    C.  Notification and Licensing Schemes                      183
    D.  Sanctions and Remedies                                  186
    E.  Inter-legal Aspects of Data Privacy Law                 190

7. Prospects for Global Consensus                               205

*Bibliography*                                                  211
    A.  Books and Journal Articles                              211
    B.  Reports and Other Documents                             222

*Index*                                                         229

# List of Abbreviations

| | |
|---|---|
| A29WP | Article 29 Data Protection Working Party (EU) |
| AFSJ | Area of Freedom, Security and Justice (EU) |
| AGPS | Australian Government Publishing Service |
| APEC | Asia Pacific Economic Cooperation |
| ASEAN | Association of South East Asian Nations |
| CJEU | Court of Justice of the European Union |
| CLSR | Computer Law and Security Review (formerly Report) |
| CoE | Council of Europe |
| DPA | Data Privacy Agency |
| DPD | Data Protection Directive (95/46/EC) |
| EC | European Community |
| ECHR | European Convention for the Protection of Human Rights and Fundamental Freedoms |
| ECOWAS | Economic Community of West African States |
| ECR | European Court Reports |
| ECtHR | European Court of Human Rights |
| EHRR | European Human Rights Reports |
| ETS | European Treaty Series |
| EU | European Union |
| FFS | Finlands författningssamling (Collection of Finnish Statutes) |
| GDPR | General Data Protection Regulation (EU) |
| HRLJ | Human Rights Law Journal |
| HMSO | Her Majesty's Stationery Office (UK) |
| ICCPR | International Covenant on Civil and Political Rights (UN) |
| ICT | information and communication technology |
| IDPL | International Data Privacy Law |
| ILO | International Labour Organisation |
| Intl | International |
| IP | Internet Protocol |
| ISP | Internet Service Provider |
| J | Journal |
| JILT | Journal of Information, Law & Technology |
| LJ | Law Journal |
| L Rev | Law Review |
| NOU | Norges Offentlige Utredninger (Official Reports to Government, Norway) |

OECD        Organisation for Economic Cooperation and Development
OJ          Official Journal of the European Communities
PDRA        Personal Data Registers Act (Norway)
PLPR        Privacy Law and Policy Reporter
rev         revised
Rt          Norsk Retstidende (Norwegian Law Reports)
SFS         Svensk författningssamling (Collection of Swedish Statutes)
SOU         Statens Offentliga Utredningar (State Official Reports, Sweden)
TFEU        Treaty on the Functioning of the European Union
UN          United Nations
USC         United States Code

# Table of Cases

## INTERNATIONAL

### UN Human Rights Committee
Coeriel and Aurik v Netherlands (1994) Comm 453/1991 (1994) 15 HRLJ 422 . . . . . . . . . . . . 85

## EUROPEAN

### European Court of Human Rights
Amann v Switzerland (27798/95) (2000) 30 EHRR 843 . . . . . . . . . . . . . . . . . . . . . . . . . . 90, 111
Association for European Integration and Human Rights and Ekimdzhiev v Bulgaria
    [2007] ECHR 533 (28 June 2007) . . . . . . . . . . . . . . . . . . . . . . . . . . . . . .! . . . . . . . . . . . . . 91, 94
B v France (A/232-C) [1992] 2 FLR 249; (1993) 16 EHRR 1; [1992] Fam Law 491 . . . . . . . . 96
Copland v United Kingdom (62617/00) (2007) 45 EHRR 37; 25 BHRC 216;
    2 ALR Int'l 785 . . . . . . . . . . . . . . . . . . . . . . . . . . . . . . . . . . . . . . . . . . . . . . . . . . . 87, 89
Cossey v United Kingdom (10843/84) [1991] 2 FLR 492; [1993] 2 FCR 97; (1991)
    13 EHRR 622; [1991] Fam Law 362 . . . . . . . . . . . . . . . . . . . . . . . . . . . . . . . . . . . . . . 96
Gaskin v United Kingdom (A/160) [1990] 1 FLR 167; (1990) 12 EHRR 36 . . . . . . . . . . . 96, 97
Golder v United Kingdom (A/18) (1979–80) 1 EHRR 524 . . . . . . . . . . . . . . . . . . . . . . . . . . 87
Guerra v Italy (1998) 26 EHRR 357; 4 BHRC 63; [1998] HRCD 277 . . . . . . . . . . . . . . . . . . 96
Halford v United Kingdom (20605/92) [1997] IRLR 471; (1997) 24 EHRR 523;
    3 BHRC 31; [1998] Crim LR 753; (1997) 94(27) LSG 24 . . . . . . . . . . . . . . . . . . . . . 89, 91
Handyside v United Kingdom (A/24) (1979–80) 1 EHRR 737 . . . . . . . . . . . . . . . . . . . . . . . 94
Huvig v France (A/176-B) (1990) 12 EHRR 528 . . . . . . . . . . . . . . . . . . . . . . . . . . . . . . . 92, 93
I v Finland (20511/03) (2009) 48 EHRR 31 . . . . . . . . . . . . . . . . . . . . . . . . . . . . . . . . . . . . . 95
Kennedy v United Kingdom (26839/05) (2011) 52 EHRR 4; 29 BHRC 341;
    [2010] Crim LR 868 . . . . . . . . . . . . . . . . . . . . . . . . . . . . . . . . . . . . . . . . . . . . . . . . . . 93
Klass v Germany (A/28) (1979–80) 2 EHRR 214 . . . . . . . . . . . . . . . . . . . . . 90, 91, 94, 95
Köpke v Germany (420/07) [2011] 53 EHRR SE26 . . . . . . . . . . . . . . . . . . . . . . . . . . . . . . . 88
Kopp v Switzerland (1999) 27 EHRR 91; 4 BHRC 277; [1998] HRCD 356 . . . . . . . . . . . . . . 93
Kruslin v France (A/176-B) (1990) 12 EHRR 547 . . . . . . . . . . . . . . . . . . . . . . . . . . . . . . 92, 93
Leander v Sweden (A/116) (1987) 9 EHRR 433 . . . . . . . . . . . . . . . . . . . . . 90, 93, 94, 97, 98
Liberty v United Kingdom (58243/00) (2009) 48 EHRR 1 . . . . . . . . . . . . . . . . . . . . . . . . . . 93
McMichael v United Kingdom (16424/90) [1995] 2 FCR 718; (1995) 20 EHRR 205;
    [1995] Fam Law 478 . . . . . . . . . . . . . . . . . . . . . . . . . . . . . . . . . . . . . . . . . . . . . . . . . . 96
Malone v United Kingdom (A/82) (1985) 7 EHRR 14 . . . . . . . . . . . . . . . . . . . . . . . . 90–3, 154
Marckx v Belgium (A/31)(1979–80) 2 EHRR 330 . . . . . . . . . . . . . . . . . . . . . . . . . . . . . . . . 87
MS v Sweden (20837/92) (1999) 28 EHRR 313; 3 BHRC 248; (1999)
    45 BMLR 133 . . . . . . . . . . . . . . . . . . . . . . . . . . . . . . . . . . . . . . . . . . . 95, 154, 162
Niemietz v Germany (A/251-B) (1993) 16 EHRR 97 . . . . . . . . . . . . . . . . . . . . . . . . . . . . . . 88
NF v Italy (37119/97) (2002) 35 EHRR 4 . . . . . . . . . . . . . . . . . . . . . . . . . . . . . . . . . . . . . . 89
Peck v United Kingdom (44647/98) [2003] EMLR 15; (2003) 36 EHRR 41;
    13 BHRC 669; [2003] Info TLR 221 . . . . . . . . . . . . . . . . . . . . . . . . . . . . . . . . . . . . . . 89
Perry v United Kingdom (63737/00) (2004) 39 EHRR 3; [2003] Info TLR 372;
    [2003] Po LR 355 . . . . . . . . . . . . . . . . . . . . . . . . . . . . . . . . . . . . . . . . . . . . . . . . . . . . 89
PG and JH v United Kingdom (44787/98) (2008) 46 EHRR 51; [2001]
    Po LR 325; [2002] Crim LR 308 . . . . . . . . . . . . . . . . . . . . . . . . . . . . . . . . . . . . . . . . . 89

Rees v United Kingdom (A/106) [1987] 2 FLR 111; [1993] 2 FCR 49; (1987)
  9 EHRR 56; [1987] Fam Law 157 . . . . . . . . . . . . . . . . . . . . . . . . . . . . . . . . . 96
Rotaru v Romania (28341/95) [2000] ECHR 192; 8 BHRC 449. . . . . . . . . . . . . . . . . . . . . 98
S and Marper v United Kingdom (30562/04) (2009) 48 EHHR 50; 25 BHRC 557;
  [2008] Po LR 403; [2009] Crim LR 355; (2008) 158 NLJ 1755 . . . . . . . . . . . . . 128, 129
SdruZení Jihočeské Matky v Czech Republic [2006] ECHR 1205 . . . . . . . . . . . . . . . . . . . . . 97
Segerstedt-Wiberg v Sweden (62332/00) (2007) 44 EHRR 2; 21 BHRC 155. . . . . . . . . . . . . . 98
Silver v United Kingdom (A/161) (1983) 5 EHRR 347 . . . . . . . . . . . . . . . . . . . . . . . . . . . 94
Társaság a Szabadságjogokért v Hungary (37374/05) (2011) 53 EHRR 3. . . . . . . . . . . . . . . 97
Tyrer v United Kingdom (A/26) (1979–80) 2 EHRR 1 . . . . . . . . . . . . . . . . . . . . . . . . . . . 87
Von Hannover v Germany (59320/00) [2004] EMLR 21; (2005) 40 EHRR 1;
  16 BHRC 545 . . . . . . . . . . . . . . . . . . . . . . . . . . . . . . . . . . . . . . . . . . . . . . . . . . . . . . 87, 90
Von Hannover v Germany (No 2) (40660/08 & 60641/08) [2012] EMLR 16;
  (2012) 55 EHRR 15; 32 BHRC 527 . . . . . . . . . . . . . . . . . . . . . . . . . . . . . . . . . . . . . . . 90
Weber and Saravia v Germany (54934/00) [2006] ECHR 1173; (2008) 46 EHRR SE5. . . . . . . 94
Z v Finland (22009/93) (1998) 25 EHRR 371; (1999) 45 BMLR 107. . . . . . . . . . . 95, 162, 165

**European Court of Justice/General Court**

Asociación Nacional de Establecimientos Financieros de Crédito (ASNEF) and
  Federación de Comercio Electrónico y Marketing Directo (FECEMD) v
  Administración del Estado (C-468/10 & C-469/10) [2012] 1 CMLR 48. . . . . . . . . . . 60, 61
Bavarian Lager v Commission of the European Communities (T-194/04) [2007]
  ECR II-4523; [2008] 1 CMLR 35 . . . . . . . . . . . . . . . . . . . . . . . . . . . . . . . . . . . . . . . . . 136
Bodil Lindqvist (C-101/01) [2004] QB 1014; [2004] 2 WLR 1385; [2004] All ER
  (EC) 561; [2003] ECR I-12971; [2004] 1 CMLR 20; [2004] CEC 117; [2004]
  Info TLR 1. . . . . . . . . . . . . . . . . . . . . . . . . . . . . . . . . . . . . .58, 143, 144, 167, 191, 192
Bonnier Audio AB v Perfect Communication Sweden AB (C-461/10) [2012]
  2 CMLR 42; [2012] CEC 1310; [2012] ECDR 21 . . . . . . . . . . . . . . . . . . . . . . . . . . 138
European Commission v Austria (C-614/10) [2013] All ER (EC) 237; [2013]
  1 CMLR 23. . . . . . . . . . . . . . . . . . . . . . . . . . . . . . . . . . . . . . . . . . . . . . . . . . . . . . . . 171
European Commission v Bavarian Lager (C-28/08 P) [2011] All ER (EC) 1007;
  [2011] Bus LR 867; [2011] 1 CMLR 1 . . . . . . . . . . . . . . . . . . . . . . . . . . . . . . . . . . . 136
European Commission v Germany (C-518/07) [2010] ECR I-1885; [2010] 3 CMLR 3 . . . . . 170
European Commission v Sweden (C-270/11) [2011] OJ C226/17. . . . . . . . . . . . . . . . . . . . . . 67
European Parliament v Council of the European Union (C-317/04 & C-318/04) [2007]
  All ER (EC) 278; [2006] ECR I-4721; [2006] 3 CMLR 9 . . . . . . . . . . . . . . . . . . . . . . 70
Huber v Germany (C-524/06) [2009] All ER (EC) 239; [2008] ECR I-9705; [2009]
  1 CMLR 49; [2009] CEC 507. . . . . . . . . . . . . . . . . . . . . . . . . . . . . . . . . . . . . . . . . . . 150
Ireland v European Parliament (C-301/06) [2009] All ER (EC) 1181; [2009] ECR I-593;
  [2009] 2 CMLR 37 . . . . . . . . . . . . . . . . . . . . . . . . . . . . . . . . . . . . . . . . . . . . . . . . . . . 67
Productores de Música de Espana (Promusicae) v Telefónica de Espana SAU (C-275/06)
  [2008] All ER (EC) 809; [2008] ECR I-271; [2008] 2 CMLR 17; [2008]
  CEC 590; [2008] ECDR 10; [2008] Info TLR 47; (2008) 31(6) IPD 31037 . . . . . . . . . 138
Rechnungshof v Österreichischer Rundfunk (C-465/00, C-138/01 & C-139/01)
  [2003] ECR I-4989; [2003] 3 CMLR 10 . . . . . . . . . . . . . . . . . . . . . . . . . . . . . . . 58, 148
SABAM v Netlog BV (C-360/10) [2012] 2 CMLR 18; [2012] CEC 1271. . . . . . . . . . . . . . . 149
Scarlet Extended v Société Belge des Auteurs, Compositeurs et Editeurs SCRL
  (SABAM) (C-70/10) [2012] ECDR 4; 31 BHRC 558 . . . . . . . . . . . . . . . . . . . . 58, 138, 149
Tietosuojavaltuutettu v Satakunnan Markkinapörssi Oy (C-73/07) [2010] All ER
  (EC) 213; [2008] ECR I-9831. . . . . . . . . . . . . . . . . . . . . . . . . . . . . . . . . . . . . . . . . . . 143
Volker und Markus Schecke GbR v Land Hessen (C-92/09 & C-03/09) [2012]
  All ER (EC) 127; [2010] ECR I-11063 . . . . . . . . . . . . . . . . . . . . . . . . . . . . . . . . . . . . 185

## DOMESTIC

**Australia**
Johns v Australian Securities Commission (1993) 178 CLR 408 . . . . . . . . . . . . . . . . . . . . . . 182

**Austria**
Case 4 Ob 41/09x 14 July 2009 Federal Supreme Ct . . . . . . . . . . . . . . . . . . . . . . . . . . . . . . 66

**Belgium**
Aff CCH v Générale de Banque (1994) 4 Droit de l'informatique et des télécoms 45
    Tribunal de commerce de Bruxelles . . . . . . . . . . . . . . . . . . . . . . . . . . . . . . . . . . . . . . . . . . 15
Aff Feprabel et Fédération des courtiers en Assurances v Kredietbank NV (1994) 4
    Droit de l'informatique et des télécoms 45 Tribunal de commerce d'Anvers . . . . . . . . . . . 15

**Canada**
Jones v Tsige [2011] ONSC 1475 . . . . . . . . . . . . . . . . . . . . . . . . . . . . . . . . . . . . . . . . . . . . . 183
Lawson Hunter v Southam Inc [1984] 2 SCR 148 . . . . . . . . . . . . . . . . . . . . . . . . . . . . . . . . 181
R v Dyment [1988] 2 SCR 417 . . . . . . . . . . . . . . . . . . . . . . . . . . . . . . . . . . . . . . . . . . . . . . . 182
R v Edwards [1996] 1 SCR 128 . . . . . . . . . . . . . . . . . . . . . . . . . . . . . . . . . . . . . . . . . . . . . . 181
R v Plant [1993] 3 SCR 281 . . . . . . . . . . . . . . . . . . . . . . . . . . . . . . . . . . . . . . . . . . . . . . . . . 182

**Denmark**
Case 2000-321-0049 Datatilysnets arsberetning 2000 [Annual Report 2000]
    (August 2001) 27 . . . . . . . . . . . . . . . . . . . . . . . . . . . . . . . . . . . . . . . . . . . . . . . . . . . . . . . . 16

**France**
Anthony G v Société Civile des Producteurs Phonographiques (SCPP)
    27 April 2007 Paris CA . . . . . . . . . . . . . . . . . . . . . . . . . . . . . . . . . . . . . . . . . . . . . . . . . . . 138
Henri S v SCPP 15 May 2007 Paris CA . . . . . . . . . . . . . . . . . . . . . . . . . . . . . . . . . . . . . . . 138

**Germany**
BVerfGE, decision of 15 December 1983, 65 BVerfGE 1 . . . . . . . . . . . . . . . . . . . . . . 28, 179, 180
BVerfGE, decision of 2 March 2010, 1 BvR 256/08, 1 BvR 263/08, 1 BvR
    586/08 . . . . . . . . . . . . . . . . . . . . . . . . . . . . . . . . . . . . . . . . . . . . . . . . . . . . . . . . . . . . . . . 67

**Hong Kong**
Eastweek Publisher Ltd v Privacy Commissioner for Personal Data [2000] 1 HKC 692 . . . . . . 137
Hall v Commissioner of ICAC [1987] HKLR 210 . . . . . . . . . . . . . . . . . . . . . . . . . . . . . . . . 182

**Hungary**
Judgment of April 1991, Constitutional Ct, Official Gazette No 30, 13 April 1991 . . . . . . . . . 180

**Ireland**
EMI Records v Eircom Ltd [2010] IEHC 108 . . . . . . . . . . . . . . . . . . . . . . . . . . . . . . . . . . . 138

**New Zealand**
Hosking v Runting [2005] 1 NZLR 1 . . . . . . . . . . . . . . . . . . . . . . . . . . . . . . . . . . . . . . . . . . 183

**Norway**
Case 1/2004 Data Privacy Tribunal . . . . . . . . . . . . . . . . . . . . . . . . . . . . . . . . . . . . . . . . . . . 161
Case 1/2012 Data Privacy Tribunal . . . . . . . . . . . . . . . . . . . . . . . . . . . . . . . . . . . . . . . . . . . 161
Rt 2013 143 Supreme Ct . . . . . . . . . . . . . . . . . . . . . . . . . . . . . . . . . . . . . . 153, 156, 157, 179

**Romania**

Decision no 1258 of 8 October 2009 Constitutional Ct . . . . . . . . . . . . . . . . . . . . . . . . . . . . . . 68

**Sweden**

B293-00 12 June 2001 Supreme Ct . . . . . . . . . . . . . . . . . . . . . . . . . . . . . . . . . . . . . . . . . .xxvii, 143
Case 285/07 8 June 2007 Stockholm Administrative CA . . . . . . . . . . . . . . . . . . . . . . . . . . 138
Case 3978/07 16 June 2009 Supreme Admin Ct . . . . . . . . . . . . . . . . . . . . . . . . . . . . . . . . . 138

**Switzerland**

Eidgenössischer Datenschutz- und Öffentlichkeitsbeauftragter (EDÖB) v Logistep
(Case 1C-285/2009) 8 September 2010 Federal Supreme Ct . . . . . . . . . . . . . . . . . . . . . . 138

**United Kingdom**

Coco v AN Clark (Engineers) Ltd 1968] FSR 415; [1969] RPC 41 . . . . . . . . . . . . . . . . . . . . 183
Durant v Financial Services Authority (Disclosure) [2003] EWCA Civ 1746; [2004]
FSR 28 . . . . . . . . . . . . . . . . . . . . . . . . . . . . . . . . . . . . . . . . . . . . . . . . . . . . . . . . . . . . . . 136
Equifax Europe Ltd v Data Protection Registrar (1991) Case DA/90 25/49/7 . . . . . . . . . . . . . 137
Marcel v Commissioner of Police of the Metropolis [1992] Ch 225; [1992] 2 WLR 50;
[1992] 1 All ER 72; (1992) 4 Admin LR 309; (1991) 141 NLJ 1224;
(1991) 135 SJLB 125 . . . . . . . . . . . . . . . . . . . . . . . . . . . . . . . . . . . . . . . . . . . . . . . . . . . 182
Morris v Director of the Serious Fraud Office [1993] Ch 372; [1993] 3 WLR 1; [1993]
1 All ER 788; [1992] BCC 934; [1993] BCLC 580 . . . . . . . . . . . . . . . . . . . . . . . . . . . . . 182
R (on application of LS) v Chief Constable of South Yorkshire Police [2004] UKHL 39;
[2004] 1 WLR 2196; [2004] 4 All ER 193; [2004] HRLR 35; [2004] UKHRR 967;
21 BHRC 408; [2004] Po LR 283; [2005] Crim LR 136; (2004) 101(34) LSG 29;
(2004) 154 NLJ 1183; (2004) 148 SJLB 914 . . . . . . . . . . . . . . . . . . . . . . . . . . . . . . . . . 128

**United States**

Katz v United States 389 US 347 (1967) . . . . . . . . . . . . . . . . . . . . . . . . . . . . . . . . . . . . . . . . 181
Roe v Wade 410 US 113 (1973) . . . . . . . . . . . . . . . . . . . . . . . . . . . . . . . . . . . . . . . . . . . . . . . 181
Sorrell v IMS Health, Inc 131 S Ct 2653 (2011). . . . . . . . . . . . . . . . . . . . . . . . . . . . . . . . . . 111
Whalen v Roe 429 US 589 (1977) . . . . . . . . . . . . . . . . . . . . . . . . . . . . . . . . . . . . . . . . . . . . . 181

# Table of Legislation

## INTERNATIONAL

Agreement Establishing the World Trade
  Organization 1994
  Annex 1B........................198
  Annex 1B Art II(1)................198
  Annex 1B Art VI(1) ...............198
  Annex 1B Art XIV(c)(ii)...........198
  Annex 1B Art XVII ...............198
First Optional Protocol to the
  International Covenant on Civil
  and Political Rights (ICCPR) ........85
General Agreement on Trade in Services
  (GATS) 1994....................198
  Art XIV ........................198
  Art XIV(c)(ii)....................198
International Covenant on Civil and
  Political Rights (ICCPR)
  1966.................31, 82, 83, 84
  Art 17.................82–6, 106, 206
  Art 40(4) .........................84

## AFRICAN

African Charter on Human and People's
  Rights 1981 .....................83
ECOWAS Treaty .....................80
Supplementary Act on Personal Data
  protection within ECOWAS
  2010....................80–2, 163
  Preamble ........................80
  Ch IV............................80
  Art 12............................81
  Art 24............................81
  Art 30............................81
  Art 35............................80
  Art 36............................80
  Art 36(1) .........................81
  Art 45(1) .........................81
  Art 48............................80

## EUROPEAN

Additional Protocol to the Convention for
  the Protection of Individuals with
  Regard to Automatic Processing of
  Personal Data (Convention 108)
  2001............. 32, 33, 39, 52, 101,
          102, 171, 173, 199

Art 1............................39
Art 1(2)(a) .......................173
Art 1(3) ..........................171
Art 1(5) ..........................174
Art 2............................39
Agreement on the European Economic
  Area (EEA) 1992 ................54
Charter of Fundamental Rights of the
  European Union 2010
  Art 7............................59
  Art 8............................58
  Art 8(2) .........................153
Convention between Belgium, Germany,
  Spain, France, Luxembourg, the
  Netherlands, and Austria on the
  stepping up of cross-border
  cooperation particularly in
  combating terrorism, cross-border
  crime, and illegal migration (Prüm
  Convention) 2005
  Art 34(1) .........................43
Convention for the Protection of Human
  Rights and Dignity of the Human
  Being with regard to the Application
  of Biology and Medicine 1997 .......42
  Art 10(1) .........................42
  Art 10(2) .........................42
  Art 10(3) .........................42
  Art 26(1) .........................42
Convention for the Protection of
  Individuals with Regard to
  Automatic Processing of Personal
  Data (Convention 108) 1981....... 26,
          31–43, 49, 52, 54–6, 58, 60,
          62, 70, 76, 82, 84, 85, 87,
          101, 102, 128, 129, 134,
          141, 142, 147, 155,
          160, 176, 187, 206
  Preamble ........................34
  Ch II .................34, 36, 38, 40
  Ch III............................38
  Art 1.....................34, 35, 119
  Art 2(a) .............129, 130, 134
  Art 2(c) ...................35, 141
  Art 3.................35, 40, 41, 141
  Art 3(2)(b) .......................35
  Art 3(2)(c) .......................35
  Art 4(1) .........................35
  Art 5............................35–8

Art 5(a) ............ 36, 45, 84, 141, 146
Art 5(b) ............... 36, 46, 85, 153
Art 5(c) ................ 36, 85, 151
Art 5(d) ................... 36, 163
Art 5(e) ................ 36, 46, 151
Art 5(1) ........................ 36
Art 6. ............ 36–8, 41, 52, 85, 165
Art 6(1) .................... 37, 165
Art 6(2) ........................ 37
Art 7. ............... 37, 38, 40, 85, 164
Art 8. ................... 35, 37, 38, 40
Art 8(a) ..................... 37, 46
Art 8(b) ..................... 37, 47
Art 8(b)–(d) ..................... 38
Art 8(c) ........................ 37
Art 8(d) ........................ 37
Art 8(2) ........................ 38
Art 9. .......................... 41
Art 9(2) ..................... 38, 47
Art 9(3) ........................ 38
Art 10. ......................... 38
Art 11. ......................... 35
Art 12. ...................... 34, 39
Art 12(2) ....................... 38
Art 12(3)(a) ................. 38, 191
Art 12(3)(b) .................... 38
Art 12(3)(c) .................... 60
Arts 13–17 ...................... 39
Art 21(6) ....................... 32
Art 23. ......................... 32
Convention on Cybercrime 2001,
    Art 1(b) ..................... 127
European Convention on Human Rights
    and Fundamental Freedoms
    (ECHR) 1950 ......... 12, 13, 31, 34,
                    40, 58, 82, 91, 94
Art 8. ............. 6, 34, 40, 58, 67, 70,
                82, 86–97, 101, 136
Art 8(1) .............. 87–93, 95, 111,
                    154, 171
Art 8(2) ............ 38, 42, 67, 86, 88,
                90–4, 148, 150, 154, 162
Art 10. ....................... 34, 97
Art 10(1) ....................... 97
Art 13. ....................... 97, 98
Art 25. ......................... 91
European Social Charter 1961 ........... 8
Art 2. ........................... 8
Art 21. .......................... 8
Art 22. .......................... 8
Art 26. .......................... 8
Schengen Convention 1990 ............. 69
Arts 102–18 ...................... 69

Treaty Establishing the European
    Community, Art 95 .............. 67
Treaty of Amsterdam 1997 ............. 69
Treaty of Lisbon 2007. ......... 58, 176, 177
Treaty on European Union (TEU) 2012
    Art 5. ....................... 60
    Art 6. ....................... 57
    Art 6(1) ..................... 58
Treaty on the Functioning of the
    European Union (TFEU)
    Art 16. ...................... 59
    Art 114. ..................... 67

## Secondary Legislation

### *Regulations*

Regulation 45/2001 on the protection of
    individuals with regard to the
    processing of personal data by the
    Community institutions and
    bodies and on the free movement of
    such data [2001] OJ L8/1 .... 59, 68, 136
    Art 1(1) ..................... 136
    Art 24(1) ..................... 68
    Art 24(1)(c) .................. 68
    Art 24(7) ..................... 69
    Art 41(1) ..................... 68
    Art 41(2) ..................... 68
    Art 46. ...................... 68
    Art 46(c) .................... 68
    Art 47(1) .................... 68
Regulation 1049/2001 on public access to
    European Parliament, Council and
    Commission documents [2001] OJ
    L145/43. ..................... 136
Regulation 1211/2009 establishing the
    Body of European Regulators for
    Electronic Communications
    (BEREC) [2009] OJ L337/1 ........ 64
Regulation 182/2011 on control by
    member states of the Commission's
    implementing powers [2011]
    OJ L55/13 .................... 176

### *Directives*

Directive 95/46 on the protection of
    individuals with regard to the
    processing of personal data and on
    the free movement of such
    data (Data Protection Directive)
    (DPD) [1995] OJ L281/31 ......... 6,
                7, 19, 38–40, 52–75, 78, 80, 99,
                101–3, 105, 107, 116, 122, 125,

127, 132, 133, 136, 138, 139, 141,
151, 155, 160–3, 170–4, 178, 179,
184, 185, 187–9, 191, 195, 199,
207, 208
Preamble . . . . . . . . . . . . . . . . . . . . . 165, 191
Recital 2 . . . . . . . . . . . . . . . . . . . . . . . . . . . 57
Recital 3 . . . . . . . . . . . . . . . . . . . . . . . . . . . 57
Recital 5 . . . . . . . . . . . . . . . . . . . . . . . . . . . 57
Recital 7 . . . . . . . . . . . . . . . . . . . . . . . . . . . 57
Recital 8 . . . . . . . . . . . . . . . . . . . . . . . . 60, 191
Recital 9 . . . . . . . . . 58, 60, 184, 188, 191
Recitals 9–11 . . . . . . . . . . . . . . . . . 134, 172
Recital 10 . . . . . . 57, 58, 60, 184, 187, 188
Recital 11 . . . . . . . . . . . . . . . . . . . . . . . 57, 58
Recital 13 . . . . . . . . . . . . . . . . . . . . . . . . . 166
Recital 14 . . . . . . . . . . . . . . . . . . . . . . . . . 129
Recital 15 . . . . . . . . . . . . . . . . . . . . . . . . . 142
Recital 19 . . . . . . . . . . . . . . . . . . . . . . . . . 201
Recital 20 . . . . . . . . . . . . . . . . . . . . . . . . . 201
Recital 26 . . . . . . . . . . . . . . . . . . . . . 131, 132
Recital 27 . . . . . . . . . . . . . . . . . . . . . . . . . 142
Recital 33 . . . . . . . . . . . . . . . . . . . . . . . . . 165
Recital 38 . . . . . . . . . . . . . . . . . . . . . . . . . 147
Recital 53 . . . . . . . . . . . . . . . . . . . . . . . . . 184
Recital 54 . . . . . . . . . . . . . . . . . . . . . 184, 185
Recital 55 . . . . . . . . . . . . . . . . . . . . . . . . . 188
Ch II . . . . . . . . . . . . . . . . . . . . . . . . . . . . . . 60
Art 1 . . . . . . . . . . . . . . . . . . . . . . . . . . . . . . 57
Art 1(1) . . . . . . . . . . . . . . . . . . . . . . . . 61, 187
Art 1(2) . . . . . . . . . . . . . . . . . . . . . . . . 63, 191
Art 2(a) . . . . . . . . . . . . . . . . 17, 129, 134
Art 2(b) . . . . . . . . . . . . . . . . . . . . . . . . 62, 141
Art 2(c) . . . . . . . . . . . . . . . . . . . . . . . . 62, 141
Art 2(d) . . . . . . . . . . . . . . . . . . . . . . . . 17, 202
Art 2(e) . . . . . . . . . . . . . . . . . . . . . . . . . . . . 18
Art 2(h) . . . . . . . . . . . . . . . 147, 160, 162
Art 3(1) . . . . . . . . . . . . . . . . . . . . . . . . 62, 141
Art 3(2) . . . . . . . . . . . . . 62, 143, 144, 202
Art 3(2)(a) . . . . . . . . . . . . . . . . . . . . . . . . 202
Art 3(2)(b) . . . . . . . . . . . . . . . . . . . . . . . . 202
Art 4 . . . . . . . . . . . . . . . . . . . . . . . . . . 200–2
Art 4(1)(a) . . . . . . . . . . . . . . . . . . . . . 63, 201
Art 4(1)(c) . . . . . . . . . . . . . . . . . . . . . . . . . 63
Art 5 . . . . . . . . . . . . . . . . . . . . . . . . . . 60, 61
Art 6 . . . . . . . . . . . . . . . . . . . . . . . . . . . . 162
Art 6(1)(a) . . . . . . . . . . . . . . . . . . . . . . . . 146
Art 6(1)(b) . . . . . . . . . . . . . . . . . . . . 153, 157
Art 6(1)(c) . . . . . . . . . . . . . . 148, 151, 163
Art 6(1)(d) . . . . . . . . . . . . . . . . . . . . 163, 164
Art 6(1)(e) . . . . . . . . . . . . . . . . . . . . . . . . 151
Art 7 . . . . . . . . . . . . . 63, 111, 148–51, 161
Art 7(a) . . . . . . . . . . . . . . . . . . . . . . . 160, 162
Art 7(a)–(e) . . . . . . . . . . . . . . . . . . . . . . . 157
Art 7(b) . . . . . . . . . . . . . . . . . . . . . . . . . . 150

Art 7(b)–(f) . . . . . . . . . . . . . . . . . . . . . . . 161
Art 7(c) . . . . . . . . . . . . . . . . . . . . . . . . . . 150
Art 7(d) . . . . . . . . . . . . . . . . . . . . . . . . . . 150
Art 7(e) . . . . . . . . . . . . . . . . . . . . . . . . . . 150
Art 7(f) . . . . . . . . . . 60, 61, 150, 157, 161
Art 8 . . . . . . . . . . . 52, 63, 111, 148, 149,
151, 160, 161, 185
Art 8(1) . . . . . . . . . . . . . . . . . . . . . 52, 165–7
Art 8(2) . . . . . . . . . . . . . . . . . . . . . . . . . . 166
Art 8(2)(a) . . . . . . . . . . . . . . . . . . . 160, 162
Art 8(3) . . . . . . . . . . . . . . . . . . . . . . . . . . 166
Art 8(4) . . . . . . . . . . . . . . . . . . . . . . . 60, 166
Art 8(5) . . . . . . . . . . . . . . . . . . . . . . 165, 166
Art 9 . . . . . . . . . . . . . . . . . . . . . . . . . 62, 143
Art 10 . . . . . . . . . . . . . . 52, 60, 63, 158, 159
Art 11 . . . . . . . . . . . . . . 52, 60, 63, 158, 159
Art 12 . . . . . . . . . . . . . . . . . . . . . . . . 159, 162
Art 12(a) . . . . . . . . . . . . . . . . . . . . . . . 63, 160
Art 12(b) . . . . . . . . . . . . . . . . . . . . . . . 72, 163
Art 13 . . . . . . . . . . . . . . 60, 61, 121, 148
Art 13(1) . . . . . . . . . . . . . . . . . . 62, 66, 143
Art 13(2) . . . . . . . . . . . . . . . . . . . . . . . . . 160
Art 14(a) . . . . . . . . . . . . . . . . . . . . . . 60, 162
Art 14(b) . . . . . . . . . . . . . . . . . . . . . . . . . 162
Art 15 . . . . . . . . . . . . . . . . . . . . . . . . 100, 162
Art 15(1) . . . . . . . . . . . . . . . . . . 63, 159, 162
Art 15(2) . . . . . . . . . . . . . . . . . . . . . . . . . 163
Art 16 . . . . . . . . . . . . . . . . . . . . . . . . . . . 164
Art 17 . . . . . . . . . . . . . . . . . . . . . . . . . . . . 73
Art 17(1) . . . . . . . . . . . . . . . . . . . . . . . . . 164
Art 17(2) . . . . . . . . . . . . . . . . . . . . . . . . . 164
Art 17(3) . . . . . . . . . . . . . . . . . . . . . 18, 164
Art 17(4) . . . . . . . . . . . . . . . . . . . . . . . . . 164
Art 18 . . . . . . . . . . . . . . . . . . . . 63, 73, 142
Art 18(1) . . . . . . . . . . . . . . . . . . . . . . . . . 184
Art 19(1) . . . . . . . . . . . . . . . . . . . . . . . . . 184
Art 20 . . . . . . . . . . . . . . . . . . . . . . . . . . . . 63
Art 20(1) . . . . . . . . . . . . . . . . . . . . . . . . . 184
Art 21(1) . . . . . . . . . . . . . . . . . . . . . . . . . 159
Art 21(2) . . . . . . . . . . . . . . . . . . . . . 159, 172
Art 22 . . . . . . . . . . . . . . . . . . . . . . . . 187, 188
Art 23 . . . . . . . . . . . . . . . . . . . . . . . . . . . 188
Art 23(1) . . . . . . . . . . . . . . . . . . . . . . . . . 188
Art 23(2) . . . . . . . . . . . . . . . . . . . . . . . . . 188
Art 24 . . . . . . . . . . . . . . . . . . . . . . . . . . . 188
Art 25 . . . . . . . . . . 54, 106, 125, 176, 191,
194, 195, 198
Art 25(1) . . . . . . . . . . . . . . . . . . . . . . 63, 191
Art 25(2) . . . . . . . . . . . . . . . . . . . . . . . . . 192
Art 25(4)–(6) . . . . . . . . . . . . . . . . . . . . . 176
Art 25(6) . . . . . . . . . . . . . . . . . . . . . . . . . 192
Art 26 . . . . . . . . . . . . . . 54, 106, 126, 191,
193, 194, 198
Art 26(1) . . . . . . . . . . . . . . . . . . . . . . . . . 194

Art 26(2) . . . . . . . . . . . . . . . . . . . . . . . .194
Art 26(3) . . . . . . . . . . . . . . . . . . . . . . . .176
Art 26(4) . . . . . . . . . . . . . . . . . . . .176, 194
Art 27. . . . . . . . . . . . . . . . . . . . . . . .63, 101
Art 28. . . . . . . . . . . . . . . . . . . . . . . . .60, 63
Art 28(1) . . . . . . . . . . . . . . . . . . . . . . . .170
Art 28(2) . . . . . . . . . . . . . . . . . . . . . . . .172
Art 28(3) . . . . . . . . . . . 172, 184, 185, 187
Art 28(4) . . . . . . . . . . . . . . . . . . . . . . . .172
Art 28(6) . . . . . . . . . . . . . . . . . . . . . . . .174
Art 29. . . . . . . . . . . . . . . . . . . . . . . . .19, 64
Art 30. . . . . . . . . . . . . . . . . . . . . . . .64, 174
Art 30(1)(a) . . . . . . . . . . . . . . . . . . . . . .192
Art 30(1)(b) . . . . . . . . . . . . . . . . . . . . . .192
Art 31. . . . . . . . . . . . . . . . . . . . . . .176, 192
Art 31(2) . . . . . . . . . . . . . . . . . . . . .176, 192
Directive 97/66 on processing personal
    data and protection of privacy in
    the telecommunications sector
    (Telecommunications Privacy Directive)
    [2008] OJ L24/1 . . . . . . . . . . . . . . . . .64
Directive 2002/19 on access to and
    interconnection of electronic
    communications networks (Access
    Directive) [2002] OJ L108/7 . . . . . . . .64
Directive 2002/20 on authorisation of
    electronic communications
    networks and services
    (Authorisation Directive) [2002]
    OJ L108/21 . . . . . . . . . . . . . . . . . . . . .64
Directive 2002/21 on a common
    regulatory framework for electronic
    communications networks and
    services (Framework Directive)
    [2002] OJ L108/33 . . . . . . . . . . . .64, 65
Recital 5. . . . . . . . . . . . . . . . . . . . . . . . . .65
Art 2(c) . . . . . . . . . . . . . . . . . . . . . . . . . .65
Directive 2002/22 on universal service
    and users' rights relating to electronic
    communications networks and
    services (Universal Service Directive)
    [2002] OJ L108/51 . . . . . . . . . . . . . . .64
Directive 2002/58 on processing
    personal data and protection of
    privacy in the electronic
    communications sector
    (Communications Privacy Directive)
    (e-privacy Directive) (EPD)
    [2002] OJ L201/37 . . . . . . . . 64, 66, 68,
                                        71, 114, 139
Preamble . . . . . . . . . . . . . . . . . . . . . . . .152
Recital 14. . . . . . . . . . . . . . . . . . . . . . . . .65
Recital 30. . . . . . . . . . . . . . . . . . . . . . . .152
Art 1(2) . . . . . . . . . . . . . . . . . . . . . . .64, 71

Art 2(c) . . . . . . . . . . . . . . . . . . . . . . . . . .65
Art 3. . . . . . . . . . . . . . . . . . . . . . . . . . . .65
Art 4. . . . . . . . . . . . . . . . . . . . . . . . . . . .65
Art 4(3) . . . . . . . . . . . . . . . . . . . . . . .66, 159
Art 5. . . . . . . . . . . . . . . . . . . . . . . . . . . .65
Art 5(3) . . . . . . . . . . . . . . . . . . . . . . . . . .66
Art 6. . . . . . . . . . . . . . . . . . . . . . . . . .65, 66
Art 8. . . . . . . . . . . . . . . . . . . . . . . . . . . .65
Art 9. . . . . . . . . . . . . . . . . . . . . . . . . . . .65
Art 12. . . . . . . . . . . . . . . . . . . . . . . . .64, 65
Art 13. . . . . . . . . . . . . . . . . . . . . . . . .65, 66
Art 13(1) . . . . . . . . . . . . . . . . . . . . . . . . .64
Art 15. . . . . . . . . . . . . . . . . . . . . . . . . . . .65
Art 15(1) . . . . . . . . . . . . . . . . . . . . . . . . .66
Directive 2006/24 on retention of data in
    connection with publicly available
    electronic communications services
    or public communications
    networks (Data Retention Directive)
    [2006] OJ L 105/54 . . . . . . . . .66–8, 114
Art 1(1) . . . . . . . . . . . . . . . . . . . . . . .66, 67
Art 1(2) . . . . . . . . . . . . . . . . . . . . . . . . . .66
Art 4. . . . . . . . . . . . . . . . . . . . . . . . . .66, 67
Art 5. . . . . . . . . . . . . . . . . . . . . . . . . .66, 67
Art 5(1) . . . . . . . . . . . . . . . . . . . . . . . . . .66
Art 5(2) . . . . . . . . . . . . . . . . . . . . . . . . . .66
Art 6. . . . . . . . . . . . . . . . . . . . . . . . . . . .66
Art 7. . . . . . . . . . . . . . . . . . . . . . . . . . . .67
Art 9. . . . . . . . . . . . . . . . . . . . . . . . . . . .67
Directive 2009/136 amending Directives
    2002/22 and 2002/58 and
    Regulation 2006/2004 [2009]
    OJ L337/11 . . . . . . . . . . . . . . . . . . . . .65

*Decisions*
Decision 92/242 on information security
    [1992] OJ L123/19 . . . . . . . . . . . . . . .56
Decision 1999/435 on the definition of
    the Schengen acquis [1999]
    OJ L176/1 . . . . . . . . . . . . . . . . . . . . . .69
Decision 2000/520 on adequacy of
    protection of safe harbor privacy
    principles (Safe Harbor Agreement)
    [2000] OJ L215/7 . . . . 50, 76, 133, 177,
                                178, 195–8, 209
Annex I . . . . . . . . . . . . . . . . . . . . . . . . .196
Annex II. . . . . . . . . . . . . . . . . . . . . .133, 196
Annex III . . . . . . . . . . . . . . . . . . . . . . . .196
Annex IV . . . . . . . . . . . . . . . . . . . . . . . .196
Decision 2001/497 on standard
    contractual clauses for transfer of
    personal data to third countries
    [2001] OJ L181/19 . . . . . . . . . . . . . .194

Decision 2002/187 on the setting up of
Eurojust [2002] OJ L63/1 . . . . . . . . .43
Recital 9. . . . . . . . . . . . . . . . . . . . . . . . .43
Art 14(2) . . . . . . . . . . . . . . . . . . . . . . . .43
Decision 1247/2002 on the regulations
and general conditions governing
the European Data-protection
Supervisor's duties [2002]
OJ L183/1 . . . . . . . . . . . . . . . . . . . . .68
Decision 2004/496 on the conclusion of
an Agreement between the EC and
the US on the processing and
transfer of PNR data [2004] OJ
L183/83. . . . . . . . . . . . . . . . . . . . . . .69
Decision 2004/535 on protection of
personal data in the Passenger Name
Record of air passengers transferred
to the US Bureau of Customs and
Border Protection [2004]
OJ L235/11 . . . . . . . . . . . . . . . . . . . .69
Decision 2004/915 amending Decision
2001/497 as regards alternative
standard contractual clauses [2004]
OJ L385/74 . . . . . . . . . . . . . . . . . . . .194
Decision 2006/729 on the signing of an
Agreement between the EU and
the US on processing and transfer
of PNR data [2006] OJ L298/27 . . . . .70
Decision 2007/551 on the signing of an
Agreement between the EU and
the US on processing and transfer
of PNR data [2007] OJ L204/16 . . . . .70
Decision 2008/615 on cooperation in
combating terrorism and cross-border
crime [2008] OJ L210/1
Art 25. . . . . . . . . . . . . . . . . . . . . . . . . . .43
Decision 2008/977 on protection of
personal data processed in the
framework of police and judicial
cooperation in criminal matters
[2008] OJ L350/60 . . . . . . 62, 70, 71, 72
Recital 39. . . . . . . . . . . . . . . . . . . . . . . .71
Art 1(2)(a) . . . . . . . . . . . . . . . . . . . . . . .70
Art 1(4) . . . . . . . . . . . . . . . . . . . . . . . . .70
Decision 2010/87 on standard contractual
clauses for transfer of personal data to
processors established in third
countries under Directive 95/46
[2010] OJ L39/5 . . . . . . . . . . . . . . . .194
Decision 2012/472 on the signing of an
Agreement between the EU and
the US on processing and transfer
of PNR data [2012] OJ L215/4 . . . . . .70

**DOMESTIC**

**Angola**
Constitution 2010
Art 69. . . . . . . . . . . . . . . . . . . . . . . . . . .27
Law No 22/11 on Data Protection . . . . . . .105

**Argentina**
Act No 25.326 on Protection of Personal
Data 2000 . . . . . . . . . . . . . . . . . . . . .103
Constitution 1994
Art 43. . . . . . . . . . . . . . . . . . . . . . . . . .103
Decree 1558/2001 of 3 December 2001. . . . .103

**Australia**
Copyright Act 1968 (Federal)
s 35(5) . . . . . . . . . . . . . . . . . . . . . . . . . .13
Government Information (Open Access)
Act 2009 (NSW)
Sch 4 cl 4(2). . . . . . . . . . . . . . . . . . . . .126
Health Records Act 2001 (Victoria) . . . . . .104
Health Records and Information Privacy
Act 2002 (NSW)
s 5(2) . . . . . . . . . . . . . . . . . . . . . . . . . .126
Information Privacy Act 2000 (Victoria). . . .104
Sch 1 . . . . . . . . . . . . . . . . . . . . . . . . . .152
Privacy Act 1988 (Federal) . . . . 104, 122, 140,
179, 182, 200
Preamble . . . . . . . . . . . . . . . . . . . . .50, 118
Pt IIIAA. . . . . . . . . . . . . . . . . . . . . . . .178
s 5B . . . . . . . . . . . . . . . . . . . . . . . . . . .200
s 6(1) . . . . . . . . . . . . . . . . . . . . . . . . . .134
s 6C(1). . . . . . . . . . . . . . . . . . . . . . . . .104
s 6D. . . . . . . . . . . . . . . . . . . . . . . . . . .104
s 6DA. . . . . . . . . . . . . . . . . . . . . . . . . .104
s 6E . . . . . . . . . . . . . . . . . . . . . . . . . . .104
s 7B(3) . . . . . . . . . . . . . . . . . . . . . . . . .104
s 29(a) . . . . . . . . . . . . . . . . . . . . . . . . .121
s 36(2) . . . . . . . . . . . . . . . . . . . . . . . . .187
s 38 . . . . . . . . . . . . . . . . . . . . . . . . . . .187
ss 38A–38C . . . . . . . . . . . . . . . . . . . . .187
s 39 . . . . . . . . . . . . . . . . . . . . . . . . . . .187
s 52(1A). . . . . . . . . . . . . . . . . . . . . . . .187
Sch 3 . . . . . . . . . . . . . . . . . . . . . . . . . .152
Privacy Amendment (Private Sector)
Act 2000 (Federal) . . . . . . . . . . . . . . .103
Privacy Amendment (Enhancing Privacy)
Act 2012 (Federal) . . . . . . . . . . . . . . .200
s 104 . . . . . . . . . . . . . . . . . . . . . . . . . .152
Privacy and Personal Information
Protection Act 1998 (NSW)
s 4(2) . . . . . . . . . . . . . . . . . . . . . . . . . .126
Surveillance Devices (Workplace Privacy)
Act 2006 (Victoria) . . . . . . . . . . . . . .104

**Austria**

Data Protection Act 2000. . . . . . . . . . . . . .132
  s 3(2) . . . . . . . . . . . . . . . . . . . . . . . . . .201
  s 4(1) . . . . . . . . . . . . . . . . . . . . . . . . . .133
Telecommunications Act 2003
  s 99 . . . . . . . . . . . . . . . . . . . . . . . . . . . .66

**Belgium**

Protection of Personal Privacy in Relation
  to the Processing of Personal Data
  Act 1992
  Art 2. . . . . . . . . . . . . . . . . . . . . . . . . . .118

**Benin**

Law No 2009-09 on the Protection of
  Personal Data in the Republic of
  Benin . . . . . . . . . . . . . . . . . . . . . . . . .105

**Brazil**

Constitution 1988
  Art 5. . . . . . . . . . . . . . . . . . . . . . . . . . .102

**Burkina Faso**

Act No 10-2004/AN on Protection of
  Personal Data . . . . . . . . . . . . . . . . . . . .105

**Canada**

Charter of Rights and Freedoms
  s 8 . . . . . . . . . . . . . . . . . . . . . . . .181, 182
Constitution Act 1982
  Pt I . . . . . . . . . . . . . . . . . . . . . . . . . . .181
Health Information Act 1999
  (Alberta) . . . . . . . . . . . . . . . . . . . . . 102
Personal Information Protection
  Act 2003 (Alberta) . . . . . . . . . . . . . . .102
Personal Information Protection Act
  2003 (British Columbia) . . . . . . . . . .102
Personal Information Protection and
  Electronic Documents Act 2000. . . . .102
  s 5(3) . . . . . . . . . . . . . . . . . . . . . . . . . .155
  Sch 1 . . . . . . . . . . . . . . . . . . . . . . . . . . .50
Privacy Act 1982 . . . . . . . . . . . . . . . . . . .102
  s 2 . . . . . . . . . . . . . . . . . . . . . . . . . . . .118
  ss 4–8. . . . . . . . . . . . . . . . . . . . . . . . . .163
  s 5(1) . . . . . . . . . . . . . . . . . . . . . . . . . .147
Protection of Personal Information in the
  Private Sector Act 1993 (Quebec). . . .102

**Cape Verde**

Constitution
  Art 46. . . . . . . . . . . . . . . . . . . . . . . . . . .27
Law No 133/V/2001 on Data Protection
  2001. . . . . . . . . . . . . . . . . . . . . . . . . .105

**China**

Constitution 1982
  Arts 38–40 . . . . . . . . . . . . . . . . . . . . . .104
General Principles of Civil Law
  Art 101. . . . . . . . . . . . . . . . . . . . . . . . .104

**Columbia**

Act No 1581 on Protection of Personal
  Data 2012 . . . . . . . . . . . . . . . . . . . . .103

**Costa Rica**

Act No 8968 on the Protectionof the
  Individual with Regards to
  Processing of Personal Data 2011. . . . 103

**Denmark**

Personal Data Act 2000 . . . . . . . . 16, 118, 201
  s 3(3) . . . . . . . . . . . . . . . . . . . . . . . . . . .16
  s 41(4) . . . . . . . . . . . . . . . . . . . . . . . . .164
Private Registers Act 1978 . . . . . . . . .118, 124
  s 4(4) . . . . . . . . . . . . . . . . . . . . . . . . . .184
  s 4(5) . . . . . . . . . . . . . . . . . . . . . . . . . .184
Public Authorities' Registers Act 1978. . . 16, 118
  s 12(3) . . . . . . . . . . . . . . . . . . . . . . . . .165

**Dubai**

Data Protection Law 2007 (DIFC Law
  No 1 of 2007) . . . . . . . . . . . . . . . . . .106

**Finland**

Personal Data Act 1999 . . . . . . . . .6, 120, 170
  s 3(1) . . . . . . . . . . . . . . . . . . . . . . . . . .135
  s 47(1) . . . . . . . . . . . . . . . . . . . . . . . . .187
Personal Data Registers Act 1987 . . . . . .6, 170
  s 1 . . . . . . . . . . . . . . . . . . . . . . . . . . . .120
  s 2(1) . . . . . . . . . . . . . . . . . . . . . . . . . .135
  s 6(6) . . . . . . . . . . . . . . . . . . . . . . . . . .165

**France**

Information Technology, Data
  Files and Civil Liberties
  Act 1978 . . . . . . . . . . . . . . . . . . .81, 142
  s 1 . . . . . . . . . . . . . . . . . . . . . . . . . . . .119
  s 2 . . . . . . . . . . . . . . . . . . . . . . . . .81, 162
  s 15 . . . . . . . . . . . . . . . . . . . . . . . . . . .142
  s 16 . . . . . . . . . . . . . . . . . . . . . . . . . . .142

**Germany**

Basic Law (Constitution)
  Art 1(1) . . . . . . . . . . . . . . . . . . . . .179, 180
  Art 2(1) . . . . . . . . . . . . . . . . . . . . .179, 180
  Art 10(1) . . . . . . . . . . . . . . . . . . . . . . . .68
Census Act 1983 (Federal) . . . . . .10, 179, 180

Data Protection Act 1970
   (Hesse) . . . . . . . . . . . . . . . . . . . . 33, 99
Data Protection Act 1990
   (Federal) . . . . . . . . . . . . . . 6, 26, 128, 132
   s 1(1) . . . . . . . . . . . . . . . . . . . . . . . . . . . 26
   s 3(1) . . . . . . . . . . . . . . . . . . . . . . . . . . 135
   s 3(6) . . . . . . . . . . . . . . . . . . . . . . . . . . 132
   s 3(a) . . . . . . . . . . . . . . . . . . . . . . 151, 152
   s 4f. . . . . . . . . . . . . . . . . . . . . . . . . . . . 178
   s 4g. . . . . . . . . . . . . . . . . . . . . . . . . . . . 178
   s 6b(2) . . . . . . . . . . . . . . . . . . . . . . . . . 159
   ss 24–26 . . . . . . . . . . . . . . . . . . . . . . . . 170
Data Protection Act 1999 (Hesse). . . . . . . 120
   s 1(2) . . . . . . . . . . . . . . . . . . . . . . . . . . 120
   s 24(2) . . . . . . . . . . . . . . . . . . . . . . . . . 121
   s 38 . . . . . . . . . . . . . . . . . . . . . . . . . . . 121
   s 39 . . . . . . . . . . . . . . . . . . . . . . . . . . . 121
Datenschutzgesetz vom 17 Dezember
   1990 (Berlin)
   s 1(1)(2) . . . . . . . . . . . . . . . . . . . . . . . . 121
   s 20 . . . . . . . . . . . . . . . . . . . . . . . . . . . 121
   s 24(3) . . . . . . . . . . . . . . . . . . . . . . . . . 121
Datenschutzgesetz vom 29 Oktober
   1991 (Thuringia)
   s 40(5) . . . . . . . . . . . . . . . . . . . . . . . . . 121
Datenschutzgesetz vom 17 Juni 1993
   (Lower Saxony) . . . . . . . . . . . . . . . . 121
Gesetz zum Schutz vor Misbrauch
   personbezogener Daten bei der
   Datenverarbeitung vom
   19 Dezember 1977 (Bremen) . . . . . . 121
Landesdatenschutzgesetz vom 5 Juli 1994
   (Rhineland-Palatinate)
   s 1(2) . . . . . . . . . . . . . . . . . . . . . . . . . . 121
   s 24(6) . . . . . . . . . . . . . . . . . . . . . . . . . 121
   s 36 . . . . . . . . . . . . . . . . . . . . . . . . . . . 121

**Hong Kong**
Personal Data (Privacy) Ordinance
   1995. . . . . . . . . . . . . . . . . . . . . . 104, 137
   s 37(2) . . . . . . . . . . . . . . . . . . . . . . . . . 187

**Hungary**
Constitution 1949 . . . . . . . . . . . . . . . . . . 180

**Iceland**
Protection of Individuals with regard
   to Processing of Personal Data
   Act 2000
   s 2(1) . . . . . . . . . . . . . . . . . . . . . . . . . . 135
   s 23 . . . . . . . . . . . . . . . . . . . . . . . . . . . 159
   s 24 . . . . . . . . . . . . . . . . . . . . . . . . . . . 159
   s 41 . . . . . . . . . . . . . . . . . . . . . . . . . . . 187

Protection of Personal Records Act 1989. . . . 118
   s 15 . . . . . . . . . . . . . . . . . . . . . . . . . . . 184
   s 29 . . . . . . . . . . . . . . . . . . . . . . . . . . . 165

**India**
Credit Information Companies
   (Regulation) Act 2005 . . . . . . . . . . . 104
   s 43 . . . . . . . . . . . . . . . . . . . . . . . . . . . 105
   s 43B . . . . . . . . . . . . . . . . . . . . . . . . . . 105
   s 66 . . . . . . . . . . . . . . . . . . . . . . . . . . . 105
   s 66B . . . . . . . . . . . . . . . . . . . . . . . . . . 105
   s 69B . . . . . . . . . . . . . . . . . . . . . . . . . . 105
   s 72A . . . . . . . . . . . . . . . . . . . . . . . . . . 105
Information Technology Act 2000 . . . . . . . 104

**Ireland**
Data Protection Act 1988. . . . . . . . . . . . . 138
   s 1(1) . . . . . . . . . . . . . . . . . . . . . . . . . . 132
   s 1(4)(a) . . . . . . . . . . . . . . . . . . . . . . . . 143
   s 13 . . . . . . . . . . . . . . . . . . . . . . . . . . . 178

**Israel**
Basic Law on Human Dignity and Liberty
   s 7 . . . . . . . . . . . . . . . . . . . . . . . . . . . . 106
Privacy Protection Act 5741-1981 . . . . . . . 106

**Japan**
Protection of Personal Information
   Act 2003 . . . . . . . . . . . . . . . . . . . . . . 103
Protection of Personal Information held
   by Incorporated Administrative
   Agencies Act 2003 . . . . . . . . . . . . . . 103
Use of Numbers to Identify Specific
   Individuals in Administrative
   Procedures Act 2013. . . . . . . . . . . . . 178

**Kenya**
Constitution 2010, Art 31 . . . . . . . . . . . . . 83

**Macau**
Personal Data Protection Act 2006 . . . . . . . 104

**Malaysia**
Personal Data Protection Act 2010 . . . . . . . 104
   s 2 . . . . . . . . . . . . . . . . . . . . . . . . . . . . 201

**Mauritius**
Data Protection Act 2004. . . . . . . . . . . . . 105

**Mexico**
Federal Law on Protection of Personal
   Data held by Private Parties 2010 . . . . 103
Regulation of 21 December 2011 . . . . . . . . 103

**Morocco**
Law No 09-08 on the Protection of
    Individuals in Relation to Processing
    of Personal Data . . . . . . . . . . . . . . . . .105

**Netherlands**
Personal Data Protection Act 2000
    Art 3(1) . . . . . . . . . . . . . . . . . . . . . . . .143
    Art 25. . . . . . . . . . . . . . . . . . . . . . . . . .178

**New Zealand**
Privacy Act 1993 . . . . . 50, 103, 122, 147, 163
    Preamble . . . . . . . . . . . . . . . . . . . . . . .118
    Pts VI–VII . . . . . . . . . . . . . . . . . . . . . .178
    s 23 . . . . . . . . . . . . . . . . . . . . . . . . . . .178

**Norway**
Intellectual Property Act 1961, s 45c . . . . . .13
Personal Data Act 2000 . . . . . . . . . . .127, 179
    s 1(2) . . . . . . . . . . . . . . . . . . . . . . . . . .120
    s 2(1) . . . . . . . . . . . . . . . . . . . . . . .134, 136
    s 2(8) . . . . . . . . . . . . . . . . . . . . . . . . . .185
    s 21 . . . . . . . . . . . . . . . . . . . . . . . . . . .159
    s 33 . . . . . . . . . . . . . . . . . . . . . . . .156, 185
    s 33(1) . . . . . . . . . . . . . . . . . . . . . . . . .185
    s 33(2) . . . . . . . . . . . . . . . . . . . . . . . . .185
    s 34 . . . . . . . . . . . . . . . . . . . . . . . . . . .122
    s 37(2) . . . . . . . . . . . . . . . . . . . . . . . . .185
    s 40 . . . . . . . . . . . . . . . . . . . . . . . . . . .159
    s 47 . . . . . . . . . . . . . . . . . . . . . . . . . . .187
    s 49(2) . . . . . . . . . . . . . . . . . . . . . . . . .186
Personal Data Registers
    Act 1978 . . . . . . . . . . . . . .118, 124, 184
    s 1(2) . . . . . . . . . . . . . . . . . . . . . . . . . .141

**Portugal**
Protection of Personal Data Act 1998,
    Art 2. . . . . . . . . . . . . . . . . . . . . . . . . . .118

**Romania**
Constitution 1991 . . . . . . . . . . . . . . . . . . . .68

**Russia**
Constitution 1993, Arts 23–25. . . . . . . . . .101
Federal Law on Information
    Technologies, and the Protection of
    Information 2006 (No 149-FZ) . . . . .102
Federal Law on Personal Data 2006
    (No 152-FZ) . . . . . . . . . . . . . . . . . . .102

**Seychelles**
Act No 9 of 2003 on Data Protection . . . . .105

**Singapore**
Personal Data Protection Act 2012 . . . . . . .104

**South Africa**
Bill of Rights
    s 14 . . . . . . . . . . . . . . . . . . . . . . . . .83, 106
    s 32 . . . . . . . . . . . . . . . . . . . . . . . . . . .106
Constitution 1996, Ch 2 . . . . . . . . . . .83, 106
Promotion of Access to Information
    Act 2000 . . . . . . . . . . . . . . . . . . . . . .106
Protection of Personal Information
    Act 2013 . . . . . . . . . . . . . . . . . . . . . .105

**South Korea**
Promotion of Information and
    Communications Network
    Utilization and Data Protection
    Act 1999 . . . . . . . . . . . . . . . . . . . . . .103

**Sweden**
Data Act 1973 . . . . . . . . 33, 99, 118, 125, 184
    s 4(2) . . . . . . . . . . . . . . . . . . . . . . . . . .165
Personal Data Act 1998
    s 1 . . . . . . . . . . . . . . . . . . . . . . . . . . . . .26
    s 5a. . . . . . . . . . . . . . . . . . . . . . . . . . . .101
    s 7 . . . . . . . . . . . . . . . . . . . . . . . . . . . .143
    s 36 . . . . . . . . . . . . . . . . . . . . . . . .101, 185
    s 37 . . . . . . . . . . . . . . . . . . . . . . . .101, 185
    s 41 . . . . . . . . . . . . . . . . . . . . . . . . . . .185
    s 48 . . . . . . . . . . . . . . . . . . . . . . . . . . .187

**Switzerland**
Federal Data Protection Act 1992
    Art 1. . . . . . . . . . . . . . . . . . . . . . . . . . . .26
    Art 3(c)(3) . . . . . . . . . . . . . . . . . . . . . .165
    Art 5. . . . . . . . . . . . . . . . . . . . . . . . . . .163
    Art 18(1) . . . . . . . . . . . . . . . . . . . . . . .159

**Trinidad and Tobago**
Data Protection Act 2011. . . . . . . . . . . . . .103

**Tunisia**
Organic Act No 2004-63 on Protection
    of Personal Data. . . . . . . . . . . . . . . . .105

**United Kingdom**
Copyright, Designs and Patents Act
    1988 (c 48), s 85(1) . . . . . . . . . . . . . . .13
Data Protection Act 1984 (c 35) . . . .118, 136
    s 1(7) . . . . . . . . . . . . . . . . . . . . . . . . . .136
Data Protection Act 1998 (c 29) . . . .118, 136
    s 1(3) . . . . . . . . . . . . . . . . . . . .132, 134, 135

s 14 . . . . . . . . . . . . . . . . . . . . . . . . . . .163
s 51(3) . . . . . . . . . . . . . . . . . . . . . . . . .178
s 51(4) . . . . . . . . . . . . . . . . . . . . . . . . .178
s 56 . . . . . . . . . . . . . . . . . . . . . . . . . . .160
Sch 1 Pt I . . . . . . . . . . . . . . . . . . .146, 155
Sch 1 Pt II s 1(1). . . . . . . . . . . . . . . . . .147
Human Rights Act 1998 (c 42) . . . . . . . . .183
Regulation of Investigatory Powers
    Act 2000 (c 23), s 5 . . . . . . . . . . . . . . .93

**United States**
15 USC §§ 41–48 . . . . . . . . . . . . . . . . . . .114
18 USC s 2701-11 . . . . . . . . . . . . . . . . . . .114
    s 2703(f) . . . . . . . . . . . . . . . . . . . . . . . .114
Children's Online Privacy Protection
    Act 1998 . . . . . . . . . . . . . . . . . .178, 200
    s 1302(2) . . . . . . . . . . . . . . . . . . . . . . .200
Civil Code (California)
    s 1798.29 . . . . . . . . . . . . . . . . . . . . . . .114
    s 1798.82 . . . . . . . . . . . . . . . . . . . . . . .114
Constitution. . . . . . . . . . . . . . . . . . .108, 181
    Bill of Rights, First Amendment . . . . . . .111
    Bill of Rights, Fourth Amendment . . . 90, 181

Electronic Communications Privacy
    Act 1986 . . . . . . . . . . . . . . . . . . . . . . .114
Fair Credit Reporting Act 1970 . . . . 33, 99, 178
Federal Trade Commission Act 1914
    s 5 . . . . . . . . . . . . . . . . . . . . . .114, 177, 178
Federal Privacy Act 1974 . . . . . . . . 18, 99, 153
    s 2(b) . . . . . . . . . . . . . . . . . . . . . . . . . . .118
    s 552a(e)(1) . . . . . . . . . . . . . . . . . .151, 163
    s 552a(e)(3) . . . . . . . . . . . . . . . . . . . . . .159
    s 552a(e)(5) . . . . . . . . . . . . . . . . . .151, 163
    s 552a(e)(6) . . . . . . . . . . . . . . . . . . . . . .163
Financial Services Modernization Act
    (Gramm-Leach-Bliley Act) 1999 . . . .178
Public Company Accounting Reform
    and Investor Protection Act
    (Sarbanes-Oxley Act) 2002. . . . . . . . .209
Stored Communications Act. . . . . . . . . . .114

**Uruguay**
Act No 18.331 on the Protection of
    Personal Data and 'Habeas Data'
    Action 2008 . . . . . . . . . . . . . . . . . . . .103
Decree 414/009 of 31 August 2009 . . . . . .103

# Introduction

The subject matter of this book is a body of law that is specifically aimed at regulating the processing of data on individual natural/physical persons. Its rules stipulate the manner and purposes of such data processing, measures to ensure adequate quality of the data, and measures to ensure that the processing is capable of being influenced by the persons to whom the data relates (that is, the data subjects). A primary formal objective of the rules is to safeguard the privacy-related interests of those persons. In Europe, such law tends to be described as 'data protection law'. In North America, Australia, and New Zealand, the preferred nomenclature tends to be 'privacy law'. A third label, 'data privacy law', is increasingly used too.

The book's core remit is to give a concise explication of the aims and principles of this body of law, along with the mechanisms for its oversight and enforcement, from an international perspective. By 'international perspective' is meant, first, that the law is predominantly presented through the prism of international codes and, secondly, that account is taken of rules in a broad range of countries. The book omits a detailed description of data privacy codes across all of the jurisdictions in which they have been adopted. Approximately one hundred countries have now adopted fairly comprehensive data privacy legislation so such a description would necessitate a mammoth (and quite likely boring) text. The book instead canvasses norms in international instruments, then selected national implementations or variations of those norms. Legislation of the European Union (EU) receives special attention because it is a key point of departure for the development of national data privacy regimes in many regions of the world. As for national codes, these are mainly selected on the basis of their ability to elucidate how the international codes may be applied in more concrete contexts. In some cases, the book elaborates upon national regimes because they possess fairly unique, innovative, contrarian, or otherwise noteworthy qualities.

The focus on international codes is justified because they embody the bulk of the central rules in national and sub-national codes. Furthermore, they provide templates for formulating the latter codes and govern the ability of individual states to determine data privacy policy on their own. Taken together, the international agreements described herein have exercised great influence on regulatory regimes at the national and sub-national level. This influence has gradually strengthened. Not only has the number of such agreements grown but their provisions have become increasingly elaborate. At the same time, ever more detailed data privacy requirements have been teased out from the relatively terse texts of treaties dealing with fundamental human rights. The overall result of this growth in regulatory density is a decreasing capacity of states to adopt data privacy regimes as they alone see fit. This increasing weight of the world is part of a more general trend in which international regulatory instruments cut ever greater swathes through areas once largely the preserve of national policy. Yet the exercise of influence in the data privacy field has not only flowed from the international to the national plane; national regimes have also shaped many international initiatives.

When canvassing data privacy law across jurisdictions, I make some attempt to highlight similarities and differences between various codes. Thus, the book could be regarded as a work of comparative law. Its central goal, though, is not so much comparative as to delineate broad patterns of normative development. Moreover, the book does not extensively compare the various data privacy regimes with the aim of assessing which regime comes closest to 'best practice'. Some scholars claim that such assessment is virtually impossible in the data privacy field.[1] I disagree, though recognize that such analysis is very difficult to do without misconstruing some element(s) of the compared regimes. Complicating the assessment is that each country's data privacy regime consists of more than formal legal rules. While the latter, together with formal oversight mechanisms, are important constituents of a data privacy regime, they are supplemented by a complex array of other instruments and institutions (information systems, industry codes, standards, etc.) which concurrently influence the practical impact of the legal rules. The functioning of a data privacy regime (including, of course, the extent to which 'law in books' equates with 'law in practice') is also shaped by a myriad of relatively informal customs and attitudes in the country concerned—for example, the extent to which the country's administrative and corporate cultures are imbued with a respect for authority and respect for data privacy principles. These factors can be easily overlooked or misunderstood.[2]

As already indicated, the presentation of data privacy law in this book is far from exhaustive. This is particularly so for coverage of sectoral, national,

---

[1] See eg, KS Selmer, 'Realising Data Protection' in J Bing and O Torvund (eds), *25 Years Anniversary Anthology in Computers and Law* (TANO 1995) 41, 42.

[2] For further discussion on the difficulties of comparative assessment of data privacy regimes, see CJ Bennett and CD Raab, *The Governance of Privacy: Policy Instruments in Global Perspective* (2nd edn, MIT Press 2006) ch 9; CD Raab and CJ Bennett, 'Taking the Measure of Privacy: Can Data Protection Be Evaluated?' (1996) 62 Intl Rev of Administrative Sciences 535.

and sub-national regimes. The book leaves many of their nooks and crannies unexplored in the interests of presenting the wood, as it were, rather than numerous trees. Further, my limited language skills and familiarity with particular jurisdictions lead to certain regimes being given greater prominence in the book than others. Particular regimes are left largely unexamined. For example, the book pays scant attention to data privacy codes that have been specifically developed to govern the activities of government agencies engaged in law enforcement, immigration, and border control or preservation of national security—that is, activities that typically fall within the 'Area of Freedom, Security and Justice' (AFSJ), to use EU terminology.[3] The data privacy regimes for these activities are usually complex, dense, and intricate. Just taking due account of the EU's supranational regime on point (in addition to the other less sector-specific regimes) would require a massive text. At the same time, comprehensive, up-to-date analysis of that regime already exists, thus compensating for the superficial treatment provided by this book.[4]

In light of these limitations in coverage, some of the book's conclusions might not accurately take account of particular idiosyncrasies at the sectoral, national, or sub-national levels. From a methodological perspective, the conclusions are probably best treated as 'extrapolations' that are *tentatively* capable of generalization for the bulk of data privacy regimes.[5]

Two other factors also necessitate such tentativeness. First is the dynamic character of law in the field—data privacy regimes tend to be revised fairly frequently, as shown at numerous points in the book. A second factor is that determining the proper meaning or ambit of data privacy rules as a matter of *lex lata* is often difficult. This kind of difficulty strikes any attempt to construe rules in a broad range of countries. Underlying the difficulty

---

[3] See further, Treaty on the Functioning of the European Union (TFEU) [2010] OJ C83/47 Title V.

[4] See F Boehm, *Information Sharing and Data Protection in the Area of Freedom, Security and Justice* (Springer 2012). For somewhat dated and less comprehensive analyses, see eg E de Busser, 'Purpose Limitation in EU–US Data Exchange in Criminal Matters: the Remains of the Day' in M Cools and others (eds), *Readings on Criminal Justice, Criminal Law & Policing* (Maklu 2009) 163–201; P de Hert and V Papakonstantinou, 'The Data Protection Framework Decision of 27 November 2008 Regarding Police and Judicial Cooperation in Criminal Matters—A Modest Achievement, However Not the Improvement Some Have Hoped for' (2009) 25 CLSR 403; SK Karanja, *Transparency and Proportionality in the Schengen Information System and Border Control Co-Operation* (Martinus Nijhoff 2008).

[5] See MQ Patton, *Qualitative Evaluation and Research Methods* (3rd edn, Sage 2002) 584 ('Extrapolations are modest speculations on the likely applicability of findings to other situations under similar, but not identical, conditions. Extrapolations are logical, thoughtful and problem oriented rather than statistical and probabilistic').

are cross-jurisdictional variations in legal dogmatic method, combined with the risk of miscalculating those variations' significance for determining valid law in a given context. In the data privacy field, the difficulty is exacerbated because much of the relevant legislation is diffusely formulated and accompanied by little authoritative source material for its interpretation. Commentary in the preparatory works and explanatory memoranda for the legislation is frequently sparse or nebulous. And in many jurisdictions, there is scant case law on point. Although there exists relatively extensive administrative practice pursuant to the legislation, not all of it is well documented. Nor can it be assumed as conforming to the views of the judiciary. Courts have occasionally overturned or questioned such practice.[6]

Finally, some words on the EU regulatory framework for data privacy are in order. As is well known, that framework is undergoing major reform. At the time of writing this book, the reform process is incomplete and considerable uncertainty attaches to its outcome. The first detailed reform proposals were issued by the European Commission in January 2012.[7] Just as the final touches were being put to this book, the European Parliament's Committee on Civil Liberties, Justice and Home Affairs agreed on amended versions of the Commission proposals.[8] However, this book's account of the reform proposals remains based on those issued by the Commission in 2012. The versions recently agreed in the European Parliament will be subject to negotiation with the European Council with a view to finding a 'common position', and they are most likely to be changed—perhaps significantly—in that process. Moreover, they do not depart radically from the Commission's approach.

Up until June 2013, the reform process looked to be in serious danger of stalling. However, the revelations over the large-scale electronic surveillance programmes run by the US National Security Agency have since galvanized European legislators into trying to complete the reform quickly and largely in line with the Commission's original vision. At its summit in late October 2013, the European Council stated that '[t]he timely adoption of a strong

---

[6] See eg, the decision of 12 June 2001 by the Swedish Supreme Court (Högsta domstolen) in case B293-00 (overturning administrative practice in relation to application of s 7 of the Personal Data Act 1998 (*Personuppgifslagen*, SFS 1998:204)). See further Ch 4 (n 110).

[7] See Proposal for a Regulation on the protection of individuals with regard to the processing of personal data and on the free movement of such data (General Data Protection Regulation) (COM(2012) 11 final); Proposal for a Directive on the protection of individuals with regard to the processing of personal data by competent authorities for the purposes of prevention, investigation, detection or prosecution of criminal offences or the execution of criminal penalties, and the free movement of such data (COM(2012) 10 final).

[8] 'Civil Liberties MEPs pave the way for stronger data protection in the EU', European Parliament Press Release, 21 October 2013.

EU General Data Protection Framework . . . is essential for the completion of the Digital Single Market by 2015'.[9] Indeed, there is a serious push to reach a final agreement on the new rules already by May 2014. Law reform, though, is often capricious, particularly when it concerns controversial matters. So any firm predictions as to the timing and outcome of the EU reform process ought to be taken with a grain of salt.

[9] Conclusions of the European Council 24/25 October 2013 (EUCO 169/13; 25 October 2013) para. 8; available at: <http://consilium.europa.eu/uedocs/cms_data/docs/pressdata/en/ec/139197.pdf>.

# 1

# Data Privacy Law in Context

## A. Definition of Field

Data privacy law specifically regulates all or most stages in the processing of certain kinds of data. It accordingly addresses the ways in which data is gathered, registered, stored, exploited, and disseminated. Not all types of data fall within its ambit. Its rules typically apply only to data that relates to, and permits identification of, individual physical/natural persons (hereinafter also termed simply 'individuals'). In rare cases, its rules apply also to data concerning corporations and other legal/juristic persons, along with organized collective entities more generally.[1] Formally, data privacy law is aimed primarily at safeguarding certain interests and rights of individuals in their role as data subjects—that is, when data about them is processed by others. These interests and rights are usually expressed in terms of privacy, and sometimes in terms of autonomy or integrity.

The central rules of data privacy law embody a set of largely procedural principles. The core of these principles may be summed up as follows:[2]

- personal data should be collected by fair and lawful means (principle of fair and lawful processing);
- the amount of personal data collected should be limited to what is necessary to achieve the purpose(s) for which the data is gathered and further processed (principle of minimality);
- personal data should be collected for specified, legitimate purposes, and not used in ways that are incompatible with those purposes (principle of purpose limitation);
- personal data should be relevant, accurate, and complete in relation to the purposes for which it is processed (principle of data quality);
- personal data should be protected against unauthorized attempts to disclose, delete, change, or exploit it (principle of data security);

---

[1] See further Ch 4 (section C(6)).    [2] For elaboration, see Ch 5.

- processing of personal data should be transparent to, and capable of being influenced by, the data subject (principle of data subject influence).

These are not the only principles found in data privacy law but they are central to it. More general principles not specific to the field come into play too. The proportionality principle is an example, particularly with respect to EU law.[3] Elements of the above principles and some of the rights to which they give rise are also found outside data privacy law, for instance in legislation on freedom of information (FOI)—that is, legislation enabling public access to government-held information.[4] Yet only legal instruments embracing all or most of the above principles are commonly considered as data privacy law—a line also taken in this book.

Data privacy is not fully commensurate with data security. This should be obvious from the above-listed principles but bears emphasis particularly since the European nomenclature for the field ('data protection') appears closely related to data security and has been conflated with the latter.[5] While data security is a component of a data privacy (or data protection) regime, the latter embraces other rules and measures too. At the same time, data security on its own may serve a broader range of concerns than data privacy. Whereas a primary goal of data privacy is protection of data subjects' privacy-related interests, data security as such can also be aimed at safeguarding the interests of controllers, processors, and users of all kinds of data (not just personal data) in the name of, say, national security or administrative efficiency. The same applies with the overlapping areas of information security and information systems security. The security measures are mainly directed towards ensuring that data is processed in accordance with the expectations of those who steer or use a given information system. The chief sub-goals for these measures are maintenance of the confidentiality, integrity/quality, and availability of information in an information system as well as appropriate protection of the system itself.[6] In many instances, these measures may serve to promote data privacy, but they can obviously come into conflict with the latter as well.

---

[3] See further Ch 5 (section C).      [4] See further section C.
[5] For an example from the field of database management, see CJ Date, *An Introduction to Database Systems* (6th edn, Addison-Wesley 1995) 373. Raab claims that such conflation is 'frequently encountered in organizational circles, including policing': CD Raab, 'Police Cooperation: The Prospects for Privacy' in Malcolm Andersen and Monica den Boer (eds), *Policing across National Boundaries* (Pinter 1994) 121, 124.
[6] See eg, Nordic Council of Ministers, *Information Security in Nordic Countries*, Nordiske Seminar-og Arbejdsrapporter 1993: 613 (Nordic Council of Ministers 1994) 12.

Data privacy (or data protection) is also not fully commensurate with privacy, at least if the latter is defined in terms of non-interference, limited accessibility, or information control.[7] Again this should be obvious from the principles listed earlier, but bears emphasis due to the tendency in some non-European countries to call the field simply 'privacy law'. In some respects, data privacy canvasses more than what are typically regarded as privacy concerns.[8] The rules aimed at ensuring adequate data quality are an example in point. In other respects, data privacy encompasses less than privacy per se. The latter has spatial, bodily, and perhaps psychological dimensions that are usually not directly addressed by data privacy law.[9]

Four more distinguishing features of the field are worth noting at this preliminary stage. The first is that data privacy law is largely statutory. This is not to say that case law or various forms of 'soft law', such as guidelines, recommendations, and codes of conduct, fall outside the field, but the central rules are usually laid down in legislation. In many jurisdictions, this legislation has been shaped, construed, and applied with little involvement from the judiciary.[10]

The second feature is that data privacy statutes usually establish special independent bodies to oversee their implementation. These bodies are commonly termed 'data protection authorities' or 'privacy commission(er)s'. In keeping with my choice of nomenclature for the legal field concerned, they are herein termed 'data privacy agencies' (DPAs). These bodies are usually given broad, discretionary powers to monitor and regulate the data-processing activities of organizations in the public and private sectors. Their functions typically extend to handling complaints, giving advice, and raising public awareness of data privacy.[11]

The third feature is that data privacy statutes often take the form of so-called 'framework' laws. Rather than stipulating in casuistic fashion detailed rules on data processing, the legislation tends to set down rather diffusely formulated, general rules for such processing, and provide for the subsequent development of more detailed rules as the need arises. This is symptomatic of legislators' desire for regulatory flexibility in the face of technological complexity and change, together with uncertainty over the nature of the interests to be

---

[7] On various common conceptualizations of 'privacy', see section F and references cited therein.

[8] See further Ch 4 (section B).

[9] For discussion of some of those dimensions and their interaction with data privacy law, see LA Bygrave, 'The Body as Data? Biobank Regulation via the "Back Door" of Data Protection Law' (2010) 2 Law, Innovation and Technology 1–7.

[10] Further on the role of the judiciary, see Ch 6 (section B).

[11] See further Ch 6 (section A).

protected.[12] Primary responsibility for developing more specific rules is often given to the respective DPA.

The second and third listed features underscore the fourth, which is that DPAs frequently play a lead role in laying down how data privacy law is understood and applied, even in contexts where their views on point are only advisory. In many countries, such as Australia, Denmark, France, NZ, Norway, and the UK, they have been able to play this role with little corrective input from the courts.

Having DPAs play that role carries obvious advantages—they are, after all, the appointed experts in the field. Yet there is also a risk that DPAs construe data privacy legislation in ways that further the cause of data privacy at the expense of other factors that require equal or greater weighting as a matter of *lex lata*. That risk is acute when promotion of data privacy is central to a DPA's formal remit. The judiciary, approaching the legislation with relatively fresh eyes and formally unencumbered by a pro-privacy mandate, will tend to be better able to resist such bias. Yet courts' frequent lack of familiarity with the legislation, combined with the time pressures of litigation, can result in their failing to appreciate the complexities of the legislation in ways that undermine the correctness of their judgments.[13] There is accordingly good reason to approach both administrative practice and case law in the field with a critical eye.

## B. Significance of Field

Processing personal data has always been integral to human interaction. It has long been central to the tasks of governmental agencies, especially since the emergence of the welfare state. Yet it has assumed unprecedented proportions and significance in our current 'information society', particularly as a source of economic productivity.[14] Personal data has thus been termed 'the new oil'.[15] A rapidly growing market exists in which personal data as such is traded

---

[12] See eg, H Burkert, 'The Law of Information Technology—Basic Concepts' (1988) Datenschutz und Datensicherheit 383, 384–5.

[13] See eg, Ch 5 (n 60).

[14] M Castells, *The Rise of the Network Society* (Blackwell 1996); D Bell, *The Coming of Post-Industrial Society: A Venture in Social Forecasting* (Basic Books 1973).

[15] World Economic Forum (WEF), *Personal Data: The Emergence of a New Asset Class* (WEF, January 2011), available at: <http://www3.weforum.org/docs/WEF_ITTC_PersonalDataNewAsset_Report_2011.pdf>. Brown and Marsden, though, aptly suggest that personal data ought to be viewed rather as the new 'silk', at least in the context of the Internet: I Brown and CT Marsden, *Regulating Code: Good Governance and Better Regulation in the Information Age* (MIT Press 2013) 184 ('Personal data accumulate with the individual's treks into cyberspace, and therefore a better metaphor is silk, woven into the tapestry of the user's online personality').

and employed as the basis for marketing and control strategies. Consider, for instance, the burgeoning trade in customer lists as commodities in their own right.[16] Consider also how much of the 'Internet economy' is fuelled by, and premised on, persons supplying data about themselves (wittingly or unwittingly) in exchange for otherwise ostensibly free online services. At the same time, the informational appetite of public sector agencies grows too. This is most obvious (though often hard to document reliably) with the surveillance schemes of national security and police agencies. Consider, for instance, the expansive ambitions behind some such schemes initiated as part of the ongoing 'war on terror'.[17] The delivery of services by other government agencies involves intensified processing of personal data as well. This intensification has traditionally been justified in terms of ensuring that services flow only to those citizens who need or legally qualify for them.[18] In recent years, fiscal imperatives have also played a prominent role in justifying agencies' push for more fine-grained knowledge of their 'clients' and 'customers'.[19]

It is in light of all these developments that the broad significance of data privacy law becomes apparent. Because it seeks to regulate directly the exploitation of personal data, such law has the potential to interfere (positively or negatively) with many of the processes mentioned. It can thereby generate considerable administrative, commercial, political, or social costs (or gains). This potential is augmented by the considerable powers that DPAs are often given to steer data-processing activities in both the public and private sectors.

Data privacy law is also important on the normative plane. In the 'information society', its principles and ideals are amongst the central counterweights to technocratic imperatives, such as increased organizational efficiency and maximization of financial profit. This is not to suggest that data privacy law is intrinsically opposed to such imperatives; in some respects, it aids their realization. Yet it also emphasizes a need to take account of other interests, thus enriching our normative sphere.

The broad significance of data privacy law is partly reflected in the heightened focus on rights to privacy and private life, with which such law is closely

---

[16] E Novak, N Sinha, and O Gandy, 'The Value of Your Name' (1990) 12 Media, Culture & Society 525.

[17] See eg, S Gorman, 'NSA's Domestic Spying Grows As Agency Sweeps Up Data', *Wall Street Journal*, 10 March 2008, A1; G Greenwald and E MacAskill, 'NSA Taps in to Internet Giants' Systems to Mine User Data, Secret Files Reveal', *The Guardian*, 6 June 2013, available at: <http://www.guardian.co.uk/world/2013/jun/06/us-tech-giants-nsa-data>.

[18] See eg, J Rule, D McAdam, L Stearns, and D Uglow, *The Politics of Privacy: Planning for Personal Data Systems As Powerful Technologies* (Elsevier 1980) 43, 45, 48–9.

[19] D Lyon, *The Electronic Eye: The Rise of Surveillance Society* (Polity Press 1994) 88ff and references cited therein.

connected. Frowein and Peukert claim that the right to private life has con-stituted the major challenge for liberal states' legal systems during the latter half of the twentieth century.[20] The claim is somewhat exaggerated yet has a kernel of truth. Debate over privacy rights has assumed a prominent place in many legal systems. For instance, the right to respect for private life set down in Article 8 of the 1950 European Convention for the Protection of Human Rights and Fundamental Freedoms (ECHR)[21] has become one of the most frequently contested rights in case law pursuant to the Convention.[22] This is symptomatic of the gradual expansion of the public sphere into previously private domains—a development partly brought on by organizations' grow-ing informational appetite. Privacy rights are being used to shield persons from the detrimental effects of this development.

The broad significance of data privacy law is further reflected in the contro-versy frequently embroiling its gestation. The birth of the Federal Republic of Germany's first Federal Data Protection Act was well nigh the hitherto most complicated, drawn out, and contentious legislative process in the country's history.[23] Subsequent revision of that Act and its replacement by new legis-lation was also far from 'short and sweet'.[24] In Finland, work on drafting the country's first main data privacy law—the Personal Data Registers Act 1987[25]—took over fifteen years and was frequently paralysed by political conflict.[26] Initial enactment of similar legislation in many other jurisdictions, such as the UK, Australia, and the Netherlands, was also controversial.[27] At the supranational level, the EU's drafting and adoption of the Data Protection

---

[20] JA Frowein and W Peukert, *Europäische MenschenRechtsKonvention: EMRK-Kommentar* (2nd edn, NP Engel 1996) 338.

[21] Opened for signature 4 November 1950; in force 3 September 1953; ETS 5 (hereinafter also 'European Convention on Human Rights' or 'ECHR').

[22] For an overview of this case law, see DJ Harris, M O'Boyle, E Bates, and C Buckley, *Harris, O'Boyle & Warbrick: Law of the European Convention on Human Rights* (2nd edn, OUP 2009) chs 8–9.

[23] S Simitis, 'Einleitung' in S Simitis, U Dammann, O Mallmann, and HJ Reh (eds), *Kommentar zum Bundesdatenschutzgesetz* (3rd edn, Nomos 1981) 69. Further on the process in English, see eg, AL Newman, *Protectors of Privacy: Regulating Personal Data in the Global Economy* (Cornell University Press 2008) 63–9.

[24] S Simitis, 'Einleitung' in S Simitis (ed), *Bundesdatenschutzgesetz* (7th edn, Nomos 2011) 97–115.

[25] *Henkilörekisterilaki/Personregisterlag* (FFS 471/87); repealed and replaced by the Personal Data Act 1999 (*Henkilötietolaki/Personuppgiftslag* (FFS 523/99)).

[26] See eg, J Kuopos, 'Finland' in D Campbell and J Fisher (eds), *Data Transmission and Privacy* (Martinus Nijhoff 1994) 161, 162.

[27] Regarding the UK, see eg, CJ Bennett, *Regulating Privacy. Data Protection and Public Policy in Europe and the United States* (Cornell University Press 1992) 82–94, 209ff. In relation to Australia, see eg, LA Bygrave, 'The Privacy Act 1988 (Cth): A Study in the Protection of Privacy and the Protection of Political Power' (1990) 19 Federal L Rev 128, 137ff. Regarding the Netherlands, see eg, VA de Pous, 'Dutch Privacy Bill Again Delayed' (1988) 11 Transnational Data Report, no. 10, 6–7.

Directive (95/46/EC)[28] took over five years and was subject to hefty debate and frenetic lobbying.[29] The legislative process currently in train with the proposal for a new EU Regulation in the field bears similar hallmarks.[30]

Although much of the controversy afflicting these legislative processes springs from the laws' putative potential to impinge negatively upon the ways in which organizations function, other factors have sometimes played a role too. For instance, the constitutional system of the UK along with its customary statutory drafting techniques hampered the initial adoption of data privacy legislation there.[31]

The legislative controversy in this area has sometimes been channelled along the traditional, Left–Right axis of political conflict—the case, for example, in Finland.[32] Yet concern for data privacy generally spans a broad range of political ideologies. In the words of Bennett:

[t]he issue [of data privacy] is so sufficiently broad that it can encompass a variety of different positions, from the civil libertarian who demands constraints on overzealous law enforcement to the conservative business group that wants tax data to be kept confidential. The issue tends to pose a dilemma for democratic socialist parties in particular; it exposes a tension between the welfare statism of the old Left, which relies on a sacrifice of individual privacy for the collective benefit, and the more antistatist individualism of the new Left. Thus below the broad liberal democratic concern for individualism and human dignity lies a complex and often contradictory set of positions. [...] The ideological foundations of the issue are inherently ambiguous because privacy and data protection do not stir partisan emotion until the debate centers on particular information in specific contexts. We then find a complexity of cross-cutting concerns.[33]

---

[28] Directive 95/46/EC on the protection of individuals with regard to the processing of personal data and on the free movement of such data [1995] OJ L281/31.

[29] See eg, N Platten, 'Background to and History of the Directive' in D Bainbridge (ed), *EC Data Protection Directive* (Butterworths 1996) 23–32; S Simitis, 'From the Market to the Polis: The EU Directive on the Protection of Personal Data' (1995) 80 Iowa L Rev 445. For a detailed description of the lobbying campaigns, see PM Regan, 'American Business and the European Data Protection Directive: Lobbying Strategies and Tactics' in CJ Bennett and R Grant (eds), *Visions of Privacy: Policy Choices for the Digital Age* (University of Toronto Press 1999) 199.

[30] See eg, C Burton, C Kuner, and A Pateraki, 'The Proposed EU Data Protection Regulation One Year Later: The Albrecht Report' *Bloomberg BNA Privacy and Security Law Report* (21 January 2013) 1. The proposed Regulation is dealt with in Ch 2 (section E(3)).

[31] PM Regan, 'Protecting Privacy and Controlling Bureaucracies: Constraints of British Constitutional Principles' (1990) 3 *Governance* 33; M Stallworthy, 'Data Protection: Regulation in a Deregulatory State' (1990) 11 Statute L Rev 130, 134ff.

[32] A Saarenpää, 'Data Protection: In Pursuit of Information. Some Background to, and Implementations of, Data Protection in Finland' (1997) 11 Intl Rev of Law, Computers & Technology 47, 48.

[33] Bennett (n 27) 147.

Its broad normative and practical significance notwithstanding, data privacy law is not the only set of legal rules impacting on organizations' informational appetite. Consider, for instance, employers' ability to engage in employee surveillance: in addition to data privacy law, rules in both statute and case law dealing specifically with labour relations may also have an impact, as may various contracts. For example, the European Social Charter[34] contains general provisions establishing workers' rights to 'just conditions of work' (Article 2), to 'information and consultation' by and from employers (Article 21), to co-determination of working conditions (Article 22), and to 'dignity at work' (Article 26). Each of these rights indirectly restricts employers' monitoring of their employees. As for contracts, collective bargaining agreements or collective employment agreements reached between employers and trade unions may contain rules limiting workplace surveillance. Further, the terms of the individual contract of employment may be important in determining how data on an employee is collected by their employer and the uses to which that data may be put, particularly in the absence of further consent by the employee.

## C.  Catalysts and Origins

The aetiology of data privacy law is complex. This section provides only a short, simplified explication.[35] In a nutshell, data privacy law results from an attempt to secure the privacy, autonomy, and integrity of individuals and thereby the bases for democratic, pluralist society in the face of massive growth in the amount of personal data gathered and shared by organizations. Other law has been perceived as unable to adequately secure these interests. Data privacy law has thus been created to fill the breach.

Looking more closely at that account, we see three categories of factors behind the emergence of data privacy law: (i) technological and organizational developments in the processing of personal data; (ii) fears about these developments; and (iii) other legal rules. Each of these categories is elaborated in the following.

---

[34] First version (ETS 35) opened for signature 18 October 1961; in force 26 February 1965. Revised version (ETS 163) opened for signature 3 May 1996; in force 1 July 1999.

[35] A fuller explanation—upon which this account builds—is given in LA Bygrave, *Data Protection Law: Approaching Its Rationale, Logic and Limits* (Kluwer Law International 2002) ch 6.

## 1. Technological and organizational developments

The first category embraces a broad range of developments in data processing. They are developments facilitated and, to some extent, driven by the growing power of information and communication technology (ICT). Yet their catalysts are also economic, social, and political. They are linked with efforts to enhance organizational efficiency, profitability, prestige, control, and service. Such efforts are symptomatic of a deep-seated concern for reflexivity and rationalization.

The most important developments are, firstly, greater dissemination, use, and re-use of personal data across organizational boundaries and, secondly, replacement or augmentation of manual control mechanisms by automated mechanisms. Corollaries of these trends include increases in:

• use of data for purposes other than the purposes for which it was originally collected ('re-purposing');
• potential for misinterpretation and misapplication of data and for dissemination of invalid or misleading data;
• automatization of organizational decision-making processes;
• the blurring and dissolution of transactional contours.

These developments result in information systems of growing complexity and diminishing transparency, at least from the perspective of individuals in their role as data subjects. At the same time, individuals are rendered increasingly transparent for the various organizations with whom they deal. An evermore pervasive, subtle, and finely spun web of mechanisms monitor and shape their activities. Individuals additionally risk being assessed or interfered with on the basis of data about them that is incorrect or otherwise of poor quality.

All of these developments figure in the discourse out of which data privacy law has emerged, though they are often less abstract than the above depiction suggests.[36] An early manifestation of them (or, more accurately, elements of them) was government initiatives during the 1960s and early 1970s to

---

[36] In the USA, see particularly, AF Westin, *Privacy and Freedom* (Atheneum 1967) chs 7 and 12; AR Miller, *The Assault on Privacy: Computers, Data Banks and Dossiers* (University of Michigan Press 1971) chs I–III. In the UK, see eg, M Warner and M Stone, *The Databank Society: Organizations, Computers, and Social Freedom* (Allen & Unwin 1970); P Sieghart, *Privacy and Computers* (Latimer 1976) esp. chs 2–3. In Norway, see eg, E Samuelsen, *Statlige databanker og personlighetsvern* (Universitetsforlaget 1972) 11–12 and ch 4; *Offentlige persondatasystem og personvern*, NOU 1975:10 esp. 10ff; *Persondata og personvern*, NOU 1974:22 esp. 6–7, 28ff. In Sweden, see particularly *Data och integritet*, SOU 1972:47 esp. 30–2, and chs 3–7. In Switzerland, see esp. *Botschaft zum Bundesgesetz über den Datenschutz vom 23.3.1988* 4–5. For a general overview of this discourse and the issues motivating it, see Bennett (n 27) ch 2.

establish centralized population databases.[37] Government plans to conduct comprehensive national population censuses were another manifestation,[38] as were efforts to introduce common criteria (for example, multi-purpose Personal Identification Numbers (PINs)) for matching stored data.[39] These and similar schemes provided much of the fuel for the public debates that helped set in train the enactment of early data privacy legislation.[40]

## 2. Fears

The debates have expressed a congeries of fears clustered about three inter-related themes: (i) increasing transparency, disorientation, and disempowerment of individuals; (ii) loss of control over technology; and (iii) dehumanization of societal processes. The central fear relates primarily to the first-mentioned theme: it is that these developments, if unchecked, will undermine the foundations of democratic, pluralist society. Experiences of systematic authoritarian repression (for example, Nazism) and attempts to subvert political due process (for example, the Watergate scandal) have fed this fear, as has dystopian literature (for example, Orwell's *Nineteen Eighty-Four*). The pervasiveness of the fear reflects growing distrust of organizations and technology. This growth in distrust reflects, in turn, a general societal trend whereby human action is increasingly weighed down by awareness of risk.[41]

Another class of fears has also played a role in the adoption of data privacy codes, though *after* these codes' initial enactment in the 1970s. The fears are primarily economic in nature and shared by governments and businesses. One anxiety is that data privacy law will unduly impede transborder flow of data. This anxiety arose because the nascent national data privacy laws of Europe restricted flow of personal data to countries not offering levels of data privacy similar to the 'exporting' jurisdiction. As elaborated in Chapter 6,

---

[37] A salient example was the proposal in the mid-1960s to set up a National Data Center in the USA which would consolidate in one database all information on US citizens held by federal government agencies: see further Miller (n 36) 54–67. Another was the implementation in France of a computerized system (SAFARI—Système automatisé pour les fichiers administratifs et le répertoire des individus) which was to aggregate data on French citizens using their social security numbers as a key for the matching: see further A Vitalis, 'France' in JB Rule and G Greenleaf (eds), *Global Privacy Protection: The First Generation* (Edward Elgar 2008) 107.

[38] The most high profile of these plans was embodied in the German federal Census Act 1983—legislation that triggered a famous decision by the German Federal Constitutional Court on the constitutional right to 'informational self-determination'. See further Ch 6 (n 45).

[39] A prominent and highly controversial example being the 'Australia Card' scheme of 1987: see further G Greenleaf, 'Australia' in JB Rule and G Greenleaf (eds), *Global Privacy Protection: The First Generation* (Edward Elgar 2008) 141–2.

[40] See too generally Bennett (n 27) 46–53.

[41] For seminal analysis on point, see U Beck, *Risk Society: Towards a New Modernity* (Sage 1992).

such restrictions have become an integral element of numerous data privacy regimes. The principal international codes in the field have all been introduced partly in order to minimize the deleterious impact that such restrictions could exercise on international commerce and freedom of expression. The other fear concerns the possibility that, in the absence of data privacy law, the general populace will lack confidence to participate in commerce, particularly as consumers/prosumers. Enactment of data privacy law can thus be partly explained as an effort to shore up public trust in the way organizations process personal data.[42]

## 3. Legal factors

Data privacy legislation would obviously not have been enacted but for perceived failings in the ability of pre-existing laws to tackle adequately the problems arising out of the earlier mentioned two categories of factors. To some extent, pre-existing laws were perceived as *aggravating* these problems. In Sweden, for example, its constitutionally entrenched, long-standing, and liberal freedom of information (FOI) regime was regarded as particularly problematic for privacy with the advent of computerization. The latter meant that the exercise of FOI rights could lead to relatively fast and easy dissemination of large amounts of personal data. Enactment of Sweden's first data privacy legislation has accordingly been described as 'a qualification of the principle of freedom of information, made in recognition of the threat to personal privacy raised by the age of computers'.[43]

Pre-existing law has also shaped data privacy law in a more positive way, by providing normative foundations or sources of inspiration for it. Statutory rules and case law laying down rights to privacy or protection of personality are the most obvious instances.[44] Rules on defamation are also pertinent. All of these rules prefigure the basic thrust of data privacy law in that they restrict various kinds of behaviour, including certain ways of processing information, in order to protect the integrity, autonomy, dignity, or privacy of individuals.

Less obvious but perhaps more important in this respect is the role played by administrative law together with general doctrines on the rule of law. Traditional rules on due administrative process embody principles that are

---

[42] See further eg, H Burkert, 'Systemvertrauen: Ein Versuch über einige Zusammenhänge zwischen Karte und Datenschutz' (1991) *á la Card Euro-Journal*, no. 1, 52.

[43] DH Flaherty, *Protecting Privacy in Surveillance Societies* (University of North Carolina Press 1989) 99.

[44] For Norwegian examples, see Bygrave (n 35) 126–7.

precursors to some of the central data privacy principles. Strong links exist between the principles of data quality and data subject influence in data privacy law on the one hand and, on the other hand, the general requirements of procedural fairness ('natural justice') under administrative law. Central amongst those requirements are that government agencies base their decisions on relevant evidence, be unbiased in the matters to be determined, and give persons who may be adversely affected by the decisions the opportunity to be heard. Moreover, the right under data privacy law of data subjects to access data on themselves kept by others parallels the information access rights under FOI legislation. This is not to say that these areas of law are fully commensurate with each other. In contrast to data privacy law, FOI legislation usually allows persons access to both personal and non-personal information held by government and, concomitantly, to information not just on themselves but other persons.[45] Thus, exercise of FOI rights can come into conflict with data privacy.[46] Whereas administrative law is traditionally limited to regulating the relationship between state organs and citizens, data privacy law often regulates the relationship between private organizations and individuals as well. And whereas large parts of administrative law focus on specific decision-making schemes, data privacy law focuses mainly on the processing of personal data, which is not necessarily tied to a specific decisional process.

Law and doctrine on human rights also pervade data privacy law. Indeed, as elaborated in the next chapter, they are now generally regarded as providing the principal normative basis for such law. Concomitantly, much of the latter is now seen as both an expression and specialized branch of the former. This is especially noteworthy as the links between data privacy and human rights were less recognized when data privacy legislation first emerged. In Norway, for instance, enactment of its first data privacy statute in 1978 was accompanied by considerable awareness of the close similarities with administrative law whilst the connection to human rights was downplayed.[47] Also noteworthy is that the Council of Europe began work on drafting its early data privacy codes due to a perception that the ECHR did not provide

---

[45] Further on the differences and similarities between FOI and data privacy law, see H Burkert, 'Data Protection and Access to Data' in P Seipel (ed), *From Data Protection to Knowledge Machines* (Kluwer Law & Taxation Publishers 1990) 49; European Data Protection Supervisor (EDPS), *Public Access to Documents and Data Protection* (EC 2005).

[46] See eg, Ch 4 (n 87).

[47] See eg, J Bing, 'Information Law?' (1982) 2 J of Law and Media Practice 219, 232 (claiming that Norwegian and other European data privacy laws are 'more closely related to the law of public administration than to the law of individual liberties'). See further Bygrave (n 35) 127–8 and references cited therein.

adequate protection for individuals in the face of computerized processing of personal data, particularly in the private sector.[48] Case law of the ECtHR since then has shown that the ECHR is a powerful data privacy instrument in its own right.[49] Other courts and lawmakers increasingly use that jurisprudence as benchmarks for developing, interpreting, and applying data privacy instruments.[50]

Numerous other areas of law have helped inspire or support data privacy law. These include rules in labour law on worker co-determination and fair workplace practices. For example, the first influential set of data privacy principles drafted in the USA—the 'Fair Information Practices' drawn up in 1973 by the federal Department of Health, Education and Welfare (DHEW)[51]— are said to have been inspired by a code of fair labour practices.[52]

Law on intellectual property rights (IPR) is a further case in point. Doctrines on copyright have been used to help ground a right to privacy, which has, in turn, helped ground data privacy law, while privacy doctrines have been used to help ground aspects of copyright.[53] The two sets of rights have also worked hand in hand on a more practical plane. For instance, the publication of certain film material in which persons are portrayed is often restricted under copyright law.[54] Nonetheless, the relationship of copyright and data privacy has grown far less cordial over the last 15 years. In their battle against digital piracy, IPR-holders have frequently been frustrated by data privacy law, particularly for hindering their ability to identify the putative pirates. A remarkably large part of recent litigation on data privacy law has been initiated by IPR-holders seeking to curtail such hindrances.[55]

---

[48] See eg, FW Hondius, *Emerging Data Protection in Europe* (North Holland Publishing Company 1975) 63ff and references cited therein.

[49] See further Ch 2 (section I(2)).        [50] See eg, Ch 2 (n 109).

[51] US Department of Health, Education and Welfare, *Records, Computers and the Rights of Citizens* (US Government Printing Office 1973) 41.

[52] WH Ware, 'A Historical Note' in US Department of Health and Human Services, Task Force on Privacy, *Health Records: Social Needs and Personal Privacy* (Conference Proceedings) (US Government Printing Office 1993) Addendum A, 50.

[53] Famous examples being S Warren and L Brandeis, 'The Right to Privacy' (1890) 4 Harvard L Rev 193, 198 (arguing, inter alia, that common law protection of intellectual, artistic, and literary property is based upon a broader principle of protection of privacy and personality); J Kohler, 'Das Autorrecht' (1880) 18 Jherings Jahrbücher für die Dogmatik des Bürgerliches Rechts 128 (basing authors' moral rights partly on the notion that the authors' works originate within their private sphere).

[54] See eg, UK Copyright, Designs and Patents Act 1988 s 85(1); Australia's federal Copyright Act 1968 s 35(5); Norway's Intellectual Property Act 1961 (*lov om opphavsrett til åndsverk mv 12 mai 1961 nr 2*) s 45c.

[55] See further LA Bygrave, 'Data Protection versus Copyright' in DJB Svantesson and S Greenstein (eds), *Internationalisation of Law in the Digital Information Society: Nordic Yearbook of Law and Informatics 2010–2012* (Ex Tuto Publishing 2013) 55.

Turning to doctrines on property rights more generally, these have undoubtedly played a part in inspiring data privacy law. However, gauging the extent of
this role is difficult. Much depends on how property rights are defined. They
can be defined so generally as to to form the basis for large tracts of the legal
system.[56] If defined more narrowly as conferring a legally enforceable claim on
the rights holder to exclude others from utilizing a particular object or thing,
we can still discern some reflection of such rights in the requirement under
data privacy law that processing of personal data is conditional on the consent
of the data subject(s).[57] However, data privacy law frequently permits circumvention of that requirement so the resultant level of data 'ownership' often has
little real traction.[58] There tend to be few, if any, other obvious manifestations
of property rights doctrines in data privacy statutes or their *travaux prépara-
toires*. Some of the early and influential contributors to the discourse out of
which data privacy law emerged championed property rights as a foundation
for such law.[59] However, others amongst them rejected this line.[60] Subsequent
advancement of a property rights approach tends to come from US scholars,[61]
although the most recent and thorough advocacy of such an approach comes
from a European.[62] Nonetheless, the majority of contributors to the debate,
especially in Europe, reject property rights doctrines as a desirable basis for
data privacy law.[63]

---

[56] See eg, Warren and Brandeis (n 53) 211 ('The right of property in its widest sense, including all
possession, including all rights and privileges, and hence embracing the right to an inviolate personality,
affords alone that broad basis upon which the protection which the individual demands can be rested').
[57] See further D Elgesem, 'Remarks on the Right of Data Protection' in J Bing and O Torvund
(eds), *25 Years Anniversary Anthology in Computers and Law* (TANO 1995) 83, 90ff.
[58] See further Ch 5 (section F).        [59] See eg, Westin (n 36) 324–5.
[60] See eg, Miller (n 36) 211ff.
[61] See eg, KC Laudon, 'Markets and Privacy' (1996) 39 Communications of the ACM 92; L
Lessig, *Code, and Other Laws of Cyberspace* (Basic Books 1999) 159–62; JB Rule and L Hunter,
'Towards Property Rights in Personal Data' in CJ Bennett and R Grant (eds), *Visions of Privacy: Policy
Choices for the Digital Age* (University of Toronto Press, 1999) 168–81; JB Rule, *Privacy in Peril*
(OUP 2007) 196–8. Cf PM Schwartz, 'Property, Privacy, and Personal Data' (2004) 117 Harvard L
Rev 2056 (critically discussing various objections to a property approach but ultimately arguing in
favour of a qualified 'propertization' of personal data).
[62] See N Purtova, *Property Rights in Personal Data: A European Perspective* (Kluwer Law International
2012) (arguing that current European law can accommodate property rights in personal data and
that such rights may strengthen data subjects' ability to exercise control over others' processing of data
on them, particularly in an era of widespread commodification of such data).
[63] See, inter alia, Hondius (n 48) 103–5; S Simitis, 'Reviewing Privacy in an Information
Society' (1987) 135 University of Pennsylvania L Rev 707, 735–6; KG Wilson, *Technologies of
Control: The New Interactive Media for the Home* (University of Wisconsin Press 1988) 91–4;
R Wacks, *Personal Information: Privacy and the Law* (Clarendon Press 1989) 49; Y Poullet, 'Data
Protection between Property and Liberties—A Civil Law Approach' in HWK Kaspersen and

The role played by the above legal factors in catalyzing or shaping data privacy law has varied from country to country and period to period. For instance, some countries adopted data privacy statutes without having comprehensive FOI legislation already in place (for example, Germany and the UK) or without specifically recognizing a right to privacy in their legal systems (for example, Australia and the UK). Some countries failed to see the close parallels between data privacy law and FOI law when these laws were first adopted (for example, France).[64] Other countries adopted the two types of law as a single legislative package (for example, Canada and Hungary).

## D. Regulatory Cross-Fertilization and Colonization

The exercise of legal influence in the data privacy field has not been simply unidirectional; data privacy law is inspiring changes in other legal fields. This cross-fertilization has come furthest in the interaction of data privacy law and human rights law. On the one hand, the emergence of data privacy law has engendered greater readiness to construe treaty provisions on the right to privacy as containing data privacy guarantees.[65] On the other, such readiness serves to stimulate the enactment or strengthening of data privacy legislation and to anchor it more firmly in traditional human rights doctrines, thereby influencing the way it is conceptualized.

In other areas, we see only the beginnings of a potential cross-fertilization process. An example is the interaction of data privacy law with competition law. In at least one jurisdiction (Belgium), elements of data privacy law have infused traditional doctrines on 'fair competition'.[66] However, the scale of

---

A Oskamp (eds), *Amongst Friends in Computers and Law: A Collection of Essays in Remembrance of Guy Vandenberghe* (Kluwer Law & Taxation Publishers 1990) 161–81; J Litman, 'Information Privacy/Information Property' (2000) 52 Stanford L Rev 1283; Bygrave (n 35) 111.

[64] See further, H Burkert, 'Access to Information and Data Protection Considerations' in C de Terwangne, H Burkert, and Y Poullet (eds), *Towards a Legal Framework for a Diffusion Policy for Data held by the Public Sector* (Kluwer Law & Taxation Publishers 1995) 23, 49.

[65] See further Ch 2 (section I(2)).

[66] See the judgment of 15 September 1994 by the Tribunal de commerce de Bruxelles in *Aff CCH v Générale de Banque*, and the judgment of 7 July 1994 by the Tribunal de commerce d'Anvers in *Aff Feprabel et Fédération des courtiers en Assurances v Kredietbank NV*, both reported in (1994) Droit de l'informatique et des télécoms, no. 4, 45–55. The plaintiffs (two federations of insurance agents in the one case; a financial credit bureau in the other) sued two banks for engaging in unfair competition occasioned by the banks' use of a particular strategy for marketing their services at the expense of similar services offered by the plaintiffs. In both cases, the strategy in dispute involved the banks analysing data on their clients which they had acquired in the course of normal banking operations, to offer the clients certain financial services (in the one case, insurance; in the other case, mortgage

such infusion appears so far to be extremely modest. We have yet to see clear evidence of competition law rubbing off on the practice or conceptualization of data privacy law.

Cross-fertilization processes are very much at work within data privacy law itself. These concern the interaction of various countries' regulatory cultures in the field. The international codes on data privacy clearly manifest the results of such interaction. Those codes are a co-production of rules by various countries that each bring to bear their own particular tradition and perspective. As elaborated in the next chapter, this co-production has occurred across fairly broad geographical and ideological divides.

Data privacy law is also being applied in a process of regulatory colonization. By this is meant that the law is applied to an area that it was not originally conceived to cover (strong colonization) or it is used as the primary model for developing *sui generis* rules for that area (weak colonization; fertilization). The most salient area in which these processes are occurring is the regulation of biobanks containing human organic material. This is an area where, in some countries, a regulatory vacuum pertains or, in other countries, the pre-existing regulation is parlous.[67]

Denmark's data privacy regime is an example of strong colonization. The Danish DPA (Datatilsynet) has determined that human biological material contains 'personal information' insofar as the material can be linked to individual persons, and that non-electronic systematic processing of such material by private sector entities falls within the ambit of Denmark's Personal Data Act 2000.[68] The DPA has further held that a structured collection of such material (that is, a biobank) constitutes a manual (non-electronic) 'filing system' ('register') for the purposes of the Act.[69] The Agency took a similar view of the status of biobanks under Denmark's previous data protection legislation.[70]

---

loans) that undercut the same sorts of services already received by the clients from the plaintiffs. The plaintiffs claimed that the strategy breached the finality principle laid down in Belgian data privacy law and that this breach also resulted in violation of doctrines on fair competition. The judges found for the plaintiffs in both cases.

[67] Bygrave (n 9) 21 and references cited therein.

[68] Case 2000-321-0049 described in *Datatilsynets årsberetning 2000 [Annual Report 2000]* (August 2001) 27–8. See further also M Hartlev, 'The Implementation of Data Protection Directive 95/46/EC in Denmark' in D Beyleveld, D Townend, S Rouillé-Mirza, and J Wright,(eds), *Implementation of the Data Protection Directive in Relation to Medical Research in Europe* (Ashgate 2004) 60, 69.

[69] Section 3(3) defines such a system as 'any structured set of personal data which are accessible according to specific criteria, whether centralized, decentralized or dispersed on a functional or geographical basis'.

[70] See eg, P Blume, *Personregistrering* (3rd edn, Akademisk 1996) 151 regarding the Public Authorities' Registers Act 1978 (*Lov nr 294 af 8 juni 1978 om offentlig myndigheders registre*) (repealed).

As for weak colonization, we see examples of this in recent recommendations from the Council of Europe and OECD dealing with biobanks.[71] The recommendations are closely modelled on data privacy law. Their rules for use of body samples largely parallel the data privacy rules that would otherwise apply to the information generated from such samples.

## E. Actors in the Field

A profusion of actors shape and apply data privacy law. Their roles may be categorized according to two main spheres of activity. One sphere concerns the operationalization of data privacy law, more specifically the ways in which the law is actually applied to specific data-processing operations or to the information systems that support these operations. I term this the 'operative sphere'. The other sphere concerns the drafting, adoption, and amendment of data privacy law. I call this the 'legislative sphere', although the term is used in a broad sense and covers some activities that are only indirectly connected to concrete legislative processes.

### 1. Actors in the operative sphere

In relation to the operative sphere, data privacy law typically accords at least three categories of actors with competence to decide how the law shall be applied in concrete situations. One category is the data subject—that is, the person to whom the data relates.[72] Data subjects typically exercise their decision-making competence pursuant to rules requiring their consent as a precondition for data processing, or rules permitting them to request access to data kept on them by others. Another category of actor is the data controller (hereinafter also termed simply 'controller'). This is the person or organization which determines the purposes and means of data processing. The controller need not be in possession of personal data; the crucial criterion is control. Under many laws, that control may also be shared.[73] Controllers bear chief liability for complying with the data-processing principles stipulated by the laws.

---

[71] Council of Europe Recommendation Rec (2006) 4 on Research on Biological Materials of Human Origin (adopted 15 March 2006); OECD Recommendation on Human Biobanks and Genetic Research Databases (adopted 22 October 2009) with accompanying guidelines.

[72] See eg, DPD Art. 2(a) which defines 'personal data' as 'any information relating to an identified or identifiable natural person ("*data subject*")' (emphasis added).

[73] See eg, DPD Art. 2(d) which defines 'controller' as the 'natural or legal person, public authority, agency or any other body which alone *or jointly with others* determines the purposes and means of the processing of personal data' (emphasis added).

A third category of actor is the DPA. The competence of DPAs tends to be more powerful than that of controllers: they usually have, for instance, the power to review (that is, to consider and overturn) the decisions of the latter.[74] They may sometimes have the power to determine the conditions for certain forms of data processing independently not just of controllers' wishes but also those of data subjects (for example, the case under a licensing regime).[75]

These actors are not the only ones with operative competence under data privacy law, yet it is they who most commonly exercise it. Courts and tribunals may also have such competence, but this will typically be exercised only on appeal from a DPA decision. In other words, the competence of the tribunal or court will typically be exercised as a power of review instigated by complaint. In many jurisdictions, this power of review tends to be exercised only exceptionally—as indicated in section A. Moreover, its 'operative' impact may be further reduced where the appeal body is limited to passing judgment on points of law rather than fact, or where the range of remedies that the body may apply is narrow.[76]

Another category of actor that figures expressly in data privacy law is the data processor (hereinafter also termed simply 'processor'). This is the person or organization which actually carries out the processing (including collection, registration, and storage) of data. For the purposes of data privacy law, processors are typically subservient to controllers—when they process personal data, they do so 'on behalf of' the latter,[77] and they act only under the latter's instructions.[78]

## 2. Actors in the legislative sphere

In developing and shaping data privacy law, the Council of Europe (CoE), Organisation for Economic Cooperation and Development (OECD), United Nations (UN), and EU have for a long time played the main roles at the

---

[74] See further Ch 6 (section A).      [75] See Ch 6 (section C).

[76] The case under the US federal Privacy Act 1974. A US federal court can only issue enforcement orders relating to the exercise of persons' rights to access and rectify information relating to themselves. The court can also order relief for damages in limited situations but cannot otherwise order US federal government agencies to change their data-processing practices. See further PM Schwartz and JR Reidenberg, *Data Privacy Law: A Study of United States Data Protection* (Michie Law Publishers 1996) 100, 114ff.

[77] See DPD Art. 2(e) which denotes a 'processor' as a person or organization engaged in processing of personal data 'on behalf of' a data controller.

[78] See eg, DPD Art. 17(3): 'The carrying out of processing by way of a processor must be governed by a contract or legal act binding the processor to the controller and stipulating in particular that…the processor shall act only on instructions from the controller'. Note, though, that the General Data Protection Regulation proposed by the European Commission in 2012 vests processors with greater independent responsibility than under the DPD: see further Ch 2 (section E(3)).

international level, although not always uniformly or concurrently. A large range of other inter- and non-governmental organizations have played a relatively marginal, though not insignificant, role in setting data privacy standards. These include the World Trade Organisation, International Labour Organisation, World Intellectual Property Organisation, International Telecommunications Union, and World Wide Web Consortium.[79] A particularly notable development over the last decade is the emergence of organizations in the Asia-Pacific and African regions as policy-brokers in the field. These include the Asia-Pacific Economic Cooperation (APEC) and Economic Community of West African States (ECOWAS).[80]

Beyond these organizations lies a vast array of bodies and interest groups which have pushed—and continue to push—particular privacy policies. Some are groups advocating relatively strong regimes for protection of personal data. Foremost among such bodies in the public sector are the regional groupings of national DPAs. These consist primarily of the Data Protection Working Party set up under Article 29 of the EU Data Protection Directive ('A29WP'),[81] the International Working Group on Data Protection and Telecommunications,[82] and the Asia-Pacific Privacy Authorities (APPA).[83] Of these, the A29WP has been the most influential in shaping policy with transnational impact.[84]

Flanking these are civil society groups with strong pro-privacy agendas. Prominent examples are the Electronic Privacy Information Center[85] and Privacy International.[86] These groups, though, tend to have relatively weak impact on the formulation of major international agreements.

Ranged usually against them are industry groups, such as the International Chamber of Commerce and the European Direct Marketing Association, determined to ensure that privacy safeguards do not unduly dent business interests. These groups were particularly active lobbyists during the drafting of the EU Data Protection Directive.[87] They are also heavily engaged in trying to shape the outcome of current negotiations over the proposed new EU Data Protection Regulation. Their efforts have been bolstered by the recent preparedness of major US-based software corporations, such as Facebook and

---

[79] For a somewhat dated, though still useful overview of these and other international players in the field, see JR Reidenberg, 'Resolving Conflicting International Data Privacy Rules in Cyberspace' (2000) 52 Stanford L Rev 1315, 1355ff. As Reidenberg makes clear, many of these bodies approach data privacy matters from a market-oriented rather than human rights perspective.

[80] The central data privacy initiatives of a selection of these organizations are presented in Ch 2.

[81] See <http://ec.europa.eu/justice/data-protection/article-29/index_en.htm>.

[82] See <http://www.datenschutz-berlin.de/content/europa-international/international-working-group-on-data-protection-in-telecommunications-iwgdpt>.

[83] See <http://www.appaforum.org/>.        [84] See further Ch 6 (sections A and E).

[85] See <http://epic.org/>.        [86] See <https://www.privacyinternational.org/>.

[87] See generally Regan (n 29).

Google, to flex financial and lobbying muscle in order to thwart the introduction of more stringent data privacy legislation.[88]

Additionally, particular individuals have frequently exercised significant influence in the shaping of data privacy law and policy.[89] These are persons who, singly and together, have combined expertise in the field with strong persuasive powers and a fairly compelling vision of how law and policy ought to be developed. Examples are Alan Westin,[90] Spiros Simitis,[91] Michael Kirby,[92] Peter Hustinx,[93] and, more recently, Viviane Reding.[94] While such policy entrepreneurs have usually exercised influence under the aegis of particular organizations, they have sometimes succeeded in stamping their personal vision on the policy of the respective organization.

## 3. Public concern for privacy

The emergence and expansion of data privacy law reflect, at least indirectly, concern for privacy on the part of the general public. That concern, though, has rarely resulted in mass political movements with privacy protection high on their agenda. In the words of Bennett, '[t]here is no concerted worldwide privacy movement that has anything like the scale, resources or public recognition of organizations in the environmental, feminist, consumer protection, and human rights fields'.[95] A rare example of mass mobilization in the name of privacy was the public protest in Australia in 1987 over the proposal for a national identity card, the Australia Card. Yet the protest's

---

[88] J Guynn and M Lifsher, 'Silicon Valley uses growing clout to kill a digital privacy bill', *Los Angeles Times*, 3 May 2013, <http://articles.latimes.com/2013/may/03/business/la-fi-digital-privacy-20130503>.

[89] Bennett (n 27) 127–9.

[90] Prior to his death in 2013, Professor of Public Law and Government, Columbia University; author of several pioneering works on data privacy; founder of the think tank, Privacy & American Business.

[91] Professor of Labour and Civil Law and of Legal Informatics, Johann Wolfgang Goethe-Üniversität, Frankfurt am Main; Data Protection Commissioner for the German State of Hessen (1975–91); Chair of the Council of Europe Committee of Experts on Data Protection (1982–86).

[92] Justice of the High Court of Australia (1996–2009); President of the International Commission of Jurists (1995–98); inaugural chair of the Australian Law Reform Commission (1975–84); head of the expert group tasked with drafting the 1980 OECD Guidelines Governing the Protection of Privacy and Transborder Flows of Personal Data.

[93] Inaugural European Data Protection Supervisor (2004–13); President of the Dutch DPA (1991–2003); Chair of the A29WP (1996–2000).

[94] Vice President of the European Commission and in charge of the Commission's 'Justice, Fundamental Rights and Citizenship' portfolio.

[95] CJ Bennett, *The Privacy Advocates: Resisting the Spread of Surveillance* (MIT Press 2008) 199. See also generally Bennett (n 27) 146, 243. See too PM Regan, 'The United States' in JB Rule and G Greenleaf (eds), *Global Privacy Protection. The First Generation* (Edward Elgar 2008) 50, 71

momentum and mass rapidly diminished once the proposal was shelved.[96] Those pushing to introduce or strengthen data privacy law tend thus to be a relatively small elite.

It is tempting to draw a parallel between this state of affairs and the way in which privacy concerns were articulated and politically pushed in the nineteenth century, at least in the USA and Germany. The movement for legal recognition of privacy rights then and there had largely genteel, elitist traits— as embodied in the Massachusetts 'Mugwump' movement of the 1880s. As Westin observes, it was 'essentially a protest by spokesmen for patrician values against the rise of the political and cultural values of "mass society"'.[97] This would be, however, an inaccurate (and unfair) characterization of the modern 'data privacy elite'. The agenda of the latter is strongly democratic and egalitarian; it is much more concerned about the welfare of the *citoyen* than simply that of the *bourgeois*. And it consciously draws much of its power from the privacy concerns of the general public.[98]

Those concerns seem to be broadly similar across the Western world.[99] Public opinion surveys provide abundant evidence that the levels of concern are relatively high,[100] at least in the abstract.[101] The concern for privacy is often

(observing that privacy concern amongst the US public tends to be latent rather than aggressive— '[p]rivacy appears to be one of those low level concerns that do not mobilize people to anger or action').

[96] Greenleaf (n 39).

[97] Westin (n 36) 348–9. See further JH Barron, 'Warren and Brandeis, The Right to Privacy, 4 Harv L Rev 193 (1890): Demystifying a Landmark Citation' (1979) 13 Suffolk University L Rev 875–922; DW Howe, 'Victorian Culture in America' in DW Howe (ed), *Victorian America* (University of Pennsylvania Press 1976) 3–28. For a similar critique with respect to the ideological and class roots of German 'Persönlichkeitsrecht', see P Schwerdtner, *Das Persönlichkeitsrecht in der deutschen Zivilordnung* (J Schweitzer Verlag 1977) 7, 85, 92.

[98] See too Bennett (n 27) 129.

[99] As Bennett notes, 'in nature and extent, the public concern for privacy is more striking for its cross-national similarities rather than for its differences': see Bennett (n 27) 43.

[100] See eg, Bygrave (n 35) 110 and references cited therein; CJ Bennett and CD Raab, *The Governance of Privacy. Policy Instruments in Global Perspective* (2nd edn, MIT Press 2006) 56–65 and references cited therein. The survey material referenced there derives mainly from the USA, Canada, Australia, Norway, Denmark, and the UK. Survey material from Hungary seems largely to fit with the findings from the other countries: see I Székely, 'New Rights and Old Concerns: Information Privacy in Public Opinion and in the Press in Hungary' (1994) Informatization and the Public Sector 99–113; I Székely, 'Hungary' in JB Rule and G Greenleaf (eds), *Global Privacy Protection: The First Generation* (Edward Elgar 2008) 174, 191ff. However, surveys of public attitudes to privacy can suffer from methodological weaknesses that make it unwise to rely upon their results as wholly accurate indications of public thinking: see eg, WH Dutton and RG Meadow, 'A Tolerance for Surveillance: American Public Opinion Concerning Privacy and Civil Liberties' in KB Levitan (ed), *Government Infostructures* (Greenwood Press 1987) 167; Regan (n 95) 71.

[101] Privacy concerns tend often to be of second-order significance for the public, with problems like public safety, unemployment, and financial security being ranked as more important: see eg, Bygrave (n 35) 110, and references cited therein.

accompanied by considerable pessimism over existing levels of privacy, along with lack of trust that organizations will not misuse personal information.[102] As noted earlier, privacy concerns tend to cut across a broad range of political leanings (within liberal democratic ideology), although there are occasional indications of statistically significant variation in attitudes to privacy issues based on party-political attachments.[103] In terms of the roles played by other demographic variables, such as age, sex, and income level, results appear to vary from country to country and from survey to survey.[104]

The survey evidence points to increasing public sensitivity to potential misuse of personal information. And we find, for example, concrete instances where items of information that previously were routinely publicized are now subject to relatively stringent requirements of confidentiality.[105] Perhaps more interesting, however, is whether indications exist of an opposite development—that is, increasing *acclimatization* of people to situations in which they are required to divulge personal information and an adjustment of what they perceive as problematic for their privacy. Such a development could lead to reductions in the stringency and scope of data privacy rules.

Prominent figures in the ICT industry have opined that privacy is now passé. The most famous case is the laconic answer given in 1999 by Scott McNealy, then head of Sun Microsystems, to a question about which privacy-enhancing measures were to be implemented in a newly launched software package: 'You already have zero privacy. Get over it'.[106] These sorts of self-serving statements are not necessarily indicative of broader public opinion. Nonetheless, it is commonly assumed that so-called 'digital natives'—those born after 1980 who are immersed in the online world—are less concerned about privacy than are those from older generations. The assumption derives

---

[102] Bygrave (n 35) 111, and references cited therein.

[103] H Becker, 'Bürger in der Modernen Informationsgesellschaft' in *Informationsgesellschaft oder Überwachungsstaat* (Hessendienst der Staatskanzlei 1984) 343, 415–16 (citing survey results from (West) Germany showing that supporters of the Green Party (*Die Grünen*) were more likely to view data protection as important than were supporters of the more conservative political parties).

[104] Compare eg, Székely, 'New Rights and Old Concerns' (n 100) 69 (Hungarian survey results appear to show that demographic variables play little role in determining public attitudes to privacy issues) with Office of Australian Federal Privacy Commissioner, *Community Attitudes to Privacy*, Information Paper 3 (AGPS 1995) (demographic variables play significant role in Australian survey results).

[105] See eg, H Torgersen, 'Forskning og personvern' in RD Blekeli and KS Selmer (eds), *Data og personvern* (Universitetsforlaget 1977) 223, 237 (noting that, in Norway, the quantity and detail of information publicly disclosed in connection with student matriculation were far greater in the 1960s than in the mid-1970s and onwards).

[106] 'Sun on Privacy: Get over It', *Wired*, 26 January 1999; available at: <http://www.wired.com/politics/law/news/1999/01/17538>.

from the apparent tendency of digital natives to disseminate a greater amount of information about themselves in online arenas than do older persons and this is also supported by some reasonably reliable evidence.[107] Yet other reliable evidence qualifies it.[108] Little solid survey evidence addressing other aspects of the 'acclimatization' issue appears to exist.[109]

## F. Issues of Nomenclature and Conceptualization

The short-hand nomenclature used to describe the field of data privacy law varies considerably. The issue of nomenclature might be dismissed as trivial since it primarily relates to 'packaging'. Yet the packaging sends important signals about the law's remit, particularly to newcomers.

In the USA and many other English-speaking countries, the term 'privacy' has figured centrally in the nomenclature given to the field. This reflects the prominence accorded to privacy, both as concept and term, in these countries' discourse about the societal challenges posed by computerization. As elaborated in section C, these challenges were instrumental in stimulating the birth of data privacy law. When extensive discussion about the societal

---

[107] See eg, C Paine U-D Reips, S Stieger, A Joinson, and T Buchanan, 'Internet Users' Perceptions of "Privacy Concerns" and "Privacy Actions"' (2007) 65 Intl J of Human-Computer Studies 526–36 (presenting survey evidence indicating that older respondents—these came from around the world, with the largest groups coming from Russia (20 per cent) and Germany (9 per cent)—were more likely than younger respondents (ie, those under 20 years of age) to be concerned about privacy in an online context); Teknologirådet, *Holdninger til personvern* (Teknologirådet 2004) (documenting that Norwegian youths are less worried than older persons about the consequences of personal data misuse).

[108] See eg, A Lenhart and M Madden, 'Teens, Privacy, and Online Social Networks' (Pew Research Center 2007), available at: <http://www.pewinternet.org/Reports/2007/Teens-Privacy-and-Online-Social-Networks.aspx>, (presenting survey evidence indicating that many American teenagers care about their privacy and take a variety of measures to safeguard it in an online context); Paine and others (n 107) (reporting that approximately 45 per cent of respondents aged under 20 were concerned about privacy online; this figure climbed to approximately 60 per cent for respondents aged 21–30 years). Cf M Madden, A Lenhart, S Cortesi, U Gasser, M Duggan, A Smith, and M Beaton, 'Teens, Social Media, and Privacy' (Pew Research Center 2013), available at: <http://www.pewinternet.org/Reports/2013/Teens-Social-Media-And-Privacy.aspx>, (presenting survey evidence that American teenagers are sharing more information about themselves on social media sites, such as Facebook, than in the past and that the majority of them are not very concerned about third parties gaining access to the information; at the same time, most of them set their Facebook profiles to 'private').

[109] For a general review of recent survey evidence on point, see the report by the European Network of Excellence in Internet Science (EINS): S Passi and S Wyatt (eds), *Overview of Online Privacy, Reputation, Trust, and Identity Mechanisms* (EINS Consortium 2013) ch 3, available at: <www.internet-science.eu/sites/internet-science.eu/files/biblio/EINS_D5_1_1_final_0.pdf>.

implications of computerized processing of personal data first took off in the USA during the 1960s, privacy was invoked as a key term for the interests that were perceived to be threatened.[110]

The focus on privacy was far from surprising. The semantics of privacy were (and are) sufficiently broad and malleable to address what was then (and still is) seen as a fundamental danger of computer (mis)use, namely the enhanced potential for large organizations to amass data on individuals and thereby subject the latter to excessive control. The notion of privacy had already enjoyed a long, although somewhat inconsistent, tradition of use in US discourse, particularly as designating a sphere in which a person could be free of unwanted intrusion by others. This dimension of privacy is most famously summed up in the phrase 'the right to be let alone'.[111] While privacy, thus conceived, can be threatened by the intrusive activities of private sector organizations,[112] Americans have usually exercised greatest concern for it in relation to state activities.[113] The latter figured centrally in the debate that began in the 1960s over the dangers of computerization. 'Privacy' was not the only term invoked to sum up what was viewed as being at stake. A variety of other, closely related terms were invoked too, such as 'freedom', 'liberty', and 'autonomy'.[114] At the same time, the semantics of privacy were reshaped to address more directly the challenges of the computer age. Thus, the seminal literature on point conceived 'privacy' essentially as a form of information control—that is, 'the claim of individuals, groups, or institutions to determine for themselves when, how, and to what extent information about them is communicated to others'.[115]

The subsequent debates in other countries over the threats posed by modern ICT generally followed the lines of the earlier US discourse. As Hondius writes, '[a]lmost every issue that arose in Europe was also an issue in the United States, but at an earlier time and on a more dramatic scale'.[116] The salience of the notion of privacy in US discourse helped to ensure its prominence

---

[110]  See eg, Westin (n 36) and Miller (n 36).

[111]  See esp. Warren and Brandeis (n 53) 205 (arguing that the right to privacy in Anglo-American law is part and parcel of a right 'to be let alone'). Further on the historical role of privacy in US discourse, see eg, PM Regan, *Legislating Privacy: Technology, Social Values, and Public Policy* (University of North Carolina Press 1995).

[112]  Indeed, it was alleged transgressions of the boundaries of decency and the law by the 'yellow press' which provoked Warren and Brandeis to pen their article.

[113]  See generally, EJ Eberle, *Dignity and Liberty: Constitutional Visions in Germany and the United States* (Praeger 2002); JQ Whitman, 'The Two Western Cultures of Privacy: Dignity versus Liberty' (2004) 113 Yale LJ 1151.

[114]  As evidenced in the title of Westin's work (n 36).          [115]  Westin (n 36) 7.

[116]  Hondius (n 48) 6.

in debate elsewhere. This is most evident in other English-speaking countries[117] and in international forums where English is a working language.[118] Yet much of the same discourse in countries where English is not the main language has also been framed, at least initially, around notions roughly equating with privacy. Examples are 'la vie privée' (French),[119] 'die Privatsphäre' (German),[120] and 'privatlivets fred' (Danish and Norwegian).[121]

The salience of 'privacy' and closely related notions in this context ultimately reflects the Western liberal democratic heritage of the countries concerned. It is in countries with such a heritage that discourse on data privacy issues first flourished. This heritage is not the sole factor behind this chronology; the relatively advanced degree of computerization in these countries played a role as well. Yet liberalism structured the basic reactions of these countries' citizens and governments to the technological development. It is an ideology that traditionally accords the privacy of individuals a great deal of value.[122] Liberal democratic states typically embrace what Bennett and Raab term the 'privacy paradigm'. This is a set of assumptions which idealizes civil society as made up of 'relatively autonomous individuals who need a modicum of privacy in order to be able to fulfil the various roles of the citizen in a liberal democratic state'.[123] This paradigm sensitized the citizens and governments concerned to the privacy-related threats posed by ICT.

Nevertheless, the regulatory field which crystallized from the early European discussions on point is often described using a bland, technocratic

---

[117] For the UK, see eg, Committee on Privacy (the Younger Committee), *Report of the Committee on Privacy*, Cmnd 5012 (HMSO 1972) and P Sieghart, *Privacy and Computers* (Latimer 1976); for Canada, see eg, Department of Communications and Department of Justice, *Privacy and Computers: A Report of a Task Force* (Information Canada 1972); for Australia, see eg, Australian Law Reform Commission (ALRC), *Privacy*, Report no. 22 (AGPS 1983) and WL Morison, *Report on the Law of Privacy to the Standing Committee of Commonwealth and State Attorneys-General*, Report no. 170/1973 (AGPS 1973).

[118] See eg, Council of Europe (CoE) Resolution (73) 22 on the Protection of the Privacy of Individuals vis-à-vis Electronic Data Banks in the Private Sector (adopted 26 September1973); CoE Resolution (74) 29 on the Protection of the Privacy of Individuals vis-à-vis Electronic Data Banks in the Public Sector (adopted 24 September 1974).

[119] See eg, G Messadie, *La fin de la vie privée* (Calmann-Levy 1974).

[120] See eg, the 1970 proposal by a (West) German Interparliamentary Working Committee for a 'Gesetz zum Schutz der Privatsphäre gegen Missbrauch von Datenbankinformationen': described in H-P Bull, *Datenschutz oder Die Angst vor dem Computer* (Piper 1984) 85.

[121] See eg, Denmark's Register Committee (Registerudvalget), *Delbetænkning om private registre*, Report no. 687 (Statens trykningskontor, 1973).

[122] See eg, S Lukes, *Individualism* (Blackwell 1973) 62; O Mallmann, *Zielfunktionen des Datenschutzes: Schutz der Privatsphäre, korrekte Information. Mit einer Studie zum Datenschutz im Bereich von Kreditinformationssystemen* (A Metzner 1977) 17.

[123] Bennett and Raab (n 100) 4.

nomenclature avoiding explicit reference to 'privacy' or closely related terms. This nomenclature is 'data protection', derived from the German term 'Datenschutz'.[124] The nomenclature has gained broad popularity in Europe and it is occasionally used elsewhere.[125] While 'privacy' and 'data protection' are closely linked, Europeans often stress that the two are not identical, reserving 'data protection' for a set of norms that serve a broader range of interests than simply privacy protection.[126]

A third term for the field is 'data privacy'. The term has entered the discourse more recently than 'privacy' and 'data protection'. It is gaining traction on both sides of the Atlantic.[127] Its use can be seen as an attempt to signal more accurately than the other two terms the focus, thrust, and rationale of the relevant norms.

Additionally, we find various countries and regions displaying terminological idiosyncrasies that partly reflect different jurisprudential backgrounds for the discussions concerned. In Western Europe, the discussion has often drawn upon jurisprudence developed there on legal protection of personality. Thus, 'Persönlichkeitsrecht' and 'Persönlichkeitsschutz' figure centrally in German and Swiss discourse on data privacy.[128] Norwegian discourse revolves around the notion of 'personvern' ('protection of person(ality)'),[129] while Swedish discourse focuses on 'integritetsskydd' ('protection of (personal) integrity').[130] By contrast, South American discourse often revolves around the notion of 'habeas data' (roughly meaning 'you should have the data'). This derives from due-process doctrine based on the writ of habeas corpus.[131] To take yet another example, US discourse (in addition to focusing

---

[124] Further on the origins of 'Datenschutz', see Simitis (n 24) 78–9.

[125] See eg, GL Hughes and M Jackson, *Hughes on Data Protection in Australia* (2nd edn, Law Book Company 2001).

[126] See eg, EDPS (n 45) 15, 21.

[127] As evidenced by the title of this book and the title of the journal, *International Data Privacy Law*, published by OUP from 2011. See too eg, Schwartz and Reidenberg (n 76); C Kuner, *European Data Privacy Law and Online Business* (OUP 2003).

[128] See eg, Germany's Federal Data Protection Act 1990 (*Bundesdatenschutzgesetz—Gesetz zum Fortentwicklung der Datenverarbeitung und des Datenschutzes vom 20. Dezember 1990*) § 1(1) (stipulating the purpose of the Act as protection of the individual from interference with their 'personality right' ('Persönlichkeitsrecht')); Switzerland's Federal Data Protection Act 1992 (*Loi fédérale du 19. juin 1992 sur la protection des données/Bundesgesetz vom 19. Juni 1992 über den Datenschutz*) Art. 1 (stating the object of the Act as, inter alia, 'protection of personality' ('Schutz der Persönlichkeit')).

[129] See Bygrave (n 35) 138–43 and references cited therein.

[130] See eg, Sweden's Personal Data Act 1998 (*Personuppgiftslagen*, SFS 1998:204) s 1; Bygrave (n 35) 126–9 and references cited therein.

[131] Habeas data is a personal right of action provided for in the constitutions of a number of Latin American countries. It may be invoked before a constitutional court to require an organization to disclose data it holds on the plaintiff, to correct inaccuracies in the data, and in some cases to destroy the data. It is said to be inspired by the CoE Convention on data protection (described in Ch 2,

on 'privacy', 'freedom', and 'autonomy') employs the notion of 'fairness' to describe core data privacy principles, referring to these as principles of 'fair information practice'.[132]

All up, the field shows bewildering conceptual and terminological diversity. This hampers easy comprehension of its remit. Adding to this difficulty is the polysemantic, diffuse character of many of the above-mentioned concepts. The most famous case in point is 'privacy'. Various definitions of the concept abound. A lengthy debate has raged, predominantly in US circles, about which definition is most correct.[133] We find parallel debates in other countries which centre on similar concepts,[134] although these debates appear less extensive than the privacy debate. Some of the latter debate concerns whether privacy is best characterized as a state/condition, a claim, or a right. That issue aside, the debate reveals four principal ways of defining privacy.[135] One set of definitions is in terms of *non-interference*,[136] another in terms of *limited accessibility*.[137] A third set conceives of privacy as *information control*.[138] A fourth set incorporates various elements of the other three sets but links privacy exclusively to *intimate* or *sensitive* aspects of persons' lives.[139]

---

section B) and the 1983 Census Act decision of the German Federal Constitutional Court (described in Ch 6 (n 45)). See A Guadamuz, 'Habeas Data: The Latin American Response to Data Protection' (2000) JILT, no. 2, available at: <http://www2.warwick.ac.uk/fac/soc/law/elj/jilt/2000_2/guadamuz/>; A Guadamuz, 'Habeas Data vs the European Data Protection Directive' (2001) JILT, no. 3, available at: <http://www2.warwick.ac.uk/fac/soc/law/elj/jilt/2001_3/guadamuz>. See also Ch 3 (section C). However, it is worth noting that Westin mentioned the possibility of developing such a writ already at the beginning of the 1970s: see AF Westin, 'Civil Liberties and Computerized Data Systems' in M Greenberger (ed), *Computers, Communications, and the Public Interest* (The Johns Hopkins Press 1971) 151, 168. The writ has also gained traction in South-East Asia and Africa. In January 2008, the Supreme Court of the Philippines formally adopted a 'Rule on the Writ of Habeas Data' (AM No. 08-1-16-SC; in force 2 February 2008) as a Rule of Court. And provision for habeas data is made in Art. 46 of the Cape Verdean Constitution (last revised 2010) and Art. 69 of the 2010 Angolan Constitution.

[132] See eg, DHEW (n 51) 41; US Privacy Protection Study Commission, *Personal Privacy in an Information Society* (US Government Printing Office 1977) esp. 17, 21.

[133] For useful overviews, see D Solove, *Understanding Privacy* (Harvard University Press 2008) chs 1–2; JC Inness, *Privacy, Intimacy, and Isolation* (OUP 1992) ch 2; JW DeCew, *In Pursuit of Privacy: Law, Ethics, and the Rise of Technology* (Cornell University Press 1997) chs 2–3.

[134] See eg, *En ny datalag* (SOU 1993:10) 150–61 (documenting difficulties experienced in Swedish data protection discourse with respect to arriving at a precise definition of 'personlig integritet').

[135] Bygrave (n 35) 128–9.  [136] See eg, Warren and Brandeis (n 53).

[137] See eg, R Gavison, 'Privacy and the Limits of Law' (1980) 89 Yale LJ 421, 428–36 (claiming that privacy is a condition of 'limited accessibility' consisting of three elements: 'secrecy' ('the extent to which we are known to others'), 'solitude' ('the extent to which others have physical access to us'), and 'anonymity' ('the extent to which we are the subject of others' attention')).

[138] See eg, Westin (n 36) 7.

[139] See eg, Inness (n 133) 140 (defining privacy as 'the state of possessing control over a realm of intimate decisions, which includes decisions about intimate access, intimate information, and intimate actions').

Definitions of privacy in terms of information control tend to be most popular in discourse dealing directly with law and policy on data privacy.[140] Indeed, the notion of information control has arisen as a leitmotif for this discourse, both in Europe and the USA. In Europe, though, the notion is not always linked directly to the privacy concept; it is either linked to related concepts, such as 'personal integrity' (for example, in the case of Swedish discourse),[141] or it stands alone. The most significant instance of the latter is the German notion of 'informational self-determination' ('informationelle Selbstbestimmung') which in itself forms the content of a constitutional right first recognized in a landmark decision of the Federal Constitutional Court (Bundesverfassungsgericht) in 1983.[142]

In this light, it is obviously very difficult if not impossible to come up with one concise formulation that accurately depicts the remit of the field. By 'concise' is meant a phrase consisting of two or three words. The term 'data protection' is problematic on multiple counts. It fails to indicate expressly the central interests served by the norms to which it is meant to apply. It is misleading insofar as it 'suggests that *the data* are being protected, instead of *the individual* whose data are involved'.[143] It has an 'unnecessary technical and esoteric air'.[144] And it has connoted in some circles concern for data security[145] and for protection of intellectual property rights.[146] It is claimed to have an advantage over a 'privacy'-focused nomenclature as it 'distinguishes the policy problem that has arisen since the late 1960s from the broad social value that has such a rich tradition and important place in the liberal democratic heritage'.[147] Yet this line-drawing capability can also underplay lines of continuity in the types of interests protected.

A term such as 'privacy protection' or 'privacy law' faces problems also. One difficulty is that 'privacy' suffers from a heritage of definitional instability and imprecision. Another is that the term fails to capture the entire remit of the law concerned. As shown in section A, this failure is a case of both

---

[140] See generally Bygrave (n 35) 130 and references cited therein.

[141] See eg *En ny datalag* (n 134) 159 (noting that the concept of 'personlig integritet' embraces information control).

[142] Decision of 15 December 15 1983, BVerfGE (*Entscheidungen des Bundesverfassungsgerichts*) vol 65, 1. See further Ch 6 (n 45).

[143] ACM Nugter, *Transborder Flow of Personal Data within the EC* (Kluwer Law & Taxation Publishers 1989) 3.

[144] Bennett (n 27) 76.        [145] See n 5 and accompanying references.

[146] Schwartz and Reidenberg (n 76) 5 (observing that the notion of data protection in the USA often 'evokes intellectual property principles of copyright and trade secrets as well as technological security measures').

[147] Bennett (n 27) 14.

under-inclusion and over-inclusion. It is a case of under-inclusion in that data privacy law embraces more than what are typically regarded as privacy concerns.[148] It is a case of over-inclusion in that 'privacy' as such has various dimensions (spatial, bodily, etc.) with which data privacy tends not to deal directly.[149]

What of a nomeclature built up around the notion of 'fairness', such as 'fair information practises law'? At first sight, this sort of terminology is attractive given that the agenda of data privacy law can be summed up quite well in terms of concern for ensuring fairness in the processing of personal data.[150] Yet 'fairness' is somewhat nebulous and has a variety of connotations, some of which have little relevance to the concerns of data privacy law.[151] Another problem is that the terminology could be applied equally well to describe, say, copyright legislation; in other words, the terminology on its own does not single out what is unique for the law concerned. Much the same criticisms can be made of a nomenclature based on the notion of 'secrecy',[152] or of attempts to subsume data privacy law under the parole of 'rule of law' or related notions, such as 'Rechtssicherheit' and 'rettssikkerhet'.[153]

My choice to employ 'data privacy' as the primary label for this area of law is not because I judge it as perfect. The label shares the problems of under-inclusion and definitional instability identified with a 'privacy'-focused nomenclature. However, it reduces the latter's over-inclusion problem. Moreover, it communicates relatively well—and far better than 'data protection'—one of the central interests at stake. It also provides a bridge for synthesizing European and non-European legal discourses.

---

[148] See further, Bygrave (n 35) ch 7.

[149] Further on those dimensions and their interaction with data privacy law, see Bygrave (n 9) 1–7.

[150] Bygrave (n 35) 155–6.

[151] Eg, the keeping of promises and bargains (quid pro quo obligations)—a dimension of 'fairness' that is central in J Rawls, *A Theory of Justice* (OUP 1972) esp. sections 18 and 52.

[152] See Inness (n 133) 60–1 (arguing that data privacy law ought to be characterized as protecting secrecy rather than privacy). An additional flaw with such a characterization is that data privacy law is about far more than just ensuring non-disclosure of information.

[153] For related criticism of the latter possibility, see eg, DW Schartum, *Rettssikkerhet og systemutvikling i offentlig forvaltning* (Universitetsforlaget 1993) 72, 85ff. Cf S Eskeland, *Fangerett* (2nd edn, TANO 1989) 79 (placing data privacy interests under the umbrella of 'rettssikkerhet'); LJ Blanck, 'Personvern—nytt navn på "gamle" rettsspørsmål?' (1979) Lov og Rett 117, 122–3 (taking a similar approach to Eskeland).

# 2

# International Data Privacy Codes

## A. Introduction

This chapter provides an overview of the principal international legal instruments on data privacy. Some account is taken too of instruments that are not legally binding yet highly influential in development of regulatory policy in the field. The chapter's primary focus is international instruments that have been central in shaping national and other international data privacy regimes. These instruments have mostly been drafted within the respective institutional frameworks of the CoE, OECD, and EU. The order in which the instruments are presented follows roughly the chronological order in which they have been drafted and adopted. Account is taken also of relevant work carried out within the framework of the UN, APEC, ECOWAS, the African Union, and the Association of South East Asian Nations (ASEAN).

The role played by catalogues of fundamental human rights set out in certain multilateral treaties is thereafter analysed. The presentation focuses on the European Convention on Human Rights and the 1966 International Covenant on Civil and Political Rights (ICCPR)[1] as both instruments have been authoritatively construed as containing data privacy guarantees.

## B. Council of Europe Initiatives

### 1. Convention 108

The Council of Europe was one of the first international bodies to begin developing normative responses to the threats posed by computer technology to privacy-related interests. It is the only international body to have drafted a multilateral treaty dealing directly with data privacy. This is the

---

[1] UN General Assembly resolution 2200A (XXI) of 16 December 1966; in force 23 March 1976.

1981 Convention for the Protection of Individuals with regard to Automatic Processing of Personal Data.[2] As of 15 September 2013, the Convention had been ratified by 45 of the 47 CoE member countries.[3] Amendments to the Convention were adopted on 15 June 1999 to permit EU accession but are not yet in force.[4] In 2001, the Convention was supplemented by an Additional Protocol which introduced more detailed rules on regulation of transborder flow of personal data and on the role of DPAs.[5]

The Convention is currently being overhauled in the name of 'modernization'. The Convention's Consultative Committee (T-PD)[6] released a proposal for a revised instrument in November 2012,[7] but without reaching agreement on all aspects. The proposal is now being considered by an ad hoc committee of the Committee of Ministers. Considerable time will pass before we know the results of the committee's deliberations, and it is likely to take a few years before any new instrument takes effect. Hence, references in the following are predominantly to the current version of the Convention, although account is taken of points where the T-PD proposal differs significantly from it.

Although a European product, the Convention is envisaged to be potentially more than an agreement between European states. The CoE Committee of Ministers may invite non-member states to accede to it (Article 23). This

---

[2] Opened for signature 28 January 1981; in force 1 October 1985; ETS 108 (hereinafter also 'Convention 108').

[3] San Marino has not even signed the Convention, while Turkey has signed but not ratified it. The latest ratification was by Russia (15 May 2013).

[4] The amendments will enter into force on the 30th day after approval by all of the Convention Parties (Art 21(6)). As of 15 September 2013, 34 Parties had registered their approval.

[5] Additional Protocol to the Convention for the Protection of Individuals with regard to Automatic Processing of Personal Data, regarding Supervisory Authorities and Transborder Data Flows (open for signature 8 November 2001; in force 1 July 2004; ETS 181). As of 15 September 2013, 33 CoE member countries have signed and ratified the Protocol. Nine member countries have signed but not ratified it: Belgium, Denmark, Greece, Iceland, Italy, Norway, Russia, Turkey, and the UK. Five member countries have not signed it: Azerbaijan, Georgia, Malta, San Marino, and Slovenia. One non-member country, Uruguay, has ratified it pursuant to ratification of Convention 108 (see n 9 and accompanying text).

[6] Full title: Consultative Committee of the Convention for the Protection of Individuals with regard to Automatic Processing of Personal Data. The Committee is established pursuant to Chapter V of the Convention. It consists primarily of state party representatives and is charged with developing proposals to improve the Convention's application.

[7] T-PD, 'Modernisation of Convention 108' (T-PD (2012) 4 Rev3_en, 29 November 2012) (hereinafter 'T-PD proposal'). The revised instrument, if adopted, is envisaged as a new Protocol to the existing Convention. For critical discussion, see G Greenleaf, '"Modernising" Data Protection Convention 108: A Safe Basis for a Global Privacy Treaty?' (2013) 29 CLSR 430; G Greenleaf, 'A World Data Privacy Treaty?: "Globalisation" and "Modernisation" of Council of Europe Convention 108' in N Witzleb, D Lindsay, M Paterson, and S Rodrick (eds), *Emerging Challenges in Privacy Law: Comparative Perspectives* (CUP forthcoming 2014) ch 6.

possibility lay long dormant but has been recently activated, partly at the instigation of civil society representatives.[8] In 2011, Uruguay became the first non-member state to request and receive such an invitation.[9] The invitation was conditional on Uruguay having taken domestic legal measures to give effect to the basic principles of the Convention and its Additional Protocol.[10] In January 2013, Morocco became the second country to request and receive an invitation, although this seems to be limited, at least initially, to the Convention and not the Additional Protocol as well.[11]

The Convention is based partly on several resolutions and recommendations emanating from the Council in the late 1960s and early 1970s. The most noteworthy of these are two resolutions adopted by the CoE Committee of Ministers: Resolution (73) 22 on the Protection of the Privacy of Individuals vis-à-vis Electronic Data Banks in the Private Sector (adopted 26 September 1973), and Resolution (74) 29 on the Protection of the Privacy of Individuals vis-à-vis Electronic Data Banks in the Public Sector (adopted 24 September 1974). The annexes to each resolution contain similar (although slightly differing) sets of basic data privacy principles which CoE member states were encouraged to implement. The committee drafting each set of principles had few models upon which to draw. The Explanatory Report accompanying Resolution (73) 22 indicates that account was at least taken of several pieces of fresh national and sub-national legislation, namely the Hessian Data Protection Act 1970, Sweden's Data Act 1973, draft data privacy legislation introduced in Belgium in 1972, and the US Fair Credit Reporting Act 1970. Interestingly, neither that report nor the equivalent report accompanying Resolution (74) 29 mention as a possible source of inspiration the contemporaneous work within the US Department of Health, Education and Welfare (DHEW) on drafting principles on 'fair information practices'—principles

---

[8] See eg, Madrid Privacy Declaration, 'Global Privacy Standards for a Global World' (3 November 2009); available at: <http://thepublicvoice.org/madrid-declaration/> (urging countries that have not yet ratified the Convention or its 2001 Protocol 'to do so as expeditiously as possible').

[9] Uruguay's accession entered into force 1 August 2013.

[10] See T-PD, 'Opinion on Uruguay's request to be invited to accede to Convention 108 and its additional Protocol' (T-PD (2011) 08 rev en, 26 May 2011).

[11] See T-PD, 'Kingdom of Morocco—request to be invited to accede to Convention 108' (T-PD (2012) 09 rev, 18 October 2012). However, the T-PD 'underlines the importance, with a view to providing a coherent and effective data protection system, for the Kingdom of Morocco to also seek accession to the additional protocol to Convention 108': T-PD, 'Kingdom of Morocco—request to be invited to accede to Convention 108' (T-PD (2012) 09 rev, 18 October 2012) 7. The criteria for issuing and accepting invitations to accede have yet to be clearly specified.

that proved influential in US policy discourse.[12] In any event, the principles laid down by the CoE resolutions are more comprehensive than the DHEW principles. Indeed, they contain the essence of most of the principles later laid down in Chapter II of Convention 108.

Work on the resolutions and Convention 108 arose out of a perception that the European Convention on Human Rights did not provide sufficiently comprehensive protection for individuals in the face of computerized processing of personal data, particularly in the private sector. Also important was the absence in many CoE member states of adequate legislative regimes to provide such protection. Work on the resolutions and the Convention was accordingly undertaken in the hope of stimulating the creation of such regimes.[13] A related object was to prevent divergence between the regimes, thereby promoting the Council's general goal of achieving greater unity between its members.[14]

For the purposes of Convention 108, this harmonization was—and remains—not only to strengthen data privacy and thereby the right to respect for private life pursuant to ECHR Article 8, but, somewhat paradoxically, to ensure also the free flow of personal data across national borders and thereby safeguard the right manifest in ECHR Article 10 'to receive and impart information and ideas without interference by public authority and regardless of frontiers'.[15] The need to harmonize national data privacy regimes in order to maintain free flow of data across borders arose in the latter half of the 1970s in the wake of a growing number of European countries passing data privacy legislation that expressly restricted flow of data to countries without similar laws. The primary aim of such rules has been to hinder data controllers from avoiding the requirements of data privacy legislation by shifting data-processing operations to countries with more lenient standards.[16]

---

[12] See DHEW, *Records, Computers and the Rights of Citizens* (US Government Printing Office 1973) 41.

[13] Thus, the Convention Art. 1 stipulates as a basic object 'to secure in the territory of each Party for every individual, whatever his nationality or residence, respect for his rights and fundamental freedoms, and in particular his right to privacy, with regard to automatic processing of personal data relating to him ("data protection")'.

[14] In this respect, note the Convention's Preamble ('Considering that the aim of the Council of Europe is to achieve greater unity between its members...'). See too *Explanatory Report on the Convention for the Protection of Individuals with regard to Automatic Processing of Personal Data* (CoE 1981) (hereinafter 'Explanatory Report') para. 21.

[15] See the Preamble which states that the goal of extending data protection is to be balanced with a 'commitment to freedom of information regardless of frontiers', and recognizes 'that it is necessary to reconcile the fundamental values of the respect for privacy and the free flow of information between peoples'. See too Art. 12 of the Convention dealt with later in this section.

[16] See generally Ch 6 (section E(1)).

Despite the legitimacy of this aim, there were—and remain—fears that its realization could obstruct the realization of other, at least equally legitimate, interests. There have also been fears that its realization could serve a less legitimate agenda: economic protectionism.[17] Hence, work on Convention 108—and, indeed, work on many of the other main international instruments on data privacy—has been informed by a desire to mitigate such fears.[18]

Convention 108 is intended primarily to cover processing of data on physical persons in both the public and private sectors, but only insofar as the processing is computerized ('automated'). Nevertheless, contracting states may apply the Convention's principles to information on 'groups of persons, associations, foundations, companies, corporations and any other bodies consisting directly or indirectly of individuals, whether or not such bodies possess legal personality' (Article 3(2)(b)),[19] and to manually processed data (Article 3(2)(c)). Moreover, a party to the Convention is free 'to grant data subjects a wider measure of protection than that stipulated in this convention' (Article 11).[20]

While the Convention requires contracting states to incorporate its principles into their domestic legislation (Article 4(1)), it is not intended to be self-executing. According to its Explanatory Report, 'individual rights cannot be derived from it'.[21] Arguments have been occasionally mounted to the contrary but are of doubtful validity.[22] The Convention was intended to be a catalyst and guide for national legislative initiatives; it was not intended

---

[17] Further on the putatively protectionist character of data privacy law, see Ch 4 (section B(3)).

[18] No such desire, though, was manifest in the work on the two above-mentioned CoE resolutions. Neither the resolution texts nor their accompanying explanatory reports mention maintenance of transborder data flow as an issue. Obviously, this is due to the paucity of national laws in the early 1970s which sought to limit such flow in the name of privacy protection.

[19] A possibility currently exploited by Albania, Austria, Italy, Liechtenstein, and Switzerland. Denmark, Norway, and Iceland exploited this possibility in their first data privacy laws but have largely dispensed with express protection of data on collective entities under their current legislation except in relation to credit reporting. See further Ch 4 (section C(3)).

[20] The T-PD proposal retains Art. 11 but deletes explicit reference to the possibility of extending protection to collective entities in Art. 3. It also does away with the focus on automated processing—ie, it proposes that the Convention apply as a point of departure to both automated and manual processing. However, manual operations are covered only inasmuch as they pertain to 'a structured set' of data 'established according to any criteria which allow to search for personal data' (revised Art. 2(c)).

[21] Explanatory Report (n 14) para. 38; see too para. 60. Note that the Explanatory Report does not provide 'an authoritative interpretation of the text of the Convention, although it might be of such nature as to facilitate the understanding of the provisions contained therein' (para. II).

[22] See eg, RJ Schweizer, 'Europäisches Datenschutzrecht—Was zu tun bleibt' (1989) Datenschutz und Datensicherheit 542, 543 (arguing that major parts of the Convention—particularly Arts. 5 and 8—may be treated as self-executing given that they are formulated sufficiently clearly to function as directly applicable rights and duties, and given the objects clause in Art. 1).

to short-circuit these initiatives by providing a finished package of directly applicable rules.[23]

## 2. Basic principles of Convention 108

The heart of the Convention lies in its Chapter II which, in broad-brush fashion, sets out basic principles for processing of personal data. As intimated earlier, these principles were hardly groundbreaking at the time of the Convention's adoption. They embody a common minimum of the standards already promulgated in the CoE resolutions and in an increasingly large number of laws passed by member states. Nonetheless, they established a key reference point for subsequent elaborations of data privacy principles in both international and national instruments.

The primary provision is Article 5 which reads:

Quality of data
Personal data undergoing automatic processing shall be:
a.  obtained and processed fairly and lawfully;
b.  stored for specified and legitimate purposes and not used in a way incompatible with those purposes;
c.  adequate, relevant and not excessive in relation to the purposes for which they are stored;
d.  accurate and, where necessary, kept up to date;
e.  preserved in a form which permits identification of the data subjects for no longer than is required for the purpose for which those data are stored.

The heading assigned to Article 5 is misleading. The provision embodies much more than simply a concern for data quality.[24] In addition to that concern (expressed in paragraphs c and d), we find the principles of fair and lawful processing (paragraph a), purpose limitation (paragraph b), and minimality (paragraphs c and e).[25]

Article 6 embodies what may be termed the sensitivity principle—that is, a principle positing that there are certain kinds of personal data which are more sensitive than others and which, therefore, ought to be subject to

---

[23] S Simitis, 'Datenschutz und Europäischer Gemeinschaft' (1990) 6 Recht der Datenverarbeitung 3, 9–10; F Henke, *Die Datenschutzkonvention des Europarates* (Peter Lang 1986) 57–60; FW Hondius, 'A Decade of International Data Protection' (1983) 30 Netherlands Intl L Rev 103, 116.

[24] The T-PD proposal retitles Art. 5 as 'Legitimacy of data processing and quality of data'.

[25] The T-PD proposal retains these core principles, albeit in slightly reworded form, and adds the principle of proportionality: 'Data processing shall be proportionate in relation to the legitimate purpose pursued and reflect at all stages of the processing a fair balance between all interests concerned, be they public or private interests, and the rights and freedoms at stake' (revised Art. 5(1)).

more stringent protection.[26] These data categories are described in resolutions 73(22) and 74(29) as data relating to a person's 'intimate private life' or data which 'might lead to unfair discrimination'. In Article 6, the data categories are described in slightly more concrete terms as data concerning a person's 'health or sexual life', their 'racial origin, political opinions, religious or other beliefs', or their 'criminal convictions'.[27]

Article 7 stipulates the need to take 'appropriate security measures' for protecting personal data 'against accidental or unauthorized destruction or accidental loss as well as against unauthorized access, alteration or dissemination'.[28]

Article 8 requires that any person shall be able to ascertain 'the existence of an automated personal data file, its main purposes, as well as the identity and habitual residence or principal place of business of the controller of the file' (paragraph a). Any person shall also be given the right 'to obtain at reasonable intervals and without excessive delay or expense confirmation of whether personal data relating to him are stored in the automated data files as well as communication to him of such data in an intelligible form' (paragraph b).[29] A person is additionally to be given the right to have the data rectified or erased if processed in breach of rules implementing Articles 5 and 6 (paragraph c). Finally, paragraph d requires that persons be given a 'remedy' in the event of non-compliance with a request for confirmation, communication, rectification, or erasure as referred to in paragraphs b and c.[30]

---

[26] See further Ch 5 (section I).

[27] The T-PD proposal adds further categories of data to this list, most notably 'genetic data', 'biometric data uniquely identifying a person', and information on 'trade-union membership' (revised Art. 6(1)). It also makes explicit the link between processing of these sorts of data and the 'risk of discrimination' (revised Art. 6(2)).

[28] The T-PD proposal adds a duty on the part of data controllers to notify 'at least' the relevant DPA of a serious security breach (new Art. 7(2)).

[29] The meaning of Art. 8(b) is discussed further on in relationship to equivalent provisions in the OECD data privacy guidelines: see n 69 and accompanying text.

[30] The T-PD proposal supplements these provisions with, inter alia, a general right to object to data processing (revised Art. 8(b)), a right not to be subject to fully automated decision making (revised Art. 8(a)), and a right 'to obtain knowledge of the reasoning underlying the data processing, the results of which are applied to [the data subject] (revised Art. 8(d)). It also adds obligations on data controllers in a new Art. 8bis. These include a duty to undertake 'risk analysis of the potential impact of the intended data processing on the rights and fundamental freedoms of the data subject and design data processing operations in such a way as to prevent or at least minimize the risk of interference with those rights and fundamental freedoms' (Art. 8bis(2)(a)). Moreover, the proposal lays down new obligations on controllers to inform data subjects of basic details of the data-processing operations, independently of the data subjects' use of their access rights (new Art. 7bis).

Derogation from the provisions of Articles 5, 6, and 8 (though not Article 7 on security measures) is permitted under Article 9(2) when such derogation

is provided for by the law of the Party and constitutes a necessary measure in a democratic society in the interests of:
a. protecting State security, public safety, the monetary interests of the State or the suppression of criminal offences;
b. protecting the data subject or the rights and freedoms of others.

These derogations echo ECHR Article 8(2),[31] but depart from it in minor respects.[32] Legal restrictions on the rights specified in Article 8(b)–(d) are also permitted with respect to data processing for the purposes of statistics or scientific research 'when there is obviously no risk of an infringement of the privacy of the data subjects' (Article 9(3)).

Under Article 10, contracting states are required to institute 'appropriate sanctions and remedies' for breach of domestic laws implementing the Chapter II principles.

Chapter III of the Convention contains rules governing the flow of personal data between states parties to the Convention. The chief rule stipulates that a party 'shall not, for the sole purpose of the protection of privacy, prohibit or subject to special authorisation transborder flows of personal data going to the territory of another Party' (Article 12(2)). Derogation from this prohibition is allowed (although not required) insofar as the data concerned is specifically protected pursuant to the state party's legislation and the regulations of the other party fail to provide 'equivalent protection' for the data (Article 12(3)(a)). Derogation is also allowed in order to prevent the transfer of data to a non-contracting state, via another state party, in circumvention of the first state party's legislation (Article 12(3)(b)).

## 3. Gaps in Convention 108

A major gap in the original version of the Convention was its lack of rules for the flow of personal data from a party to non-party state. While initially of small significance, this gap became increasingly anachronistic, particularly after adoption of the EU Data Protection Directive, which contains extensive

---

[31] See further section I(2(c)).
[32] For instance, whereas Art. 9(2) refers to 'suppression of criminal offences', ECHR Art. 8(2) employs the apparently more permissive formulation 'prevention of disorder and crime'. Hondius claims that the difference was intended to curb 'the setting up of data files to keep an eye on people, just in case': Hondius (n 23) 117. However, it is difficult to read such an intention out of the Convention's Explanatory Report.

rules on flow of personal data from EU member states to other countries.[33] The CoE remedied the anomaly by adopting the additional Protocol to the Convention in 2001. The Protocol contains provisions on flow of data from party to non-party states (see Article 2) which follow the broad thrust of the equivalent provisions of the Directive.[34]

The same Protocol fills others gaps in the original version of the Convention as well. Although the Convention has always contained fairly detailed provisions envisaging both the establishment of authorities to help oversee implementation of the Convention and a high level of cooperation between these authorities (Articles 13–17), it originally fell short of mandating that each contracting state establish a special control body in the form of a DPA or the like.[35] It also failed to specify minimum requirements regarding the competence and independence of such an agency. Again, these gaps became increasingly anomalous, particularly after adoption of the EU Data Protection Directive which requires each EU member state to establish one or more DPAs and prescribes in detail their independence, competence, and functions along with provision for judicial review of their decisions.[36] Article 1 of the Protocol lays down broadly similar requirements.[37]

Although the Protocol has plugged some gaps, others remain. For instance, the Convention omits provisions regulating the issues of choice and collision of laws. This is remarkable given the practical significance of the issues, the transnational focus of the Convention, and the inclusion in the Data Protection Directive of provisions on applicable law. The experts drafting the Convention were evidently reluctant to include such provisions for fear that inclusion would delay the Convention's adoption.[38] The T-PD proposal only

[33] See further Ch 6 (section E(1)).

[34] The T-PD proposal integrates a modified version of Art. 2 of the Protocol in a revised version of Art. 12 of the Convention. The effect of the modifications is to make the criteria for transfers of personal data to non-party states follow more closely the provisions of the Data Protection Directive. It extends these criteria to govern transfers of data to international organizations as well. However, it reformulates the basic criterion for transfer in terms of the recipient state or organization having to offer an 'appropriate' level of protection rather than an 'adequate' level. While this does not necessarily signal a relaxation of the transfer standard, 'appropriate' is prima facie more diffuse and open-textured than that of adequacy. For discussion, see eg Greenleaf, ' "Modernising" Data Protection Convention 108' (n 7) 434–5.

[35] See also the Convention's Explanatory Report (n 14) para. 73.

[36] See further Ch 6 (section A).

[37] The T-PD proposal integrates these requirements, in modified form, in a new Art. 12bis of the Convention. The new provisions follow the provisions of the Data Protection Directive more faithfully.

[38] Hondius (n 23) 120.

goes as far as stipulating that each party 'undertakes to apply this Convention to data processing subject to its jurisdiction, thereby protecting the right to protection of personal data of any person subject to its jurisdiction' (revised Article 3) but omits specifying criteria for how such jurisdiction is to be asserted. The continuing failure to make a more ambitious move on these issues is perhaps rooted in the controversy surrounding the Directive's provisions on applicable law.[39]

Another gap is that the Convention does not set up an agency specifically charged with overseeing and enforcing its implementation. The Consultative Committee fills this gap somewhat but has only advisory status. That status persists under the T-PD proposal, although the proposed new committee is to be given additional powers and functions which resemble those of the EU's A29WP (see proposed new Article 19). Another mitigating factor is that breach of the principles in Chapter II of the Convention would most likely constitute interference with the right to respect for private life under ECHR Article 8 and thus fall within the jurisdiction of the ECtHR. The Convention is clearly envisaged as an elaboration of the protection provided under EHCR Article 8, and ECtHR jurisprudence confirms this.[40] Yet the ability of the ECtHR to function as an effective oversight and enforcement organ in the field is hampered by its enormous caseload and procedural limitations (for example, it does not hear complaints until all possibilities for domestic remedies have been exhausted). Moreover, doubt pertains as to whether all breaches of Chapter II principles would be regarded by the Court as interferences with rights under the ECHR.[41]

Still other problems afflict implementation of the Convention. The Chapter II principles are formulated in a general, abstract way, and many key words are left undefined by the Convention and its Explanatory Report. Admittedly, the diffuseness and generality of the Convention's principles have certain strengths. Their generality has helped them battle obsolescence in the face of technological developments. This battle has not been made easy by the focus of some of the principles on the notion of 'file' (Articles 7 and 8), which, on its face, fits awkwardly with a world of distributed data networks.[42] On the other hand, the diffuseness of the principles has undoubtedly facilitated their ready acceptance by a large group of contracting states

---

[39] See further Ch 6 (section E(2)).          [40] See further section I(2).
[41] See further section I(2).
[42] Cf Explanatory Report (n 14) para. 30 (stating that the term 'file' in the Convention 'covers not only data files consisting of compact sets of data, but also sets of data which are geographically distributed and are brought together via computer links for purposes of processing'). However, the T-PD proposal fortunately discards all references to 'file'.

that represent markedly different legal-political cultures. Yet the principles' diffuseness detracts from their ability to harmonize the data privacy regimes of the contracting states. This weakness is exacerbated by the Convention otherwise permitting discretionary derogation on numerous significant points (see for example, Articles 3, 6, and 9). This in turn quickly undermined the ability of the Convention to guarantee the free flow of personal data across national borders.[43] The abstract level at which the principles are pitched further detracts from their ability to function as practical 'rules for the road' in concrete situations.

## 4. Sectoral recommendations

The latter problem has been mitigated by a series of CoE recommendations dealing specifically with data processing in particular sectors, such as telecommunications, scientific research, and insurance.[44] These recommendations function as useful supplements to the general principles of the Convention. Although not legally binding, the recommendations have strong persuasive force, not least politically, as they are drafted with participation from

---

[43] See further eg, ACM Nugter, *Transborder Flow of Personal Data within the EC* (Kluwer Law & Taxation Publishers 1989) ch 8 (showing that, as of 1990, the Convention had failed to establish more than a minimal, formal equivalence between the national data privacy regimes of Germany, France, the Netherlands, and UK).

[44] In chronological order, these are: Recommendation R (81) 1 on regulations for automated medical data banks (adopted 23 January 1981); Recommendation R (83) 10 on the protection of personal data used for scientific research and statistics (adopted 23 September 1983; replaced by Recommendation R (97) 18—see following); Recommendation R (85) 20 on the protection of personal data used for the purposes of direct marketing (adopted 25 October 1985); Recommendation R (86) 1 on the protection of personal data for social security purposes (adopted 23 January 1986); Recommendation R (87) 15 regulating the use of personal data in the police sector (adopted 17 September 1987); Recommendation R (89) 2 on the protection of peronal data used for employment purposes (adopted 18 January 1989); Recommendation R (90) 19 on the protection of personal data used for payment and other operations (adopted 13 September 1990); Recommendation R (91) 10 on the communication to third parties of personal data held by public bodies (adopted 9 September 1991); Recommendation R (95) 4 on the protection of personal data in the area of telecommunication services, with particular reference to telephone services (adopted 7 February 1995); Recommendation R (97) 5 on the protection of medical data (adopted 13 February 1997); Recommendation R (97) 18 on the protection of personal data collected and processed for statistical purposes (adopted 30 September 1997); Recommendation R (99) 5 on the protection of privacy on the internet (adopted 23 February 1999); Recommendation R (2002) 9 on the protection of personal data collected and processed for insurance purposes (adopted 18 September 2002); Recommendation CM/Rec (2010) 13 on the protection of individuals with regard to automatic processing of personal data in the context of profiling (adopted 23 November 2010); Recommendation CM/Rec (2012) 3 on the protection of human rights with regard to search engines (adopted 4 April 2012); and Recommendation CM/Rec (2012) 4 on the protection of human rights with regard to social networking services (adopted 4 April 2012).

all member states. The authority of the recommendations is reflected in the fact that when they are adopted, individual member states frequently issue reservations on points of contention. The recommendations are also highly influential on the policies and practices of national DPAs.

Other relevant examples are recommendations on genetic testing which provide that genetic information should be processed in conformity with basic data privacy principles.[45] The latter recommendations are supplemented by the 1997 Convention for the Protection of Human Rights and Dignity of the Human Being with regard to the Application of Biology and Medicine.[46] This Convention contains several provisions on data privacy in relation to the processing of health information. The central provision in this regard is Article 10(1) stipulating that '[e]veryone has the right to respect for private life in relation to information about his or her health'.[47]

Furthermore, the CoE has issued a range of other instruments which, whilst directly concerning issues other than data privacy, indirectly promote privacy-related interests. Examples are recommendations on government administrative procedure which attempt to ensure that government decision-making is carried out fairly and that citizens are given access to government-held information.[48]

Hence, while Convention 108 is, in many respects, the Council of Europe's crowning achievement in the field of data privacy, the Council has gone on to generate a large number of other instruments relevant to the field. Many of these have more practical bite in their respective fields of application than does the Convention. Yet the Convention is far from passé. It continues to be a key reference point for shaping regulatory policy, also outside the aegis of the Council. This is evidenced, for example, by its use as a benchmark for regulatory standards in the development of EU data privacy rules for policing and

---

[45] See eg, Recommendation R (90) 13 on Prenatal Genetic Screening, Prenatal Genetic Diagnosis and Associated Genetic Counselling (adopted 21 June 1990) esp. Principles 8–13; Recommendation R (92) 1 on Use of Analysis of Deoxyribonucleic Acid (DNA) within the Framework of the Criminal Justice System (adopted 10 February 1992), esp. Principles 3, 7, 8, and 12; Recommendation R (92) 3 on Genetic Testing and Screening for Health Care Purposes (adopted 10 February 1992) esp. Principles 11–13.

[46] Adopted 4 April 1997; in force 1 December 1999; ETS 164.

[47] See too Art. 10(2) which provides that '[e]veryone is entitled to know any information collected about his or her health'; at the same time, 'the wishes of individuals not to be so informed shall be observed'. These provisions appear to create both a right to know and a right *not* to know, in relation to health information. The exercise of both rights, however, may be restricted by law '[i]n exceptional cases' and 'in the interests of the patient' (Art. 10(3)). See also Art. 26(1) which allows for derogations from Art. 10 in accordance with the criteria set down in ECHR Art. 8(2).

[48] See eg, Recommendation R (80) 2 on Exercise of Discretionary Powers by Administrative Authorities (adopted 11 March 1980) esp. Principles 1–3; and Recommendation R (81) 19 on Access to Information Held by Public Authorities (adopted 25 November 1981).

judicial cooperation.[49] The current push to get states that are not CoE members to accede to it, combined with its ongoing revision, ought to assure that the Convention remains important for future law and policy in the field, both within and outside Europe.[50]

# C. OECD Initiatives

## 1. Guidelines on privacy protection and transborder data flow

The OECD began taking an interest in data privacy not long after the CoE. In the early 1970s, it commissioned a number of reports on the issue as part of a series of 'Informatics Studies'.[51] Later in that decade, it began work on drafting its own regulatory instrument. This work was undertaken in close liaison with the CoE. The initial fruits of its efforts are guidelines published in 1980 bearing the title 'Guidelines Governing the Protection of Privacy and Transborder Flows of Personal Data'. The core of the Guidelines is a set of eight data privacy principles (elaborated in the following) intended to apply to manual and electronic processing of personal data in both the public and private sectors.

The Guidelines are not legally binding on OECD member states. Their publication was simply accompanied by an OECD Council Recommendation stating that account should be taken of them when member countries develop domestic legislation on privacy and data protection.[52] The recommendation also stressed that member countries should 'endeavour to remove or avoid creating, in the name of privacy protection, unjustified obstacles to transborder data flows of personal data'.

---

[49] See eg, Council Decision 2002/187/JHA setting up Eurojust with a view to reinforcing the fight against serious crime [2002] OJ L63/1, Art. 14(2) and Recital 9. Eurojust is an EU body set up in 2002 to coordinate efforts by EU member states' judicial authorities in countering serious crime. See too Council Decision 2008/615/JHA on the stepping up of cross-border cooperation, particularly in combating terrorism and cross-border crime [2008] OJ L210/1, Art. 25; and the earlier Prüm Convention of 2005: Convention between the Kingdom of Belgium, the Federal Republic of Germany, the Kingdom of Spain, the French Republic, the Grand Duchy of Luxembourg, the Kingdom of the Netherlands, and the Republic of Austria on the stepping up of cross-border cooperation, particularly in combating terrorism, cross-border crime, and illegal migration (opened for signature 27 May 2005; fully in force 26 August 2008) Art. 34(1).

[50] For fairly upbeat assessment of the likely importance of the Convention in future years, see Greenleaf, 'A World Data Privacy Treaty?' (n 7). On the prospects of Convention 108 becoming a global data privacy treaty, see Ch 7.

[51] See eg, GBF Niblett, *Digital Information and the Privacy Problem*, OECD Informatics Studies No. 2 (OECD 1971).

[52] Recommendation of the Council concerning Guidelines governing the Protection of Privacy and Transborder Flows of Personal Data (adopted 23 September 1980; (C(80)58/FINAL).

The Guidelines were recently revised and issued in a new version in September 2013. The revision followed the OECD's announcement five years previously that it would carry out a broad-ranging assessment of the various OECD instruments 'addressing consumer protection and empowerment, privacy and security in light of changing technologies, markets and user behaviour and the growing importance of digital identities'.[53] The principal changes introduced by the revised Guidelines concern implementation and enforcement mechanisms (spelled out further on in this section). The Guidelines' legal status remains otherwise unchanged. The same may be said of their eight core principles and, to a large extent, their rationale. The decision to leave the core principles untouched is remarkable given that the principles are over 30 years old, were formulated in an environment that was markedly different from today's, and could arguably be fine-tuned or otherwise improved in light of such change. The Expert Group responsible for drafting the 2013 revision were nonetheless of the view 'that the balance reflected in the eight basic principles of Part Two of the 1980 Guidelines remains generally sound and should be maintained'.[54] One might also read into this statement an unwillingness to reopen a debate which could have led to diminishment of the protection offered by the existing principles.

According to Michael Kirby, who headed the Expert Group responsible for drafting the original Guidelines, the OECD's work in the field was motivated primarily by economic concerns:

It was the fear that local regulation, ostensibly for privacy protection, would, in truth, be enacted for purposes of economic protectionism, that led to the initiative of the OECD to establish the expert group which developed its Privacy Guidelines. The spectre was presented that the economically beneficial flow of data across national boundaries might be impeded unnecessarily and regulated inefficiently producing a cacophony of laws which did little to advance human rights but much to interfere in the free flow of information and ideas.[55]

These concerns are particularly prominent in the Council Recommendation accompanying the original Guidelines which pronounces a determination 'to further advance the free flow of information between Member countries and to avoid the creation of unjustified obstacles to the development of economic and social relations among them'. This determination is repeated word for word in the Council Recommendation accompanying the revised

---

[53] Seoul Declaration for the Future of the Internet Economy (18 June 2008; C(2008)99).

[54] 'Supplementary Explanatory Memorandum to the Revised Recommendation of the Council concerning Guidelines governing the Protection of Privacy and Transborder Flows of Personal Data (2013)'—hereinafter 'Supplementary Explanatory Memorandum'.

[55] MD Kirby, 'Legal Aspects of Transborder Data Flows' (1991) 5 Intl Computer Law Adviser no. 5, 4, 5–6.

Guidelines.[56] Nevertheless, the Guidelines affirm the need for member states to 'adopt laws protecting privacy' (paragraph 19(b)).[57] The Guidelines stipulate that they 'should be regarded as minimum standards which can be supplemented by additional measures for the protection of privacy and individual liberties, which may impact transborder flows of personal data' (paragraph 6).[58]

## 2. Core principles

It is remarkable that, despite the difference in the traditional focus of the OECD from that of the CoE—the latter being customarily regarded as more concerned than the former with human rights protection—the chief data privacy instruments of both organizations expound broadly similar principles. The similarities are partly attributable to the extensive cooperation between the bodies charged with drafting the respective instruments.[59]

In significant respects, the OECD Guidelines are broader than Convention 108. The Guidelines dispense with the potentially restrictive concept of 'data file' and focus instead on the processing of personal data regardless of the way in which the data is organized. The Guidelines also cover manual (non-computerized) data processing in addition to automated (computerized) processing. Further, their revision has resulted in the addition of a considerable number of provisions on implementation and enforcement mechanisms (dealt with further on in this section) which the Convention lacks. Finally, several of the Guidelines' basic principles are more comprehensive than the equivalent principles in the Convention. This is the case with the Guidelines' 'Collection Limitation Principle': whereas the Convention contains only a requirement that personal data be obtained 'fairly and lawfully' (Article 5(a)), the Guidelines state additionally that data collection should be

[56] Recommendation of the Council concerning Guidelines governing the Protection of Privacy and Transborder Flows of Personal Data (adopted 11 July 2013; (C(2013)79). Note also the Guidelines para. 3(b)—introduced in the 2013 revision—which stipulates that the Guidelines 'should not be interpreted . . . in a manner which unduly limits the freedom of expression'.

[57] The term 'laws protecting privacy' is defined as 'national laws or regulations, the enforcement of which has the effect of protecting personal data consistent with these Guidelines' (para. 1(c)). The Explanatory Memorandum for the revised Guidelines states that the term 'can refer not only to horizontal privacy laws that are common in Member countries, but also to sectoral privacy legislation (e.g. credit reporting or telecommunications laws) or other types of legislation that contain provisions which protect personal data so as to give effect to the Guidelines in practice (e.g. consumer protection laws)'.

[58] Note too para. 3: 'The principles in these Guidelines . . . should not be interpreted (a) as preventing the application of different protective measures to different categories of personal data, depending upon their nature and the context in which they are collected, stored, processed or disseminated'.

[59] See para. 14 of the Convention's Explanatory Report (n 14) and para. 20 of the Guidelines' original Explanatory Memorandum. See also Hondius (n 23) 112; H Seip, 'Data Protection, Privacy and National Borders' in J Bing and O Torvund (eds), *25 Years Anniversary Anthology in Computers and Law* (TANO 1995) 67.

'with the knowledge and consent of the data subject' and not without 'limits' (paragraph 7).[60] Secondly, the Guidelines' 'Purpose Specification Principle' states, inter alia, that '[t]he purposes for which personal data are collected should be specified not later than at the time of data collection' (paragraph 9); by contrast, Article 5(b) of the Convention appears to permit purpose specification at a stage later than when data is first obtained. Finally, the Guidelines contain an 'Openness Principle' (paragraph 12) which is more broadly formulated than Article 8(a) of the Convention.[61]

Yet the Guidelines fall short of the Convention's reach on numerous points. Unlike the Convention, the Guidelines avoid specific mention of the need for special safeguards for certain kinds of particularly sensitive data. While acknowledging that sensitivity of data is a central factor in determining the nature of protective measures (paragraph 3(a)), the Guidelines refrain from listing data that is putatively more sensitive than other data. This appears to be due partly to the failure by the Expert Group responsible for drafting the Guidelines to agree on which categories of data deserve special protection, and partly to a belief that the sensitivity of personal data is not an a priori given but dependent on the context in which the data is used.[62] The Guidelines omit specifically mentioning the possibility of protecting data on collective entities.[63] They do not contain a specific requirement that data is processed for 'legitimate' purposes,[64] or that data is deleted or anonymized after a certain period.[65] Moreover, the conditions for permitting use of data

---

[60] Arguably, though, the criteria 'fairly and lawfully' in the Convention could be read to imply a requirement that data subjects know of, and consent to, the collection of data on them.

[61] The 'Openness Principle' reads: 'There should be a general policy of openness about developments, practices and policies with respect to personal data. Means should be readily available of establishing the existence and nature of personal data, and the main purposes of their use, as well as the identity and usual residence of the data controller.'

[62] See the Guidelines' original Explanatory Memorandum paras 43 and 51; P Seipel, 'Transborder Flows of Personal Data: Reflections on the OECD Guidelines' (1981) 4 Transnational Data Report, no. 1, 32, 36.

[63] However, the possibility is intimated in para. 45 of the original Explanatory Memorandum which recognizes that '[i]n one country, protection may be afforded to data relating to groups and similar entities whereas such protection is completely nonexistent in another country'.

[64] Cf Art. 5(b) of the Convention which requires personal data to be stored and used for 'legitimate' purposes.

[65] Cf Art. 5(e) of the Convention which requires personal data to be 'preserved in a form which permits identification of the data subjects for no longer than is required for the purpose for which those data are stored'. Nevertheless, para. 54 of the Guidelines' original Explanatory Memorandum recognizes that the 'Purpose Specification Principle' may require the erasure or anonymization of personal data. Note that the Guidelines' original Explanatory Memorandum continues to be relevant for interpreting those provisions which remain unchanged after the 2013 revision—provisions that

for purposes that are incompatible with the original purpose(s) for which it is collected, are not as stringent in the Guidelines as in the Convention.[66] And whereas Article 8(b) of the Convention appears to require that both confirmation of whether or not a data controller has data stored on a data subject, and communication of these data to the data subject, be carried out within a reasonable time and for a charge that is not excessive,[67] the Guidelines apply the latter requirements (that is, timeliness and reasonable cost) only to communication of data to the data subject (paragraph 13(b)).[68]

It has been argued, though, that Article 8(b) of the Convention poses only one requirement in relation to *communication* from a controller to a data subject of data relating to the latter, this requirement being that the data is communicated 'in an intelligible form'. Concomitantly, the argument runs, the other requirements ('without excessive delay or expense') pertain only to a controller's *confirmation* of whether personal data relating to a data subject is stored by the controller. From this, the conclusion is drawn that data subjects' interests are better served by paragraph 13(b) of the Guidelines than by Article 8(b).[69] In contrast, I read Article 8(b) as applying the timeliness and expense requirements to communication as well as confirmation. In my view, this reading conforms better with the provision's syntax and basic purpose.[70]

Part 3 of the Guidelines contains provisions on 'implementing accountability'. These provisions were introduced in the 2013 revision. As their title suggests, they elaborate the 'accountability principle' in paragraph 14 which

include the core principles set out in Part 2 of the Guidelines. The Supplementary Explanatory Memorandum accompanying the 2013 revision states that it 'is intended to supplement—not replace—the original Explanatory Memorandum'.

[66] Para. 10 of the Guidelines permits such use if the data subject consents to it or it is legally authorized. Cf Art. 9(2) of the Convention which does not permit such use when it is simply 'provided for by...law' but when it also 'constitutes a necessary measure in a democratic society in the interests of...protecting State security, public safety, the monetary interests of the State or the suppression of criminal offences;...protecting the data subject or the rights and freedoms of others'.

[67] Art. 8(b) reads: '[Any person shall be enabled] to obtain at reasonable intervals and without excessive delay or expense confirmation of whether personal data relating to him are stored in the automated data files as well as communication to him of such data in an intelligible form'.

[68] The relevant parts of para. 13 read: '[An individual should have the right] a) to obtain from a data controller, or otherwise, confirmation of whether or not the data controller has data relating to him; b) to have communicated to him, data relating to him within a reasonable time; at a charge, if any, that is not excessive; in a reasonable manner; and in a form that is readily intelligible to him'.

[69] J Bing, 'The Council of Europe Convention and the OECD Guidelines on Data Protection' in *Regulation of Transnational Communication: Michigan Yearbook of International Legal Studies* (Clark Boardman Company 1984) 271, 280–1.

[70] See the Convention's Explanatory Report (n 14) para. 53: 'The wording of littera *b* is intended to cover various formulas followed by national legislation: communication at the request of the data subject or at the initiative of the controller of the file; communication free of charge at fixed intervals as well as communication against payment at any other time, etc.'. Henke seems also to read Art. 8(b) in the way I do: see Henke (n 23) 127ff.

stipulates that data controllers 'should be accountable for complying with measures which give effect to' the other Part 2 principles. The key element of the new Part 3 provisions is the need for a controller to draw up a 'privacy management programme' that 'provides for appropriate safeguards based on privacy risk assessment' (paragraph 15(a)(iii)). Another central element is a requirement for security breach notification. This means that a controller should '[p]rovide notice, as appropriate, to privacy enforcement authorities or other relevant authorities where there has been a significant security breach affecting personal data'; notification should also extend to those data subjects who are 'likely' to be 'adversely affect[ed]' by the breach (paragraph 15(c)).[71]

## 3. Transborder data flow

Part 4 deals specifically with regulating the flow of personal data across national borders. The rules here were modified in the 2013 revision but retain much the same approach as the original Guidelines. They begin with a re-elaboration of the accountability principle in the context of transborder data flow: 'a data controller remains accountable for personal data under its control without regard to the location of the data' (paragraph 16). The central rules are laid down in paragraphs 17 and 18. According to paragraph 17:

A Member country should refrain from restricting transborder data flows of personal data between itself and another country where (a) the other country substantially observes these Guidelines or (b) sufficient safeguards exist, including effective enforcement mechanisms and appropriate measures put in place by the data controller, to ensure a continuing level of protection consistent with these Guidelines.

An important difference between this and the previous version of paragraph 17 is that the latter dealt primarily with data flow between OECD member states; the new version is of more general application. Another important difference concerns the criteria for permitting restrictions on transborder data flow. The previous version of paragraph 17 permitted a member country to restrict such flow 'where re-export of ... data would circumvent its domestic privacy legislation' or where the restrictions concerned 'certain categories of personal data for which its domestic privacy legislation includes specific regulations in view of the nature of those data and for which the other member country provides no equivalent protection'. The new version dispenses with these criteria. 'Equivalency with domestic legislation' is replaced by 'consistency with the Guidelines'. This seems to raise the bar for permitted restrictions.

---

[71] According to the Supplementary Explanatory Memorandum, 'the term "adverse effect" should be interpreted broadly to include factors other than just financial loss'.

An important prop for that bar is paragraph 18:

18. Any restrictions to transborder flows of personal data should be proportionate to the risks presented, taking into account the sensitivity of the data, and the purpose and context of the processing.[72]

Paragraphs 17 and 18 ought to be read in the light of paragraph 21, which encourages member countries to develop 'international arrangements that promote interoperability among privacy frameworks that give practical effect to these Guidelines'. The latter paragraph was introduced in the 2013 revision. Achievement of 'interoperability' is a goal that has been pushed particularly hard by US government and business organizations. Like 'multistakeholderism', 'interoperability' is fast becoming a mantra for discourse on 'good' transnational governance of data privacy matters. Its precise meaning remains unclear. Neither the OECD Guidelines nor their Supplementary Explanatory Memorandum defines the term. In essence, however, 'interoperability' seems to denote a situation in which different data privacy regimes co-exist harmoniously and, as a result, permit personal data to flow between countries and organizations but without unduly compromising the privacy-related interests of the data subjects. The vexing issue, of course, concerns the degree of compromise tolerated—an issue that neither the OECD Guidelines nor their Supplementary Explanatory Memorandum meet head on. It bears emphasis, though, that the thrust of paragraphs 17 and 18 seems somewhat undercut by paragraph 6, which recognizes that the 'minimum standards' of the Guidelines 'can be supplemented by additional' data privacy measures 'which may impact transborder flows of personal data'. The import of the latter clause on transborder data flow impact—introduced in the 2013 revision—is rather enigmatic. Yet it does signal that a more stringent regulation of transborder data flow (as provided, say, under EU law)[73] is permissible even if in tension with paragraph 17.[74]

## 4. Implementation mechanisms

Parts 5 and 6 of the Guidelines deal with their implementation and international cooperative efforts to advance their aims. Particularly noteworthy with these provisions is that they now recommend member countries to establish 'privacy enforcement authorities' (paragraph 19(c)). This is in contrast

[72] The previous version of para. 18 was essentially along the same lines: 'Member countries should avoid developing laws, policies and practices in the name of the protection of privacy and individual liberties, which would create obstacles to transborder flows of personal data that would exceed requirements for such protection'.

[73] See further Ch 6 (section E(1)).

[74] The Supplementary Explanatory Memorandum states that para. 17 does not preclude application of para. 6.

to the original Guidelines which (like the CoE Convention as originally adopted) did not. 'Privacy enforcement authorities' embrace not just traditional DPAs but also other regulators with a role in enforcing data privacy law.[75] Such authorities should be invested 'with the governance, resources and technical expertise necessary to exercise their powers effectively and to make decisions on an objective, impartial and consistent basis' (paragraph 19(c)). Further, the Guidelines exhort member countries 'to facilitate cross-border privacy law enforcement co-operation, in particular by enhancing information sharing among privacy enforcement authorities' (paragraph 20).[76]

Also noteworthy is the Guidelines' encouragement of 'self-regulation, whether in the form of codes of conduct or otherwise' (paragraph 19(d)), and their recommendation (added in the 2013 revision) that countries 'consider the adoption of complementary measures, including education and awareness raising, skills development, and the promotion of technical measures which help to protect privacy' (paragraph 19(g)).

## 5. Influence

Although not legally binding, the Guidelines have been highly influential on the development of data privacy law in countries outside Europe, particularly Japan, Australia, New Zealand, Canada, and Hong Kong. For example, the Preamble to Australia's federal Privacy Act 1988 lists both the Guidelines and the accompanying Recommendation of the OECD Council as part of the reasons for the passing of the Act. Similarly, the Preamble to New Zealand's Privacy Act 1993 states that the Act is to 'promote and protect individual privacy in general accordance with [the OECD Council's] Recommendation'. In Canada, the Guidelines form the basis for the Canadian Standards Association's Model Code for the Protection of Personal Information,[77] incorporated into Canadian legislation as Schedule 1 to the Personal Information Protection and Electronic Documents Act 2000. The Guidelines are also used as a benchmark in the Safe Harbor Agreement of 2000 between the European Commission and US Department of Commerce.[78] And as elaborated in

---

[75] According to the Supplementary Explanatory Memorandum, '[a] "privacy enforcement authority" refers not only to those public sector entities whose primary mission is the enforcement of national privacy laws, but may for example also extend to regulators with a national consumer protection mission, provided they have the powers to conduct investigations or bring proceedings in the context of enforcing "laws protecting privacy"'.

[76] This stems from, and gives effect to, the OECD's Recommendation on Cross-Border Co-operation in the Enforcement of Laws Protecting Privacy (adopted 12 June 2007; C(2007)67).

[77] CAN/CSA-Q830-96; adopted March 1996. These were the first comprehensive set of data privacy standards to be developed by a national standards association.

[78] See Frequently Asked Question (FAQ) 8 in Annex II to the Safe Harbor Agreement. The Agreement is described in Ch 6 (section E(1)).

section F of this chapter, the Guidelines are touted as a significant source of inspiration for the APEC Privacy Framework of 2005.

Since 1980, the OECD has adopted other normative instruments relevant to data privacy. These include guidelines dealing with information security,[79] cryptography policy,[80] and consumer protection in electronic commerce.[81] While these instruments develop OECD information policy along new avenues, all of them pay deference to, and reaffirm the vision embodied in, the 1980 Guidelines.

## D. UN Initiatives

The first UN instrument dealing directly with data privacy matters was a 1968 resolution of the General Assembly inviting the UN Secretary-General to examine, inter alia, individuals' right to privacy 'in the light of advances in recording and other techniques'.[82] The resulting study by the Secretary-General led to the publication of a report in 1976 urging states to adopt data privacy legislation covering computerized personal data systems in the public and private sectors, and listing minimum standards for such legislation.[83]

In 1990, the UN General Assembly adopted a set of Guidelines on data privacy which repeat and strengthen this call.[84] Work on the Guidelines was rooted primarily in human rights concerns; commercial anxieties about restrictions on transborder data flows appear to have taken a back seat.[85] The adoption of the Guidelines underlined at the time that data privacy had ceased to be exclusively a 'first world', Western concern.

The Guidelines are two-pronged: one prong lays down 'minimum guarantees' for inclusion in national data privacy laws (Part A). The field of

---

[79] Guidelines for the Security of Information Systems (adopted November 26, 1992); since replaced by Guidelines for the Security of Information Systems and Networks: Towards a Culture of Security (adopted 25 July 2002).

[80] Guidelines for Cryptography Policy (adopted 27 March 1997).

[81] Guidelines for Consumer Protection in the Context of Electronic Commerce (adopted 9 December 1999).

[82] UN General Assembly Resolution 2450 of 19 December 1968 (Doc E/CN.4/1025).

[83] See 'Points for Possible Inclusion in Draft International Standards for the Protection of the Rights of the Individual against Threats Arising from the Use of Computerized Personal Data Systems' (Doc E/CN.4/1233). Cf Doc E/CN.4/1116 dealing more generally with surveillance technology.

[84] Guidelines Concerning Computerized Personal Data Files (UN General Assembly Resolution 45/95 of 14 December 1990) (Doc E/CN.4/1990/72) (hereinafter also termed 'UN Guidelines').

[85] On the background to the Guidelines, see generally J Michael, *Privacy and Human Rights. An International and Comparative Study, with Special Reference to Developments in Information Technology*, (Dartmouth/Aldershot 1994) 21–6.

application of these guarantees is primarily intended as 'all public and private computerized files', although states are also given the express option to extend application to manual files and to data on legal persons (paragraph 10).

The other prong is aimed at encouraging international organizations (governmental and non-governmental) to process personal data in a responsible, fair, and privacy-friendly manner (Part B). This is a particularly progressive element of the Guidelines—one not specifically found in Convention 108, the OECD Guidelines, or EU Data Protection Directive.

Other progressive elements are present too. First, the UN Guidelines stipulate a 'principle of accuracy' which obligates data controllers to carry out *regular* checks of the quality of personal data (paragraph 2). The equivalent provisions in the OECD Guidelines, Convention 108, and EU Directive omit explicit mention of this obligation, although it can arguably be read into them.

Secondly, the 'principle of purpose specification' in the UN Guidelines requires that the purpose of a file be actively publicized (paragraph 3). Such a requirement is also present in Articles 10 and 11 of the EU Directive but can at best be read into Convention 108 and the OECD Guidelines.[86]

Thirdly, the 'principle of interested-party access' in the UN Guidelines goes further than Convention 108 and the OECD Guidelines, although not the Directive, by stating that a data subject should have the right to be informed of the recipients ('addressees') of data relating to him/her (paragraph 4).

Fourthly, the Guidelines address the need to establish national DPAs that are impartial, independent, and technically competent (paragraph 8). This is a point upon which the original version of the OECD Guidelines and Convention 108 (minus additional Protocol) are silent, although not the Directive.

The Guidelines also augment the range of specially sensitive data listed in Article 6 of Convention 108 and Article 8 of the Directive, by expressly treating these as instances of a broader category of data—that is, 'data likely to give rise to unlawful or arbitrary discrimination'.[87] It is fairly clear that data relating to criminal convictions would fall within this category, even though the UN Guidelines do not expressly refer to such information. Also

---

[86] Cf para. 54 of the Explanatory Memorandum to the original version of the OECD Guidelines which states that 'specification of purposes' pursuant to para. 9 of the Guidelines 'can be made in a number of alternative or complementary ways, e.g. by public declarations, information to data subjects, legislation, administrative decrees, and licences provided by supervisory authorities'.

[87] Note, though, that the list of sensitive data in Convention 108 Art. 6 is not meant to be exhaustive: see the Convention's Explanatory Report (n 14) para. 48. The opposite appears to be the case with respect to the list of 'special categories' of data in the EU Directive Art. 8(1): see Ch 5 (section I).

noteworthy is that the Guidelines—in contrast to the Directive—treat data on membership of associations in general (not just trade unions) as deserving special protection.

Regarding flow of data across borders, the Guidelines stipulate in paragraph 9:

When the legislation of two or more countries concerned by a transborder data flow offers comparable safeguards for the protection of privacy, information should be able to circulate as freely as inside each of the territories concerned. If there are no reciprocal safeguards, limitations on such circulation may not be imposed unduly and only insofar as the protection of privacy demands.

Both 'comparable' and 'reciprocal' are more diffuse, loose, and confusing than the criterion of 'equivalent' protection (which is also nebulous) used in Convention 108. It is probable, though, that paragraph 9 seeks to apply essentially the same standards as the latter.

Despite their progressive character, the UN Guidelines have had a lower public profile and practical impact than the majority of the other main international instruments on point. Their 'soft law' status might account for part of this, although only to a small degree given that the more influential OECD Guidelines have the same status, as do the CoE sectoral recommendations. A more significant factor is probably the UN Guidelines' greater stringency on key points relative to their 'competitors'. Yet at least part of the problem is undoubtedly due to the absence of definitions of central terms, such as 'personal data', 'personal data file', and 'comparable' or 'reciprocal' safeguards. This diminishes the Guidelines' practical utility.

# E. EU Initiatives

## 1. Data Protection Directive

The institutional organs of the EU and its predecessors (the European Economic Community and European Community) were slower off the mark than their counterparts in the CoE, OECD, and UN to develop data privacy instruments. The EU instruments that were eventually adopted have nonetheless been the most ambitious, comprehensive, and complex in the field. The central instrument is the Data Protection Directive (95/46/EC)(DPD). Since its adoption in October 1995, it has constituted the most important point of departure for national data privacy initiatives within and, to a large extent, outside the EU.

Although the DPD's scope is delimited in several major respects (spelled out in the following), its rules are capable of broad application and impact. It is incorporated into the 1992 Agreement on the European Economic Area (EEA) such that states which are not EU members but party to the EEA Agreement (that is, Norway, Iceland, and Liechtenstein) are legally bound to bring their respective laws into conformity with it. Moreover, the Directive has exercised considerable influence over other countries outside the EU not least because it prohibits (with some qualifications) the transfer of personal data to these countries unless they provide 'adequate' levels of data privacy (Articles 25–26). Accordingly, the following presentation treats the Directive in considerably more detail than the other international instruments.

## (a) Gestation

The adoption of the DPD is the culmination of a series of proposals, strung over two decades, urging EU member states to take legal action in the field of data privacy. The initially most active institutional actor in this context was the European Parliament (EP). Concerned to protect human rights in the face of developments in computer technology, it made repeated calls for the drawing up of a Directive on data privacy and for EU member states to sign and ratify Convention 108.[88] Hondius drily observes that the issue of data privacy was fervently pursued by the Parliament not simply because of the importance of the issue itself but also because 'this subject was ideally suited to demonstrate that the European Communities, and especially the Parliament, were doing something to defend the fundamental freedoms of the individual Community citizen'.[89] The European Commission, along with the Council of Ministers, was considerably more reserved in taking up the issue. The Commission directed

[88] See esp. EP Resolution on the protection of the rights of the individual in the face of developing technical progress in the field of automatic data processing [1975] OJ C60/48; EP Resolution on the protection of the rights of the individual in the face of developing technical progress in the field of automatic data processing [1976] OJ C100/27; EP Resolution on the protection of the rights of the individual in the face of technical developments in data processing [1979] OJ C140/34; EP Resolution on the protection of the rights of the individual in the face of technical developments in data processing [1982] OJ C87/39. In addition, the Parliament's Legal Affairs Committee commissioned two studies on data privacy issues, resulting in the so-called 'Bayerl' and 'Sieglerschmidt' reports: see *Report on the Protection of the Rights of the Individual in the Face of Technical Developments in Data Processing* (the 'Bayerl Report') (EP Doc 100/79, PE 56.386 final, 4 May 1979), and *Second Report on the Protection of the Rights of the Individual in the Face of Technical Developments in Data Processing* (the 'Sieglerschmidt Report') (EP Doc 1-548/81, PE 70.166 final, 12 October 1981).

[89] FW Hondius, *Emerging Data Protection in Europe* (North Holland Publishing Company 1975) 72–3.

its energies primarily to development of the internal market and a European computer industry.[90]

The first major initiative taken by the Commission with respect to data privacy was to issue a Recommendation in 1981 echoing calls by the Parliament for member states to sign and ratify Convention 108.[91] Towards the end of the 1980s, the Commission began work on drafting a framework Directive on data privacy. Although the Commission appears to have been partly motivated by a desire to protect basic human rights,[92] the more predominant concern in its pronouncements was to prevent conflicting national data privacy regimes from impeding the realization of the internal market and growth of the European computer industry.[93] Only when faced with clear signs that the uneven nature of EU member states' respective rules in the field threatened such realization did the Commission put serious effort into drafting a framework Directive.[94] The unevenness between national regimes at the time—with some EU member states (for example, Italy, Spain, and Greece) lacking even rudimentary data privacy laws—partly reflected the weakness of Convention 108 and the OECD Guidelines in prompting nation states to adopt comprehensive and relatively uniform data privacy regimes. This weakness was exacerbated by the Convention and Guidelines also permitting derogation on numerous significant points. As of 1990, the Convention had failed to establish more than a minimal, formal equivalence between the national data privacy laws of the Federal Republic of Germany, France, the UK, and the Netherlands.[95] This meant that the free flow of personal data between a large number of EU states could not be guaranteed.

[90] See generally WJ Kirsch, 'The Protection of Privacy and Transborder Flows of Personal Data: the Work of the Council of Europe, the Organization for Economic Co-operation and Development and the European Economic Community' (1982) Legal Issues of European Integration, no. 2, 21, 34–7; H Geiger, 'Europäischer Informationsmarkt und Datenschutz' (1989) 5 Recht der Datenverarbeitung 203.

[91] Commission Recommendation 81/679/EEC relating to the Council of Europe convention for the protection of individuals with regard to automatic processing of personal data [1981] OJ L246/31.

[92] See eg, Commission Communication on the protection of individuals in relation to the processing of personal data in the Community and information security (COM(90) 314 final) 15 (noting that deficient legal regimes for data protection in some member states are problematic because they 'do not reflect the Community's commitment to the protection of fundamental rights').

[93] (COM(90) 314 final) 4 ('The diversity of national approaches and the lack of a system of protection at Community level are an obstacle to completion of the internal market...A Community approach towards the protection of individuals in relation to the processing of personal data is also essential to the development of the data processing industry and of value-added data communication services').

[94] See further AL Newman, *Protectors of Privacy: Regulating Personal Data in the Global Economy* (Cornell University Press 2008) 90ff.

[95] Nugter (n 43) ch 8.

The Commission issued its first proposal for a framework Directive on data privacy in 1990.[96] Accompanying this initiative were, inter alia, a proposal for a more specialized Directive on data privacy in the context of telecommunications,[97] a recommendation that the European Communities become a party to Convention 108,[98] and a proposal on information security measures.[99]

The 1990 proposal for a framework Directive on data privacy was met with much criticism from, amongst others, the business community and privacy advocates.[100] The Commission issued an amended proposal in 1992 after extensive input from the European Parliament.[101] Although critical response to the new proposal was milder, another three years of intensive discussion, lobbying, and bargaining occurred before the Directive was adopted.

## (b) Interpretation and policy thrust

Interpreting the DPD is no easy task. This is due largely to the nebulous manner in which many of its provisions are formulated, combined with a paucity of authoritative guides on their meaning. The nebulousness is symptomatic of the political compromises reached after extensive tugs-of-war between various member states, organizations, and interest groups during the drafting process. Such vagueness is not unique to the Directive; as seen in the preceding

---

[96] See Proposal for a Council Directive concerning the protection of individuals in relation to the processing of personal data (COM(90) 314 final—SYN 287); [1990] OJ C277/3.

[97] Proposal for a Council Directive concerning the protection of personal data and privacy in the context of public digital telecommunications networks, in particular the integrated services digital network (ISDN) and public digital mobile networks (COM(90) 314 final—SYN 288); [1990] OJ C277/12.

[98] See Recommendation for a Council Decision on the opening of negotiations with a view to the accession of the European Communities to the Council of Europe Convention for the protection of individuals with regard to the automatic processing of personal data (COM(90) 314 final). A similar proposal was made earlier by the European Parliament: see EP Resolution of 9 March 1982 [1982] OJ C87/41 para. 16.

[99] Proposal for a Council Decision in the field of information security (COM(90) 314 final). This was subsequently adopted as Council Decision 92/242/EEC in the field of information security [1992] OJ L123/19 (establishing an Action Plan to develop comprehensive strategies for the security of information systems).

[100] For a general overview of critical responses, see C Tapper, 'New European Directions in Data Protection' (1992) 3 J of Law and Information Systems 9, 14ff.

[101] See Amended proposal for a Council Directive on the protection of individuals with regard to the processing of personal data and the free movement of such data (COM(92) 422 final—SYN 287); [1992] OJ C311/30. An amended proposal for a Directive on data protection in the context of telecommunications was issued later: see Amended proposal for a European Parliament and Council Directive concerning the protection of personal data and privacy in the context of digital telecommunications Networks, in particular the Integrated Services Digital Network (ISDN) and digital mobile networks (COM(94) 128 final—COD 288); [1994] OJ C200/4.

sections of this chapter, it afflicts many of the provisions found in other international data privacy instruments.

The general policy thrust of the Directive, particularly as expressed in the recitals in its preamble, points in at least two directions. On the one hand, the recitals register a concern to promote realization of the internal market of the EU, in which goods, persons, services, capital, and, concomitantly, personal data are able to flow freely between member states.[102] In furtherance of this concern, a major function of the Directive is to secure harmonization of member states' respective data privacy laws.

On the other hand, the Directive also emphasizes the importance of protecting basic human rights, notably that of privacy, in the face of technological and economic developments.[103] Indeed, it was the first Directive expressly to accord a prominent place to the protection of human rights. As such, it reflects and reinforces the gradual incorporation of law and doctrine on human rights into the EU legal system.[104]

The ambivalence in the aims of the Directive is neatly manifested in Article 1:

1. In accordance with this Directive, member states shall protect the fundamental rights and freedoms of natural persons, and in particular their right to privacy, with respect to the processing of personal data.
2. Member states shall neither restrict nor prohibit the free flow of personal data between member states for reasons connected with the protection afforded under paragraph 1.

We see a similar ambivalence in the other main international instruments in the field. However, the Directive is unique in its absolute prohibition on restricting the flow of personal data between certain states on the grounds of protecting privacy and other basic human rights. This absolute prohibition could be construed as evidence that the Directive is ultimately concerned with realizing the effective functioning of the EU's internal market and only penultimately concerned with data privacy.

---

[102] See esp. Recitals 3, 5, 7. The need to ensure free flow of personal data throughout the EU was not rooted entirely in commercial considerations; the pan-EU ambit of government administration also played a role. In this respect, see Recital 5 (noting, inter alia, that 'national authorities in the various Member States are being called upon by virtue of Community law to collaborate and exchange personal data so as to be able to perform their duties or carry out tasks on behalf of an authority in another Member State within the context of the area without internal frontiers as constituted by the Internal Market').

[103] See eg Recitals 2, 3, 10, 11.

[104] See particularly the Treaty on European Union (TEU) [2012] OJ C326/13 Art. 6.

Nevertheless, the Directive strives to bring about a 'high' level of data protection across the EU.[105] It seeks not just to 'give substance to' but to 'amplify' Convention 108.[106] Thus, the Directive should not be viewed as merely constituting the lowest common denominator of rules found in member states' pre-existing laws.[107] The importance of human rights in the Directive's agenda is recognized in jurisprudence of the Court of Justice of the EU (hereinafter 'CJEU'). The seminal judgment on point is the *Rechnungshof* decision from 2003 in which the Court held that the Directive is rooted in more than simply a concern to promote realization of the internal market and has the safeguarding of fundamental human rights as one of its principal goals.[108] It further held that interpretation of the Directive must turn partly on the ECHR as interpreted by the ECtHR. Subsequent jurisprudence confirms this approach.[109]

### (c) Data protection as fundamental right

The EU's constitutional framework, as amended by the Treaty of Lisbon, now recognizes protection of personal data as a fundamental right in itself—that is, a right separate to the more traditional right to respect for private life. The key provision is Article 8 of the Charter of Fundamental Rights of the European Union:[110]

1. Everyone has the right to the protection of personal data concerning him or her.
2. Such data must be processed fairly for specified purposes and on the basis of the consent of the person concerned or some other legitimate basis laid down by law. Everyone has the right of access to data which has been collected concerning him or her, and the right to have it rectified.

---

[105] See esp. Recital 10 ('Whereas the object of the national laws on the processing of personal data is to protect fundamental rights and freedoms, notably the right to privacy, which is recognized both in Article 8 of the European Convention for the Protection of Human Rights and Fundamental Freedoms and in the general principles of Community law; whereas, for that reason, the approximation of those laws must not result in any lessening of the protection they afford but must, on the contrary, seek to ensure a high level of protection in the Community').

[106] Recital 11.

[107] See also Recital 9 (providing that member states 'shall strive to improve the protection currently provided by their legislation').

[108] Joined Cases C-465/00, C-138/01, and C-139/01 *Rechnungshof v Österreichischer Rundfunk and Others* [2003] ECR I-4989 paras 39–45, 71ff.

[109] See eg, Case C-101/01 *Bodil Lindqvist* [2003] ECR I-12971; Case C-70/10 *Scarlet Extended v Société belge des auteurs, compositeurs et éditeurs SCRL (SABAM)* [2011] ECR I-0000.

[110] [2010] OJ C83/389. As of 1 December 2009, the Charter has the same legal value as the EU Treaties: see TEU Art. 6(1) as amended by the Treaty of Lisbon (adopted 13 December 2007; in force 1 December 2009) [2007] OJ C306/1. This status of the Charter applies to all EU member states except for the UK and Poland.

3. Compliance with these rules shall be subject to control by an independent authority.[111]

A specific right to data protection is also provided by TFEU Article 16:

1. Everyone has the right to the protection of personal data concerning them.
2. The European Parliament and the Council, acting in accordance with the ordinary legislative procedure, shall lay down the rules relating to the protection of individuals with regard to the processing of personal data by Union institutions, bodies, offices and agencies, and by the Member States when carrying out activities which fall within the scope of Union law, and the rules relating to the free movement of such data. Compliance with these rules shall be subject to the control of independent authorities.[112]

The recognition of data protection as a fundamental right in itself is a hitherto unique development internationally. It bolsters the normative status of data protection in the EU legal system, including the DPD's provisions. It ought to make derogations from basic data privacy norms more difficult and breaches of such norms more readily sanctioned. We see signs of such a development in CJEU jurisprudence. The Court is increasingly stringent when assessing data-processing practices in light of the principle of proportionality as manifest in the DPD and associated instruments.[113]

## (d) Harmonization efforts

The harmonization efforts represented by the DPD go further than those of the other main international instruments in the field. The Directive introduces a relatively comprehensive vision of what protection of data privacy should involve and it lays down a relatively rigorous set of rules. Concomitantly, it specifies in relatively great detail a baseline for data privacy from which member states cannot derogate. It introduces, for instance, not just a simple requirement that member states establish independent authorities to monitor and enforce their

---

[111] Cf Art. 7 which stipulates: 'Everyone has the right to respect for his or her private and family life, home and communications'.

[112] The effect of this provision is to ensure that the right to data protection is respected by EU institutions. It thus provides part of the normative basis for Regulation (EC) 45/2001 (see n 151 and accompanying text). Article 16 adds that the rules adopted on its basis 'shall be without prejudice to the specific rules laid down in Article 39 of the Treaty on European Union'. The latter provision stipulates that the Council shall adopt a decision setting out rules on protection of personal data in respect of activities pertaining to exercise of EU foreign and security policy, and that compliance with the rules shall be 'subject to the control of independent authorities'. To my knowledge, such a decision has not been adopted.

[113] See further Ch 5 (section C).

data privacy laws; it lays down a large number of attributes for such authorities (Article 28).[114]

Implementation of the Directive is assumed to bring about an 'approximation' of national laws, resulting in 'equivalent' levels of data privacy across the EU.[115] Attainment of such equivalency is important not least in light of Article 12(3)(c) of Convention 108.[116] Yet the Directive's baseline specifications also afford member states a 'margin for manoeuvre'.[117] This is manifested in, inter alia, Article 5 which provides that 'Member States shall, within the limits of the provisions of [Chapter II], determine more precisely the circumstances in which the processing of personal data is lawful'. Recital 9 recognizes, as a result, that 'disparities could arise in the implementation of the Directive', but diplomatically refrains from elaborating on the eventual consequences. This margin for manoeuvre follows partly from the Directive's basic nature *qua* Directive (as opposed to Regulation).[118] It reflects also the principle of subsidiarity that generally informs EU regulatory policy,[119] along with the extensive controversy accompanying the Directive's gestation.

Particularly in light of Recitals 9 and 10, it is open for a member state to establish or maintain a higher level of data privacy than the baseline that the Directive seeks to establish. Yet a member state cannot derogate from any of the Directive's mandatory requirements. Nor can it introduce more narrowly framed exemptions to the Directive's general rules than the mandatory exemptions specified in the Directive.

CJEU jurisprudence reinforces limits on the margin for manoeuvre under the Directive. The *ASNEF* judgment is important in this respect.[120] The case concerns Spanish transposition of DPD Article 7(f), which provides:

[Member States shall provide that personal data may be processed only if, inter alia,] processing is necessary for the purposes of the legitimate interests pursued by the controller or by the third party or parties to whom the data are disclosed, except where

---

[114] See further Ch 6 (section A).     [115] Recitals 8 and 9.

[116] As Recital 9 notes (with implicit reference to the Convention), achieving equivalency will make it legally impossible for member states to prevent flow of personal data to other member states on privacy-related gounds.

[117] Recital 9. Examples of points in the Directive where member states are given an obvious margin for manoeuvre are Arts 7(f), 8(4), 10, 11, 13, and 14(a). See further following.

[118] Basically, a Directive requires achievement of a specified result, leaving member states some discretion as to how to achieve the result. A Regulation, however, does not provide any such discretion. Further on the differences between Directives and Regulations, see eg, P Craig and G de Búrca, *EU Law* (5th edn, OUP 2011) 105–6.

[119] See esp. TEU Art. 5.

[120] Joined Cases C-468/10 and C-469/10 *Asociación Nacional de Establecimientos Financieros de Crédito (ASNEF) and Federación de Comercio Electrónico y Marketing Directo (FECEMD) v Administración del Estado* [2011] ECR I-0000.

such interests are overridden by the interests for fundamental rights and freedoms of the data subject which require protection under Article 1(1).

Spanish transposition of these provisions effectively limited their application to public source data. The CJEU held that such a limitation was precluded. Acknowledging that DPD Article 5 permits member states to issue guidelines on the interest-balancing processes at stake and thus to create more precision as to those processes, the Court nonetheless held that this does not allow states to

exclude the possibility of processing certain categories of personal data by definitively prescribing, for those categories, the result of the balancing of the opposing rights and interests, without allowing a different result by virtue of the particular circumstances of an individual case.[121]

Accordingly, DPD Article 7(f)

precludes a Member State from excluding, in a categorical and generalised manner, the possibility of processing certain categories of personal data, without allowing the opposing rights and interests at issue to be balanced against each other in a particular case.[122]

Moreover, the Court found Article 7(f) suffiently precise and unconditional as to have direct effect,[123] thus allowing an individual to rely on it in proceedings before a national court of a member state that has failed to punctually or correctly transpose the Directive.

The *ASNEF* case notwithstanding, the Directive lays the way open for significant disparities between member states' respective data privacy regimes. This follows not just from Article 5 but from Articles 9 and 13 which permit exemptions from many of the Directive's central rules (see directly below). And it follows, of course, from the Directive's numerous textual ambiguities. Not surprisingly, member states' transposition of the Directive has fallen woefully short of the original harmonization objective.[124]

---

[121] *ASNEF* (n 120) [47].     [122] *ASNEF* (n 120) [48].     [123] *ASNEF* (n 120) [52], [55].
[124] See further European Commission, 'First Report on the Implementation of the Data Protection Directive (95/46/EC)' (COM(2003) 265).

## (e) Field of application

The Directive applies to 'processing' (broadly defined in Article 2(b)) of personal data in both the private and public sectors, largely regardless of the way in which the data is structured.[125] The notion of 'file' is retained, however, with respect to manual processing: such processing is covered by the Directive insofar as the data forms or is intended to form part of a 'filing system' (Article 3(1))—that is, 'any structured set of personal data which are accessible according to specific criteria, whether centralized, decentralized or dispersed on a functional or geographical basis' (Article 2(c)).

The Directive does not apply to data processing carried out as part of activities relating to 'public security, defence, State security... and the activities of the State in areas of criminal law' (Article 3(2)). These are activities that used to fall within the ambit of the EU's old 'third pillar' and 'second pillar' and, as such, outside the scope of the former European Community (the old 'first pillar'). The formal division of EU competence and activity under the pillar system was abolished when the Lisbon Treaty entered into force in 2009. However, the effects of the system continue to mark the ambit of legal instruments that were borne of it—the DPD being one such instrument. Member states are nonetheless free to subject the earlier listed activities to data privacy regimes modelled on the Directive, although other legal instruments impinge on that freedom.[126] At the same time, the Directive empowers member states to restrict the scope of many of the general rights and obligations it sets down, when the restriction is 'necessary' to safeguard, inter alia, national security, public security, law enforcement, or 'important' economic or financial interests of the member states (Article 13(1)).

The processing of data 'by a natural person in the course of a purely personal or household activity' is also exempt from the Directive's scope (Article 3(2)). Member states must additionally lay down exemptions from the central provisions of the Directive with respect to data processing 'carried out solely for journalistic purposes or the purpose of artistic or literary expression', insofar as is 'necessary to reconcile the right to privacy with the rules governing freedom of expression' (Article 9).[127]

---

[125] Cf the 1990 Directive proposal which, like Convention 108, focused primarily on creation and use of 'personal data files'.

[126] Eg, Council Framework Decision 2008/977/JHA on the protection of personal data processed in the framework of police and judicial cooperation in criminal matters [2008] OJ L350/60. See further n 164 and accompanying text.

[127] The above rules on field of application are dealt with in more detail in Ch 4 (section C(5)).

## (f) Content

The basic principles in the DPD for processing personal data are similar to, and modelled on, the earlier international instruments on point, especially Convention 108. Yet many go considerably further than those in the other instruments. For instance, the Directive requires data controllers to provide data subjects with basic information about the scope of data-processing operations, independently of the data subjects' use of access rights (Articles 10–11). It extends access rights to include the right of a person to obtain 'knowledge of the logic involved in any automated processing of data concerning him' (Article 12(a)). It grants a person the qualified right to object to certain types of fully automated decision-making processes (Article 15(1)). Also unique is its explicit prohibition on processing of personal data unless specified conditions are satisfied (Articles 7–8).[128]

The Directive lays down extensive provisions dealing with inter-legal issues.[129] It is the first and only international data privacy instrument to tackle directly the vexed issue of which national law is applicable to a given case of data processing. The basic rule specifies the applicable law as being that of the member state in which the data controller is established (Article 4(1)(a)). More controversially, the Directive also provides for the law of a member state to apply outside the EU in certain circumstances, most notably if a controller, based outside the EU, utilizes 'equipment' located in the state to process personal data for purposes other than merely transmitting the data through that state (Article 4(1)(c)). Further, it specifies relatively strong controls on trans-border transfers of personal data. While proscribing privacy-based restrictions on the flow of personal data between EU member states (Article 1(2)), it places a qualified prohibition on flow of personal data from EU member states to countries outside the EU (so-called 'third countries') unless the latter offer an 'adequate level of protection' for the data (Article 25(1)). Both sets of rules have proven controversial.

Another special aspect of the Directive is its relatively detailed provisions on monitoring and supervisory regimes.[130] As noted above, the Directive requires member states to establish one or more independent authorities to monitor and enforce their data privacy laws, and it lays down a large number of attributes for such authorities (Article 28). It provides for notification and licensing regimes (Articles 18 and 20), encourages the drafting of sectoral codes of conduct (Article 27), and establishes a special advisory body in the

---

[128] These rules and principles are dealt with in more detail in Ch 5.
[129] See further Ch 6 (section E).     [130] See generally Ch 6.

form of the 'Working Party on the Protection of Individuals with regard to the Processing of Personal Data' (Article 29). The latter (A29WP) is composed largely of representatives from each member state's DPA. Its chief task is to provide independent advice to the European Commission on a range of issues, including uniformity in the application of national measures adopted pursuant to the DPD, and privacy protection afforded by non-member states (Article 30).

## 2. Sectoral instruments

### (a) Electronic communications

Beyond the DPD, the EU has adopted several data privacy instruments dealing specifically with electronic communications. The first of these was the Telecommunications Privacy Directive (97/66/EC).[131] It was aimed at regulating aspects of the then nascent market for digital telecommunications services, although its provisions bore the imprint of notions of traditional telephony. Its application to Internet-based communication was plagued by uncertainty. Hence, it was soon repealed and replaced by the Electronic Communications Privacy Directive (2002/58/EC)[132] which more clearly covers Internet-based communication.

The provisions of the E-Privacy Directive 'particularise and complement' the DPD with respect to electronic communications (Article 1(2)). In some respects, they have a broader ambit than the DPD. For example, they protect the 'legitimate interests' of legal persons (Article 1(2)) as subscribers or users of electronic communications services, although this protection is not fully commensurate with the protection afforded individuals (see Articles 12 and 13(1) dealing with respectively subscriber directories and automated calling systems).

The EPD forms part of a comprehensive regulatory framework dealing specifically with provision of electronic communications networks and services.[133] Its scope is limited by the scope of that framework. It thus applies to the

---

[131] Directive 97/66/EC concerning the processing of personal data and the protection of privacy in the telecommunications sector [2008] OJ L24/1.

[132] Directive 2002/58/EC concerning the processing of personal data and the protection of privacy in the electronic communications sector [2002] OJ L201/37 (hereinafter 'e-privacy Directive' or 'EPD').

[133] The core of the framework comprises five Directives (2002/21/EC, 2002/19/EC, 2002/20/EC, 2002/22/EC, and 2002/58/EC) and a Regulation ((EC) 1211/2009). These are supplemented by sector-specific recommendations, guidelines, and notices along with rules of more general application. See further P Nihoul and P Rodford, *EU Electronic Communications Law: Competition and Regulation in the European Telecommunications Market* (2nd edn, OUP 2011); I Walden (ed), *Telecommunications Law and Regulation* (4th edn, OUP 2012).

'processing of personal data in connection with the provision of publicly available electronic communications services in public communications networks in the Community' (Article 3). The phrase 'electronic communications services' covers services that are essentially concerned with provision of communications infrastructure, not the information content of the transmitted data.[134] Nonetheless, maintaining a strict separation between transmission and content is difficult in practice, and some of the EPD's provisions (for example, Articles 5 and 13, elaborated further on in this section ) appear to apply to provision of information services as much as to communication services.[135]

The EPD contains rules on security and confidentiality of electronic communications (Articles 4–5), storage and use of electronic communications traffic data (Articles 6 and 15),[136] processing of location data other than traffic data (Article 9),[137] calling and connected line identification (Article 8), content of subscriber directories (Article 12), and unsolicited communications for direct marketing purposes (Article 13). In 2009, the EPD underwent several significant amendments.[138] One introduced a requirement that providers of

---

[134] See Framework Directive 2002/21/EC on a common regulatory framework for electronic communications networks and services [2002] OJ L108/33: 'electronic communications service means a service normally provided for remuneration which consists wholly or mainly in the conveyance of signals on electronic communications networks, including telecommunications services and transmission services in networks used for broadcasting, but exclude [sic] services providing, or exercising editorial control over, content transmitted using electronic communications networks and services; it does not include information society services, as defined in Article 1 of Directive 98/34/EC, which do not consist wholly or mainly in the conveyance of signals on electronic communications networks' (Art. 2(c)).

[135] Cf Directive 2002/21/EC: 'The separation between the regulation of transmission and the regulation of content does not prejudice the taking into account of the links existing between them, in particular in order to guarantee media pluralism, cultural diversity and consumer protection' (Recital 5).

[136] 'Traffic data' is defined as 'any data processed for the purpose of the conveyance of a communication on an electronic communications network or for the billing thereof' (Art. 2(b)). Recital 15 elaborates: '[t]raffic data may, inter alia, consist of data referring to the routing, duration, time or volume of a communication, to the protocol used, to the location of the terminal equipment of the sender or recipient, to the network on which the communication originates or terminates, to the beginning, end or duration of a connection. They may also consist of the format in which the communication is conveyed by the network'.

[137] 'Location data' is defined as 'any data processed in an electronic communications network, indicating the geographic position of the terminal equipment of a user of a publicly available electronic communications service' (Art. 2(c)). Recital 14 elaborates: 'Location data may refer to the latitude, longitude and altitude of the user's terminal equipment, to the direction of travel, to the level of accuracy of the location information, to the identification of the network cell in which the terminal equipment is located at a certain point in time and to the time the location information was recorded'.

[138] See Directive 2009/136/EC amending Directive 2002/22/EC on universal service and users' rights relating to electronic communications networks and services, Directive 2002/58/EC concerning the processing of personal data and the protection of privacy in the electronic communications sector and Regulation (EC) No. 2006/2004 on cooperation between national authorities responsible for the enforcement of consumer protection laws [2009] OJ L337/11.

public electronic communications networks notify data subjects and relevant authorities of personal data security breaches (Article 4(3)). Another sharpened (at least on paper) the conditions for placement of cookies (Article 5(3)). A third strengthened the anti-spamming provisions of Article 13.[139] However, Article 6 has been the most practically important of all the above provisions, at least in the first few years after the Directive was adopted. It limits the use and storage of traffic data for purposes other than subscriber billing and interconnection payments. That limitation has, for example, frustrated IPR-holders' campaign against digital piracy.[140] However, it has since been short-circuited to a considerable degree by broadly formulated derogations under EPD Article 15(1), DPD Article 13(1), and the Data Retention Directive (elaborated in the following paragraphs).

The Data Retention Directive was adopted in 2006.[141] It owes most of its existence to the terrorist attacks in Madrid and London in 2004 and 2005 respectively, and the concomitant interests of law enforcement agencies in gaining access to traffic and location data as part of their 'war' on terror and serious crime.[142] It requires EU member states to ensure that providers of public electronic communications networks store such data (specified in detail in Article 5), along with related data necessary to identify subscribers or users of such networks, for a minimum of six months and maximum of two years (Article 6). The purpose of storage is to facilitate 'the investigation, detection and prosecution of serious crime' (Article 1(1)). The stored data is to be made available to 'competent authorities' pursuant to requirements of legal due process (Article 4). The Directive is not intended to cover data 'revealing the content of… communication' (Article 5(2)). This includes 'information consulted using an electronic communications network' (Article 1(2)). Stored data is to be subject to security

---

[139] Further on the EPD and its transposition into UK law, see C Millard, 'Communications Privacy' in Walden (n 133) ch 13, esp. 632–40.

[140] See eg, decision of 14 July 2009 by the Austrian Federal Supreme Court (*Oberster Gerichtshof*) in Case 4 Ob 41/09x; available at: <http://www.internet4jurists.at/entscheidungen/ogh4_41_09x.htm>. Here the Court held that IP addresses, as traffic data, were subjected to special protection under Austria's Telecommunications Act 2003 s 99 (which transposes Art. 6 of the EPD) (see particularly para. 5.4 of the judgment). Under Austrian criminal law at the time, copyright infringement was not sufficiently serious to permit disclosure of traffic data to IPR-holders.

[141] Directive 2006/24/EC on the retention of data generated or processed in connection with the provision of publicly available electronic communications services or of public communications networks and amending Directive 2002/58/EC [2006] OJ L105/54.

[142] Traffic and location data comprises, inter alia, data on the source, date, duration, and recipient of a communication, along with the location of the communication device: see further Art. 5(1).

safeguards (Article 7) the implementation of which is to be monitored by independent supervisory authorities, such as DPAs (Article 9).

Controversy has dogged the Directive from its gestation. Part of the controversy stems from its legal foundations. The Directive was adopted as a first pillar instrument pursuant to the Treaty establishing the European Community Article 95 (now TFEU Article 114). Ireland (joined by Slovakia) filed a challenge before the CJEU claiming that the Directive should have been adopted as a third pillar instrument as its main objective is to combat crime. The CJEU rejected the claim, holding that the Directive is predominantly concerned with the functioning of the internal market, more specifically with ensuring that communication service providers in the various EU member states are subject to harmonized data retention requirements.[143] Most controversy, though, stems from the Directive's incursion on privacy-related interests. Privacy advocates have rightly questioned its necessity and thereby its compatibility with the right to respect for private life and correspondence under ECHR Article 8.[144] The absence of definitions of key terms, such as 'serious crime' (Article 1(1)) and 'competent authorities' (Article 4), coupled with ambiguity in the delineation of some of the types of data that are to be retained (Article 5), is also problematic, at least in light of the general ideal of establishing legal certainty.[145] Moreover, while the Directive is not intended to cover information about the content of communications, one cannot discount the possibility of such information being derived from analysis of traffic and location data in combination.

National transposition of the Directive has been very uneven.[146] And it has often been slow.[147] The tardiness is due to a variety of factors. These include the Directive's textual ambiguity, local political opposition to its implementation, and obstacles in domestic law. In Germany, the first legislation that attempted to transpose the Directive into domestic law was struck down for breaching the country's Constitution.[148] The German Federal Constitutional

---

[143] Case C-301/06, *Ireland v European Parliament and Council of the European Union* [2009] ECR I-593.

[144] See eg, P Breyer, 'Telecommunications Data Retention and Human Rights: The Compatibility of Blanket Traffic Data Retention with the ECHR' (2005) 11 European LJ 365–75. Further on ECHR Art. 8 and case law pursuant thereto, see section I(2).

[145] Whether the definitional omissions breach ECHR Art. 8(2) is more difficult to gauge. See further n 249 and accompanying text.

[146] See further European Commission, 'Evaluation report on the Data Retention Directive (Directive 2006/24/EC)' COM (2011) 225 final.

[147] Sweden, for example, was recently fined for delaying transposition of the Directive. See judgment of 30 May 2013 in Case C-270/11, *European Commission v Kingdom of Sweden* [2013] ECR I-0000.

[148] BVerfGE, 1 BvR 256/08.

Court held that storage of traffic data seriously encroaches on the right to communications secrecy under Article 10(1) of the Constitution. At the same time, the Court made clear that such storage need not violate that right if based on legislation with well-defined data privacy provisions ensuring the security of the data, transparency of its use, and limitations on that use. The Court majority found that the legislation in dispute did not meet those standards. By contrast, the Romanian Constitutional Court held that the very storage of traffic data violated the proportionality principle inherent in the Romanian Constitution.[149] The legal obstacles to implementation of the Directive in Romanian law seem thereby greater than with respect to German law.[150]

## (b) EU institutions

Regulation 45/2001 is the chief data privacy instrument governing the processing of personal data by the institutional organs of the EU.[151] It embodies (with some modifications) the core principles of the DPD. It also sets out data privacy rules in respect of telecommunications networks and terminal equipment operated by EU organs (chapter IV). These rules parallel the provisions of the EPD.

Additionally, the Regulation establishes the office of European Data Protection Supervisor (EDPS)(Article 41(1)) and lays down the main rules regarding his or her duties and competence.[152] The EDPS has monitoring and control functions with respect to EU institutions (Articles 41(2) and 46), with the exception of the CJEU acting in its judicial capacity (Article 46(c)). He or she can issue legally binding orders (Article 47(1)), which may be appealed to the CJEU.[153] Each EU institution must also appoint a data protection officer (Article 24(1)) who, in liaison with the EDPS, shall ensure, inter alia, 'the internal application of the...Regulation' (Article 24(1)(c)). Like the EDPS,

---

[149] Decision no. 1258 of 8 October 2009.

[150] See further T Mahler, MR Ranheim, and DI Cojocarasu, 'Hvordan vurderer nasjonale domstoler datalagringsdirektivet opp mot grunn- og menneskerettigheter?' in DW Schartum (ed), *Overvåking i en rettsstat* (Fagbokforlaget 2010) 147.

[151] Regulation (EC) 45/2001 on the protection of individuals with regard to the processing of personal data by the institutions and bodies of the Community and on the free movement of such data [2001] OJ L8/1.

[152] Provisions regarding the remuneration and seat of the EDPS are set out in Decision 1247/2002/EC on the regulations and general conditions governing the performance of the European Data-protection Supervisor's duties [2002] OJ L183/1.

[153] Further on the competence and role of the EDPS, see H Hijmans, 'The European Data Protection Supervisor: The Institutions of the EC Controlled by an Independent Authority' (2006) 43 CML Rev 1313; HCH Hofmann, GC Rowe, and AH Türk, *Administrative Law and Policy of the European Union* (OUP 2011) 740–6.

the officers are to exercise their functions under the Regulation independently of the institutions that appoint them (Article 24(7)). As Hofmann, Rowe, and Türk comment, 'the institutional framework of the EDPS should not be regarded as a single, or at least not a centralized, institutional unit, but rather as a type of network within the Union institutions'.[154]

## (c) Area of freedom, security, and justice

The EU has long struggled to enact comprehensive data privacy rules governing police operations and other AFSJ-related activities. The bulk of its respective sets of data privacy rules for this area are each of fairly narrow application.[155] They concern, for example, the operations of particular EU agencies, such as Europol and Eurojust,[156] or the use of particular information systems, such as the Schengen Information System (SIS),[157] or particular arrangements for transferring data to non-European agencies, such as the schemes for transfer of Air Passenger Name Records (PNR data) to US border-control authorities.[158] The resulting congeries of codes is extremely complex and difficult to navigate. Part of the complexity stems from various divisions of legal competence—manifest most saliently in the former pillar system—which are not always clear-cut in practice.

[154] Hofmann and others (n 153) 741.

[155] For comprehensive analysis, see F Boehm, *Information Sharing and Data Protection in the Area of Freedom, Security and Justice* (Springer 2012) ch B.

[156] See eg, Rules of procedure on the processing and protection of personal data at Eurojust [2005] OJ C68/1.

[157] See eg, 1990 Schengen Convention (Convention implementing the Schengen Agreement of 14 June 1985 between the Governments of the States of the Benelux Economic Union, the Federal Republic of Germany and the French Republic on the gradual abolition of checks at their common borders [2000] OJ L239/19) Arts 102–118. Further on these and associated rules, see SK Karanja, *Transparency and Proportionality in the Schengen Information System and Border Control Co-Operation* (Martinus Nijhoff 2008) and Boehm (n 155) 260–80. While the Schengen acquis has non-EU origins, it was incorporated into the EU legal system by the 1997 Treaty of Amsterdam: see Council Decision of 20 May 1999 concerning the definition of the Schengen acquis for the purpose of determining, in conformity with the relevant provisions of the Treaty establishing the European Community and the Treaty on European Union, the legal basis for each of the provisions or decisions which constitute the acquis [1999] OJ L176/1.

[158] See initially Commission Decision 2004/535/EC on the adequate protection of personal data contained in the Passenger Name Record of air passengers transferred to the United States' Bureau of Customs and Border Protection (notified under document number C(2004) 1914) [2004] OJ L235/11 (subsequently annulled—see following); approved in Council Decision 2004/496/EC on the conclusion of an Agreement between the European Community and the United States of America on the processing and transfer of PNR data by Air Carriers to the United States Department of Homeland Security, Bureau of Customs and Border Protection [2004] OJ L183/83 (subsequently annulled—see following).

Those divisions of competence have occasionally tripped up the rule-makers themselves.

For instance, the CJEU nullified the first of the PNR data transfer schemes for being *ultra vires*.[159] The Commission and Council had adopted the scheme as a first pillar instrument but the Court held that it applied to matters falling outside the first pillar—namely, public security and prevention of crime. A new scheme with new legal legs had to be quickly adopted a few months later.[160]

The absence of an overarching EU instrument for data privacy in the AFSJ has been partly compensated for by CoE codes—primarily Convention 108, ECtHR case law pursuant to ECHR Article 8,[161] and Recommendation R (87) 15.[162] Effort has nonetheless gone into drafting an EU framework instrument, equivalent to the DPD, that would lay down basic rules on data privacy for police and judicial cooperation. The Commission issued a proposal for such an instrument in 2005.[163] However, the instrument adopted on the basis of that proposal is considerably circumscribed.[164] It does not cover intra-state processing of personal data by police, only data that 'are or have been transmitted or made available between Member States' (Article 1(2)(a)). It is 'without prejudice to essential national security interests and specific intelligence activities in the field of national security' (Article 1(4)). Many AFSJ-related activities fall outside its scope—for example, it does not apply

---

[159] Joined Cases C-317/04 and C-318/04, *European Parliament v Council of the European Union and Commission of the European Communities* [2006] ECR I-4721.

[160] Council Decision 2006/729/CFSP/JHA on the signing, on behalf of the European Union, of an Agreement between the European Union and the United States of America on the processing and transfer of Passenger Name Record (PNR) data by air carriers to the United States Department of Homeland Security [2006] OJ L298/27. That agreement expired in July 2007 and was replaced by two successive agreements: (i) Council Decision 2007/551/CFSP/JHA on the signing, on behalf of the European Union, of an Agreement between the European Union and the United States of America on the processing and transfer of Passenger Name Record (PNR) data by air carriers to the United States Department of Homeland Security (DHS) (2007 PNR Agreement) [2007] OJ L204/16; and (ii) Council Decision of 26 April 2012 on the conclusion of the Agreement between the United States of America and the European Union on the use and transfer of passenger name records to the United States Department of Homeland Security [2012] OJ L215/4.

[161] See section I(2).

[162] Recommendation R (87) 15 (n 44). See further n 171 and accompanying text.

[163] Proposal for a Council Framework Decision on the protection of personal data processed in the framework of police and judicial cooperation in criminal matters COM (2005) 475 final, Brussels, 4 October 2005.

[164] Council Framework Decision 2008/977/JHA on the protection of personal data processed in the framework of police and judicial cooperation in criminal matters [2008] OJ L350/60. For analyis of its background and aims, see P de Hert and V Papakonstantinou, 'The Data Protection Framework Decision of 27 November 2008 Regarding Police and Judicial Cooperation in Criminal Matters – A Modest Achievement, However Not the Improvement Some Have Hoped for' (2009) 25 CLSR 403. For critical analysis of its provisions, see Boehm (n 155) 128ff.

to Europol, Eurojust, or SIS (Recital 39). And many of its basic data privacy rules are significantly watered down relative to, say, the DPD.[165]

## 3. Current reform

The EU regulatory framework for data privacy is undergoing major reform. This is chiefly due to the considerable differences that persist between national data privacy regimes across the EU, along with points of uncertainty and inefficiency in their application, particularly regarding the online environment. The principal aim of the reform is accordingly to mitigate these problems. Associated objectives include strengthening data privacy in line with its status as a fundamental right in the EU constitutional order, increasing public trust in online services, and minimizing data controllers' compliance burdens.[166] In the optimistic words of the reform's principal proponent, 'the European Commission is now proposing a strong and consistent legislative framework across Union policies, enhancing individuals' rights, the Single Market dimension of data protection and cutting red tape for businesses'.[167]

More concretely, the reform—at least as initially envisaged—involves adopting two new instruments: (i) a General Data Protection Regulation (GDPR) which is to replace Directive 95/46/EC; and (ii) a Police and Criminal Justice Data Protection Directive which is to replace Framework Decision 2008/977/JHA. After several years of consultation, the Commission issued proposals for both instruments in January 2012.[168] Other existing sectoral legislation is to be retained, albeit with minor adjustments.[169]

Little point is to be had in describing the proposed new instruments in great detail here. They are undergoing intensive negotiation at the time of writing this book and the outcome of this negotiation is not yet clear. Exacerbating the uncertainty is that both instruments—especially the proposed GDPR—envisage extensive use of delegated legislation to cover particular fields of

---

[165] See De Hert and Papakonstantinou (n 164); Boehm (n 155).

[166] See generally, Commission Communication, 'Safeguarding Privacy in a Connected World: A European Data Protection Framework for the 21st Century' (COM(2012) 9 final).

[167] Commission Communication, 'Safeguarding Privacy in a Connected World', 4.

[168] Proposal for a Regulation on the protection of individuals with regard to the processing of personal data and on the free movement of such data (General Data Protection Regulation) (COM(2012) 11 final); Proposal for a Directive on the protection of individuals with regard to the processing of personal data by competent authorities for the purposes of prevention, investigation, detection, or prosecution of criminal offences or the execution of criminal penalties, and the free movement of such data (COM(2012) 10 final).

[169] For example, the E-Privacy Directive is no longer to be treated as a type of *lex specialis* in respect of the DPD or its replacement: the proposed GDPR Art. 89 accordingly deletes EPD Art. 1(2), which states that the EPD provisions 'particularise and complement Directive 95/46/EC'.

data processing,[170] and drafts of such legislation have yet to be publicly disclosed. It suffices here to describe the broad thrust of the reform proposals. References to more specific aspects of them are provided, where relevant, in ensuing chapters of this book.

The main change envisaged by the proposed Police and Criminal Justice Data Protection Directive is to introduce data privacy rules applying not just to inter-state data processing but domestic, intra-state data processing as well (Article 2). Its rules parallel those of the proposed GDPR to a greater degree than do the rules of Framework Decision 2008/977/JHA in relation to the DPD. At the same time, the proposed Directive distinguishes between various classes of data subjects (for example, witnesses as opposed to suspects) (Article 5) and differentiates data privacy requirements accordingly (see, for example, Article 6).[171]

The proposed Directive appears to have figured relatively little in the ensuing negotiations over the reform package: centre stage has so far been taken by the proposed Regulation. Indeed, the proposed Directive seems to have been placed on the 'back burner' until agreement is reached on the other instrument. The GDPR-related negotiations are complex, intense, and ridden by deep-seated conflict, so we could well be waiting for considerable time before the proposed Directive faces the full brunt of politicians' attention.

The proposed GDPR is more detailed and stringent than the DPD in many respects. As a Regulation, it obviously aims at a much higher degree of harmonization of national regimes than is possible under the DPD. And with 139 recitals and 91 articles (many comprising multiple clauses), it far exceeds the DPD's length. At the same time, its sheer size and density make comprehension of it extremely challenging, even for legal experts in the field.

In terms of strengthening data privacy, the proposed Regulation both increases the bite of current rights and introduces new ones. For example, it enhances the ability of data subjects to gain erasure of data on them (Article 17; cf DPD Article 12b). The provisions on point—often flagged somewhat misleading as 'the right to be forgotten'—have proved to be one of the most controversial elements of the reform, particularly amongst US stakeholders.[172] Other noteworthy enhancements of current data privacy rules include:

- a new right of 'data portability'—that is, a right of data subjects to transfer data about themselves from one information system to another (Article 18);

---

[170] See draft GDPR esp. Arts 81–83, 86–87; draft Directive esp. Art. 56.

[171] An approach inspired by CoE Recommendation R (87) 15 (n 44): see explanatory comments by the Commission in COM(2012) 10 final (n 168) 7.

[172] See further Ch 7.

- new requirements of 'data protection by design and by default'—that is, an obligation on controllers to hardwire, as it were, data privacy norms into information systems development (Article 23; cf DPD Article 17);
- new restrictions on processing of data on children under the age of 13 years (Article 8);
- a new obligation on controllers and processors to carry out *ex ante* 'data protection impact assessments' of risky processing operations (Article 33);
- a new obligation on controllers to notify DPAs and data subjects of 'personal data breaches' (Articles 31–32);
- stronger sanctions, with DPAs able to impose fines on both controllers and processors of up to €1 million or 2 per cent of an enterprise's annual turnover (Article 79(6));
- replacement of the A29WP by an 'European Data Protection Board' which is also composed of representatives of national DPAs but given a broader (although still largely advisory) mandate (Articles 64ff).

In terms of cutting compliance burdens, the proposed Regulation introduces a 'one-stop shop' scheme whereby a controller or processor established in multiple states need only engage with the DPA of the country of the controller's or processor's 'main establishment', with that DPA being deemed 'competent for the supervision of the processing activities of the controller or the processor in all Member States' (Article 51(2)). Further, the proposed Regulation abolishes the general requirement under DPD Article 18 that controllers notify DPAs of processing operations. This is offset, though, by a range of other obligations on controllers and, in many instances, processors too. These obligations include duties on controllers and processors to document in detail all processing operations under their responsibility (Article 28), a general duty of accountability on controllers (Article 22), and, in particular cases, duties on controllers and processors to appoint internal 'data protection officers' (DPOs)(Article 35).

The increase in processor responsibilities under the proposed Regulation relative to the DPD is noteworthy. As Blume observes, the proposed Regulation 'moves towards giving the processor an independent existence. The processor is emerging from the shadows'.[173] While acknowledging that the increased salience of the processor role generally makes sense in light of technological developments, Blume rightly points out that the allocation of responsibilities seems somewhat arbitrary: why, for instance, do processors have responsibility for ensuring data security (Article 30) but not for

---

[173] P Blume, 'Controller and Processor: Is There a Risk of Confusion?' (2013) 3 IDPL 140, 144.

notifying DPAs or data subjects of security breaches (responsibility for the latter resting solely on controllers: Articles 31–32)?[174]

Although the harmonization efforts inherent in the proposed Regulation go much further than the DPD, member states are still left with some discretion in development and application of their respective data privacy regimes. This is the case regarding their implementation of the numerous derogations permitted by the proposed GDPR to its basic rules (see particularly Articles 21(1) and 80(1)). It is also the case regarding member states' development of data privacy regimes for the processing of personal data related to health, processing in the employment context, processing for historical, statistical, and scientific research purposes, and processing by churches and religious associations (chapter IX). Moreover, many of the basic principles laid down in the proposed Regulation are susceptible to divergent interpretation—the case, for instance, with legal standards formulated in terms of 'reasonableness' or 'fairness'.

The Commission recognizes the potential for divergence between national regimes, and the proposed Regulation accordingly introduces special measures to counter it. An elaborate 'consistency mechanism' is established (Articles 57ff) by which draft measures of national DPAs are vetted, first by the 'European Data Protection Board', and secondly by the Commission, with the latter able ultimately to force a national DPA to alter its measures in order to ensure correct application of the Regulation (Articles 60, 62). Moreover, the Commission is given power to adopt delegated acts with respect to an extensive range of processing operations (see, for example, Chapter IX).

It goes without saying that these reform proposals, taken as a whole, are extremely ambitious. They involve far more than a cosmetic makeover of the current regulatory framework. Some commentators have gone so far as to characterize them as a 'root-and-branch revision of the law' and 'the end of the beginning'.[175] However, they do not constitute a fundamental break with the current framework; they embody essentially the same ideals as the latter and replicate the broad thrust of the current rules, albeit in modified form. For example, while the proposed GDPR introduces more flexibility to the current regime for regulating flow of personal data from European countries to third countries (see Chapter V), it still imposes *ex ante* restrictions on such flow using an adequacy test as point of departure (Article 41). And its provisions on extraterritorial application follow the thrust of those in the DPD.[176]

---

[174] Blume (n 173) 140, 144.
[175] C Kuner, FH Cate, C Millard, and DJB Svantesson, 'The End of the Beginning' (2012) 2 IDPL 115.
[176] See further Ch 6 (section E(2)).

It will take considerable time before the dust settles around the legislative reform. The process is complex and cumbersome. This is underlined by the fact that the European Parliament has been debating several thousand proposed amendments to the Commission's GDPR initiative, while the Council of Ministers debates its own set of amendments. Burton, Kuner, and Pateraki aptly remark: 'The reform is a marathon, not a sprint. The process is likely to take at least two more years to complete, if not longer, and there will be further important steps along the way'.[177]

# F. APEC Initiatives

In 2003, the 21 member states of the Asia–Pacific Economic Cooperation formally began work on drafting a set of common principles to guide their respective regulatory approaches in the field.[178] The principal outcome of this work is an agreement in the form of a 'Privacy Framework', the final version of which was adopted in 2005. Work on the Framework signals a readiness by the APEC states to forge an approach to data privacy tailored to their own needs rather than those of European states. As shown in the following, it is an approach which appears to foster data privacy regimes less because of desire to protect basic human rights than to engender consumer confidence in business.

The Framework is inspired by, and modelled upon, the OECD Guidelines rather than EU and CoE instruments. Indeed, the Framework goes out of its way to laud the Guidelines' continuing importance. Footnote 1 in the preamble to the Framework states:

[t]he OECD Guidelines were drafted at a high level that makes them still relevant today. In many ways, the OECD Guidelines represent the international consensus on what constitutes honest and trustworthy treatment of personal information.

While concern for privacy is far from absent in the formal rationale for the Framework as expressed in its preamble,[179] economic concerns are clearly predominant. Of the latter, one is the familiar interest in preventing

---

[177] C Burton, C Kuner, and A Pateraki, 'The Proposed EU Data Protection Regulation One Year Later: The Albrecht Report', *Bloomberg BNA Privacy and Security Law Report* (21 January 2013) 1, 7.

[178] The APEC states are Australia, Brunei, Canada, Chile, China, Hong Kong, Indonesia, Japan, Korea, Malaysia, Mexico, New Zealand, Papua New Guinea, Peru, Philippines, the Russian Federation, Singapore, Taiwan, Thailand, the USA, and Vietnam.

[179] The preamble states that the Framework 'reaffirms the value of privacy to individuals and to the information society' (para. 5).

commercially harmful restrictions on transborder data flow. The other is to bolster consumer confidence and thereby ensure growth of commerce. The preamble to the Framework seems implicitly to treat privacy safeguards not as valuable in themselves but as principally valuable for their ability to facilitate the realization of the 'potential' of electronic commerce (paragraph 1). Privacy safeguards are not alluded to as fundamental human rights or as stemming from such rights.

The heart of the Framework is a set of 'Information Privacy Principles' (IPPs) based mostly on the core principles of the OECD Guidelines. Some of the principles' nomenclature (for example, 'notice', 'choice') also reflect possible influence from the Safe Harbor Agreement.[180] Few traces of Convention 108 or the DPD are evident. The standards set by the IPPs are generally lower than those of the European instruments although consistent with the broad thrust of the OECD Guidelines. For instance, the Framework does not embrace the sensitivity principle, and it applies the criteria of 'fair' and 'lawful' only to the *collection* of personal information (paragraph 18) as opposed to further stages of information processing as well.

As its nomenclature suggests, the Framework is an instrument with a mild prescriptive bite. It does not prescribe that it be implemented in a particular way—for example, through legislation and establishment of DPAs—but recognizes that a variety of implementation methods may be appropriate (paragraphs 31–32). The provision for flexibility is augmented by the diffuse and cautious manner in which many of the IPPs are formulated, together with the extensive allowance that is made for derogation from them. Derogations are permitted according to criteria that are more lax than those specified under the European codes. Derogations are to be 'limited and proportional to meeting the objectives' to which they relate, and they are either to be 'made known to the public' or 'in accordance with law' (paragraph 13).

At various other points, the Framework spells out that the requirements it lays down for promotion of privacy-related interests may be relaxed or dispensed with in particular situations. For instance, the basic rule of the principle on 'choice'—stating that 'individuals should be provided with clear, prominent, easily understandable, accessible and affordable mechanisms to exercise choice in relation to the collection, use and disclosure of their personal information'—applies only '[w]here appropriate' (paragraph 20). Further, the IPPs have limited application to publicly available information (paragraph 11). Thus, adjustments are made for such information with respect to implementing the principles on 'notice' (paragraph 17) and 'choice' (paragraph 20).

---

[180] The Safe Harbor Agreement is dealt with in Ch 6 (section E(1)).

As for transborder data flow, the Framework does not expressly permit restrictions on such flow on the basis of the recipient jurisdiction lacking equivalent or adequate protection for the data. Nonetheless, the possibility of restriction is broached under the Accountability Principle (paragraph 26), which states, *inter alia*, that

[w]hen personal information is to be transferred to another person or organization, whether domestically or internationally, the personal information controller should obtain the consent of the individual or exercise due diligence and take reasonable steps to ensure that the recipient person or organization will protect the information consistently with these Principles.

An innovative element is the Framework's encouragement that member economies allow non-governmental bodies—including groups concerned with privacy and consumer protection—to participate in development of law and policy in the field (paragraph 37). Another innovative element is the 'preventing harm principle' in the IPPs—a principle not found in any of the other main international instruments. The principle has two chief elements: (i) 'personal information protection should be designed to prevent the misuse of [personal] information'; (ii) 'remedial measures should be proportionate to the likelihood and severity of the harm threatened' by the processing of personal information (paragraph 14). The apparent aim of the principle is to prevent regulatory overkill. Yet apart from signalling the desirability of such an aim, the principle's practical utility is questionable.

An early draft of the Framework was aptly described as 'OECD Lite'.[181] Although the final version goes further to meet OECD standards, the description is still pertinent.[182] It has been argued that the Framework represents an important step towards the adoption of a truly international agreement in the field.[183] However, the Framework has so far had little substantial influence on

---

[181] G Greenleaf, 'Australia's APEC Privacy Initiative: The Pros and Cons of "OECD Lite"' (2003) 10 PLPR 1.

[182] See too G Greenleaf, 'APEC's Privacy Framework Sets a New Low Standard for the Asia-Pacific' in AT Kenyon and M Richardson (eds), *New Dimensions in Privacy Law: International and Comparative Perspectives* (CUP 2005) 91–120; G Greenleaf, 'Five Years of the APEC Privacy Framework: Failure or Promise?' (2009) 25 CLSR 28. For less critical views of the APEC initiative, see N Waters, 'The APEC Asia-Pacific Privacy Initiative—A New Route to Effective Data Protection or a Trojan Horse for Self-regulation?' (2009) 6 SCRIPTed 75, available at: <www.law.ed.ac.uk/ahrc/script-ed/vol6-1/waters.asp>; JG Tan, 'A Comparative Study of the APEC Privacy Framework—A New Voice in the Data Protection Dialogue?' (2008) 3 Asian J of Comparative L, issue 1, available at: <http://www.degruyter.com/view/j/asjcl.2008.3.1071.xml>.

[183] Tan (n 182).

the shape of national data privacy laws in the region, relative to the influence exercised by the DPD and OECD Guidelines.[184]

Subsequent to the Framework's adoption, APEC has put effort into facilitating cross-border flow of personal data in conformity with the above-cited Accountability Principle. The effort was formalized in September 2007 as the 'Data Privacy Pathfinder'. Its first palpable result is the establishment of a Cross-Border Privacy Enforcement Arrangement (CPEA) in July 2010. This is a mechanism for the region's DPAs (or 'Privacy Enforcement Agents' in the APEC terminology) to share information and assist each other in cross-border enforcement of data privacy rules. A second result is the endorsement of a Cross-Border Privacy Rules (CBPR) system in November 2011. This is a voluntary certification scheme whereby an organization may choose to develop internal policies governing transborder flow of personal data, then submit these policies to scrutiny by an independent, nationally based Accountability Agent (AA). The AA role may be filled by a national DPA, although it does not have to be.[185] Scrutiny by an AA involves assessing whether the policies submitted by the organization comply with a set of standards based on the principles in the APEC Privacy Framework. If the AA's assessment is positive, the organization's policies are certified as CBPR-compliant and the organization is listed in a publicly accessible directory of CBPR-compliant bodies. When certified, the organization's CBPRs may be open to enforcement by the AA or local DPA.[186] It bears emphasis that the benchmark for certification is not necessarily as stringent as the data privacy rules of the particular APEC state in which the organization is established. The organization will still have to comply with the local rules if these are more stringent.

Although the CBPR system has been touted by the FTC as a 'model for global interoperability among privacy regimes',[187] just two APEC member states have so far signed on as formal participants—the USA in September 2012 and Mexico in January 2013. Japan announced in June 2013 that it would follow suit. The prospects for broad take-up are far from promising as many APEC member states (for example, Singapore, Malaysia, New Zealand,

---

[184] See too G Greenleaf, 'The Influence of European Data Privacy Standards outside Europe: Implications for Globalization of Convention 108' (2012) 2 IDPL 68, 80.

[185] For instance, the US Federal Trade Commission (FTC) has been approved as AA for the USA.

[186] See further APEC Electronic Commerce Steering Group, 'APEC Cross-Border Privacy Rules System: Policies, Rules and Guidelines' (no date specified), available at: <http://www. apec.org/Groups/Committee-on-Trade-and-Investment/~/media/Files/Groups/ECSG/CBPR/ CBPR-PoliciesRulesGuidelines.ashx>.

[187] Quoted in APEC Electronic Commerce Steering Group, 'APEC Cross-Border Privacy Rules System goes public', press release, 12 June 2012, available at: <http://www.apec.org/press/ news-releases/2012/0731_cbpr.aspx>.

Australia) have adopted national data privacy regimes with stricter rules for offshore transfer of personal data than those established under the APEC Privacy Framework.[188] Thus, there may be little significant benefit for businesses to participate in the system. Taking an Australian perspective, Burnett and Leonard state:

> For Australian organisations, there appears to be no compelling reason to participate in a resource-intensive scheme that ultimately falls below the high-water mark set by the Privacy Act—other than any corporate reputational benefits that may flow from an Australian organisation submitting itself to minimum standards in such APEC jurisdictions as do not currently have general privacy regulation.[189]

## G. ASEAN Initiatives

APEC is not the only regional organization in the Asia-Pacific with expressed ambitions on data privacy. The Association of South East Asian Nations (ASEAN), composed of ten member states,[190] agreed in 2007 to establish harmonized data privacy regimes by 2015.[191] The initiative is part and parcel of an aim to develop harmonized legal infrastructure for e-commerce. This is, in turn, part and parcel of ASEAN's push to turn itself into an integrated 'Economic Community' within which goods, services, labour, investment, and capital can move freely. Thus, parallels exist between ASEAN's data privacy agenda and that of the European Commission, particularly when the latter first entered the field.

The time frame set by ASEAN for realizing its agenda is overly ambitious, although one commentator is more optimistic.[192] Little information is publicly available as to precisely what kind of harmonized regimes ASEAN is aiming at, apart from the fact that they are to accord with 'best practices/guidelines'.

---

[188] See further Ch 6 (section E(1)).

[189] M Burnett and P Leonard, 'The APEC Cross-Border Privacy Rules System: An Australian Perspective' (2013) 9 Privacy Law Bulletin 128, 130.

[190] Brunei Darussalam, Cambodia, Indonesia, Laos, Malaysia, Myanmar, Philippines, Singapore, Thailand, and Vietnam.

[191] See *ASEAN Economic Community Blueprint* (January 2008) 53; available at: <http://www.asean.org/archive/5187-10.pdf>.

[192] See C Connolly, 'A New Regional Approach to Privacy in ASEAN', Galexia, October 2008, available at: <http://www.galexia.com/public/research/articles/research_articles-art55.html> (stating that ASEAN 'has a successful track record in implementing harmonised legal infrastructure' related to e-commerce and in doing so fairly quickly).

# H. African Initiatives

Until recently, African organizations scarcely figured as policy entrepreneurs in the field of data privacy. The situation today is different. Africa is now home to some of the most prescriptively ambitious data privacy initiatives at the regional and sub-regional levels. The leading initiative comes from the 15 members of the Economic Community of West African States (ECOWAS).[193] It takes the form of a Supplementary Act on Personal Data Protection within ECOWAS, adopted in 2010.[194] The Supplementary Act is annexed to the ECOWAS Treaty of which it forms an integral part.[195] Thus it is legally binding on the member states. Further, the East African Community (EAC)[196] has issued a recommendation that its member states adopt data privacy laws in line with best international practice.[197] Unlike the ECOWAS instrument, the EAC recommendation does not set out substantive data privacy rules nor is it legally binding.

The preamble to the Supplementary Act makes clear that the instrument is largely rooted in concern to secure human rights. It refers in this regard to the provisions of the ECOWAS Treaty which demand 'Member States' adherence to the promotion and protection of human and peoples' rights in accordance with the ... African Charter on Human Rights and Peoples' Rights'. The Supplementary Act accordingly lays down relatively demanding requirements for member states' data privacy regimes. The requirements show strong influence from EU norms. They devote, for example, considerable space to the powers and functions of DPAs, treating these in conformity with the DPD (Chapter IV). French influence over and above that of the EU is also evident in the dirigist nature of some of the Supplementary Act's provisions relative to the minimum requirements set by the DPD. Article 35 is the most obvious instance in point: it prohibits fully automated decision making by courts and fully automated decision making based on personality profiles.[198] Both

---

[193] The ECOWAS states are Benin, Burkina Faso, Cape Verde, Cote d'Ivoire, Gambia, Ghana, Guinea, Guinea Bissau, Liberia, Mali, Niger, Nigeria, Senegal, Sierra Leone, and Togo.

[194] Supplementary Act A/SA.1/01/10 on Personal Data Protection within ECOWAS, adopted 16 February 2010.

[195] See Art. 48 of the Supplementary Act.

[196] Composed of Tanzania, Rwanda, Kenya, Uganda, and Burundi.

[197] Legal Framework for Cyber Laws (Phase 1) November 2008, formally adopted 7 May 2010.

[198] Article 36 reads: '1) No court decision implying an assessment of the behaviour of an individual shall be based on the processing by automatic means of personal data for the purpose of evaluating certain aspects of their personality; 2) No decision that has legal effect on an individual shall be based solely on processing by automatic means of personal data for the purpose of defining the profile of the subject or evaluating certain aspects of their personality'.

types of prohibition derive from Article 10 of France's principal data privacy law passed in 1978.[199] Another instance is Article 12 which subjects a large range of data-processing operations to licensing by DPAs.[200] French law has traditionally operated with relatively extensive licensing obligations.[201]

The provisions on transborder data flow are also stringent. Article 36(1) provides:

The data controller shall transfer personal data to a non-member ECOWAS country only where such a country provides an adequate level of protection for privacy, freedoms and the fundamental rights of individuals in relation to the processing or possible processing of such data.

Surprisingly, this stipulation seems to be absolute; there is at least no provision in the Supplementary Act which permits derogation from it.

The Supplementary Act is otherwise remarkable for several innovative additions to the standard body of data privacy rules. First, it adds a criterion of 'non-fraudulent' to the basic principle of fair and lawful processing—that is, collection and further processing of personal data 'must be carried out in a legal, fair, and non-fraudulent manner' (Article 24). This addition, though, would seem to play a pedagogical function only; substantively, both 'legal' and 'fair' imply absence of fraud. Secondly, it adds 'genetic data' and data revealing a person's 'parentage' to the list of sensitive data the processing of which is subject to more stringent data privacy rules (Article 30). Finally, it lays down an 'obligation of durability', meaning that '[t]he data controller shall take all the necessary measures to ensure that the personal data processed can be utilized, no matter the technical medium' (Article 45(1)). Taken at face value, this requirement seems strange—one might argue that data privacy is not an issue when personal data cannot be utilized! However, its place seems justified inasmuch as it facilitates data subject access rights.

The Supplementary Act has spurred other regional and sub-regional initiatives on data privacy. Most notably, it appears to form the basis of the data privacy provisions of a draft Convention on cyber security proposed by the

---

[199] Act on Information Technology, Data Files and Civil Liberties 1978 (*Loi no. 78–17 du 6 janvier 1978 relative à l'informatique, aux fichiers et aux libertés*). The provisions of Art. 10 were originally found in Art. 2.

[200] These operations are: '1) Processing of personal data relating to genetic data and health research; 2) Processing of personal data relating to offences, sentences, or security measures; 3) Processing of personal data for the purpose of combining files . . .; 4) Processing relating to a national identification number or any such other identification; 5) Processing of personal data that includes biometric data; 6) Processing of personal data for reasons of public interest, in particular for historical, statistical or scientific purposes'.

[201] See further Ch 4 (n 106).

African Union in 2011.[202] All of the characteristics of the Supplementary Act highlighted above are present in the draft Convention, albeit with slightly different phrasing.[203]

As its name suggests, the draft Convention covers more than data privacy; it sets out rules on electronic commerce, information security, and computer crime as well. According to its explanatory text:

> It lays the foundation for an African Union-wide cyber ethics and enunciates fundamental principles in the key areas of cyber security. It also defines the basis for electronic commerce, puts in place a mechanism for combating intrusions into private life likely to be generated by the gathering, processing, transmission, storage and use of personal data and sets broad guidelines for incrimination and repression of cyber crime.

Despite this broad remit, the drafters of the Convention recognize the human rights dimension of its data privacy rules. In the words of its explanatory text, the Convention 'seeks to . . . [e]stablish the legal and institutional mechanisms likely to guarantee normal exercise of human rights in cyber space'.

## I. Special Role of Human Rights Treaties

Forty years ago, the principal multilateral instruments setting out catalogues of fundamental human rights were generally perceived as having little direct relevance for resolving data privacy issues. To be sure, some recognition existed of these instruments' place amongst the normative foundations of data privacy law but they were usually not regarded as sufficiently detailed to function usefully as data privacy tools in themselves. As noted in section B, this perception helped stimulate work on Convention 108.

Today that perception has changed. Major human rights treaties, most notably the 1966 International Covenant on Civil and Political Rights (ICCPR)[204] and the ECHR, are now commonly seen as providing the central normative roots for data privacy law, and they are increasingly used as data privacy instruments in themselves. Jurisprudence developed pursuant to the right to privacy in ICCPR Article 17 and ECHR Article 8 provides the

---

[202] Draft African Union Convention on the Establishment of a Credible Legal Framework for Cyber Security in Africa, version 01/01.2011. The African Union embraces all 54 African states except for Morocco.

[203] See esp. Arts II-29 (non-fraudulent processing), II-35 (genetic data and data on parentage), II-40 (fully automated decision making), II-41 (transborder data flow), and II-50 (sustainability).

[204] UN General Assembly resolution 2200A (XXI) of December 16, 1966; in force 23 March 1976.

backbone for this development. As elaborated here, both sets of provisions have been authoritatively construed as requiring national implementation of the basic principles of data privacy laws. Moreover, the jurisprudence provides an important touchstone for interpreting ordinary data privacy instruments. The jurisprudence builds principally on the provisions dealing with the right to privacy, although it occasionally leverages off other human rights as well, such as freedom from discrimination and freedom of expression.

The operationalization of the human rights dimension of data privacy law is, however, far from uniform. It is much more developed in Western Europe than in, say, the Asia-Pacific. As highlighted in sections F and G, the APEC Privacy Framework shows scant regard for the connection between data privacy and human rights, while the ASEAN push for harmonized data privacy regimes is driven primarily by economic concerns. By contrast, Africa would seem to occupy a position closer to the European than Asian. Its chief human rights treaty—the 1981 African Charter on Human and People's Rights[205] — omits express mention of a right to privacy. It accordingly lacks an important human rights pillar upon which to base local data privacy law. However, this is offset by the inclusion of a right to privacy in ICCPR Article 17 (see the section directly following) and in some of the constitutions of African countries.[206] Moreover, the ECOWAS and African Union initiatives (described in section H) firmly acknowledge their roots in human rights.

## 1. ICCPR Article 17

The UN Human Rights Committee[207] was the first to clearly recognize that the right to privacy in ICCPR Article 17 provides certain data privacy guarantees. Article 17 states:

1. No one shall be subjected to arbitrary or unlawful interference with his privacy, family, home or correspondence, nor to unlawful attacks upon his honour and reputation.
2. Everyone has the right to the protection of the law against such interference or attacks.

---

[205] OAU Doc CAB/LEG/67/3 rev 5; adopted 27 June 1981; in force 21 October 1986.

[206] Eg, both Kenya and the Republic of South Africa make express provision for a right to privacy in their constitutions. For Kenya, see Art. 31 of its Constitution of 2010; for South Africa, see s 14 of the Bill of Rights set out in ch 2 of its Constitution of 1996.

[207] The Committee is charged with overseeing states parties' implementation of the ICCPR and with handling complaints about putative breaches of the Covenant. See generally D McGoldrick, *The Human Rights Committee: Its Role in the Development of the International Covenant on Civil and Political Rights* (2nd edn, Clarendon Press 1994).

In its General Comment 16 of 1988,[208] the Committee held that processing of personal data in both the public and private sectors must be regulated in accordance with basic data privacy principles:

The competent public authorities should only be able to call for such information relating to an individual's private life the knowledge of which is essential in the interests of society as understood under the Covenant.... The gathering and holding of personal information on computers, databanks and other devices, whether by public authorities or private individuals and bodies, must be regulated by law. Effective measures have to be taken by States to ensure that information concerning a person's private life does not reach the hands of persons who are not authorized by law to receive, process and use it, and is never used for purposes incompatible with the Covenant. In order to have the most effective protection of his private life, every individual should have the right to ascertain in an intelligible form, whether, and if so, what personal data is stored in automatic data files, and for what purposes. Every individual should also be able to ascertain which public authorities or private individuals or bodies control or may control their files. If such files contain incorrect personal data or have been collected or processed contrary to the provisions of the law, every individual should have the right to request rectification or elimination.[209]

This statement is particularly significant as the ICCPR has—on paper at least—the greatest reach of treaties on human rights, having been ratified by the majority of the world's nation states.[210]

Remarkably, the data privacy requirements listed by the Committee are truncated compared with the principles specified in, say, Convention 108 and many other ordinary data privacy instruments. The Committee mentions the need to limit collection of personal data but fails to specify the need to ensure that collection is carried out fairly.[211] It mentions the need

---

[208] General Comment 16 issued 23 March 1988 (UN Doc A/43/40, 181–183; UN Doc CCPR/C/21/Add.6; UN Doc HRI/GEN/1/Rev 1, 21–23). General Comments are 'a means by which a UN human rights expert committee distils its considered views on an issue which arises out of the provisions of the treaty whose implementation it supervises and presents those views in the context of a formal statement of its understanding to which it attaches major importance': P Alston, 'The Historical Origins of the Concept of "General Comments" in Human Rights Law' in L Boisson de Chazournes and VG Debbas (eds), *The International Legal System in Quest of Equity and Universality: Liber Amicorum Georges Abi-Saab* (Martinus Nijhoff 2001) 763, 775. The competence to issue General Comments derives from ICCPR Art. 40(4). General Comments are best seen as policy recommendations rather than legally binding pronouncements. They are nonetheless influential in delineating states parties' obligations under the Convention. For discussion, see H Keller and L Grover, 'General Comments of the Human Rights Committee and Their Legitimacy' in H Keller and G Ulfstein (eds), *UN Human Rights Treaty Bodies: Law and Legitimacy* (CUP 2012) 116, 124ff.

[209] General Comment 16 (n 208) paras 7 and 10.

[210] As of 12 June 2013, the ICCPR had been signed and ratified by 167 states.

[211] Cf Convention 108 Art. 5(a) (personal data must be 'obtained and processed fairly and lawfully').

for security measures but relates these only to ensuring the confidentiality of personal data. No mention is made of the need to ensure that personal data is also safeguarded against unauthorized alteration or destruction or is otherwise adequate, relevant, and not excessive in relation to the purposes for which it is processed.[212] Nor is mention made of special categories of data that may require a more stringent level of protection.[213] Further, the principle of purpose limitation laid down by the Committee is looser than the equivalent principle set down in Convention 108 Article 5(b).[214] The principles dealt with most comprehensively by the Committee concern rights on information access and rectification, but they seem to be formulated only in relation to computerized ('automatic') files.

These shortcomings are surprising as the Committee had at the time it issued General Comment 16 several well-established sets of relatively comprehensive data privacy principles from which it could draw inspiration—Convention 108 being one such set. Are, then, the principles it laid down intended to delineate exhaustively the data privacy requirements of Article 17? In keeping with conceptions of 'privacy' in terms of seclusion or limited accessibility, one could argue that the Committee purposefully angled General Comment 16 to give priority to safeguarding the interest of persons in keeping information about themselves out of the hands of others and that the Committee's relatively narrow conception of the purpose of security measures evidences this prioritization. However, the argument is tenuous. The Committee's specification of access and rectification rights points to broader concerns, such as ensuring that persons are able to orient themselves in, and maintain some sort of control over, their informational environs. Further, when hearing complaints pursuant to the first Optional Protocol to the Covenant, the Committee has adopted an expansive view of the notion of privacy in Article 17, stating, inter alia, that privacy denotes more than simply a sphere of seclusion; it embraces also 'a sphere of a person's life in which he or she can freely express his or her identity, be it by entering into relationships with others or alone'.[215] All in all, the better view is that General

---

[212] Cf Convention 108 Art. 5(c) (personal data must be 'adequate, relevant and not excessive in relation to the purposes for which they are stored'); Art. 7 ('appropriate security measures' must be taken to protect personal data 'against accidental or unauthorised destruction or accidental loss as well as against unauthorised access, alteration or dissemination').

[213] Cf Convention 108 Art. 6 (singling out certain types of personal data, such as data on a person's ethnic origins, religious beliefs, sexual habits, or criminal convictions) as warranting special protection.

[214] Art. 5(b) states that personal data shall be 'stored for specified and legitimate purposes and not used in a way incompatible with those purposes'.

[215] *Coeriel & Aurik v the Netherlands* (1994) Comm 453/1991 [10.2], reported in (1994) 15 HRLJ 422.

Comment 16 lays down some but not all of the data privacy guarantees inherent in Article 17.[216]

## 2. ECHR Article 8

Whereas ICCPR Article 17 is framed essentially in terms of a prohibition on 'interference with privacy', ECHR Article 8 is framed in terms of a right to, inter alia, 'respect for private life' followed by an enumeration of criteria permitting interference with that right:

1. Everyone has the right to respect for his private and family life, his home, and correspondence.
2. There shall be no interference by a public authority with the exercise of this right except such as is in accordance with the law and is necessary in a democratic society in the interests of national security, public safety or the economic well-being of the country, for the prevention of disorder or crime, for the protection of health or morals, or for the protection of the rights and freedoms of others.

Over a long series of cases, the European Court of Human Rights (ECtHR) has gradually reached a standpoint in line with the broad thrust of General Comment 16.[217] Its jurisprudence on data privacy, though, is richer and more exacting than the latter, and has had more tangible effect in improving data privacy, both nationally and internationally. Its greatest practical contribution to the field has been to ratchet up data privacy standards for surveillance and control activities carried out by the police or other state security services in Europe. This is particularly important given the paucity of a comprehensive EU data privacy framework for the AFSJ. As elaborated later in this chapter, the ECtHR has enhanced data privacy standards in this area first and foremost by insisting, pursuant to Article 8(2), that processing of personal data by state security services is: (i) subject to legal controls that conform with the ideals of 'rule of law' and thereby promote the foreseeability of data-processing outcomes; and (ii) proportionate in relation to the aims of the processing operations. The Court has additionally delineated these procedural safeguards in considerable detail.

---

[216] See too LA Bygrave, 'Data Protection Pursuant to the Right to Privacy in Human Rights Treaties' (1998) 6 Intl J of Law and Information Technology 247, 254.

[217] For an extensive, fairly up-to-date, though rather repetitive analysis, see Boehm (n 155) 26–91. For a more concise critical treatment, see P De Hert and S Gutwirth, 'Data Protection in the Case Law of Strasbourg and Luxemburg: Constitutionalisation in Action' in S Gutwirth, Y Poullet, P de Hert, C de Terwangne, and S Nouwt (eds), *Reinventing Data Protection?* (Springer 2009) 14–29. For the seminal but now outdated analysis, see Bygrave (n 216) 254–83.

## (a) Object and ambit

The Court takes a broad, evolutive view of the aims and scope of Article 8. This reflects its intention to apply the ECHR as a 'living instrument which...must be interpreted in the light of present-day conditions'.[218] The Court has thus readily applied the Convention in general and Article 8 in particular to new forms of technology. It has held, for example, that the term 'correspondence' in Article 8(1) embraces electronic mail and 'personal Internet usage'.[219] Concomitantly, the Court has been willing to read into the Convention additional requirements for improving the protection of persons in relation to problems that may not have been specifically addressed or contemplated by the Convention's drafters. Yet it has done so only with requirements that it views as 'inherent' in a stated right—that is, as 'based on the very terms of the...[stated right] read in its context and having regard to the object and purpose of the Convention'.[220]

The Court's readiness to read additional requirements into the Convention is partly influenced by the development of common legal and ethical standards in the CoE member states. Its readiness to read data privacy requirements into ECHR Article 8 has accordingly been engendered by member states' enactment of data privacy laws, together with the conclusion of international agreements on data privacy—most notably Convention 108. Yet we cannot assume that the Court will invariably interpret the ECHR in complete conformity with these laws' requirements. The Court has insisted that the provisions of the ECHR have an autonomous meaning.[221]

The 'essential' object of Article 8 has been stated as protecting 'the individual against arbitrary interference by the public authorities in his private or family life'.[222] Article 8, though, does not merely oblige a state party to abstain from interfering with private life; it additionally creates 'positive obligations' on the state party to take action to ensure that private life is effectively respected.[223] As part of these obligations, a state party must take steps to safeguard the right(s) in Article 8(1) from threats originating in the privacy-invasive behaviour of entities in the private sector.[224] Thus, Article 8 serves indirectly to regulate relations between private bodies. As such, it is

---

[218] *Tyrer v UK* (1978) 2 EHRR 1 [31].     [219] *Copland v UK* (2007) 45 EHRR 37 [41].
[220] *Golder v UK* (1975) 1 EHRR 524 [36].
[221] See DJ Harris, M O'Boyle, C Warbrick, and E Bates, *Harris, O'Boyle & Warbrick: Law of the European Convention on Human Rights* (2nd edn, OUP 2009) 16 and references cited therein.
[222] See eg, *Marckx v Belgium* (1980) 2 EHRR 330 [31].
[223] See eg, *Marckx* (n 222) [31].
[224] See eg, *Von Hannover v Germany* (2005) 40 EHRR 1.

relevant to, say, private media organizations' publication of photos of celebrities,[225] or private employers' surveillance of their employees.[226] However, litigation arising as a result of such activity and seeking a remedy based on Article 8 must ultimately be directed at the state authorities of the jurisdiction concerned. The argument by the putative victim (the applicant) will be that a failure by the authorities to prevent or remedy the harm incurred by the actions of the private body is a breach of the state party's positive obligation under Article 8(1) to ensure respect for the right(s) laid down therein. If properly called upon to assess the validity of this argument, the ECtHR will essentially attempt to determine whether the domestic legal framework created by the state concerned, strikes a fair balance between the applicant's privacy-related interests and the legitimate interests of the private body in carrying out the actions concerned. As elaborated in the following, this parallels the proportionality assessment that would follow under Article 8(2) were the private body a state agency.

Regarding the basic ambit of the right to respect for private life, the Court has stressed that this embraces more than merely safeguarding a sphere of seclusion in which the individual may act autonomously; it also protects interpersonal relationships outside the domestic realm. Thus, in *Niemietz v Germany*, the Court held:

it would be too restrictive to limit the notion [of 'private life'] to an "inner circle" in which the individual may live his own personal life as he chooses and to exclude therefrom entirely the outside world not encompassed within that circle. Respect for private life must also comprise to a certain degree the right to establish and develop relationships with other human beings. There appears, furthermore, to be no reason of principle why this understanding of the notion of "private life" should be taken to exclude activities of a professional or business nature since it is, after all, in the course of their working lives that the majority of people have a significant, if not the greatest, opportunity of developing relationships with the outside world.[227]

The right to respect for private life may also be engaged even in relation to activities of persons in the public sphere beyond their workplace. However, the application of Article 8(1) to such activities is far from automatic. The Court will only be prepared to find interference in respect of such activities

---

[225] See eg, *Von Hannover* (n 224).

[226] See eg, *Köpke v Germany* (2010) application no. 420/07; admissibility decision 5 October 2010; unreported.

[227] (1992) 16 EHRR 97 [29]. The Court went on to find that a search of a lawyer's office by a state agency and the subsequent seizure of documents from the office interfered with the lawyer's right(s) in Art. 8(1). The Court further found that this interference was not justified pursuant to Art. 8(2) because it was disproportionate in the circumstances.

after a relatively searching assessment involving consideration of several factors:

> There are a number of elements relevant to a consideration of whether a person's private life is concerned in measures effected outside a person's home or private premises. Since there are occasions when people knowingly or intentionally involve themselves in activities which are or may be recorded or reported in a public manner, a person's reasonable expectations as to privacy may be a significant, although not necessarily conclusive, factor. A person who walks down the street will, inevitably, be visible to any member of the public who is also present. Monitoring by technological means of the same public scene (for example, a security guard viewing through closed-circuit television) is of a similar character. Private life considerations may arise, however, once any systematic or permanent record comes into existence of such material from the public domain.[228]

Thus, while softening the distinction between 'private' and 'public' realms of activity, the Court has not dispensed with it altogether as a demarcation of the scope of Article 8(1). An example in point—highlighted in the above citation—concerns CCTV (closed-circuit television) surveillance of public space: 'the normal use of security cameras *per se* whether in the public street or on premises, such as shopping centres or police stations where they serve a legitimate and foreseeable purpose, do [sic] not raise issues under Article 8 § 1 of the Convention'.[229] Another example concerns disclosure by the press of personal information that is already publicly available: this will not be interference unless it can be shown as harming the person's 'physical or psychological integrity'.[230] Yet Article 8(1) may be engaged once information from the public sphere is systematically recorded, stored, and used, particularly in ways that go beyond the reasonable expectations of the person(s) concerned.[231]

The factor of 'reasonable expectations' increasingly figures in the Court's assessment of what constitutes 'private life'.[232] This development parallels

---

[228] *PG and JH v UK* (2001) 46 EHRR 1272 [57].

[229] *Perry v UK* (2004) 39 EHRR 3 [40].     [230] *NF v Italy* (2002) 35 EHRR 4 [39].

[231] See eg, *Peck v UK* (2003) 36 EHRR 41 esp. [62] (disclosure of CCTV footage of aftermath of man's suicide attempt in a public space deemed an interference as the 'relevant moment was viewed to an extent which far exceeded any exposure to a passer-by or to security observation . . . and to a degree surpassing that which the applicant could possibly have foreseen').

[232] See eg, *Halford v UK* (1997) 24 EHRR 523 and *Copland* (n 219). Both cases concerned instances of employers in the public sector engaging in covert surveillance of communications from their employees, without the latter being adequately warned that such monitoring might occur. The Court held that because of the absence of adequate warning, the employees had a reasonable expectation as to the privacy of their communications sent from their workplace. In both cases, the Court found that the covert surveillance was not in accordance with the employees' reasonable expectations and accordingly interfered with their right(s) under Art. 8(1).

(and is perhaps partly inspired by) US Supreme Court jurisprudence on the Fourth Amendment to the Bill of Rights in the US Constitution.[233] The precise nature of the 'reasonable expectations' criterion in ECtHR jurisprudence remains unclear: for instance, whose expectations set the benchmark for reasonableness, how does the Court determine what is reasonable, and what weight does the criterion carry?[234] The lack of clarity is unfortunate given the slipperiness of the criterion and its potential (particularly if based on actual or subjective expectations) to undercut the purchase of privacy safeguards in tact with behavioural 'conditioning' caused by increased surveillance.[235]

The distinction between public and private realms arises also in relation to states parties' positive obligations under Article 8(1). In the two cases of *Von Hannover v Germany*,[236] the Court held that celebrities and other public figures have a right to respect for their private life and cannot be 'free game' for the mass media. Nonetheless, it made clear that public figures must tolerate greater exposure than others when they carry out public duties or when the information published about them contributes to a debate of general societal interest (as opposed to publication purely to satisfy curiosity).[237]

## (b) Interference

The bulk of the Article 8 case law dealing with data privacy issues concerns covert or otherwise non-consensual surveillance activities by state security agencies. The case law makes clear that such activities generally constitute interference with Article 8(1) rights, and thus fall to be justified under Article 8(2).[238] Indeed, the covert storage of personal information by a state security agency may constitute interference, regardless of whether or not the information is subsequently used.[239] Further, the mere existence of laws and practices allowing state agencies to carry out secret surveillance may be sufficient to constitute

---

[233] T Gomez-Arostegui, 'Defining Private Life Under the European Convention on Human Rights by Referring to Reasonable Expectations' (2005) 35 California Western Intl LJ 153, 163.

[234] See n 233, 169, 173, 175–7.

[235] A potential demonstrated by the US Supreme Court's Fourth Amendment case law: see n 233, 195–6 and references cited therein.

[236] *Von Hannover v Germany* (n 224); *Von Hannover v Germany* (no. 2) (2012) 55 EHRR 15.

[237] See particularly the elaboration of the criteria for balancing the privacy interests of public figures with the right to freedom of expression in the second of the *Von Hannover* cases: *Von Hannover v Germany* (no. 2) (2012) 55 EHRR 15 [108]–[113].

[238] Leading cases are *Klass v Germany* (1978) 2 EHRR 214; *Malone v UK* (1984) 7 EHRR 14; *Leander v Sweden* (1987) 9 EHRR 433.

[239] *Amann v Switzerland* (2000) 30 EHRR 843 [69].

interference.[240] This considerably eases an applicant's burden of showing that he or she has been the victim of an interference occasioned by such surveillance.[241] In the absence of laws and practices permitting surveillance, victim status will only be recognized when applicants can prove a 'reasonable likelihood' that the actions allegedly constituting interference have occurred.[242]

The Court is not always clear in specifying exactly which elements of the contested data-processing practices constitute an interference and the weight each element is given. Similarly, it has frequently failed to describe the threatened interest. Typically, the Court has reached a briefly reasoned decision on interference and then gone straight over to an assessment of whether the interference is justified pursuant to Article 8(2). One example of uncertainty concerns the re-purposing of personal data—that is, a situation in which personal data is utilized for purposes that differ from those for which it was originally processed. Re-purposing of data is in tension with the principle of purpose limitation. The Court has yet to fully throw its weight behind this principle such that we can be sure that breach of it is presumptively an interference with Article 8(1) rights.[243]

A second example concerns the element of consent (or lack of it). All decisions by the ECtHR on data privacy issues have hitherto involved *non*-consensual processing of personal data. This raises the question as to what may constitute interference with the rights laid down in Article 8(1) in the case of consensual processing of personal data. Concomitantly, to what extent will the Court restrict data-processing operations which, although consented to by data subjects, nevertheless contribute to the erosion of pluralistic, democratic society? These questions have yet to be squarely addressed by the Court.

Yet another example concerns data subjects' opportunity to gain access to data kept on them by others, and to challenge its validity. Older case law suggests that denial of such an opportunity does not ordinarily constitute interference, but the Court's pronouncements on point are ambiguous.[244] However,

---

[240] *Klass* (n 238) [34], [41]; *Malone* (n 238) [64], [86]. For more recent confirmation, see eg, *Association for European Integration and Human Rights and Ekimdzhiev v Bulgaria* (2007) ECHR 533 (28 June 2007) [58]–[59].

[241] According to ECHR Art. 25, a private party may only bring an action before the ECtHR on the basis that they are a victim of a breach of the Convention. The conditions under which a person may claim victim status without having to prove victimization 'are to be determined in each case according to the Convention right or rights alleged to have been infringed, the secret character of the measures objected to, and the connection between the applicant and those measures': *Klass* (n 238) [34]. See also *Malone* (n 238) [64], [86].

[242] *Halford* (n 232) [47], [57].     [243] See further Ch 5 (section E).

[244] See Bygrave (n 216) 261.

as shown further below, denial of such an opportunity may be in breach of a state's positive obligations under Article 8(1). It may also aggravate the seriousness of an interference incurred by the (non-consensual) processing of the data. And it is germane to the issue of whether or not such interference is justified under Article 8(2).

### (c) Justification for interference

Turning to justification for interferences, Article 8(2) tends to play the dominant role in the Court's case law on data privacy. In other words, the salient issue tends to be whether interference with the right(s) under Article 8(1) can be justified under Article 8(2). Resolution of this issue depends on the fulfilment of the cumulative criteria stipulated therein—that is, that the interference was (i) 'in accordance with the law', (ii) 'necessary in a democratic society', and (iii) in furtherance of at least one of the enumerated aims. The first two of these criteria tend to be most crucial in the case law; the last-mentioned criterion is usually satisfied.

The requirement that an interference be 'in accordance with the law' means that there must be a legal basis for the interference. This basis does not have to be found in statutes; it may also be found in rules made pursuant to delegated powers, or in judicial practice.[245] The legal measure must also satisfy the ideals of 'rule of law'; that is, it must be accessible to the person concerned and sufficiently precise to allow the person reasonably to foresee its consequences.[246] Thus, it 'must indicate the scope of any...discretion conferred on the competent authorities and the manner of its exercise with sufficient clarity...to give the individual adequate protection against arbitrary interference'.[247]

The stringency of these requirements of the quality of a legal measure depends on the seriousness of the interference. For instance, the Court emphasized in *Kruslin* that

interception of telephone conversations represent[s] a serious interference with private life and correspondence and must accordingly be based upon a 'law' that is particularly precise. It is essential to have clear, detailed rules on the subject, especially as the technology available for use is continually becoming more sophisticated.[248]

At the same time, the requirement of foreseeability may be relaxed for the purposes of police investigations and the safeguarding of national security:

the requirements of the Convention, notably in regard to foreseeability, cannot be exactly the same in the special context of interception of communications for the

---

[245] See eg, *Kruslin v France* (1990) 12 EHRR 547 [29]; *Huvig v France* (1990) 12 EHRR 528 [28].
[246] *Malone* (n 238) [66]–[68].        [247] *Malone* (n 238) [66]–[68].
[248] *Kruslin* (n 245) [33]; *Huvig* (n 245) [32].

purposes of police investigations as they are where the object of the relevant law is to place restrictions on the conduct of individuals. In particular, the requirement of foreseeability cannot mean that an individual should be enabled to foresee when the authorities are likely to intercept his communications so that he can adapt his conduct accordingly.[249]

Nonetheless, a considerable number of cases have resulted in the Court finding that the quality of the legal measures relied upon by the state party concerned are inadequate to justify police telephone-tapping practices pursuant to Article 8(2). In *Kruslin* and *Huvig*, for instance, serious deficiencies were identified with the quality of French law regulating the surreptitious tapping of telephones by the police. The Court pointed out, inter alia, that the law failed to specify safeguards against possible abuses of the telephone-tapping system. There were, for instance, insufficiently detailed rules defining whose telephones should be tapped and under which circumstances, and the conditions upon which the recordings should be destroyed.[250] The judgments in these and similar cases highlight that when interference with rights under Article 8(1) is serious, there must be comprehensive regulation of the activities that incur the interference. As De Hert observes, the Court's insistence on comprehensive regulation places it in the role of European legislator.[251] With regard to covert telecommunications surveillance by state security agencies, the governing rules must at least specify:

the nature of the offences which may give rise to an interception order; a definition of the categories of people liable to have their telephones tapped; a limit on the duration of telephone tapping; the procedure to be followed for examining, using and storing the data obtained; the precautions to be taken when communicating the data

---

[249] *Malone* (n 238) [67]. See too *Leander* (n 238) [51]. For more recent elaboration, see *Kennedy v UK* (2011) 52 EHRR 4. In the latter case, the Court rejected the applicant's argument that the UK Regulation of Investigatory Powers Act 2000 s 5 was insufficiently clear. Section 5 permits interception of communications when necessary in the interests of 'national security', for the purposes of, inter alia, preventing or detecting 'serious crime'. The Court observed: 'the term "national security" is frequently employed in both national and international legislation and constitutes one of the legitimate aims to which Article 8 § 2 itself refers…. By the nature of things, threats to national security may vary in character and may be unanticipated or difficult to define in advance…. Similar considerations apply to the use of the term in the context of secret surveillance. Further, additional clarification of how the term is to be applied in practice in the United Kingdom has been provided by the Commissioner…. As for "serious crime", this is defined in the interpretative provisions of the Act itself and what is meant by "detecting" serious crime is also explained in the Act' [159].

[250] *Kruslin* (n 245) [35]; *Huvig* (n 245) [34]. See too eg, *Kopp v Switzerland* (1998) 27 EHRR 91 [73]–[75]; *Liberty and Others v UK* (2009) 48 EHRR 1 [69].

[251] P de Hert, 'Balancing Security and Liberty within the European Human Rights Framework: A Critical Reading of the Court's Case Law in the Light of Surveillance and Criminal Law Enforcement Strategies after 9/11' (2005) 1 Utrecht L Rev 68, 79.

to other parties; and the circumstances in which recordings may or must be erased or the tapes destroyed.[252]

Recent case law also emphasizes the need to subject surveillance operations to review by an independent authority,[253] and to notify the targeted persons that they have been monitored, as soon as notification can occur without jeopardizing the purpose of the surveillance.[254]

Regarding the 'necessity' of an interference (that is, the second cumulative requirement for justification under Article 8(2)), this criterion has been generally interpreted by the Court as satisfied when the interference 'corresponds to a pressing social need' and is 'proportionate to the legitimate aim pursued'.[255] At the same time it has stated that 'the adjective "necessary" is not synonymous with "indispensable", neither has it the flexibility of such expressions as "admissible", "ordinary", "useful", "reasonable" or "desirable"'.[256]

In applying the necessity criterion, the Court accords states parties a 'margin of appreciation'. This allows the assessment of what is necessary in the circumstances of the particular case to be determined to some extent by the national authorities. The extent of this margin of appreciation varies from case to case and depends on the Court's appraisal of a variety of factors. These include the seriousness of the interference with the right concerned, the importance of this right, the importance of the 'legitimate aim' for the interference, and the conformity of the interference to a relevant pan-European practice.[257]

In cases involving state agencies' surreptitious surveillance of persons, the Court has viewed the criterion of necessity more stringently than in other cases: 'Powers of secret surveillance of citizens, characterising as they do the police state, are tolerable under the Convention only insofar as *strictly* necessary for safeguarding the democratic institutions'.[258] At the same time, the Court has held that when the aim of such surveillance is to safeguard national security (as it often is), the margin of appreciation available to states parties in assessing what is necessary for fulfilling that aim is wide.[259] It could be argued,

---

[252] *Weber and Saravia v Germany* [2006] ECHR 1173 (29 June 2006) [95].

[253] *Association for European Integration and Human Rights and Ekimdzhiev* (n 240) [85], [87].

[254] *Weber and Saravia* (n 252) [135]; *Association for European Integration and Human Rights and Ekimdzhiev* (n 240) [90], [91].

[255] See eg, *Leander* (n 238) [58].

[256] *Handyside v UK* (1976) 1 EHRR 737 [48]; *Silver and Others v UK* [1983] 5 EHRR 347 [97].

[257] See further HC Yourow, *The Margin of Appreciation Doctrine in the Dynamics of the European Court of Human Rights Jurisprudence* (Martinus Nijhoff Publishers 1996); Harris and others (n 221) 11–14, 349–59.

[258] *Klass* (n 238) [42] (emphasis added).            [259] *Leander* (n 238) [59].

though, that in cases involving the processing of personal data for *other* purposes, the existence of a large body of European data privacy laws based on common principles is a factor that would tend to reduce state parties' margin of appreciation.

In assessing the necessity/proportionality of a data-processing operation that interferes with an Article 8(1) right, the Court pays regard to the nature of the data in question. Generally speaking, the more intimate or sensitive the data is judged to be, the more stringent will be the application of the necessity/proportionality criterion.[260] The Court also pays regard to the existence or otherwise of sufficient safeguards against abuse of the measure(s) leading to the interference. Assessment of these safeguards is similar to, and overlaps with, the assessment of the quality of the legal basis for the interference.[261] Thus, the safeguards deemed appropriate are generally the same as those highlighted in the latter assessment.

One safeguard that bears emphasis due to its direct relevance for data privacy law generally is the existence of rules to ensure data confidentiality—that is, rules that are typically present in ordinary data privacy statutes. This safeguard is seen as especially important with respect to medical data.[262] At the same time, it is important to note that this safeguard, at least with respect to medical data, needs to be complemented by technological–organizational measures to ensure implementation of the rules on point. The need for such measures arises as a positive obligation on states parties—that is, in addition to their obligation to abstain from interference with the right(s) under Article 8(1). In *I v Finland*,[263] the Court held that Finland had violated Article 8 due to its failure to secure the confidentiality of patient data at a public hospital. While Finnish data privacy law contained rules to ensure confidentiality of such data and to provide compensation for their breach, these rules were not transposed in the design of the hospital's information system for accessing medical files. The system did not limit access to health professionals who

---

[260] See eg, *Z v Finland* (1998) 25 EHRR 371 [96] ('In view of the highly intimate and sensitive nature of information concerning a person's HIV status, any State measures compelling communication or disclosure of such information without the consent of the patient call for the most careful scrutiny on the part of the Court, as do the safeguards designed to secure an effective protection').

[261] See eg, *Klass* (n 238) [50] ('The court must be satisfied that, whatever system of surveillance is adopted, there exist adequate and effective guarantees against abuse. This assessment has only a relative character: it depends on all the circumstances of the case, such as the nature, scope and duration of the possible measures, the grounds required for ordering such measures, the authorities competent to permit, carry out and supervise such measures, and the kind of remedy provided by the national law').

[262] *Z v Finland* (n 260) [95]; *MS v Sweden* [1997] ECHR 49 (27 August 1997) [41].

[263] (2009) 48 EHRR [31].

were directly involved in the treatment of the applicant, nor did it record who accessed the files. According to the Court:

> the mere fact that the domestic legislation provided the applicant with an opportunity to claim compensation for damages caused by an alleged unlawful disclosure of personal data was not sufficient to protect her private life. What is required in this connection is practical and effective protection to exclude any possibility of unauthorised access occurring in the first place. Such protection was not given here.[264]

### (d)  Access and rectification rights

An area in which the Court has been reticent in requiring strict data privacy safeguards concerns access and rectification rights in respect of personal data. To be sure, the Court has recognized that states parties are under a positive obligation to secure a person's interest in gaining access to certain types of information about themself and to rectify it if it is inaccurate. However, the degree to which states parties must secure this interest will depend on the importance of the information for the applicant's private and family life. Generally, the Court has upheld this interest only when the information is of crucial importance for the psychological well-being or physical health of the applicant.[265] Such importance is merely a necessary condition for enforcing access, not a sufficient condition. In *Gaskin*, for example, the Court refrained from enforcing access, requiring instead that the UK authorities establish a procedure for independently determining access requests of the type made by the applicant.[266] Moreover, the Court was initially reluctant to find breach of Article 8 occasioned by public authorities' refusal to rectify birth certificates or other official records so as to reflect the changed sexual identities of transsexuals.[267] This reluctance was incongruous with the Court's recognition otherwise of the importance of Article 8 for cultivating the interest in autonomous development of one's personality.

Article 8 may require, in some circumstances, public authorities to divulge certain information to citizens independent of requests for the information. Further, that information may encompass non-personal information that can

---

[264] (2009) 48 EHRR [47].

[265] See eg *Gaskin v UK* (1990) 12 EHRR 36; *McMichael v UK* (1995) 20 EHRR 205; *Guerra and Others v Italy* (1998) 26 EHRR 357.

[266] *Gaskin* (n 265) [49].

[267] *Rees v UK* (1987) 9 EHRR 56; *Cossey v UK* (1991) 13 EHRR 622. Later decisions, however, have found such refusal to violate Art. 8: see esp. *B v France* (1993) 16 EHRR 1 and *Goodwin v UK* (2002) 35 EHRR 18.

increase citizens' understanding of their health situation. In *Guerra*, the Court unanimously found that the failure by public authorities to fulfil certain legislative obligations to inform the citizens of a town about serious nearby environmental hazards was in violation of the authorities' positive obligation to secure the citizens' right(s) under Article 8.[268]

The Court seems also increasingly prepared to recognize a right of access to personal information under the right to freedom of expression in ECHR Article 10(1), which includes 'the freedom to … receive … information … without interference by public authority'. In *Leander*, the Court held that 'the right to freedom to receive information basically prohibits a Government from restricting a person from receiving information that others wish or may be willing to impart to him', but added that 'Article 10 does not, in circumstances such as those of the present case, confer on the individual a right of access to a register containing information on his personal position, nor does it embody an obligation on the Government to impart such information to the individual'.[269] This view was reaffirmed by the Court in *Gaskin*.[270] Both judgments, though, concerned demands for access to information that was only of a personal nature and only of importance for the data subjects. In recent case law, the Court signals readiness to adopt a different approach where the information in question concerns a matter of general public concern and denial of access to it can be cast as an interference 'with the exercise of the functions of a social watchdog, like the press, rather than a denial of a general right of access to official documents'.[271]

## 3. Article 13

ECHR Article 13 is also relevant for data privacy. It states:

Everyone whose rights and freedoms as set forth in [the] Convention are violated shall have an effective remedy before a national authority notwithstanding that the violation has been committed by persons acting in an official capacity.

---

[268] *Guerra* (n 265) [60].      [269] *Leander* (n 238) [74].      [270] *Gaskin* (n 265) [52].

[271] *Társaság a Szabadságjogokért v Hungary* (2011) 53 EHRR 3 [36]. In this case, the Court paid lip-service to its line in *Leander* but, citing *SdruZení Jihočeské Matky v Czech Republic* [2006] ECHR 1205 (10 July 2006), noted that 'the Court has recently advanced towards a broader interpretation of the notion of "freedom to receive information" … and thereby towards the recognition of a right of access to information': [35]. It went on to find breach of Art. 10 occasioned by the Hungarian Constitutional Court withholding information that was necessary for debate on a matter of public importance (the information cast doubt on the legality of changes to criminal law regarding drug-related offences).

A precondition for applying Article 13 is that the applicant 'has an arguable claim to be the victim of a violation of the rights set forth in the Convention'.[272] It is not necessary that the national authority concerned be a judicial body 'but, if it is not, the powers and the guarantees which it affords are relevant in determining whether the remedy before it is effective'.[273] Assessment of effectiveness comprises the remedy's practical as well as legal effect.[274]

In *Rotaru v Romania*, the ECtHR held that the absence of any proven possibility for the applicant to challenge the continued storage of information about him by the Romanian Intelligence Service or to challenge the veracity of the information amounted to a breach of Article 13.[275] The same result was reached in *Segerstedt-Wiberg and Others v Sweden*, in part because the applicants 'had no direct access to any legal remedy as regards the erasure of the information in question'.[276] Breach was additionally due to the fact that particular Swedish agencies involved in enforcing the relevant data privacy rules lacked the power to issue legally binding decisions, and, in the case of the Swedish DPA (Datainspektionen) which did have greater legal powers, no evidence had been adduced to show its effectiveness in practice.[277]

---

[272] *Leander* (n 238) [77].　　　[273] *Leander* (n 238) [77].
[274] *Rotaru v Romania* [2000] ECHR 192 (4 May 2000) [67].
[275] [2000] ECHR 192 (4 May 2000) [70]–[71].　　　[276] (2007) 44 EHRR 2 [121].
[277] (2007) 44 EHRR 2 [119]–[120].

# 3

# National Data Privacy Laws

## A. Introduction

Data privacy law emerged at the beginning of the 1970s on both sides of the Atlantic. Initially it was a sub-national code in the main—the very first legislation dealing substantially and directly with data privacy was the Hessian Data Protection Act (Hessisches Datenschutzgesetz) enacted on 7 October 1970. On 11 May 1973, Sweden enacted the first such legislation at the national level—the Data Act (Datalagen). In the USA, federal legislation in the field was enacted in the form of the Privacy Act 1974, although the Fair Credit Reporting Act 1970 already contained rudimentary data privacy rules for the credit reporting industry.

Legislative development in the field during the ensuing two decades was largely a European affair. Although an increasing number of non-European countries passed data privacy legislation in this period and thereafter, the majority of national laws in the field were still European by the early 2000s. The inclusion of ten largely East European states in the EU in 2004 prolonged this European preponderance.[1]

In the last few years, however, we have witnessed an exponential rise in the rate at which countries are enacting data privacy statutes. Most of that growth has occurred outside Europe, although under considerable influence from the latter.[2] The result is that approximately 100 countries have enacted data privacy statutes at national or federal level, and that number is expected to grow.

This chapter provides a broad-brush overview of national regimes on a regional basis. The US regime is singled out for special attention as it

---

[1] Adoption of national legislation transposing the EU Data Protection Directive is a prerequisite for EU membership.

[2] The development is charted in detail in G Greenleaf, 'The Influence of European Data Privacy Standards outside Europe: Implications for Globalization of Convention 108' (2012) 2 IDPL 68.

constitutes the predominant counterweight to regulatory developments initiated in Europe. The chapter also canvasses the transatlantic dialogue on data privacy issues. This dialogue has dominated much of the international policy development in the field and will continue to do so, at least in the short term. Thus, the chief similarities and differences between US and European approaches to data privacy are analysed, along with the reasons for these differences.

## B. Europe

Europe is home to the oldest, most comprehensive, and most bureaucratically cumbersome data privacy laws at both national and sub-national levels. Moreover, as shown in the previous chapter, Europe—through its supranational institutions—is a springboard for the most extensive international initiatives in the field.

Common points of departure for national data privacy regimes in Europe are as follows:[3]

- coverage of both public and private sectors;
- coverage of both automated and manual systems for processing personal data largely irrespective of how the data is structured;
- application of broad definitions of 'personal data';
- application of extensive sets of procedural principles some of which are rarely found in data privacy regimes elsewhere;[4]
- more stringent regulation of certain categories of sensitive data (for example, data relating to philosophical beliefs, sexual preferences, ethnic origins);
- *ex ante* restrictions on transborder flow of personal data to countries lacking adequate protection for the data;
- establishment of independent DPAs with broad discretionary powers to oversee implementation and development of data privacy rules;
- channelling of privacy complaints to these agencies rather than courts;

---

[3] See further C Kuner, *European Data Protection Law: Corporate Compliance and Regulation* (2nd edn, OUP 2007); D Korff, *Data Protection Law in the European Union* (Direct Marketing Association/Federation of European Direct and Interactive Marketing, 2005); LA Bygrave, *Data Protection Law: Approaching Its Rationale, Logic and Limits* (Kluwer Law International 2002) chs 2–4.

[4] An example of a principle that is rarely found other than in European laws concerns fully automated profiling. The principle—embodied in Art. 15 of the EU Data Protection Directive—is that fully automated assessments of a person's character should not form the sole basis of decisions that impinge upon the person's interests. See further Ch 5 (section F).

- availability of judicial remedies for enforcement of data privacy rights;
- extensive subjection of data processing to notification or licensing requirements administered by the DPAs;
- extensive use of 'opt-in' requirements for valid consent by data subjects;
- little use of industry-developed codes of practice.

These characteristics reflect the requirements of Convention 108, the DPD and ECHR Article 8. While most of them are typical for national data privacy regimes in Europe, each country has its own unique mix of rules; concomitantly, a good deal of variation exists in the degree to which each country shares these listed traits. For example, the Netherlands has always made relatively extensive use of industry-based codes of practice, and the DPD itself encourages greater use of such codes (see Article 27), as does the proposed GDPR (Article 38). Moreover, data privacy regimes in each country are far from static. For example, Swedish legislation originally operated with extensive licensing and notification requirements; it subsequently dispensed entirely with a licensing scheme, cut back significantly on notification requirements, and introduced 'light-touch', misuse-oriented regulation for the processing of unstructured electronic data.[5] There has been movement too at a broader European level. For instance, while many early European data protection regimes relied heavily on paternalistic control mechanisms—that is, control exercised by government bodies (primarily DPAs) on behalf (and supposedly in the best interests) of citizens (data subjects)—they now rely to a greater degree on participatory control (that is, control exercised by citizens themselves). This notwithstanding, European jurisdictions (in contrast to, say, the USA)[6] generally maintain a relatively non-negotiable legislative baseline for the private sector.

It bears emphasis that Europe is more than the EU. Further, the traction of EU data privacy norms on European countries that are not member states of the EU or EEA can be weak. The Russian Federation is a principal instance here. While it has signed and ratified Convention 108 (although not the Additional Protocol), introduced provisions on rights related to data privacy in its Constitution,[7] and enacted data privacy legislation formally incorporating many of the elements of the DPD and Convention 108,[8]

---

[5] Personal Data Act 1998 ss 5a, 36, 37. By 'misuse-oriented' regulation is meant regulation that applies only insofar as the data processing in question violates the personal integrity of the data subject: see further *Översyn av personuppgiftslagen*, 2004: 6; S Öman, 'Implementing Data Protection in Law' (2004) 47 Scandinavian Studies in Law 389, 392–8.

[6] See further section F.     [7] See Constitution of the Russian Federation 1993 Arts 23–25.

[8] See esp. Federal Law on Personal Data 2006 (No. 152-FZ) along with Federal Law on Information, Information Technologies, and the Protection of Information 2006 (No. 149-FZ).

its data privacy regime falls short of the requirements of the DPD and the Convention's Additional Protocol. For example, its DPA (the Federal Service for Supervision of Telecommunications, Information Technologies, and Mass Media (Roskomnadzor)) is under the wing of the federal Ministry of Communications and is headed by a government appointee. Roskomnadzor accordingly lacks the independence demanded by the DPD and Additional Protocol.[9] Further, there are very broadly drawn exemptions from core data privacy requirements for government agencies in the name of safeguarding national security and public order.

## C. The Americas

Across the Atlantic, a large number of countries have adopted data privacy regimes that embrace or are largely in harmony with the European approach. The oldest of these regimes is the Canadian. Canada introduced federal legislation covering data privacy in relation to the federal government sector in 1982.[10] Federal legislation covering the private sector was introduced in 2000.[11] All Canadian provinces and territories have enacted data privacy laws covering provincial and territorial government agencies; the legislation of several provinces covers the private sector too.[12] DPAs exist at both federal and provincial levels.

In South America, rudimentary rules on data privacy initially manifested themselves in the form of constitutional rights of habeas data. As noted earlier,[13] habeas data enables a person to gain, by way of court order, access to data kept on them in government databases and, if appropriate, have the data rectified or erased. Brazil was the first to introduce such a right, which was incorporated in Article 5 of its Constitution of 1988. This was a reaction to the repression of civil liberties under the country's former military dictatorship, particularly the activities of the infamous Serviço Nacional de Informações (National Information Service), which had established an

---

[9] Further on the stringency of those demands, see Ch 6 (section A).
[10] Privacy Act 1982.
[11] Personal Information Protection and Electronic Documents Act 2000.
[12] See eg, Quebec's Act on Protection of Personal Information in the Private Sector 1993; British Columbia's Personal Information Protection Act 2003; Alberta's Personal Information Protection Act 2003 and Health Information Act 1999.
[13] See Ch 1 (section F).

extensive database of the Brazilian population.[14] Brazil has not yet supplemented the habeas data writ with comprehensive data privacy legislation, but other countries in the region have. Argentina was the first to do so, in 2000.[15] Its legislation is formally based on the right of habeas data in Article 43 of its Constitution and otherwise modelled on the DPD and equivalent Spanish legislation. Other countries in the region which have enacted fairly comprehensive data privacy legislation include Uruguay,[16] Mexico,[17] Costa Rica,[18] Colombia,[19] and Trinidad and Tobago.[20]

However, the economically and militarily most powerful nation in the region and, indeed, the world, has steadfastly eschewed omnibus legislative solutions for data privacy. The US regulatory approach in the field is dealt with in detail in section F of this chapter.

# D. Asia and Oceania

In the regions of Asia and Oceania, there exist a handful of relatively comprehensive legislative data privacy regimes, most notably those in Australia, New Zealand, Hong Kong, South Korea, and Japan. The bulk of these jurisdictions have also established DPAs. New Zealand was the first to enact legislation applying across the public and private sectors.[21] Australian, South Korean, and Japanese legislation in the field was initially limited largely to the public sector but has since been extended to cover the private sector too.[22]

---

[14] See eg, JC Júnior, *Comentários à Constituição Brasileira de 1988* (3rd edn, Forense Universitária 1994) 770 § 3.

[15] Act No. 25.326 on Protection of Personal Data (adopted 4 October 2000); supplemented by Decree 1558/2001 of 3 December 2001.

[16] Act No. 18.331 on the Protection of Personal Data and 'Habeas Data' Action (adopted 11 August 2008); supplemented by Decree 414/009 of 31 August 2009.

[17] Federal Law on Protection of Personal Data held by Private Parties (adopted 6 July 2010); supplemented by Regulation of 21 December 2011, Privacy Notice Guidelines of 17 January 2013, and Parameters for Mandatory Self-Regulation of 17 January 2013.

[18] Act No. 8968 on the Protection of the Individual with Regards to Processing of Personal Data (adopted 7 July 2011).

[19] Act No. 1581 on Protection of Personal Data (adopted 17 October 2012).

[20] Data Protection Act 2011 (although only partially in force as of 6 January 2012).

[21] Privacy Act 1993.

[22] For Australia, see federal Privacy Amendment (Private Sector) Act 2000. For Japan, see Act on Protection of Personal Information 2003. For South Korea, see Act on Promotion of Information and Communications Network Utilization and Data Protection 1999. The latter Act covers private sector entities insofar as these process personal data for profit using telecommunication networks; medical records and credit information are protected under other laws. Regarding Japan, there is also a separate law for incorporated administrative agencies: see Act on Protection of Personal Information Held by Incorporated Administrative Agencies 2003. The Japanese legislative regime is augmented by sets of ministerial guidelines. Further on the Japanese regime, see H Miyashita, 'The Evolving Concept of Data Privacy in Japanese Law' (2011) 1 IDPL 229. Several of the Australian States have enacted data

Some of these extensions, however, still leave large gaps in private sector coverage.[23] Other aspects of the laws in question also diverge from the EU model(s).[24]

Data privacy regimes in other Asia–Pacific jurisdictions tend to be even patchier in coverage. Malaysia and Singapore, for instance, have introduced data privacy legislation to cover parts of the private sector but lack equivalent legislation for personal information processed by government agencies.[25] As for the People's Republic of China, there exists formal protection for privacy-related interests in its Constitution[26] and General Principles of Civil Law,[27] augmented by a small amount of case law,[28] along with a patchwork of sectoral laws and guidelines on point.[29] There have been signals in recent years that the country is on the verge of introducing a relatively comprehensive data privacy law, but these signals have not yet been followed up by concrete legislative enactment. However, the Special Administrative Regions (SAR) of Hong Kong and Macau both have European-style data privacy laws.[30]

With respect to India, sectoral laws have been adopted but yet to be put effectively in operation. The most significant of these is the Credit Information Companies (Regulation) Act 2005 which lays out a relatively comprehensive data privacy code for the credit-reporting industry. Another is the Information Technology Act 2000, together with amending legislation of 2008. The Act

privacy laws covering their respective government agencies and, to a lesser extent, other sectors: see eg, Victoria's Information Privacy Act 2000, Health Records Act 2001, and Surveillance Devices (Workplace Privacy) Act 2006.

[23] For example, with a few exceptions, the Australian federal Privacy Act does not apply to 'small business operators' (operators of one or more businesses each of which has an annual turnover of AU$3 million or less)(ss 6C(1), 6D, 6DA, and 6E)). Nor does the Act apply to employer processing of employee records when the processing is 'directly related' to a 'current or former employment relationship' between the employer and the employee concerned (s 7B(3)).

[24] The Japanese legislation, for example, does not formally distinguish between sensitive and non-sensitive data, and makes relatively extensive use of 'opt-out' consent mechanisms.

[25] For Singapore, see Personal Data Protection Act 2012; for Malaysia, see Personal Data Protection Act 2010.

[26] See Constitution of the People's Republic of China 1982 Arts 38–40.

[27] General Principles of the Civil Law of the People's Republic of China 1986 Art. 101 (concerning protection of reputation).

[28] For analysis, see R Ong, 'Recognition of the Right to Privacy on the Internet in China' (2011) 1 IDPL 172–9. For more general analysis of the ways in which the Chinese legal system provides data privacy safeguards, see H Wang, *Protecting Privacy in China: A Research on China's Privacy Standards and the Possibility of Establishing the Right to Privacy and the Information Privacy Protection Legislation in Modern China* (Springer 2011).

[29] See further G Greenleaf and GY Tian, 'China Expands Data Protection through New 2013 Guidelines' (2013) Privacy Laws & Business Intl Report, No. 122, 1, 4–6.

[30] For Hong Kong, see Personal Data (Privacy) Ordinance 1996 as amended by the Personal Data (Privacy) (Amendment) Ordinance 2012. For Macau, see Personal Data Protection Act 2006.

contains several provisions dealing with security and wrongful disclosure of personal data (see for example, sections 43, 43B, 66, 66B, 72A) but, as indicated above, these are yet to be applied in practice.[31] Although India has been reported to be considering enactment of a law modelled on the DPD (largely due to fear that its burgeoning outsourcing industry will otherwise flounder),[32] no such law has emerged.

## E. Africa and the Middle East

Legal regimes for data privacy are least developed in Middle Eastern and African countries taken as a whole. As noted in the previous chapter, however, there is a significant push by African states to enact data privacy legislation. In 2001, Cape Verde became the first African state to enact a European-style data privacy law,[33] although it has yet to establish a national DPA (despite provision being made for such a body). Ten other African states have followed suit, including the Seychelles,[34] Burkina Faso,[35] Benin,[36] Tunisia,[37] Morocco,[38] Mauritius,[39] Angola,[40] and, most recently, the Republic of South Africa.[41] Some of the data privacy laws in these countries are not yet fully operational. For example, Angola and Cape Verde have yet to establish DPAs (although their laws require establishment of such bodies). A sizeable number of other states (including Madagascar, Niger, and Mali) have legislative bills pending.

Some African countries have enacted complementary elements for a data privacy regime well before enacting legislation dealing specifically with data

---

[31] Moreover, the small privacy gains they represent are dwarfed by the extensive surveillance measures that are authorized by other provisions in the legislation (see eg, s 69B) along with other laws. Further on recent surveillance trends in India, see G Greenleaf, 'Data Surveillance in India: Multiple Accelerating Paths' (2010) Privacy Laws & Business Intl Report, No. 105, 15–17.

[32] See S Dresner, 'India Gives Commitment on New Privacy Initiative' (2004) Privacy Laws & Business Intl Report, No. 72, 1, 3, 17.

[33] Law No. 133/V/2001 on Data Protection. This is but one element of a wide-ranging statutory framework on data privacy, with firm constitutional underpinning. See further JL Traça and B Embry, 'An Overview of the Legal Regime for Data Protection in Cape Verde' (2011) 1 IDPL 249.

[34] Act No. 9 of 2003 on Data Protection.

[35] Act 10-2004/AN on Protection of Personal Data.

[36] Law No. 2009-09 on the Protection of Personal Data in the Republic of Benin.

[37] Organic Act No. 2004-63 on Protection of Personal Data.

[38] Law No. 09-08 on the Protection of Individuals in Relation to Processing of Personal Data.

[39] Data Protection Act 2004.

[40] Law No. 22/11 on Data Protection. See further JL Traça and B Embry, 'The Angolan Data Protection Act: First Impressions' (2012) 2 IDPL 40.

[41] Protection of Personal Information Act 2013.

privacy. The Republic of South Africa, for instance, included a right to privacy in section 14 of its Bill of Rights set out in Chapter 2 of its Constitution of 1996. Also included (in section 32) is a broad right of access to information held in both the public and private sectors. Freedom of information legislation based on the latter right was enacted back in 2000.[42]

The development of data privacy law in Africa reflects multiple factors. These include: a desire to meet the adequacy requirements of DPD Articles 25–26 and thereby attract foreign investment, particularly in use of the local outsourcing industry; recent first-hand experience of political oppression; the requirements of ICCPR Article 17; and old lines of colonial influence. The latter are particularly noteworthy. They are most salient in the efforts by the French DPA (Commission de l'Informatique et des Libertés (CNIL)) to cultivate data privacy in former French colonies of north-west Africa, such as Morocco, Tunisia, Mauritius, Benin, and the Seychelles. We see also traces of Portuguese inspiration for the laws enacted in former Portuguese colonies (Angola, Cape Verde).

No African data privacy regime has yet received a positive adequacy finding by the EU. Consultants engaged by the European Commission to undertake preliminary assessments of four African regimes (Burkina Faso, Mauritius, Tunisia, and Morocco) in 2010 refused to conclude that any of them met the EU adequacy standard. This was partly due to substantive legal discrepancies and partly due to insufficient time having passed to properly assess how the regimes actually function.[43]

As for the Middle East, Israel has long had a legislative regime for data privacy in place,[44] and has passed the EU adequacy test. The only Arab state to enact data privacy legislation is Dubai, in 2007. The legislation, however, applies only to the Dubai International Financial Centre (DIFC), not to data-processing operations in the rest of the state.[45]

---

[42] Promotion of Access to Information Act 2000. Further on the Act, see I Currie and J Klaaren, *The Promotion of Access to Information Act Commentary* (Siber Ink 2002). A unique feature of the legislation is that it provides, as a point of departure, for FOI rights not just in relation to information held by government agencies but also information held in the private sector.

[43] For critical appraisal, see AB Makulilo, 'Data Protection Regimes in Africa: Too Far from the European "Adequacy" Standard?' (2013) 3 IDPL 42.

[44] Privacy Protection Act 5741-1981 (as amended) together with s 7 of the Basic Law on Human Dignity and Liberty.

[45] Data Protection Law 2007 (DIFC Law No. 1 of 2007).

## F. The USA and the Transatlantic Data Privacy Divide

It is impossible to understand the transnational development of law and policy in the field without understanding US attitudes to data privacy regulation. These attitudes have played a key role in co-producing many of the international instruments outlined earlier in the chapter. This is especially the case with the OECD Guidelines and APEC Privacy Framework. US actors have also lobbied aggressively for outcomes favourable to their interests during EU legislative processes. They did so in the negotiations that led to the adoption of the DPD and they are doing so in the current negotiations concerning the proposed GDPR. Although their policy preferences have not come up trumps, they have held some sway over negotiation outcomes.

Moreover, US policy preferences continue to shape real levels of data privacy in online worlds. They are embodied in the culture of the US-based corporations that maintain a powerful grip over much of Internet development and set many of the default standards for the routine processing of data on Internet end-users. For a huge proportion of the latter, the Internet has become largely a Google-, Facebook-, and Apple-mediated experience. The data privacy standards governing this experience remain primarily rooted in US law, even if EU law increasingly holds influence.

While the interplay of US policy preferences with those of other policy entrepreneurs has often been harmonious, it has also generated conflict and regulatory divergence. This is most apparent in the interplay of US and European actors. The transatlantic dialogue over data privacy issues has at times been intense, with each side engaged in open power struggles with the other.[46] Additionally, the tensions in this dialogue have affected not just the USA and Europe but large parts of the rest of the world. Thus, depiction of the dialogue as a 'clash of data titans' is apposite,[47] even if it underplays the policy convergence that also exists. Similar tensions have arisen between other constellations of countries, but the tensions inherent in the US–Europe relationship have generated most noise and had the greatest impact on policy development at the international level. They are unlikely to disappear in the near future.

---

[46] See further Chs 6 and 7.
[47] A Charlesworth, 'Clash of the Data Titans? US and EU Data Privacy Regulation' (2000) 6 European Public Law 253.

## 1. Transatlantic commonality

Despite tensions in the transatlantic dialogue, Europe and the USA share a great deal in their respective attitudes to protecting privacy and closely related interests, such as personal autonomy and integrity. In other words, the divergence between them over regulatory approaches to data privacy occurs on top of a transatlantic view that privacy safeguards are important. This commonality is evident in the shared commitment of Americans and Europeans (particularly West Europeans) to upholding civil liberties and liberal democratic ideals of government. Both sides of the Atlantic are firmly under the grip of the 'privacy paradigm' identified in Chapter 1. Legislators on both sides of the Atlantic recognize a need for statutory regulation of the processing of personal data. While the US legislation on point is generally less stringent and comprehensive than its European counterparts, it still makes up a hefty corpus of code. Moreover, the USA was far from being a legislative laggard in the field. As noted at the start of this chapter, it was one of the first countries in the world to enact data privacy legislation. Further, the US legal system already recognized a right to privacy more generally, both at common law (in tort) and under the US Constitution. It also boasted an extensive amount of case law dealing with both types of right.[48]

The central US and European statutes on data privacy expound a core set of broadly similar principles for protection of personal data. These principles were first drawn up in the early 1970s on both sides of the Atlantic by expert committees working contemporaneously yet independently of each other. The first body appointed by the British Parliament to investigate the putative privacy problems with the operation of computerized personal data records drafted a set of regulatory principles[49] that are remarkably similar to the code of 'fair information practices' recommended a short time later by the US Department of Health, Education and Welfare (DHEW).[50] It is impossible to determine how, if at all, one committee influenced the other.[51] Subsequent

---

[48] See generally PM Schwartz and JR Reidenberg, *Data Privacy Law: A Study of United States Data Protection* (Michie Law Publishers 1996).

[49] Younger Committee, *Report of the Committee on Privacy*, Cmnd 5012 (HMSO 1972).

[50] DHEW, *Records, Computers and the Rights of Citizens* (US Government Printing Office 1973) 41. The Younger Committee principles, however, reach further than the DHEW principles. For example, the former (unlike the latter) stipulate that information systems should be designed so that information is not held indefinitely (principle 7) and that 'care should be taken in coding value judgments' (principle 10).

[51] See too CJ Bennett, *Regulating Privacy. Data Protection and Public Policy in Europe and the United States* (Cornell University Press 1992) 99.

policy development by experts in the field involved considerably greater—and better documented—cross-jurisdictional exchange of viewpoints. This is particularly evident with the work of the CoE and OECD on their chief data privacy codes.[52]

The OECD Guidelines show that early convergence on basic principles for data privacy occurred not only between the USA and Europe but also between a considerable number of other advanced industrial nations, including Australia, New Zealand, Japan, and Canada. It would be misconceived, though, to see this convergence as simply the result of transnational agreement between expert policy entrepreneurs; other factors were at work as well. Bennett canvasses five hypotheses for explaining the convergence: (1) similarity of perceived technological threats, which forced policy makers to adopt similar solutions; (2) desire by policy makers to draw lessons from, and emulate, policies adopted earlier in other countries; (3) agreement amongst a small, cross-national network of experts as to appropriate data privacy policy; (4) harmonization efforts of international organizations, such as the OECD; and (5) 'penetration' (a process in which countries are forced to adopt certain policies because of the actions of other countries). After extensive analysis, Bennett finds that none of these hypotheses on its own adequately explains the policy convergence but that they have considerable explanatory utility in combination with each other.[53]

## 2. Transatlantic difference

While the OECD Guidelines represent a highpoint in transatlantic agreement on basic data privacy principles, their broad-brush, abstract formulation papered over tensions that most likely prevented a drafting of the principles with greater detail, precision, and bite. The chair of the Expert Group charged with formulating the Guidelines describes these tensions as follows:

Within the Expert Group there were brilliant antagonists. The chief US delegate, Mr William Fishman, expressed with great clarity the American commitment to the free flow of data and of ideas. The head of the French delegation, Mr Louis Joinet, led those in the Expert Group who were alarmed by the dangers to individual privacy of completely unrestrained collections of personal data, vastly expanded in quantity and kind by the new technology. Each protagonist spoke with sincere conviction and gathered supporters. The contemporary state of technology meant that US business interests stood to gain from the growth of informatics and the spread of transborder

---

[52] See Ch 2 (sections B and C).     [53] Bennett (n 51) ch 4.

data flows. The French and European business interests, on the other hand, coincided generally with restrictions insistent upon privacy protection.[54]

Kirby's observations here highlight a basic difference between US and European regulatory approaches to data privacy: generally, the US approach is less restrictive than the European. Concomitantly, US law affords market mechanisms greater latitude in setting data privacy standards than does European law. The 'non-negotiable' baseline for data privacy set by US legislation or case law is accordingly lower than in Europe, where the status of data privacy as a fundamental right places relatively comprehensive legislative limits on the ability to contract around data privacy rules.[55]

While the USA has enacted a large number of data privacy statutes, these tend to be narrowly circumscribed. The coverage they offer, particularly with respect to processing of personal data by private sector bodies, is haphazard and riddled with gaps.[56] This reflects a piecemeal legislative strategy. As Regan states, '[g]enerally it takes an incident to focus attention on the issue of information privacy—and such incidents tend to focus on one type of record system at a time'.[57] Schwartz characterizes this approach as one of 'regulatory parsimony': 'before the U.S. legal system acts, the lawmaker will wait for strong evidence that demonstrates the need for a regulatory measure'.[58]

When legislative protection for data privacy interests does obtain, it is usually not as far-reaching as European rules. For example, US legislation refrains from imposing privacy-related restrictions on export of personal data to other countries. It also refrains from imposing a stringent form of the principle of purpose limitation—indeed, the principle is largely absent from its core data privacy codes. It permits a considerable degree of contractual override of data subjects' privacy interests. Monitoring and enforcement schemes for data privacy are far less developed than in Europe. There is no federal regulatory authority with the mandate and powers of European DPAs. The authority that comes closest to fulfilling the role of the latter is the US Federal Trade Commission (FTC) which may uphold data privacy standards in contexts involving misleading or deceptive business practices. As elaborated further

---

[54] MD Kirby, 'Privacy Protection, a New Beginning: OECD Principles 20 Years On' (1999) 6 PLPR 25.

[55] See further Ch 5 (section F).

[56] See further generally DJ Solove and PM Schwartz, *Information Privacy Law*, (4th edn, Wolters Kluwer Law & Business 2011). For earlier concurring analysis, see Schwartz and Reidenberg (n 48).

[57] PM Regan, 'The United States' in JB Rule and G Greenleaf (eds), *Global Privacy Protection. The First Generation* (Edward Elgar 2008) 50, 51.

[58] PM Schwartz, 'The E.U.-U.S. Privacy Collision: A Turn to Institutions and Procedures' (2013) 126 Harv L Rev 1966, 1977.

on in this section, the FTC may apply penalties for such practices which go far beyond the sanctions that are ordinarily available to European DPAs. Nonetheless, the FTC has itself acknowledged that the current data privacy regime in the USA lacks sufficient legal deterrents to companies intent on undermining the privacy of consumers.[59] It has further pointed to a lack of clear standards to guide companies that intend to respect consumers' data privacy interests.[60]

Proposed legislative measures in the field usually face strong opposition from affected business groups. The latter typically have well-oiled lobbyist machinery at their disposal, along with a considerable number of 'veto points' through which to exert pressure.[61] A recent case in point, from May 2013, was the defeat of a bill introduced into the Californian legislature which would have given consumers a right to gain insight into their personal profiles compiled by online data brokers.[62] Even if legislation gets enacted, it will often face challenge in the courts, the litigation typically centring on putative infringement of the First Amendment to the Bill of Rights in the US Constitution.[63] An example is *Sorrell v IMS Health, Inc.*[64] in which the US Supreme Court overturned a Vermont statute restricting marketeers' use of pharmacy records, on the grounds that the law unduly violated free speech.

The latter case is one of many examples of the strong emphasis on freedom of expression by the US legal system. In line with this prioritization, a basic point of departure under US law is that processing of personal data is permitted. Under EU law, however, a great deal of such processing is prohibited unless it has a legal basis.[65] Recall too ECtHR jurisprudence which holds that mere storage of personal data (albeit without consent or knowledge of the data subject) can constitute an interference with the right(s) under ECHR Article 8(1) even if there is no evidence that the data was used to the practical detriment of the data subject or even at all.[66]

---

[59] FTC, 'Protecting Consumer Privacy in an Era of Rapid Change: Recommendations for Businesses and Policymakers' (March 2012); available at: <http://ftc.gov/os/2012/03/120326privacyreport-pdf>.

[60] FTC, 'Protecting Consumer Privacy' (n 59).

[61] AL Newman, *Protectors of Privacy: Regulating Personal Data in the Global Economy* (Cornell University Press 2008) 54.

[62] J Guynn and M Lifsher, 'Silicon Valley uses growing clout to kill a digital privacy bill', *Los Angeles Times*, 3 May 2013, <http://articles.latimes.com/2013/may/03/business/la-fi-digital-privacy-20130503>.

[63] Regan (n 57) 51.      [64] 131 S Ct 2653 (2011).

[65] See esp. DPD Arts 7 and 8 dealt with in Ch 5 (sections C and D).

[66] *Amann v Switzerland* (2000) 30 EHRR 843 [69].

## 3. Explanations for transatlantic divergence

The aetiology of these transatlantic differences is complex. The relative laxity of US legislative safeguards, particularly regarding the private sector, reflects multiple factors. One set of factors are ideological. Americans tend to see privacy as important primarily in ensuring freedom from government intrusion. In Whitman's words, American concern for privacy centres upon 'the right to freedom from intrusions by the state, especially in one's own home'.[67] This is part and parcel of Americans' general constitutional vision, which focuses on 'the limits of government, reflecting the original American republican revolution, and securing a basis for the pursuit of liberty and happiness'.[68] Americans tend also to view privacy as an interest that is mainly, if not exclusively, valuable for individual persons *qua* individuals, and therefore often in tension with the needs of wider society.[69]

In much of Europe, however, protection of privacy tends to be intimately tied to protection of dignity and honour.[70] It is also often perceived as valuable not just for individual persons but society generally, particularly for maintaining civility, pluralism, and democracy.[71]

Lindsay neatly sums up the contrasting ideologies as follows:

On the one hand, the American approach takes autonomous individuals as given, and conceives the role of the law as one of setting limits on government in order to secure pre-existing individual autonomy. On the other hand, the European approach regards individual autonomy as being only fully realised in society, and conceives an important role for the law in creating the conditions for autonomous individuals as participating members of a community.[72]

Lindsay further portrays the division between the US and European approaches in this area as reflecting a tension between 'consequentialist', harms-focused ideology that is closely aligned with utilitarian thinking (the US approach), and a 'deontological' ideology that is grounded in the thought

---

[67] JQ Whitman, 'The Two Western Cultures of Privacy: Dignity versus Liberty' (2004) 113 Yale LJ 1151, 1161.

[68] EJ Eberle, *Dignity and Liberty. Constitutional Visions in Germany and the United States* (Praeger 2002) 257.

[69] See generally PM Regan, *Legislating Privacy: Technology, Social Values, and Public Policy* (University of North Carolina Press 1995) chs 2, 8.

[70] See generally Eberle (n 68); Whitman (n 67).

[71] See Bygrave (n 3) ch 7 and references cited therein.

[72] D Lindsay, 'An Exploration of the Conceptual Basis of Privacy and the Implications for the Future of Australian Privacy Law' (2005) 29 Melbourne University L Rev 131, 169.

of Kant and emphasizes respect for persons as morally autonomous beings (the European approach).[73]

Going beyond ideology, a strong case can be made that the relative laxity of US data privacy rules is partly symptomatic of the paucity of first-hand domestic experience of totalitarian oppression in the USA (at least for the bulk of 'white society'), particularly given the strength of consequentialist ideology there. On the other side, the traumas from first-hand experience of such oppression in large parts of Europe have imparted to European regulatory policy an anxiety and gravity that is considerably more subdued in US policy. Lindsay too emphasizes the importance of first-hand experience of totalitarianism in explaining the European approach to data privacy:

The European experience of mid-20th century totalitarianism resulted in a deep suspicion of any attempts by centralised authorities to increase their capacity for surveillance of individuals. Moreover, the activities of the secret police in the totalitarian regimes of Eastern Europe and the Soviet Union, which focused on monitoring individuals and collecting personal information in extensive (and often inaccurate) filing systems, provided a continuing example of the repressive use of information management techniques. European data protection law is part of the broader European project of building institutions and practices, including the EU itself, which are intended to ensure that the horrors of European totalitarianism are not revisited.[74]

Newman, however, downplays the purchase of the 'fascist legacy' argument in explaining the rise of comprehensive data privacy laws in Europe and the absence of such laws in the USA. He highlights a lack of empirical correlation between the fascist legacy of a nation state and the form of its subsequent data privacy regime. For example, he correctly points to the fact that Italy and Spain were slow to adopt comprehensive data privacy legislation. Nonetheless, he recognizes that 'the Nazi experience sensitized the advanced industrial societies on both sides of the Atlantic to the potential of government abuse'.[75] I would go further and claim that this sensitization was generally greater on the European than the US side.

Care must be taken not to cast transatlantic divergence in this area along clear-cut lines in which US legal protections for data privacy are presented as being uniformly weaker than those of Europe. For instance, while the USA has federal legislation requiring providers of public electronic communications networks to preserve, in particular cases, electronic traffic data that they have

---

[73] See too, inter alia, PM Schwartz, 'The Computer in German and American Constitutional Law: Towards an American Right of Informational Self-Determination' (1989) 37 The American Journal of Comparative Law 675.

[74] Lindsay (n 72) 157–8.        [75] Newman (n 61) 54.

already recorded,[76] it has not (yet) passed legislation that generally requires, in the manner of the EU Data Retention Directive,[77] network providers to record and store traffic data for a particular period of time independent of a specific court order or warrant.

To take another example, data on personal income is publicly available as a matter of course in some Nordic countries (for example, Norway). Such a disclosure practice is unthinkable in the USA (and, indeed, in many other parts of Europe).

A third example concerns security breach notification. In 2002, California was the first jurisdiction in the world to enact legislation requiring notification of security breaches involving personal information.[78] Most US states have since enacted similar rules, although their notification criteria vary.[79] Under EU law, mandatory notification requirements (inspired by the Californian rules) have only been imposed on providers of public electronic communications networks, pursuant to amendments to the E-Privacy Directive in 2009. The European Commission's GDPR proposal, though, provides for more general application of such requirements (Articles 31–32).

A fourth example concerns sanctions. For certain types of privacy-invasive conduct, the US regime imposes higher and more wide-ranging penalties than are typical under European regimes. The principal enforcement body in this respect is the FTC which regulates unfair trade practices under section 5 of the Federal Trade Commission Act 1914.[80] Section 5 prohibits 'unfair methods of competition in or affecting commerce, and unfair or deceptive acts or practices in or affecting commerce'. This provision is usually applied in cases where a company fails to comply with the public representations it makes in its privacy policy. Application of the provision may also be triggered when a company fails to institute adequate data security measures. Breach of section 5 may result in imposition of sanctions that are extraordinary or unavailable under European regimes. For instance, upon finding Facebook and Google to have engaged in deceptive processing of personal data, the FTC entered into settlement agreements with each company in 2011, requiring them, inter

---

[76] See Stored Communications Act, enacted as part of the Electronic Communications Privacy Act 1986 and codified at 18 USC s 2701-11; see esp. s 2703(f).

[77] See Ch 2 (section E(2)).

[78] Codified in Californian Civil Code ss 1798.82 and 1798.29.

[79] See further National Conference of State Legislatures, 'State Security Breach Notification Laws', 20 August 2012; available at: <http://www.ncsl.org/issues-research/telecom/security-breach-notification-laws.aspx>.

[80] Codified at 15 USC §§ 41–48. Note, however, that the FTC's jurisdiction under the Act is limited in some respects. For example, it does not have competence in relation to the telecommunications or financial services sectors.

alia, to set up a comprehensive programme to address privacy risks associated with new and existing products and services, and to undergo biannual independent auditing for 20 years with a view to certifying their compliance with the FTC orders.[81] In August 2012, the FTC fined Google a record US$ 22.5 million for violating the terms of the settlement.[82]

The Obama Administration recently announced some important new policy goals on data privacy. In February 2012, it released a report setting out a comprehensive data privacy framework targeted at commercial use of personal data.[83] The initiative is basically aimed at promoting a more consistent regulatory response to data privacy concerns in the USA, particularly regarding provision and use of 'networked technologies'. Another stated aim of the initiative is to improve the 'interoperability' of the US data privacy regime with the equivalent regimes of other countries.

The heart of the framework is a Consumer Privacy Bill of Rights incorporating a new set of 'fair information practice principles' (FIPPs) to govern private-sector handling of personal data in commercial contexts.[84] The FIPPs have been crafted with the Internet environment in mind—an environment 'in which processing of data about individuals is far more decentralized and pervasive than it was when FIPPs were initially developed'.[85] Thus, the FIPPs differ in some respects from previous US elaborations of such principles. Especially noteworthy is a new principle entitled 'respect for context': '[c]onsumers have a right to expect that companies will collect, use, and disclose personal data in ways that are consistent with the context in which consumers provide the data'. According to the Obama Administration, '[c]ontext should shape the balance and relative emphasis of particular principles in the Consumer Privacy Bill of Rights'.[86]

The privacy framework is envisaged as being implemented primarily through sector-specific codes of conduct. At the same time, the Obama Administration states that it will work with Congress to transpose the FIPPs into legislation applicable to sectors not currently covered by Federal statutes.

[81] Agreement Containing Consent Order, In the Matter of Facebook Inc, FTC File No. 092-3184 (November 2011; finalized August 2012); Agreement Containing Consent Order, In the Matter of Google Inc, FTC File No. 102-3136 (October 2011; finalized August 2012).

[82] FTC Press Release, 'Google Will Pay $22.5 Million to Settle FTC Charges it Misrepresented Privacy Assurances to Users of Apple's Safari Internet Browser', 9 August 2012; available at: <http://www.ftc.gov/opa/2012/08/google.shtm>.

[83] The White House, *Consumer Data Privacy in a Networked World: A Framework for Protecting Privacy and Promoting Innovation in the Global Digital Economy* (US Government Printing Office 2012).

[84] The White House (n 83) appendix A.     [85] The White House (n 83) 9.

[86] The White House (n 83) 10.

It also wants to empower the FTC (and State Attorneys General) to enforce the FIPPs.[87] These legislative ambitions align the framework closer to the European regulatory approach. Yet as indicated earlier in this section, their realization faces a tough uphill domestic battle.

The FIPPs are less stringent than their European equivalents in some respects. For example, their emphasis on 'context' arguably permits greater repurposing of data than the purpose limitation principle permits under the DPD.[88] The framework does not impose restrictions on TBDF, nor does it establish a DPA. The Obama Administration goes out of its way to laud the benefits of pursuing a distinctly American approach to data privacy regulation which is putatively flexible, anchored in bottom-up multi-stakeholder dialogue, and conducive to business innovation. Right-wing commentators nonetheless criticize the framework for being tainted by European-style dirigiste thinking. Their criticism also alleges that the framework will detrimentally affect the competitiveness of the US Internet industry and increase consumer prices for Internet-based services.[89] On the other hand, data privacy advocates offer only lukewarm support for the framework on account of its failure to stipulate data privacy safeguards that meet international (European) standards.[90]

---

[87] The White House (n 83) ch VI.          [88] See further Ch 5 (section E).

[89] See eg, A Thierer, 'The Problem with Obama's "Let's Be More like Europe" Privacy Plan', *Forbes*, 23 February 2012; available at: <http://www.forbes.com/sites/adamthierer/2012/02/23/the-problem-with-obamas-lets-be-more-like-europe-privacy-plan/>.

[90] G Greenleaf and N Waters, 'Obama's Privacy Framework: An Offer to Be Left on the Table?' (2012) Privacy Laws & Business Intl Report, No. 119, 6.

# 4

# Aims and Scope of Data Privacy Law

## A. Introduction

The preceding chapters depict privacy protection as one of the primary formal aims of data privacy law. They further highlight that, in many jurisdictions, this remit is regarded as part of a broader endeavour to secure privacy as a basic human right. As for the scope of data privacy law, the preceding chapters depict this as essentially limited to the processing of personal data—that is, data that can be linked to identifiable individual natural/physical persons—with additional limits being imposed with respect to various sectors of activity. While correct, this depiction of the aims and scope of data privacy law is simplistic. The purpose of this chapter is to provide a more nuanced picture that does justice to the field's complexity.

## B. Aims

### 1. Obscurity of aims

Data privacy law has long been afflicted by absence of clarity over its aims and conceptual foundation. In the early 1990s, Napier noted that, in the UK, 'the conceptual basis for data protection laws remains unclear'.[1] Towards the end of the 1990s, Korff observed 'a lack of clarity, of focus, over the very nature, aims and objects of data protection in the [EU] Member States which is, not surprisingly, reflected in the international data protection instruments'.[2] A similar observation has been made for Australian law, with Lindsay writing in

---

[1] BW Napier, 'International Data Protection Standards and British Experience' (1992) *Informatica e diritto*, no. 1–2, 83, 85.

[2] D Korff, *Study on the Protection of the Rights and Interests of Legal Persons with regard to the Processing of Personal Data relating to such Persons*, final report to European Commission (October 1998) 42; available at: <http://papers.ssrn.com/sol3/papers.cfm?abstract_id=1288583>.

2005 that 'the conceptual underpinnings of Australia's information privacy laws have not been clearly enunciated'.[3]

The obscurity is reflected in the absence in some data privacy statutes of objects clauses formally specifying the interest(s) that the legislation is intended to serve. This is the case, for instance, with the legislation of Denmark and the UK,[4] and with the first legislation passed by Sweden, Norway, and Iceland.[5]

## 2. Formal aims

Despite obscurity of aims, privacy protection figures prominently in the objects clauses or titles of many data privacy laws. For instance, Australian, Canadian, NZ, and US statutes enacted at the federal/national level all bear the title 'Privacy Act' and set down the safeguarding of privacy as one of their basic objects.[6] The equivalent statutes of several European countries also expressly point to privacy as a fundamental interest to be protected.[7] Other statutes in the field omit explicit reference to the safeguarding of privacy, but refer to closely related interests, such as protection of 'personality',[8] or protection of 'personal integrity'.[9]

---

[3] D Lindsay, 'An Exploration of the Conceptual Basis of Privacy and the Implications for the Future of Australian Privacy Law' (2005) 29 Melbourne University L Rev 131, 133.

[4] For Denmark, see Personal Data Act 2000 (*Lov nr 429 af 31 maj 2000 om behandling af personoplysninger*). Denmark's previous legislation in the field also lacked an objects clause: see the Private Registers Act 1978 (*Lov nr 293 af 8 juni 1978 om private registre mv*) and the Public Authorities' Registers Act 1978 (*Lov nr 294 af 8 juni 1978 om offentlige myndigheders registre*). For the UK, see Data Protection Act 1998 and its predecessor (Data Protection Act 1984; repealed).

[5] For Sweden, see Data Act 1973 (*Datalagen* (SFS 1973:289)), repealed. For Iceland, see Protection of Personal Records Act 1989 (*Lög nr 121 28 desember 1989 um skráningu og meðferð persónuupplýsinga*), repealed. For Norway, see Personal Data Registers Act 1978 (*Lov om personregistre mm 9 juni 1978 nr 48*)(PDRA), repealed. Nonetheless, some of this legislation gave indications of the interests it served by way of other provisions. Sweden's Data Act stipulated that creation of personal files was only permitted if it did not unduly encroach upon the 'personal integrity' of registered persons (s 3), while the preparatory works for Norway's PDRA described the legislation as aimed at safeguarding 'personal integrity': Innstilling Odelsting [Parliamentary Recommendation] no. 47 (1977–78) 1. In both of these cases, however, the notion of 'personal integrity' was not clearly defined.

[6] See preamble to Australia's federal Privacy Act 1988 and to NZ's Privacy Act 1993, Canada's Privacy Act 1982 s 2, and the US Privacy Act 1974 s 2(b).

[7] See eg, Belgium's 1992 Act Concerning the Protection of Personal Privacy in Relation to the Processing of Personal Data (*Wet van December 8, 1992 tot bescherming van de persoonlijke levensfeer ten opzichte van de verwerking van persoonsgegevens / Loi du 8 décembre 1992 relative à la protection de la vie privée à l'égard des traitements de données à caractère personnel*) Art. 2; and Portugal's Protection of Personal Data Act 1998 (*Lei no. 67/98 de 26 de Outubro 1998, da Protecção de Dados Pessoais*) Art. 2.

[8] The case with Swiss and German legislation: see Ch 1 (n 128).

[9] The case with current Swedish legislation: see Ch 1 (n 130).

However, privacy and these related interests are never directly defined in the laws that explicitly refer to them. This undoubtedly reflects the notorious difficulties that have plagued attempts to give the concepts delineating these interests a precise, analytically serviceable, and generally accepted meaning. This lack of definition is not necessarily a weakness. It can provide room for flexibility in the implementation of data privacy law. It can enable such law to address a broad range of fears related to increasingly intrusive data-processing practices. Moreover, privacy advocates have probably found it useful to adopt, in the words of Freund, 'a large concept in order to offset an equally large rhetorical counter-claim: freedom of inquiry, the right to know, liberty of the press' and so on.[10] Nonetheless, the failure to define privacy and related interests in data privacy laws detracts from the capacity of these laws for prescriptive guidance. It also perpetuates the lack of clarity over these laws' conceptual basis. And, more generally, it perpetuates the vulnerability of the privacy concept to criticisms that it is incapable of definition, has no independent, coherent meaning, and should be subsumed by other concepts.[11]

While privacy does occupy a central place in data privacy law, it is not the sole concern of such law. Legislation on data privacy serves a multiplicity of interests, which in some cases extend well beyond traditional conceptualizations of privacy. This is sometimes manifest in the broad wording of the laws' objects clauses. Convention 108 Article 1, for example, stipulates as its principal object

to secure in the territory of each Party for every individual, whatever his nationality or residence, respect for his rights and fundamental freedoms, and in particular his right to privacy, with regard to automatic processing of personal data relating to him ('data protection').

Similarly, the objects clause of the French legislation provides:

Information technology should be at the service of every citizen. Its development shall take place in the context of international co-operation. It shall not violate human identity, human rights, privacy, or individual or public liberties.[12]

These sorts of goal formulations provide the laws with an extremely large register of interests upon which their formal rationale may be grounded. Yet even those laws with objects clauses or titles referring simply to the safeguarding of privacy must be viewed as being concerned with more than such protection. The safeguarding of privacy serves a large range of other interests,

---

[10] PA Freund, 'Privacy: One Concept or Many' in JR Pennock and JW Chapman (eds), *Privacy: Nomos XIII* (Atherton Press 1971) 182, 193.

[11] Such criticisms are advanced in eg, JJ Thomson, 'The Right to Privacy' (1975) 4 Philosophy and Public Affairs 295.

[12] See Act on Information Technology, Data Files and Civil Liberties 1978 Art. 1.

which must accordingly form part of the rationale and agenda of data privacy law. Important examples are personal autonomy, integrity, and dignity. These interests have been summed up as being largely concerned with 'achieving individual goals of self-realization'.[13] However, such interests, like privacy, are not only relevant to the well-being of individual persons; they have a broader societal significance as well. Their protection helps to constitute a society infused with the values of civility, stability, pluralism, and democracy.[14] Realization of these general societal values must, therefore, also be recognized and treated as an integral part of data privacy law.

At the same time, data privacy laws are expressly concerned with setting standards for the quality of personal data. Indeed, Norway's principal legislation on data privacy contains an objects clause specifically referring to the need for 'adequate quality of personal information' ('tilstrekkelig kvalitet på personopplysninger') in addition to the needs for privacy and personal integrity.[15] While adequate data quality can serve to secure the privacy of individuals, it breaks down into a multiplicity of interests (including concern for, inter alia, the validity, integrity, availability, relevance, and completeness of data) that have little *direct* connection to privacy-related values.[16]

A handful of data privacy laws have gone so far as to show express concern for safeguarding interests directly related to the state. A case in point is Finland's first data privacy law: its purposes were stipulated as being 'to protect the privacy, interests and rights of the person, to ensure the security of the State and to maintain good data file practice'.[17] The data privacy laws of some of the German *Länder* provide other cases in point. One aim of these laws is to maintain state order based on the principle of separation of powers. The Hessian Data Protection Act 1999,[18] for example, sets down as one of its purposes:

to safeguard the constitutional structure of the State, in particular the relationship between the constitutional organs of the *Land* and those of local government, based on the principle of separation of powers, against all risks entailed by automatic data processing (section 1(2)).[19]

---

[13] AF Westin, *Privacy and Freedom* (Atheneum 1967) 39.

[14] See further LA Bygrave, *Data Protection Law: Approaching Its Rationale, Logic and Limits* (Kluwer Law International 2002) ch 7 (sections 7.2.2, 7.2.5).

[15] Personal Data Act 2000 (*Lov om behandling av personopplysninger av 14 april 2000 nr 31*) § 1(2).

[16] For an elaboration of these interests, see Bygrave (n 14) ch 7 (section 7.2.5).

[17] Personal Data Registers Act 1987 s 1. The reference to protecting the interests of the State was dropped from the objects clause of the Finnish Personal Data Act 1999 which replaced the 1987 legislation.

[18] *Hessisches Datenschutzgesetz vom 7 January 1999*.

[19] The German text reads: 'das auf dem Grundsatz der Gewaltenteilung beruhende verfassungsmäßige Gefüge des Staates, insbesondere der Verfassungsorgane des Landes und der Organe

This declaration is followed up by provisions aimed at maintaining what Simitis terms an 'Informationsgleichgewicht' ('informational equilibrium') between the legislature and other state organs in Hesse.[20] This 'equilibrium' refers principally to a situation in which the legislature is able to get access to information (personal or non-personal) that is available to the executive.[21] Similar provisions are found in the data protection statutes of Rhineland-Palatinate, Berlin and, to a lesser extent, Thuringia.[22]

As shown in Chapter 2, a major formal aim of the principal *international* data privacy instruments is to stimulate the creation of adequate national regimes and to prevent divergence between them. This harmonization is not just to strengthen data privacy but to minimize disruption to the flow of personal data across national borders and thereby safeguard the interests that profit from such flow.

## 3. Less formal aims

### (a) Serving controller interests

Data privacy law also serves less formal aims. By 'less formal' is meant that the aim does not figure in an objects clause but appears more obliquely, even though it is sometimes expressly referenced in other provisions of the legislation or in the relevant preparatory works. The main such aim of data privacy law is to uphold the legitimate data-processing interests of controllers. This concern is manifest in various ways, most clearly in provisions permitting derogation from core data privacy principles,[23] or in provisions specifying the considerations that DPAs must take into account when carrying out their functions generally[24] or when exercising their discretionary powers in specific

der kommunalen Selbstverwaltung untereinander und zueinander, vor einer Gefährdung infolge der automatisierten Datenverarbeitung zu bewahren'.

[20] See ss 24(2), 38, and 39. This concern has also been present in the earlier data protection legislation of Hesse.

[21] See further S Simitis, 'Einleitung' in S Simitis (ed), *Bundesdatenschutzgesetz* (7th edn, Nomos 2011) 84–5.

[22] For Rhineland-Palatinate, see *Landesdatenschutzgesetz vom 5 Juli 1994*, ss 1(2), 24(6), 36. For Berlin, see *Datenschutzgesetz vom Dezember 17, 1990* ss 1(1)(2), 20, 24(3). For Thuringia, see *Datenschutzgesetz vom 29 Oktober 1991* s 40(5). Similar provisions were also included in the early data protection statutes of Bremen (see *Gesetz zum Schutz vor Misbrauch personbezogener Daten bei der Datenverarbeitung vom Dezember 19, 1977*) and Lower Saxony (see *Datenschutzgesetz vom 17 Juni 1993*) but have since been taken out.

[23] See eg, DPD Art. 13 (permitting derogation from central obligations and rights in the Directive insofar as is necessary to safeguard, inter alia, 'national security', 'defence', or 'public security').

[24] See eg, Australia's federal Privacy Act s 29(a) (stating that, in carrying out his or her functions, the Privacy Commissioner is to 'have due regard for the protection of important human rights and interests that compete with privacy, including the general desirability of a free flow of information and the recognition of the right of government and business to achieve their objectives in an efficient way').

contexts.[25] More subtle manifestation of this concern occurs in the very fact that data privacy legislation tends to operate with largely procedural rules that avoid fundamentally challenging the bulk of established patterns of information use. In the language of road signs, it usually posts the warning 'Proceed with Care!'; it rarely orders 'Stop!'.

Further, data privacy law tends to manage these patterns of information use in a manner that makes them more palatable to (and, hence, legitimate from the perspective of) the general populace.[26] Extending this point, data privacy law has much the same aim and function that policies of 'sustainable development' have in the field of environmental protection. Just as the latter policies seek to preserve the natural environment at the same time as they allow for economic growth, data privacy law seeks to safeguard the privacy-related interests of data subjects at the same time as it secures the legitimate interests of controllers in processing personal data. Both strategies promote a belief that the potential for conflict between these respective sets of interests can be significantly reduced through appropriate management strategies. Concomitantly, both strategies can be used to create an impression that the interests of data subjects and the natural environment are adequately secured, even when their respective counter-interests are also secured.

In some jurisdictions, enactment of data privacy legislation has been closely connected with a wish to create public acceptance for new or existing information systems. This is the case with Australia's federal Privacy Act which was enacted partly from the federal government's desire to win support for a proposed national PIN scheme aimed largely at reducing fraud of the income-tax system and welfare programmes.[27] Similarly, enactment of NZ's Privacy Act was closely connected with the government's desire to create acceptance for data-matching operations aimed at combating abuse of government services.[28] A third example is the DPD, which was adopted partly in order to engender public confidence in using new systems of electronic commerce.[29]

---

[25] See eg, Norway's Personal Data Act s 34 (providing that when the Data Inspectorate assesses an application for a license to process personal data, consideration shall be given to whether or not problems which are caused for the individual person by the proposed processing and which cannot be solved satisfactorily by rules prescribed under other parts of the Act, 'are outweighed by *such considerations as favour* the processing' (emphasis added)).
[26] See further J Rule, D McAdam, L Stearns, and D Uglow, *The Politics of Privacy: Planning for Personal Data Systems as Powerful Technologies* (Elsevier 1980) 71ff.
[27] See Bygrave (n 14) 138 and references cited therein.
[28] See E Longworth and T McBride, *The Privacy Act: A Guide* (GP Publications 1994) 19ff and references cited therein.
[29] See eg, European Commission press release of 25 July 1995 (IP/95/822) accompanying adoption of the DPD (citing comments by then Commissioner Mario Monti to the effect that '[t]he

Thus, while concern for privacy and related interests has been uppermost in the minds of citizens when they have clamoured for the introduction of data privacy laws, this concern has not necessarily been shared to the same degree by the legislators. The latter have been mainly interested in finding a balance between citizens' concerns as data subjects and the data-processing interests of controllers (especially government agencies). Legislators' concern for citizens' privacy was perhaps greatest in the early years of legislating in the field. From the late 1970s, this concern increasingly lost ground to other, predominantly economic, concerns.

A principal instance of the latter relates to transborder data flow (TBDF). As shown in Chapter 2, much of the impulse behind the main international data privacy initiatives has stemmed from a wish to harmonize national data privacy laws in order to maintain the flow of data across borders. And national legislators have frequently passed data privacy laws in order to avoid restrictions on the flow of data into their respective countries being imposed pursuant to the data privacy laws of other countries. At the same time, they have been pressured to provide for the same sorts of restrictions under their own laws, in order to meet the adequacy requirements of the other countries' laws.

### (b) Economic protectionism?

Allegations have been made that the restrictions imposed on TBDF are motivated by economic protectionism. These allegations came largely from North American quarters during the late 1970s and early 1980s and were directed at the then newly enacted data privacy legislation of European countries. This legislation, it was alleged, was grounded in a desire to protect the nascent, European ICT industries from foreign (US) competition.[30] Such allegations reflected unease, especially on the part of US trade representatives, that the legislation had been introduced too quickly, without adequate discussion of its economic consequences, and would hinder the international growth of the ICT industry, which was—and remains—dominated by American firms.[31] Criticism focused not just upon the European laws' restrictions on TBDF but also on the

---

Directive will...help to ensure the free flow of Information Society services in the Single Market by fostering consumer confidence').

[30] See eg, KR Pinegar, 'Privacy Protection Acts: Privacy Protectionism or Economic Protectionism?' (1984) 12 Intl Business Lawyer 183; Office of the US Special Trade Representative, 'Trade Barriers to Telecommunications, Data and Information Services' (1981) 4 Transnational Data Report, no. 5, 53; GS Grossman, 'Transborder Data Flow: Separating the Privacy Interests of Individuals and Corporations' (1982) 4 Northwestern J of Intl Law and Business 1; RP McGuire, 'The Information Age: An Introduction to Transborder Data Flow' (1979–80) 20 Jurimetrics J 1.

[31] See generally DP Farnsworth, 'Data Privacy: An American's View of European Legislation' (1983) 6 Transnational Data Report, no. 5, 285.

fact that some of them protect(ed) data on legal persons in addition to data on individuals.[32] It was claimed that, because of this fact, these laws could not have been passed simply in order to protect the right of privacy; they must also have been passed for the purpose of economic protectionism.[33]

The latter claim rests upon two assumptions: (i) that the purpose of 'pure' data privacy laws is only to safeguard privacy; and (ii) that privacy as a concept and legal right can only embrace natural/physical persons. Both assumptions are highly questionable.[34] There is also little if any solid evidence to suggest that economic protectionism motivated the protection of legal person data.[35]

The same can be said for evidence in support of the allegation that TBDF restrictions have been grounded in economic protectionism. The preparatory works for the Norwegian Personal Data Registers Act, for instance, make no mention of the need to protect Norwegian industry from foreign competition,[36] and empirical studies have failed to find evidence of the Act's regulation of TBDF being practised in a protectionist manner. The same applies with respect to TBDF regulation pursuant to the first data privacy laws of Germany, Austria, Sweden, France, and the UK.[37] A recent study cites evidence documenting that in the 1970s, protection of 'informational sovereignty' was at least discussed as a concern in Sweden and put into practice by Brazil when the latter was ruled by a military government.[38] However, Brazil's regulation of TBDF was not carried out pursuant to data privacy

---

[32] Further on the protection of legal person data, see section C(3).

[33] Pinegar (n 30) 188; Grossman (n 30) 12, 20; McGuire (n 30) 4.

[34] See generally Bygrave (n 14) chs 12, 16.          [35] Bygrave (n 14) ch 9.

[36] See the discussion on regulating transborder data flows in Odelstingsproposisjon (Government Bill) 2 (1977–78) 9–10, 96. See also H Seip, 'Unfair Competition in Computer Services?' (1981) 4 Transnational Data Report, no. 8, 33.

[37] See R Ellger, *Der Datenschutz im grenzüberschreitende Datenverkehr: eine rechtsvergleichende und kollisionsrechtliche Untersuchung* (Nomos 1990) 428–30 (concluding on the basis of an in-depth examination of the data privacy regimes of Austria, Sweden, Denmark, Norway, France, the Federal Republic of Germany, and the UK that, at least up until 1990, no solid evidence exists that rules for restricting TBDF under these regimes operated as 'non-tariff trade barriers'). Ellger points out also (pp. 429 and 270) that only an extremely small percentage of cross-border transfers of personal data were stopped. The findings of an earlier, albeit narrower, study by Bing are in line with Ellger's findings: see J Bing, *Data Protection in Practice—International Service Bureaux and Transnational Data Flows*, CompLex 1/85 (Universitetsforlaget 1985). However, the rules in Denmark's Private Registers Act on TBDF were not concerned solely with protection of individual persons; they were also grounded upon a desire to build up a national computer industry, such that public or private enterprise in Denmark could continue to operate independently of events in other countries: see P Blume, *Personregistrering* (3rd edn, Akademisk 1996) 129 and references cited therein. Nevertheless, the latter concern apparently did not reflect a desire for economic protectionism as such but a desire to ensure that enterprises in the country could continue functioning in the event of a foreign crisis.

[38] C Kuner, *Transborder Data Flows and Data Privacy Law* (OUP 2013) 28–30.

law. It is also difficult to link the Swedish discussion on this point with the provision for TBDF restrictions under Sweden's Data Act. And the concern to safeguard 'informational sovereignty' appears not have been fully commensurate with economic protectionism but to have embraced general vulnerability issues arising as a result of a country becoming overly reliant on foreign data-processing services.

While the protectionism theory lacks firm credibility in relation to national data privacy laws passed in Europe in the 1970s and 1980s, it is perhaps less easily refuted with respect to the DPD. As noted in Chapter 2, the European Commission, together with the Council of Ministers, first took up the issue of data privacy largely out of concern for fostering development of the internal market and European IT industry.[39] Traces of such a concern appear also in the Commission Communication setting out the first proposal for the DPD.[40] Yet to what extent this concern accurately reflects a desire for economic protectionism is unclear. Equally unclear is the extent to which final adoption of the Directive took place in order to fulfil such a desire. Nevertheless, implementation of the Directive—particularly Articles 25 and 26—could have incidental protectionist benefits for data controllers established within the EU.

In the current era of cloud computing in which personal data from one country is increasingly stored on servers in another country, concerns about 'informational sovereignty' are likely to rise to the fore. As Kuner states:

The ever-increasing globalisation of data processing may cause a counter-reaction and motivate States to assert their sovereignty interests in data processing and transborder data flow regulation more aggressively, both because of privacy concerns and for economic reasons.[41]

The recent revelations about the US National Security Agency's large-scale tapping of personal data from US-based online services appear to be reinforcing such motivations.[42]

---

[39] See generally WJ Kirsch, 'The Protection of Privacy and Transborder Flows of Personal Data: The Work of the Council of Europe, the Organization for Economic Co-operation and Development and the European Economic Community' (1982) Legal Issues of European Integration, no. 2, 21, 34–7; H Geiger, 'Europäischer Informationsmarkt und Datenschutz' (1989) 5 Recht der Datenverarbeitung, no. 5/6, 203.

[40] See COM(90) 314 final 4.　　[41] Kuner (n 38) 31.

[42] See eg, 'Boom Triggered by NSA: German Email Services Report Surge in Demand', *Der Spiegel*, 26 August 2013; available at: <http://www.spiegel.de/international/germany/growing-demand-for-german-email-providers-after-nsa-scandal-a-918651.html>; B Brooks and F Bajak, 'Brazil Looks to Break from US-centric Internet', *SFGate*, 18 September 2013; available at <http://www.sfgate.com/news/world/article/Brazil-looks-to-break-from-US-centric-Internet-4819946.php>.

## C. Scope

### 1. Scope with regard to data

Data privacy law applies to certain kinds of data and information which can be linked to persons. Exactly what is meant by 'data' or 'information' has usually been taken for granted in the regulatory discourse. Most attention has been directed instead to the nature of the link between data or information and persons—the subject of the next section (C(2)). However, elucidation of the meaning of data and information is increasingly necessary. This is due to technological developments that are challenging the feasibility of maintaining a logical boundary between data/information and the physical material that constitutes its medium. The challenge is most evident in our increasing capacity to derive myriad types of information from biological material. Advances in genetic testing are one example of this capability.[43] Growth in deployment of biometrics (that is, systems for determining or verifying the identity of persons based on their bodily characteristics)[44] is another. As biological material is increasingly mined for information, justifying a distinction between the former and the latter—that is between the medium and the message—becomes more difficult.

Not surprisingly, discussion over the meaning of data and information for the purposes of data privacy law has arisen precisely in relation to biological material. The question is whether the terms 'personal data' and 'personal information' in data privacy law may extend to human biological material per se (for example, blood cells as opposed to any data or information that can otherwise be derived from the cells).[45] Most data privacy legislation fails on its face to provide a definite answer to the question.[46] It simply defines 'personal data' or 'personal information' as data or information which can be linked, directly or indirectly, to identifiable individual persons.[47] To be sure,

---

[43] See generally FS Collins, *The Language of Life: DNA and the Revolution in Personalized Medicine* (HarperCollins 2010).

[44] See generally N Liu, *Bio-Privacy: Privacy Regulations and the Challenge of Biometrics* (Routledge 2011) ch 2.

[45] The issue is explored at length in LA Bygrave, 'The Body as Data? Biobank Regulation via the "Back Door" of Data Protection Law' (2010) 2 Law, Innovation and Technology 1.

[46] An exception is the legislation of the Australian state of New South Wales which defines 'personal information' as encompassing 'such things as an individual's fingerprints, retina prints, *body samples* or genetic characteristics' (emphasis added): see Privacy and Personal Information Protection Act 1998 s 4(2), Health Records and Information Privacy Act 2002 s 5(2), and Government Information (Open Access) Act 2009 schedule 4 clause 4(2).

[47] See section C(2).

the legislators have generally intended to give these terms a broad ambit and to draft the legal provisions in a largely technology-neutral way. The preparatory works for the DPD are a case in point.[48] Yet they fail to conclusively indicate that the term 'personal data' in the Directive is intended to embrace human biological material as such.[49] The same can be said for many other data privacy laws and their preparatory works.

Scholars, lawmakers, and other policy entrepreneurs diverge considerably in their respective stances on the matter.[50] Many of those who take the view that biological material does not constitute data or information ground their stance in conceptual logic. They claim that data comprise a formalized representation of some entity (object, process, etc.) which is intended to communicate information about that entity, while information comprises a cognitive element involving comprehension of the representation. This conception of data and information is fairly common in the field of informatics.[51] It is also embraced by the International Organization for Standardization (ISO).[52] On the basis of this conception, biological material as such cannot be treated as information and its treatment as data is doubtful.[53] In Norway, this line of thinking has led the Data Privacy Tribunal (Personvernnemnda) to reject a claim by the DPA (the Data Inspectorate; Datatilsynet) that Norway's Personal Data Act covers blood samples as such.[54] The A29WP appears to take a similar line.[55]

---

[48] See eg, Amended proposal for a Council Directive on the protection of individuals with regard to the processing of personal data and the free movement of such data (COM(92) 422 final—SYN 287) 9.

[49] See further Bygrave (n 45) 14–15 and references cited therein.

[50] See generally D Beyleveld, D Townend, S Rouillé-Mirza, and J Wright (eds), *Implementation of the Data Protection Directive in Relation to Medical Research in Europe* (Ashgate 2004); Bygrave (n 45) 16–20.

[51] See eg, L Floridi, *Information: A Very Short Introduction* (OUP 2010) 20–21; P Rob and C Coronel, *Database Systems: Design, Implementation, and Management* (8th edn, Thomson 2009) 5–6; C Avgerou and T Cornford, *Developing Information Systems: Concepts, Issues and Practice* (2nd edn, Macmillan 1998) 115.

[52] See ISO 2382-1, *Information Technology—Vocabulary—Part 1: Fundamental Terms* (1993) (defining 'data' as 'a representation of facts, concepts or instructions in a formalized manner suitable for communication, interpretation or processing by human beings or by automatic means'; and defining 'information' as 'the meaning assigned to data by means of conventions applied to that data'). See too CoE Convention on Cybercrime 2001 (opened for signature 23 November 2001; in force 1 July 2004; ETS 185) Art. 1(b) which builds on the ISO definition of 'data'.

[53] Bygrave (n 45) 15–17, 19–20.

[54] See appeal decision in case 8/2002; available at: <http://www.personvernnemnda.no/vedtak/2002_8.htm>; confirmed in appeal decision in case 1/2013, <http://www.personvernnemnda.no/vedtak/2013_01.htm>. The Tribunal is a quasi-judicial body charged with deciding appeals against decisions of the Data Inspectorate. Its decisions may be appealed to ordinary courts of law but are otherwise binding on the Inspectorate.

[55] A29WP, Opinion 4/2007 on the concept of personal data (20 June 2007; WP 136) 8.

Those pushing the view that biological material may be personal data or information tend to pay more regard to pragmatic considerations than conceptual logic. Chief amongst such considerations are the need to fill lacunae in biobank regulation, the growing ease with which persons can be identified from biological material, and the fact that such material is often only stored for the purpose of generating information.[56]

The conceptual barriers to treating biological material as data are not as profound as they appear. In the first place, if separated from its natural environment (more specifically, the body of which it is a part) and structured as a sample or set of samples with the intention of providing information, such material can function at the very least analogously to data in the above-described sense. This will typically be the case with biobanks.

We see manifestation of such a view in judicial pronouncements that human cellular samples are to be treated, in particular contexts, as personal data and subjected to the same legal safeguards as apply to the storage of data profiles of human DNA (deoxyribonucleic acid) and fingerprints. The pronouncements have come in litigation dealing with the legality of police agencies retaining DNA profiles, fingerprints, and cellular samples taken from persons who have been suspected but not convicted of legal offences. In the relevant UK litigation, Baroness Hale in the then House of Lords (now Supreme Court) stated that 'the only reason [the samples] . . . are taken or kept is for the information which they contain', that the samples therefore 'are kept as information . . . and nothing else', and that '[t]he same privacy principles should apply to' the samples as to the fingerprints and profiles.[57] In subsequent litigation of the same case, the ECtHR held that the samples (along with the DNA profiles and fingerprints) 'constitute personal data within the meaning of the Data Protection Convention [Convention 108] as they relate to identified or identifiable individuals'.[58] Independently of these pronouncements, academic commentary on particular national data privacy laws states that biological material may become personal data pursuant to the legislation concerned, from the time the material is isolated and structured for the purpose of generating information that facilitates identification of individuals.[59]

---

[56] For examples, see Bygrave (n 45) 16, 19, and references cited therein.

[57] *LS, R (on application of) v South Yorkshire Police (Consolidated Appeals)* [2004] UKHL 39, [2004] 1 WLR 2196 [70].

[58] *S and Marper v UK* (2009) 48 EHHR 50 [68]. Remarkably, the Court gave no further reason for its stance. For criticism, see Bygrave (n 45) 8–11.

[59] The case with the German Federal Data Protection Act, according to the most authoritative academic commentary on it: see U Dammann, '§3 Weitere Begriffsbestimmungen' in S Simitis (ed), *Bundesdatenschutzgesetz* (7th edn, Nomos 2011) 297, 302–3.

Such a stance, however, is far from universally embraced and the status of biological material under data privacy law remains unresolved in many jurisdictions. It is also important to remember that the ECtHR decision in *Marper* does not create legally binding precedent for interpretation of Convention 108. Nonetheless, it is a highly persuasive authority and creates pressure to apply the Convention to a range of activities that would fall outside the Convention's ambit were samples or other biological material not regarded as personal data. It also creates pressure to treat other 'lower-order' data privacy codes more directly as instruments of biobank regulation (or transform them into such) in the interest of maintaining regulatory consistency down the normative chain. However, such an extension will not necessarily sit happily with the respective history, rationale, and customary application of the lower-order instruments or enable their sensible application to biobanks.[60]

## 2. Scope with regard to type of data

Data privacy law generally applies solely to 'personal' data or information. Thus, when determining whether data privacy law applies to a given set of data, the first question one asks is whether the data is 'personal'. If the answer is negative, one can generally disregard data privacy law. So what exactly makes data or information 'personal' for the purposes of data privacy law?

Article 2(a) of Convention 108 along with paragraph 1(b) of the OECD Guidelines define 'personal data' as 'any information relating to an identified or identifiable individual'. A more elaborate definition is provided by DPD Article 2(a) which defines 'personal data' as

any information relating to an identified or identifiable natural person ('data subject'); an identifiable person is one who can be identified, directly or indirectly, in particular by reference to an identification number or to one or more factors specific to his physical, physiological, mental, economic, cultural or social identity.[61]

From these definitions, we can discern two cumulative conditions for data to be 'personal': first, the data must relate to or concern a person; secondly, the data must enable the identification of such a person. However, there is usually no prima facie requirement that the data relate to a particular (for example, private, intimate) sphere of a person's activity.[62] Hence, in most cases, it may not be appropriate to talk of two separate (although cumulative) conditions for making data 'personal'; the first condition can be embraced by the second,

---

[60] See further Bygrave (n 45) 11–12, 22–4.
[61] According to Recital 14, the definition encompasses sound and image data on natural persons.
[62] Although see the UK case law referenced in n 86.

in the sense that data will normally relate to, or concern, a person if it enables that person's identification. In other words, the basic criterion appearing in these definitions is that of identifiability—that is, the potential of data to enable identification of a person.

Six further issues are relevant for determining what is 'personal' data pursuant to data privacy laws:

(1) What exactly is meant by identification/identifiability?
(2) How easily or practicably must a person be identified from data in order for it to be regarded as 'personal'?
(3) Who is the legally relevant agent of identification (that is, the person who is to carry out identification)?
(4) To what extent must the link between a set of data and a person be objectively valid?
(5) To what extent is the use of auxiliary data or information permitted in the identification process? Can data be 'personal' if it allows a person to be identified only in combination with other (auxiliary) data or information?
(6) To what extent must data be linkable to just *one* person in order to be 'personal'?

These issues tend to be interrelated, the answer to one partly determining the answers to the others.

### (a)  Concept of identification/identifiability

The ability to identify a person is essentially the ability to distinguish that person from others by linking him or her to pre-collected information of some kind. As such, identification does not require knowledge of a person's name but it does require knowledge of some unique characteristics of the person relative to a set of other persons.[63]

### (b)  Ease of identification

The Explanatory Report for Convention 108 states that an 'identifiable person' pursuant to Article 2(a) of the Convention is one 'who can be *easily* identified: it does not cover identification of persons by means of *very sophisticated* methods'.[64] It is not clear if this statement should be read as introducing two separate criteria (ease and sophistication of methods) or just one (that

---

[63] See also the following commentary by the European Commission (COM(92) 422 final—SYN 287) 9: 'A person may be identified directly by name or indirectly by a telephone number, a car registration number, a social security number, a passport number or by a combination of significant criteria which allows him to be recognized by narrowing down the group to which he belongs (age, occupation, place of residence, etc)'.

[64] *Explanatory Report on the Convention for the Protection of Individuals with regard to Automatic Processing of Personal Data* (CoE 1981) para. 28 (emphasis added).

is, the reference to 'very sophisticated methods' being simply an elaboration of the ease criterion). In any case, the focus on 'sophistication' of methods is problematic as it rests on a misguided perception that as sophistication increases, ease of identification decreases. In reality, enhanced sophistication often results in greater ease of identification. Thus, subsequent elaborations of the ease criterion in the CoE's various sectoral recommendations on data privacy introduce (more appropriately) the factors of reasonableness, time, resources, and, to a decreasing extent, cost.[65]

Recital 26 of the DPD lays down a relatively broad and flexible criterion for identifiability:

to determine whether a person is identifiable, account should be taken of all the means likely reasonably to be used either by the controller or by any other person to identify the said person.

The phrase 'likely reasonably' could be read as introducing two criteria for identifiability: the term 'likely' pointing to an assessment of *probability* of identification; the term 'reasonably' pointing to an assessment of the *difficulty* (for example, in terms of time and resource utilization) of identification. However, the two criteria will tend to be interlinked in practice. The French, German, and Swedish versions of Recital 26 formulate the criteria for identifiability in terms of those means for identification which are *reasonably capable* (as opposed to likely) of being put to use.[66] Nevertheless, these differences between the Recital versions are probably insignificant as a probability criterion can be read into the notion of reasonableness. It is also doubtful that the Directive's criteria for identifiability differ substantially from the criteria laid down in the CoE Recommendations.

As for the OECD Guidelines, these are relatively non-committal on the issue,[67] as are the UN Guidelines.[68] However, both sets of Guidelines most

---

[65] See eg, Recommendation R (89) 2 on the protection of peronal data used for employment purposes para. 1.3 ('[a]n individual shall not be regarded as "identifiable" if the identification requires an unreasonable amount of time, cost and manpower'). More recent Recommendations have dropped the reference to 'cost' on account of technological developments: see eg, the Explanatory Memorandum to Recommendation R (97) 5, on the protection of medical data, para. 36 ('in view of the developments in computer technology, the aspect of 'costs' was no longer a reliable criterion for determining whether an individual was identifiable or not').

[66] The French version refers to 'l'ensemble des moyens susceptibles d'être raisonnablement mis en œuvre'; the German version refers to 'alle Mittel...die vernüftigerweise...eingesetzt werden könnten'; and the Swedish version to 'alla hjälpmedel som...rimligen kan komma att användas'. Cf the Danish version which expresses the relevant criteria in terms of the means that can reasonably be *thought* to be used ('alle de hjælpemidler...der med rimelighed kan tænkes bragt i anvendelse'). The Danish version is probably much the same in effect as the other versions.

[67] See Explanatory Memorandum to the original OECD Guidelines para. 41.

[68] As noted above, the UN Guidelines fail to provide definitions of their key terms, such as 'personal data'. It seems safe to assume, though, that these are to be defined in basically the same way as they are defined in the other major international data protection instruments.

probably embrace criteria for identifiability similar to those found in the DPD and CoE Recommendations. Some national laws which expressly qualify degree of identifiability have employed similar criteria as well.[69]

It bears emphasis that, at least for some laws, such as the DPD, what is of legal importance is the *capability* or *potential* of identification rather than the actual achievement of identification. Hence, data will not fail to be personal merely because the data controller refrains from linking it to a particular person.[70]

## (c) Legally relevant agent of identification

Closely related to the issue of ease/probability of identification is the issue of who is the legally relevant agent of identification. Most data privacy codes refrain from broaching the latter issue. A notable exception is DPD Recital 26 which indicates that *any* person may be the legally relevant agent for identification—that is, legally decisive is not just the ability of the controller to link a person to data but any person's ability to do so.[71] This lowers the threshold for determining the circumstances under which data is personal.

Nevertheless, the criteria for ease/practicability of identification discussed in the preceding paragraphs exclude from consideration any persons who do not employ means that are reasonably capable of being used for identification. The notion of reasonableness implies that account ordinarily should not be taken of persons who are only able to carry out identification by *illegal* means (for example, computer hacking).[72] Given that reasonableness also connotes a probability criterion, account should also not be taken of persons who are only able to carry out identification by (objectively) *unexpected* or

---

[69] For instance, a criterion of proportionality applies with respect to the identification process envisaged by Germany's Federal Data Protection Act so as to exclude cases where identification is only possible through a data controller making an effort that is 'disproportionate' in relation to his/her/its 'normal' means and activities. This proportionality criterion is derived from s 3(6) of the Act which defines anonymized data in terms of information which 'can no longer or only with a disproportionately great expenditure of time, money and labour be attributed to an identified or identifiable natural person'.

[70] Cf the case law referenced in nn 90 and 92.

[71] Cf s 1(3) of the UK Data Protection Act which defines 'personal data' as 'data which relate to a living individual who can be identified (a) from those data, or (b) from those data and other information which is in the possession of, or is likely to come into the possession of, the data controller'. The equivalent definition in s 1(1) of the Irish Data Protection Act is similar. Both definitions indicate that account is only to be taken of the controller's ability to carry out identification. See further case law on point at n 92.

[72] Cf Austria's Data Protection Act 2000 (*Datenschutzgesetz 2000* (DSG 2000), BGBl I Nr 165/1999) which operates with a sub-category of personal data termed 'only indirectly person-related' ('nur indirekt personenbezogen'). This sub-category is defined as data that the controller or processor cannot link (on his/her/its own) to a specific person using '*legally permitted* means' ('rechtlich zulässigen

*unusual* means. In most cases, illegal means will be unexpected or unusual means, but not always. Thus, a situation of conflicting standards might arise. It goes without saying that neither the Directive nor its preparatory works provide guidance on how to resolve this potential conflict. In light of the intention behind the Directive to encourage a flexible approach to the issue of identification and thereby a broad basis for data privacy, the probability criterion should be given priority over the legality criterion in the event of conflict—that is, account should be allowed of persons who are able to carry out identification by illegal yet probable means. In practice, assessment of probability here will involve analysing security measures for the data concerned in light of the history of attempts at gaining unauthorized access to this data. At the same time, the criterion of probability might need to be construed more stringently if the means are illegal.

It is also noteworthy that the Safe Harbor agreement between the European Commission and US Department of Commerce states that an organization in the USA which receives, from Europe, pseudonymized medical research data—that is data to which a unique code is given such that the identity of the data subject is masked—does not need to process the data in conformity with the Safe Harbor data privacy principles if the company does not possess the 'key' that may reveal the data subject's identity, even though that key is possessed by the person or organization that sends the data from Europe.[73] This presupposes, of course, that the US organization is not legally able to demand that key. The rule is expressed only in relation to pharmaceutical and medical research data. Whether the rule applies to other categories of data that are transferred from Europe to US organizations is unclear but it is logically difficult to see why it ought not to.

### (d) Accuracy of link between data and individual

The accuracy of the connection between a set of data and an individual has rarely been raised as an issue. The matter comes to a head in cases where a set of data (for example, about a company) is incorrectly perceived to relate to an individual. Does this lack of objective validity mean that the data is not properly to be regarded as 'personal' pursuant to data privacy legislation? In support of a negative answer to this question, one could point to the

---

Mitteln'; emphasis added) (§ 4(1)). Processing of this category of data is subjected under the Act to less stringent controls than the processing of other personal data.

[73] Decision 2000/520/EC on the adequacy of the protection provided by the Safe Harbor privacy principles and related frequently asked questions issued by the US Department of Commerce [2000] OJ L215/7 Annex II FAQ 14 para. 7.

rules in the legislation dealing with rectification of incorrect or misleading data:[74] such rules would seem not to make sense if an affirmative answer were adopted. However, by and large, these rules seem to operate only once data is established as being 'personal'; that is, they do not relate to the quality (accuracy) of the way in which a set of data is initially connected to an individual.

It could be argued that the manner of such connection must be objectively valid in the sense that data, in order to be 'personal', must be capable, in truth, of being linked to one person; concomitantly, it is not possible under data privacy law for data to become 'personal' primarily on the basis of a *mis*-perception that the data is so capable. This argument works best with those laws that define 'personal data' (or 'personal information') as excluding mere opinions. However, some laws allow for opinions to qualify as personal data;[75] some even allow for *false* opinions to qualify as such.[76] It is not entirely clear if the definition of 'personal data' in DPD Article 2(a) embraces opinions, let alone false ones. However, neither the Directive nor its preparatory works specifically exclude opinions from coverage, and the preparatory works indicate an intention to make the definition of 'personal data' in the Directive 'as general as possible, so as to include all information concerning an identifiable individual'.[77] In light of this intention, together with the Directive's express aim of providing for a high level of data protection (Recitals 9–11), solid grounds exist for including opinions—even false ones—within the ambit of Article 2(a). The risk of regulatory over-reaching that such inclusion brings could be mitigated by limiting inclusion to those opinions that are shared by many people and harbour likely adverse consequences for the individual concerned.

### (e)  Use of auxiliary information

The issue of auxiliary information is not specifically addressed by Convention 108, the OECD Guidelines, or UN Guidelines. However, the inclusion of the term 'identifiable' in their definitions of 'personal data' would seem to open up for the use of some such information. Article 2(a) of the Directive is more helpful, providing that

an identifiable person is one who can be identified, directly or indirectly, in particular by reference to an identification number or to one or more factors specific to his physical, physiological, mental, economic, cultural or social identity.

---

[74] See further Ch 5 (section F).
[75] See eg, s 6(1) of Australia's federal Privacy Act, s 1(3) of the UK Data Protection Act, and s 2(1) of Norway's Personal Data Act.
[76] The case with the Australian Act.          [77] COM(92) 422 final—SYN 287, 9.

On the national plane, many data privacy laws open up for the use of certain auxiliary information, either by making specific mention of such information,[78] or by providing that identification may occur 'indirectly'.[79] Inclusion of the adjective 'identifiable' in the definition of 'personal data' has also been interpreted as allowing for the use of some auxiliary information in identifying a person.[80]

## (f) Requirement of individuation

The sixth and final issue concerns the extent to which data must allow for individuation—that is, be capable of being linked to *one* person as opposed to an aggregate of persons. Data privacy laws typically require that data must allow for individuation in order to qualify as 'personal'. However, some variation exists from jurisdiction to jurisdiction as to how stringent the requirement of individuation is applied. Finnish law, for example, expressly opens up for some relaxation of the requirement by providing that data may be 'personal' even if it can be linked only to a 'family' or 'household' unit.[81] Such provision is rare. Nevertheless, relaxation of the individuation requirement would seem to be possible under some other national regimes. For the purposes of Norwegian law, for instance, it seems that data may be 'personal' even if it can be linked to a small group of individuals, although this is somewhat dependent on there existing a pronounced threat to data privacy.[82]

## (g) Restricting expansive potential

From the analysis above, it is clear that many of the definitions of personal data are capable in theory of embracing a great deal of data that has prima facie little direct relationship to a particular person. At the same time as this capability has obvious benefits from a data privacy perspective, it threatens the semantic viability of the notion of 'personal data/information' and incurs a risk that data privacy laws will over-reach themselves. Thus, in some jurisdictions, attempts have been made to delimit this capability. For example, under German law, data over material goods is, as a general rule, 'personal' only insofar as it can be linked to a particular person and its processing can

---

[78] See eg, s 1(3) of the UK Data Protection Act.
[79] See eg, s 2(1) of Iceland's Act on the Protection of Individuals with regard to Processing of Personal Data 2000 (*Lög nr 77 23 mai 2000 um persónuvernd og medferd persónuupplýsninga*).
[80] The case eg, in relation to the definition of 'personal data' in s 3(1) of Germany's Federal Data Protection Act: see Dammann (n 59) 312–14.
[81] See the definitions of 'personal data' in s 2(1) of the 1987 Act and s 3(1) of the 1999 Act.
[82] MW Johansen, K-B Kaspersen, and ÅM Bergseng Skullerud, *Personopplysningsloven. Kommentarutgave* (Universitetsforlaget 2001) 69.

affect, in a given context, that person's legal, economic, or social standing.[83] Moreover, the preparatory works for the Norwegian Personal Data Act suggest that some data that would fit within the Act's literal definition of 'personal information' (in s 2(1)) may not warrant protection in light of the Act's objects clause.[84] As Dammann makes clear, such delimitations are not fixed along abstract logical or semantic lines but are reached pragmatically.[85]

Courts have also read down the literal scope of statutory definitions of 'personal data'. The most controversial instance is a 2003 decision of the UK Court of Appeal which restricted the term, as defined in the UK Data Protection Act 1998, to information that is 'biographical in a significant sense' or has the data subject as its focus, such that it 'affects his privacy, whether in his personal or family life, business or professional capacity'.[86] This line is controversial as neither the Act nor the DPD provide firm support for it. Moreover, it sits uncomfortably with the thrust of CJEU case law, which suggests that EU data privacy regulation is not to be restricted to situations in which the processing of personal data would infringe the privacy or integrity of the data subject.[87] It does, however, sit relatively comfortably with the old UK legislation. The Data Protection Act 1984 (repealed) only applied to the processing of personal data when the processing occurred 'by

---

[83] Dammann (n 59) 324.
[84] NOU 1997:19, 131; Odelstingsproposisjon (Government Bill) no. 92 (1998–99) 101.
[85] Dammann (n 59) 324.
[86] *Durant v Financial Services Authority* [2003] EWCA Civ 1746 [28].
[87] See Case C-28/08 *European Commission v Bavarian Lager* [2010] ECR I-06055 esp. [59]–[61]. Here the CJEU overruled a decision of the General Court (formerly Court of First Instance) in Case T-194/04 *Bavarian Lager v Commission* [2007] ECR II-4523. The central issue concerned the relative strength of FOI requirements under Regulation (EC) 1049/2001 regarding public access to European Parliament, Council, and Commission documents ([2001] OJ L145/43) and confidentiality requirements under Regulation (EC) 45/2001 on the protection of individuals with regard to the processing of personal data by the institutions and bodies of the Community and on the free movement of such data ([2001] OJ L8/1). The General Court held, in effect, that the latter requirements only trumped the former in cases where the personal data that is subject to an FOI access request, is capable of undermining the privacy and integrity of the data subject for the purposes of ECHR Art. 8: [2007] ECR II-4523 [111]–[120]. The CJEU (Grand Chamber) rejected this line, stating: 'According to Article 1(1) of Regulation No. 45/2001, the purpose of that regulation is to "protect the fundamental rights and freedoms of natural persons, and in particular their right to privacy with respect to the processing of personal data". That provision does not allow cases of processing of personal data to be separated into two categories, namely, a category in which that treatment is examined solely on the basis of Article 8 of the ECHR and the case law of the European Court of Human Rights relating to that article and another category in which that processing is subject to the provisions of Regulation No. 45/2001' [61]. The Court went on to uphold the European Commission's refusal to disclose the names of several persons who were mentioned in the minutes of a Commission meeting as the company requesting disclosure (Bavarian Lager) had not shown the necessity for it, nor had the data subjects' consent to disclosure been obtained.

reference to the data subject' (s 1(7)). The UK Data Protection Tribunal (now 'Information Tribunal') read the latter phrase as excluding from the purview of the Act processing operations in which the data subject is not intended to be in focus.[88]

A majority judgment of the Hong Kong Court of Appeal has read a broadly similar delimitation into Hong Kong's Personal Data (Privacy) Ordinance 1995.[89] The Court majority held that the collection of data falls within the scope of the Ordinance only if the 'data user' is 'thereby...compiling information about an *identified* person or about a person *whom the data user intends or seeks to identify*'.[90]

### (h)  IP addresses as personal data?

One of the most vexed issues in this area is whether Internet protocol (IP) addresses may constitute 'personal data'. The issue has arisen frequently in litigation and generated extensive debate otherwise. Inconsistency and ambiguity mark many of the outcomes. European DPAs have generally taken the view that IP addresses are personal data.[91] Courts, on the other hand, have been divided. This division partly reflects differences in statutory definitions of 'personal data'.

---

[88]  See *Equifax Europe Ltd v The Data Protection Registrar* (1991) Case DA/90 25/49/7 [49] ('using the Land Registry's computer to change the boundaries of a plot of land, or perhaps to extract a copy of a restrictive covenant, would in no way concern the individual identity or attributes of a data subject, and need not attract the control over processing'). The Tribunal contrasted such a processing operation with a situation in which 'the object of the exercise is to learn something about the individual [data subject], not about the land' [50].

[89]  *Eastweek Publisher Ltd v Privacy Commissioner for Personal Data* [2000] 1 HKC 692 (per Ribeiro JA and Godfrey VP; Wong JA dissenting). The case concerned the non-consensual publication by a magazine of a photograph taken at long range by one of its journalists of a woman in a public place without her knowledge. The photograph was one of a series published in a feature article on the fashion sense of Hong Kong women. In the article, derisive comments were made about the dress style of the photographed woman although no additional information was supplied as to her identity, which was immaterial for and unknown to the magazine. The main issue before the Court was whether the publisher of the magazine had breached the Ordinance's requirement that personal data be collected fairly and lawfully. The Court majority found that there had been no breach as the magazine had neither sought nor intended to identify the woman. Although this finding formally relates to the meaning of 'collection' under the Ordinance, it implicitly rests on a view of the meaning of 'personal data'.

[90]  *Eastweek* (n 89) 700 (emphasis added). The conclusion was grounded partly in a concern not to unduly restrict photojournalistic activity and thereby freedom of expression and partly in the assumption underlying several of the basic rules of the Ordinance (eg, data access and rectification rights) that a data controller is able to readily identify the data subject (*Eastweek* (n 89) 701–3).

[91]  See A29WP (n 55) 16.

For instance, the Irish High Court has ruled that, for the purposes of the Irish Data Protection Act 1988, an IP address gathered on behalf of the holders of intellectual property rights (IPR) is not personal data in the hands of the latter when it is unlikely that they will try to find the name and contact details of the person behind the address.[92] As noted earlier,[93] the Act defines 'personal data' such that the controller (in this context, an IPR-holder) is the only legally relevant agent of identification. This is different to the DPD which requires account to be taken of the means of identification likely reasonably to be used not just by the controller but by 'any other person'.

Some national courts applying legislation that faithfully transposes the DPD have regarded IP addresses in the hands of IPR-holders as personal data if an ISP can (without great effort) connect the addresses to particular persons.[94] Other courts have not.[95] The CJEU, however, has repeatedly held that IP addresses are personal data, although its decisions on point are cursory and fail to clearly distinguish the status of IP addresses vis-à-vis IPR-holders and their status vis-à-vis ISPs.[96] The failure could imply that the CJEU considers the distinction legally irrelevant for the purposes of the Directive but we cannot be sure.

---

[92] *EMI Records and Others v Eircom Ltd* [2010] IEHC 108 [24]–[25]. Here, the IPR-holders were seeking injunctive relief from an Internet service provider (ISP) whereby the latter was being asked to restrict Internet access for those of its customers who persistently infringe copyright. The judge noted that 'the plaintiffs have left behind what they reasonably regard as an expensive and futile pursuit of the identity of copyright tortfeasors in favour of injunctive relief that has been expressed . . . as a protocol to choke off the problem in a three stage process that never involves the identification of any wrongdoer' [24]. The reasoning is not dissimilar to the approach taken to pseudonymous medical research data for the purposes of the Safe Harbor agreement: see n 73 and accompanying text.

[93] See n 71.

[94] See eg, decision of 8 September 2010 by Switzerland's Federal Supreme Court (Bundesgericht) in *Eidgenössischer Datenschutz- und Öffentlichkeitsbeauftragter (EDÖB) v Logistep* (case 1C-285/2009); available at: <http://jumpcgi.bger.ch/cgi-bin/JumpCGI?id=08.09.2010_1C_285/2009>. See too decision of 8 June 2007 by the Stockholm Administrative Court of Appeal (Kammarrätten) in Case 285/07—upheld by the Swedish Supreme Administrative Court (Regeringsrätten) in decision of 16 June 2009 (Case 3978-07); both decisions available at: <http://arkiv.idg.se/it24/SthlmRRejpt_3978_07.pdf>.

[95] See eg, decision of 27 April 2007 by the Paris Court of Appeal in *Anthony G v Société Civile des Producteurs Phonographiques (SCPP)* and its decision of 15 May 2007 in *Henri S v SCPP*; both decisions available via <http://www.legalis.net>.

[96] See eg, Case C-275/06 *Productores de Música de España (Promusicae) v Telefónica de España SAU* [2008] ECR I-271 [45]; Case C-70/10 *Scarlet Extended v Société belge des auteurs, compositeurs et éditeurs SCRL (SABAM)* [2011] ECR I-0000 [41]; Case C-461/10 *Bonnier Audio AB and Others v Perfect Communication Sweden AB* [2012] ECR I-0000 [52].

## 3. Scope with regard to data on collective entities

The bulk of the hitherto most influential data privacy codes worked out at an international level are drafted to protect data on individuals only. However, none of these codes expressly exclude the possibility of individual countries extending protection to data on collective entities. As noted in Chapter 2 (section E(2)), the Electronic Privacy Directive provides express protection for the 'legitimate interests' of corporate entities ('legal persons') in their role as 'subscribers' to electronic communication services. This protection is largely (but not fully) commensurate with the protection afforded to individuals.

The data privacy legislation of the overwhelming majority of countries does not provide express protection for data on collective entities. A handful of countries (including Austria, Italy, Argentina, South Africa, and Switzerland) have data privacy laws expressly providing collective entities (primarily corporations) with safeguards and rights. Several countries (Denmark, Norway, and Iceland) provided for such safeguards and rights under their *first* data privacy laws but have either entirely dispensed with express protection of data on collective entities under their current legislation (the case with Iceland) or have retained such protection only in relation to credit reporting (the case with Norway), or in relation to credit reporting and blacklisting (Denmark).

The extension of protection to data on organized collective entities has been grounded in various reasons some of which are connected not just with a concern to provide more complete protection for individuals but also to protect the interests of the collective entities as such.[97] Particularly important for the decision of some countries to provide protection for both corporate and natural persons has been pre-existing legal traditions. A fundamental premise of the Austrian, Swiss, and South African legal systems, for example, is that legal persons are to be treated as far as possible in the same way as natural persons. Another noteworthy factor—and one that appears to have motivated at least the Italian decision on point—is concern to increase the general transparency of data processing and, concomitantly, the diffusion of knowledge for the benefit of wider society.

Nevertheless, most countries with data privacy legislation have refrained from expressly safeguarding data on corporate and other collective entities under that legislation. This does not always mean, though, that data on such entities has been left without any protection in their respective countries. There are several ways in which these entities may still be protected.[98] For instance, the country's DPA could have used its powers to give such entities

---

[97] See further Bygrave (n 14) ch 9 and references cited therein.
[98] For details see Bygrave (n 14) ch 10.

some data privacy rights without this extension of protection being reflected in actual legislation. This has occurred, for example, in France with respect to data access rights. Alternatively, collective entities could have been given some rights as data subjects in relation to a specific type or sector of data processing, these rights being set down expressly in sectoral legislation. This has been the case, for example, in Sweden in relation to the credit-reporting and debt-recovery industries.

The exclusion of data on legal persons and other collective entities from explicit protection under the bulk of data privacy instruments is due to a multiplicity of factors.[99] The primary factor is a generally held view that the main interests served by data privacy law are only applicable to individuals. A second factor is a view that many collective entities, particularly corporations, do not need protection because the individuals constituting them enjoy such protection already, or because the interests of the entities as such are protected sufficiently under other law. Accompanying this view is a perception that many collective entities are robust bodies capable of looking after themselves to a greater degree than are individuals. A third factor is the natural disinclination of governments to introduce rules that might further curtail their agencies' ability to process information on collective entities. Yet another factor is trenchant opposition from major business groups to extending the ambit of data privacy law to cover legal person data. This opposition has been grounded in uncertainty over the ways in which such an extension would affect market dynamics. One fear is that expanding the class of data subjects under data privacy law will expand the potential to restrict transborder flows of data that are important for international business transactions. Another fear is that corporations will use their data privacy rights to distort economic competition between themselves.

Each of these factors has been critically analysed and found, in sum, as not amounting to a watertight case against giving collective entities safeguards and rights under data privacy law.[100] Yet support for the case against giving data privacy rights to collective entities is too entrenched to be overthrown by academic surmising. Recent years have not seen any significant shift towards greater protection of data on collective entities.[101]

---

[99] Bygrave (n 14) ch 9 (section 9.4).     [100] Bygrave (n 14) ch 16.

[101] The Australian Law Reform Commission (ALRC) considered the matter in depth as part of its general review of Australia's regulatory framework on data privacy. It referred to my arguments on the matter but recommended against extending the scope of Australia's federal Privacy Act to

## 4. Scope with regard to type of data processing

Current data privacy laws typically regulate all or most stages of the data-processing cycle, including registration, storage, retrieval, and dissemination of personal data. Thus, the DPD broadly defines 'processing' as

> any operation or set of operations which is performed upon personal data, whether or not by automatic means, such as collection, recording, organization, storage, adaptation or alteration, retrieval, consultation, use, disclosure by transmission, dissemination or otherwise making available, alignment or combination, blocking, erasure or destruction (Article 2(b)).

The term 'processing' in Convention 108 is a little narrower: it does not cover collection of data, nor data processing carried out by entirely manual (non-automated) means (Article 2(c)). However, states parties may apply its rules to data processed manually (Article 3). And some of its provisions (notably Article 5(a)) pertain directly to the collection of data.

Some national laws have focused mainly on the registration, as opposed to collection, of personal data—the case, for instance, with Norway's PDRA. This was part of a more general focus on the creation and use of personal data *registers*; that is, files, records, and the like in which 'personal information is systematically stored so that information concerning an individual person may be retrieved' (PDRA section 1(2)). The focus on registers is shared by Convention 108 and the UN Guidelines. Indeed, it is typical for data privacy instruments drafted in the 1970s and early 1980s, with the OECD Guidelines as a notable exception.

The regulatory focus of the DPD is on the 'processing' of personal data regardless (almost) of the way in which the data is organized. The register/file concept has not been totally ditched by the Directive; it lives on with respect to manually processed data. Purely manual data processing is to be regulated insofar as the data forms or is intended to form part of a 'filing system' (Article 3(1)). By 'filing system' is meant 'any structured set of personal data which are accessible according to specific criteria, whether centralized, decentralized or dispersed on a functional or geographical basis' (Article 2(c)). As this definition suggests, retainment of the register/file concept here is

---

cover data on corporations and commercial entities for essentially the same reasons as outlined above: see ALRC, *For Your Information: Australian Privacy Law and Practice*, Report no. 108 (ALRC 2008) [7.58]–[7.60]. The Commission also rejected any extension of data privacy rights to groups as this would, inter alia, 'require a fundamental and radical change to the scope and operation of the *Privacy Act*' [7.18] and 'could result in a group asserting privacy rights in a way that conflicts with the interests of individual members of the group' [7.21].

essentially a consequence of a concern to limit the application of data privacy laws to data that can be linked to a particular person without great difficulty,[102] as it is in relation to this sort of data that the risk to privacy-related interests primarily lies.[103] Retainment is also symptomatic of a concern to minimize regulatory overreaching.[104]

Otherwise, the provisions of the Directive are largely technology-neutral. This is in contrast to Convention 108 and the UN Guidelines (but not the OECD Guidelines) which cover automated data-processing practices to the almost total exclusion of manual (non-automated) processing, though allow for optional coverage of non-automated files. The legislation of a large number of countries, such as Austria, Ireland, Japan, Luxembourg, Sweden, and the UK, also initially covered automated data-processing practices only. This focus on automation was symptomatic of a belief that the increasing usage of computers, particularly for decision-making purposes, represented the main threat to data protection interests.[105]

Most current laws, however, extend to both manual and computerized processing of personal data. This does not mean that manual and automated techniques are uniformly regulated. The DPD, for instance, does not require national DPAs to be notified of purely manual data-processing operations (Article 18).

## 5. Scope with regard to type of sector

All of the international data privacy instruments are intended to apply to the processing of personal data in both the public and private sectors. Many national data privacy laws have a similar ambit, particularly in Europe. Under some previous national regimes, however, differentiated regulation for each sector has occurred, with the processing practices of public sector bodies being subjected to more stringent regulation than those of private sector bodies.[106]

---

[102] Recital 27 qualifies the notion of accessibility in Art. 2(c) with the adjective 'easy'; ie in order to fall within the scope of the Directive, the filing system 'must be structured according to specific criteria relating to individuals allowing easy access to the personal data'. See also Recital 15.

[103] On the latter point, see eg, COM(92) 422 final—SYN 287, 10.

[104] See reference in n 103.

[105] See eg, para. 1 of the Explanatory Report for Convention 108.

[106] This was the case with, inter alia, the Danish and French regimes. For example, the French Act Regarding Data Processing, Files and Individual Liberties 1978 subjected automatic processing of personal data by public sector bodies to prior authorization by the country's data protection authority, unless the processing was already authorized by law. In contrast, private bodies were able to undertake automated processing of personal data simply upon notifying the authority of the basic details of their processing plans. This differentiation disappeared with amendments to the Act in 2004.

Such differentiation has largely disappeared in Europe, particularly given its absence from the DPD.

As indicated in Chapter 3, the public–private divide has greater purchase under non-European regimes. For example, the data privacy legislation of Singapore and Malaysia is largely restricted to the private sector or parts thereof, while the US legislation regulates the data-processing activities of government agencies to a greater extent than those of private sector entities.

Data privacy laws generally operate with other limitations in their coverage as well. Exemptions from the laws in their entirety or from their central provisions are often made, for instance, with respect to national security services,[107] journalism, and artistic endeavour,[108] and data processing for purely personal or domestic purposes.[109] Considerable uncertainty surrounds the exact ambit of these exemptions, although case law increasingly offers authoritative guidance.

Two significant cases in point are the decisions of the CJEU in *Satamedia* and *Lindqvist*. In *Satamedia*, the Court adopted a liberal reading of the term 'journalistic purposes' in DPD Article 9. According to the Court, the term covers 'disclosure to the public of information, opinions or ideas, irrespective of the medium which is used to transmit them' and is 'not limited to media undertakings and may be undertaken for profit-making purposes'.[110]

In *Lindqvist*, the Court was called upon to consider, inter alia, whether dissemination of personal data via personal Internet 'homepages' constituted data processing 'in the course of a purely personal or household activity' and thus fell within the exception to the ambit of the Directive provided for in the second indent of Article 3(2).[111] The Court held that this exception 'must ... be interpreted as relating only to activities which are carried out in the course of private or family life of individuals, which is clearly not the case

---

[107] See eg, Ireland's Data Protection Act 1988 s 1(4)(a). Cf DPD Arts 3(2) and 13(1).

[108] See eg, Sweden's Personal Data Act 1998 s 7; the Netherlands' Personal Data Protection Act 2000 (*Wet bescherming persoonsgegevens*) Art. 3(1). The DPD requires EU member states to lay down exemptions from the central provisions of the Directive with respect to data processing 'carried out solely for journalistic purposes or the purpose of artistic or literary expression', insofar as is 'necessary to reconcile the right to privacy with the rules governing freedom of expression' (Art. 9).

[109] See eg, DPD Art. 3(2) which exempts coverage of data processing 'by a natural person in the course of a purely personal or household activity'.

[110] Case C-73/07 *Tietosuojavaltuutettu v Satakunnan Markkinapörssi Oy, Satamedia Oy* [2008] ECR I-09831 [61]. An earlier decision of the Swedish Supreme Court took the same line with respect to the Swedish provisions transposing DPD Art. 9: see decision of 12 June 2001 in case B293-00. For analysis, see LA Bygrave, 'Balancing Data Protection and Freedom of Expression in the Context of Website Publishing—Recent Swedish Case Law' (2002) 18 CLSR 56.

[111] Bodil Lindqvist worked on a voluntary basis for her local parish church in Sweden, preparing parishioners for their confirmation. In that role she posted information about some of her fellow parish workers on Internet homepages that she had set up using her personal computer at home, without first informing her colleagues or getting their consent.

with the processing of personal data consisting in publication on the internet so that those data are made accessible to an indefinite number of people'.[112] Unfortunately, the Court otherwise provided no guidance as to when or how a lesser degree of accessibility may make a website private for the purposes of Article 3(2).[113]

---

[112] Case C-101/01 *Bodil Lindqvist* [2003] ECR I-12971 [47].

[113] In Norway, disagreement has arisen over whether the country's first major online social network, 'Nettby', which at the height of its popularity had 750,000 registered members but closed down in the face of competition from Facebook, was a private space falling within the exception under Norwegian law that equates with DPD Art. 3(2). The Data Inspectorate has taken the view that the exception applies with respect to those elements of Nettby that were only accessible to the registered members, even though the membership size was extremely large. The Tribunal has disagreed, arguing that the size of membership took Nettby beyond what could properly be deemed a 'private' space: see appeal decision in case 3/2012; available at: <http://www.personvernnemnda.no/vedtak/2012_03.htm>.

# 5

# Core Principles of Data Privacy Law

## A. Definition and Role of Principles

This chapter provides an overview of the basic principles applied by data privacy laws to the processing of personal data.[1] Its purpose is to present the constituent elements of these principles, along with the main similarities and differences in the way they are elaborated in the more influential international codes. Account is occasionally taken of their elaboration in national regimes as well.

As shown in the following, considerable overlap exists between the principles. Further, each of them can be broken down into multiple sub-principles. As 'principles', they are primarily abstractions denoting the pith and basic thrust of a set of legal rules. At the same time, they have a normative force of their own. This force is exercised in several ways. First, the principles have been expressly incorporated in some data privacy codes as fully fledged legal rules in their own right (though not always using exactly the same formulations as given in this chapter). Secondly, the principles function as guiding standards for, say, DPAs when conducting interest-balancing processes in the exercise of discretionary powers. Thirdly, and closely related to the latter function, the principles help to shape the drafting of new data privacy codes.

It bears emphasis that the rules giving effect to these principles are seldom set down as absolutes. The derogations from them are numerous and complex. Doing full justice to their intricate tapestry would require a far larger text than is the ambition of this chapter. Thus, in the interests of keeping the following presentation concise, these derogations are not dealt with in detail.

---

[1] The chapter builds on and updates where necessary the account in LA Bygrave, *Data Protection Law: Approaching Its Rationale, Logic and Limits* (Kluwer Law International 2002) chs 3 and 18.

The final preliminary point to note is that the following presentation focuses considerably on European norms. The reasons for this focus are, first, that these norms have been the internationally most influential and are likely to continue to be for the near future. Secondly, there exists a comparatively rich degree of jurisprudence and scholarship that casts light on their meaning. In this sense, their study can be said to offer relatively high 'heuristic value'.

## B. Fair and Lawful Processing

The primary principle of data privacy law is that personal data shall be 'processed fairly and lawfully'.[2] This principle is 'primary' as it embraces and generates the other principles presented below.[3] Concomitantly, the twin criteria of fairness and lawfulness are manifest in all of these principles even if, in some instruments, they are expressly linked only to the means for collecting personal data,[4] or not specifically mentioned at all.[5]

Of the criteria 'fairly' and 'lawfully', the latter is relatively self-explanatory. Less obvious in meaning but potentially broader is the criterion of fairness. It is impossible to explicate exhaustively this criterion in the abstract, and general agreement on what it connotes will inevitably change over time. Nonetheless, fairness undoubtedly means that data controllers must take account of the interests and reasonable expectations of data subjects; they cannot ride roughshod over the latter. The collection and further processing of personal data must accordingly be carried out so that it does not interfere unreasonably with data subjects' privacy-related interests. In other words, requirements of balance and proportionality lie inherent in the criterion. These requirements apply not just to individual data-processing operations; they speak equally to the way in which the *information systems* supporting such operations are designed and managed.[6]

In light of these requirements, fairness also implies that persons are not unduly pressured into supplying data on themselves to others or agreeing to new uses of the data once supplied. Fairness thus arguably implies protection from abuse by data controllers of their monopoly position. It is rare to find

---

[2] See eg, Convention 108 Art. 5(a); DPD Art. 6(1)(a); DPP 1 in Part 1 of Schedule 1 to the UK Act.

[3] See too Bygrave (n 1) ch 18 (section 18.4.1).

[4] The case, eg, with the OECD Guidelines para. 7.

[5] The case, eg, with the Norwegian PDA.          [6] See further Bygrave (n 1) ch 19.

data privacy codes expressly addressing this matter,[7] though some protection from abuse of monopoly can be read into the relatively common provisions on data subject consent, particularly the requirement that such consent be 'freely given'.[8]

The notion of fairness further implies that the processing of personal data be transparent for the data subjects.[9] This militates not only against surreptitious processing of personal data, but also against deception of data subjects as to the nature of, and purposes for, the processing.[10] Arguably, another requirement flowing from the link between fairness and transparency is that, as a point of departure, personal data shall be collected directly from the data subject, not from third parties. This requirement is expressly laid down in some but not the majority of data protection instruments.[11]

As mentioned above, fairness implies that data controllers must take some account of the reasonable expectations of data subjects. This implication has direct consequences for the purposes for which data may be processed. It helps to ground rules embracing the purpose limitation principle dealt with in section E following. Concomitantly, it sets limits on the secondary purposes to which personal data may be put. More specifically, it arguably means that when personal data obtained for one purpose is subsequently used for another purpose, which the data subject would not reasonably anticipate, the data controller may have to obtain the data subject's positive consent to the new use.[12]

## C. Proportionality

One of the most striking developments over the last decade in European data privacy law is the emergence of a requirement of proportionality as a data privacy principle in its own right. As elaborated below, this development is mainly manifest in case law. We see it too in the recent proposal to add a principle of proportionality to the core principles of Convention 108.[13]

---

[7] A lonely instance is the Australian Privacy Charter (adopted December 1994; set out in (1995) 2 PLPR 44): 'People should not have to pay in order to exercise their rights of privacy... nor be denied goods or services or offered them on a less preferential basis for wishing to do so. The provision of reasonable facilities for the exercise of privacy rights is part of the normal operating costs of organisations' (Principle 18). The Charter is the private initiative of a group of concerned citizens and interest groups; it has not been conferred any official status by a government body.

[8] See eg, DPD Art. 2(h).    [9] See eg, DPD Recital 38.

[10] See eg, UK Act sch 1 pt II s 1(1).

[11] See eg, Canada's federal Privacy Act 1982 s 5(1); NZ Privacy Act 1993 IPP 2.

[12] See further Bygrave (n 1) ch 18 (section 18.4.1).    [13] See Ch 2 (n 25).

Concern for proportionality is far from unique to data privacy law. Such concern is, for instance, firmly established as a general principle in EU law, manifesting itself in a multitude of legal instruments and judicial decisions covering a broad range of contexts. In EU law, the proportionality principle is generally recognized as having three prongs:

(i) suitability—is the measure concerned suitable or relevant to realizing the goals it is aimed at meeting?;

(ii) necessity—is the measure concerned required for realizing the goals it is aimed at meeting?; and

(iii) non-excessiveness (proportionality *stricto sensu*)—does the measure go further than is necessary to realize the goals it is aimed at meeting?[14]

The proportionality principle per se (as delineated above) is not included as one of the classic 'fair information practice' principles,[15] though it underpins these and shines through in their interstices. As noted above, the principle of fair and lawful processing connotes proportionality in the balancing of interests of data subjects and controllers. Proportionality requirements are further manifest in a variety of relatively concrete rules. A central example is the stipulation that personal data must be 'relevant' and 'not excessive' in relation to the purposes for which it is processed.[16] Provisions incorporating a criterion of 'necessity' also embody a requirement of proportionality. This is established most clearly in the ECtHR case law pursuant to ECHR Article 8(2).[17] It is also the case with the criterion of necessity in certain provisions of the DPD (primarily Articles 7, 8, and 13).[18] At the same time, elements of the classic 'fair information practice' principles serve to enable application of the proportionality principle. Indeed, there is a close, symbiotic relationship between the latter and elements of the former. The first element of the principle of purpose limitation (that is, that personal data should be collected for specified legitimate purposes)[19] is key in this respect. Any assessment of the proportionality of a particular action relies on identification of that action's purpose(s).

---

[14] See further P Craig and G de Búrca, *EU Law* (5th edn, OUP 2011) 526–33.

[15] For an overview of these principles and their evolution, see FH Cate, 'The Failure of Fair Information Practice Principles' in JK Winn (ed), *Consumer Protection in the Age of the 'Information Economy'* (Ashgate 2006) 341. The proportionality principle as such does not figure in that overview nor does it figure in the elaboration of core data privacy principles in Bygrave (n 1).

[16] See eg, DPD Art. 6(1)(c). The connection of this rule with a requirement of proportionality is recognized by the CJEU: see esp. Joined Cases C-465/00, C-138/01, and C-139/01 *Rechnungshof v Österreichischer Rundfunk and Others* [2003] ECR I-4989 [91].

[17] See Ch 2 (section I(2)).		[18] See eg, *Rechnungshof* (n 16) [91].

[19] See further section E of this chapter.

The proportionality principle must be observed not just by data controllers but also by DPAs when exercising their respective decision-making competence. At the same time, because of its ubiquity across many codes and contexts, application of the principle to these decisions may follow not just from data privacy legislation but other sets of legal norms too. For instance, a DPA decision will often have to comply with the principle as a matter of general administrative law. The same goes for decisions of data controllers which exercise public authority. Nevertheless, the precise status and content of the proportionality principle in terms of general administrative law may vary from jurisdiction to jurisdiction.[20]

Part and parcel of the increasing salience of the proportionality principle in European data privacy law is growing judicial readiness to impose limits on data-processing operations in the principle's name. Indeed, the CJEU is increasingly prepared to make the principle bite. Rather than leaving the requisite proportionality assessment to the national authorities, the Court itself is now often carrying out the assessment and doing so stringently.[21]

The Court's *Scarlet Extended* judgment is a case in point.[22] It deals with the lawfulness of a requirement, sought for by IPR-holders, that an ISP introduce a system for systematically monitoring and filtering all of its customers' Internet usage, at its own expense and for an unlimited period of time, with a view to enabling the ISP to block the transfer of particular files containing works in which copyright inheres. Applying a proportionality test, the Court held that the required system did not strike a fair balance between the various rights concerned. These rights included not just data privacy rights but, inter alia, the ISP's freedom to conduct business.[23] A subsequent case, which dealt with the imposition of a similar system on the provider of an online social networking service, ended with the same result.[24]

As noted above, elements of proportionality inhere in DPD Articles 7 and 8. These provisions stipulate that the processing of personal data without data subject consent is prohibited unless 'necessary' for certain specified

[20] For example, while the principle is firmly entrenched as a key norm in German and EU administrative law, its status in the respective administrative law regimes of the Scandinavian countries is less certain. See generally C Bagger Tranberg, *Nødvendig behandling af personoplysninger* (Thomson 2007) chs 6–8 and references cited therein.

[21] See generally C Bagger Tranberg, 'Proportionality and Data Protection in the Case Law of the European Court of Justice' (2011) 1 IDPL 239.

[22] Case C-70/10 *Scarlet Extended v Société belge des auteurs, compositeurs et éditeurs SCRL (SABAM)* [2011] ECR I-0000.

[23] This was on account of the ISP having 'to install a complicated, costly, permanent computer system at its own expense': *Scarlet Extended* (n 22) [48].

[24] Case C-360/10 *SABAM v Netlog* [2012] ECR I-0000.

purposes: concluding a contract with the data subject (Article 7(b)); complying with a 'legal obligation to which the controller is subject' (Article 7(c)); protecting the 'vital interests' of the data subject (Article 7(d)); performing a task executed in the 'public interest' or in exercise of official authority (Article 7(e)), or pursuing 'legitimate interests' that override the conflicting interests of the data subject (Article 7(f)). A key operational issue concerns the precise meaning of the 'necessity' criterion in these provisions. The preparatory works to the Directive fail to elaborate on the criterion. However, in the *Huber* case,[25] the CJEU cast light on the criterion in Article 7(e). The case arose from a request by Mr Huber to have data relating to him deleted from the Central Register of Foreign Nationals ('Ausländerzentralregister'; 'AZR') maintained by the German state. A crucial question was whether the register was 'necessary' for the purposes of Article 7(e). In tackling this question, the CJEU interpreted the necessity criterion in terms of effectiveness:

with respect to the necessity that a centralised register such as the AZR be available in order to meet the requirements of the authorities responsible for the application of the legislation relating to the right of residence, even if it were to be assumed that decentralised registers such as the district population registers contain all the data which are relevant for the purposes of allowing the authorities to undertake their duties, the centralisation of those data could be necessary, within the meaning of Article 7(e) of Directive 95/46, if it contributes to the *more effective application* of that legislation as regards the right of residence of Union citizens who wish to reside in a Member State of which they are not nationals.[26]

Thus, 'necessary' is not as stringent as 'indispensable', at least for the purposes of Article 7(e). This reading of 'necessary' is in conformity with ECtHR case law pursuant to ECHR Article 8(2).[27] The same interpretation ought probably to be applied to the other clauses of Article 7. At the same time, the Court held as another requirement for satisfying the necessity criterion that the AZR 'contains only the data which are necessary for the application by those authorities of that legislation'.[28] Further, it held that storage and processing of *non-anonymized* data in the AZR for *statistical* purposes 'cannot, on any basis' meet the necessity criterion in Article 7(e).[29]

---

[25] Case C-524/06 *Huber* [2008] ECR I-9705.
[26] *Huber* (n 25) [62]; emphasis added. See too [66].        [27] See Ch 2 (section I(2)).
[28] *Huber* (n 25) [66].        [29] *Huber* (n 25) [68].

# D. Minimality

The principle of minimality stipulates that the amount of personal data collected should be limited to what is necessary to achieve the purpose(s) for which the data is gathered and further processed. The principle goes under a variety of other terms as well, such as 'data avoidance' and 'data frugality'.[30]

The principle is manifest in DPD Article 6(1)(c) which provides, inter alia, that personal data must be 'relevant and not excessive in relation to the purposes for which they are collected and/or further processed'. Article 5(c) of Convention 108 is in almost identical terms though relates the requirements of relevance and non-excessiveness to the purposes for which data is 'stored'. These provisions of the Directive and, to a lesser extent, the Convention are primarily directed at ensuring minimality at the stage of data collection. Both instruments also contain provisions directed prima facie at ensuring minimality subsequent to that stage. These provisions require personal data to be erased or anonymized once it is no longer required for the purposes for which it has been kept.[31] The minimality principle is also manifest in one of the Directive's basic regulatory premises, which is that the processing of personal data is prohibited unless it is necessary for the achievement of certain specified goals (Articles 7 and 8).

The minimality principle does not shine so clearly or broadly in all data privacy codes as it does in the Directive. For instance, neither the OECD Guidelines nor UN Guidelines expressly require minimality at the stage of data collection, though such a requirement can arguably be read into the more general criterion of fairness as set out in section B. The OECD Guidelines also omit specific provision for the destruction or anonymization of personal data after a certain period. Again, though, erasure or anonymization may be required pursuant to other provisions, such as those setting out the principle of purpose limitation (see section E following).[32] Many (but not all)[33] national laws make specific provision for the erasure etc. of personal data once the data is no longer required.

---

[30] See Germany's Federal Data Protection Act s 3(a) which employs the notions of 'Datenvermeidung' and 'Datensparsamkeit'.

[31] See DPD Art. 6(1)(e); Convention 108 Art. 5(e).

[32] A point noted in the Explanatory Memorandum to the original Guidelines para. 54.

[33] The US federal Privacy Act being an example. However, a requirement of erasure/anonymization can arguably be read into other provisions of the Act: see s 552a(e)(1) and (5).

Rules encouraging transactional anonymity are also direct manifestations of the minimality principle. However, express concern in data privacy laws for the interest in anonymity tends to be muted. Very few laws contain rules expressly mandating transactional anonymity or, indeed, stipulating that active consideration be given to crafting technical solutions for ensuring its possibility. A rare example is Germany's Federal Data Protection Act which stipulates that '[t]he design and selection of data processing systems shall be oriented to the goal of collecting, processing or using no personal data or as little personal data as possible' (section 3a).[34] The proposed GDPR contains somewhat similar provisions,[35] as does the preamble to the EPD,[36] along with the 2010 CoE Recommendation on profiling.[37] It is arguable, though, that such requirements may be read into the more commonly found provisions (described earlier in this section) in which the minimality principle is manifest, particularly when these provisions are considered as a totality.[38]

---

[34] 'Gestaltung und Auswahl von Datenverarbeitungssystemen haben sich an dem Ziel auszurichten, keine oder so wenig personenbezogene Daten wie möglich zu erheben, zu verarbeiten oder zu nutzen'.

[35] 'The controller shall implement mechanisms for ensuring that, by default, only those personal data are processed which are necessary for each specific purpose of the processing and are especially not collected or retained beyond the minimum necessary for those purposes...' (Art. 23(2)).

[36] 'Systems for the provision of electronic communications networks and services should be designed to limit the amount of personal data necessary to a strict minimum. Any activities related to the provision of the electronic communications service that go beyond the transmission of a communication and the billing thereof should be based on aggregated, traffic data that cannot be related to subscribers or users...' (Recital 30). Cf National Privacy Principle (NPP) 8 in sch 3 to Australia's federal Privacy Act ('Wherever it is lawful and practicable, individuals should have the option of not identifying themselves when entering transactions') and Information Privacy Principle 8 in sch 1 to Victoria's Information Privacy Act ('Wherever it is lawful and practicable, individuals must have the option of not identifying themselves when entering transactions with an organisation'). The provisions that will replace the NPPs in the federal legislation also make qualified provision for anonymity, with pseudonymity as a further option: see Privacy Amendment (Enhancing Privacy) Act 2012 (due to commence in March 2014) s 104.

[37] Recommendation CM/Rec (2010) 13 on the protection of individuals with regard to automatic processing of personal data in the context of profiling para. 2.2 ('Member states should encourage the design and implementation of procedures and systems in accordance with privacy and data protection, already at their planning stage, notably through the use of privacy-enhancing technologies. They should also take appropriate measures against the development and use of technologies which are aimed, wholly or partly, at the illicit circumvention of technological measures protecting privacy'). See too para. 3.7 ('As much as possible, and unless the service required necessitates knowledge of the data subject's identity, everyone should have access to information about goods or services or access to these goods or services themselves without having to communicate personal data to the goods or services provider. In order to ensure free, specific and informed consent to profiling, providers of information society services should ensure, by default, non-profiled access to information about their services').

[38] See further Bygrave (n 1) ch 18 (section 18.4.3).

# E. Purpose Limitation

The principle of purpose limitation stipulates, in short, that personal data should be collected for specified, legitimate purposes and not used in ways that are incompatible with those purposes. The principle has several other names, most notably 'finality' and 'purpose specification'. It is prominent in all of the main international data privacy codes.[39] It is also prominent in most (but not all)[40] of the national laws.

Purpose limitation is frequently singled out by experts in the field as an especially important principle.[41] The Norwegian Supreme Court recently reiterated this, stating that the principle 'is internationally considered as a fundamental and important principle in the field of data protection'.[42] At the same time, the principle presents special challenges in practice. As the A29WP observes, '[a]ssessing the compatibility of any given operation with the purpose for which the data were originally collected... is one of the most difficult and important tasks in supervising compliance with data protection legislation'.[43] This difficulty is exacerbated in the current era of 'Big Data' when increasingly refined methods of data analytics are improving the ability to draw meaningful correlations between ever larger data sets.

The principle is grounded partly in concern for ensuring foreseeability in data-processing outcomes. It aims to ensure that both the way in which personal data is processed and the results of such processing conform with the reasonable expectations of data subjects. It is additionally grounded in concern for ensuring that personal data is used for purposes to which it is suited. In other words, the principle is also concerned with ensuring adequate information quality and that data-processing outcomes conform with the expectations of data controllers.

---

[39] See Convention 108 Art. 5(b); DPD Art. 6(1)(b); UN Guidelines principle 3; OECD Guidelines para. 9; APEC Privacy Framework paras 15b and 19. Surprisingly, though, the EU Charter of Fundamental Rights expressly refers to just one component of the principle (ie, specification of purposes), although the other components are arguably inherent in its reference to 'fair' processing: see Art. 8(2) ('data must be processed fairly for specified purposes').

[40] It is reflected only obliquely in the US federal Privacy Act.

[41] See A29WP, Opinion 03/2013 on purpose limitation (2 April 2013; WP 203) 4 (describing the principle as a 'cornerstone of data protection'). See too S Öman and H-O Lindblom, *Personuppgiftslagen: En kommentar* (4th edn, Norstedts Juridik 2011) 203; H Waaben and K Korfits Nielsen, *Lov om behandling af personoplysninger med kommentarer* (2nd edn, Jurist-og Økonomforbundets Forlag 2008) 146.

[42] Rt 2013 143 [47].

[43] A29WP, Working document on notification (3 December 1997; WP 8) 6.

Despite its acknowledged importance, the principle is far from salient in ECtHR case law. Some emphasis is arguably put on the principle in the case of *MS v Sweden*.[44] The case concerned the communication by a hospital, without the applicant's consent, of medical data about the applicant to the Swedish Social Insurance Office so that the latter could settle a compensation claim by the applicant. The Court found the communication to interfere with the applicant's rights under Article 8(1) but held it justified under Article 8(2). In finding interference, the Court stated:

> Although the records remained confidential, they had been disclosed to another public authority and therefore to a wider circle of public servants.... Moreover, whilst the information had been collected and stored at the clinic in connection with medical treatment, its subsequent communication had served a *different purpose*, namely to enable the Office to examine her [the applicant's] compensation claim. It did not follow from the fact that she had sought treatment at the clinic that she would consent to the data being disclosed to the Office.[45]

From this statement, it seems that the Court did not see the re-purposing of the medical data as solely constitutive of the interference; rather, the Court seems to have placed primary weight on the absence of consent, with the re-purposing of the data serving merely to establish the parameters of the consent. Nevertheless, the Court was apparently alert to, and respectful of, the applicant's reasonable expectations as to what would happen with the data, inasmuch as the parameters of the applicant's consent reflected the parameters of these expectations.

Some weight is also placed on the purpose limitation principle in *Malone v UK*.[46] This case concerned, inter alia, the secret disclosure to the British police of certain data obtained from the 'metering' of Malone's telephone by the British telecommunications authority.[47] The Court found interference on the basis of this disclosure.[48] In a separate, concurring opinion, Judge Pettiti suggested that the mere application of metering data for purposes other than 'accounting' would be sufficient to constitute interference.[49] Here, Pettiti seems to have drawn on the principle of purpose limitation. His colleagues, however, failed to signal support for his view on this point.

---

[44] (1999) 28 EHRR 313.          [45] *MS* (n 44) [35] (emphasis added).

[46] *Malone v UK* (1984) 7 EHRR 14.

[47] 'Metering' denotes the registration of data on telephone usage, including numbers dialled and the time and duration of each call, but not the call's content: *Malone* (n 46) [56].

[48] *Malone* (n 46) [84].

[49] Publications of the European Court of Human Rights, Series A, 1984, vol. 82, 47.

The purpose limitation principle is really a cluster of three sub-principles:

(1) the purposes for which data is collected shall be defined and made explicit;
(2) these purposes shall be lawful or legitimate;
(3) the purposes for which the data is further processed shall not be incompatible with the purposes for which the data is originally collected.

Some laws stipulate that the purposes for which data is processed shall be 'lawful'.[50] Other laws, such as Convention 108 and the DPD, stipulate that such purposes shall be 'legitimate'.

The first of these sub-principles is relatively free of ambiguity. The purposes for which a data controller collects personal data must be defined and documented in advance of collection, and they must be delineated in fairly concrete, precise terms.[51]

The second sub-principle is more problematic: what does 'legitimate' mean? Does it simply mean 'lawful'? Or does it denote a broader criterion of social acceptability? Arguably, it embraces the latter criterion, such that personal data should only be processed for purposes that do not run counter to ethical and social mores that are generally deemed appropriate to govern the relationship of the controller and data subject(s).[52] If so, how are these mores to be defined? Are they to be defined essentially as a procedural norm—more specifically, that the purposes for which personal data is processed should be compatible with, or fall naturally within, the ordinary (and lawful) ambit of the particular controller's activities? Or do they also have substantive elements—more specifically, that the controller's activities promote or do not detract from some generally valued state of affairs? Most data privacy codes seem to comprehend legitimacy primarily in terms of procedural norms.[53] Nevertheless, the discretionary powers given by some laws to DPAs have enabled the latter to apply a relatively wide-ranging test of social justification, particularly in connection

---

[50] See eg, Data Protection Principle 2 in pt I of sch 1 to the UK Act, and the OECD Guidelines para. 9.

[51] See too COM(92) 422 final—SYN 287, 15; A29WP (n 41) 15–17.

[52] See too A29WP (n 41) 20 ('Within the confines of law, other elements such as customs, codes of conduct, codes of ethics, contractual arrangements, and the general context and facts of the case, may also be considered when determining whether a particular purpose is legitimate. This will include the nature of the underlying relationship between the controller and the data subjects, whether it be commercial or otherwise').

[53] Cf Canada's Personal Information Protection and Electronic Documents Act s 5(3) ('An organization may collect, use or disclose personal information only for purposes that a reasonable person would consider are appropriate in the circumstances'). This comes close to a broad substantive criterion of social justification.

with the licensing of certain data-processing operations.[54] Although this ability has been cut back in line with reductions in the scope of licensing schemes, it has not disappeared completely.[55]

Turning to the third sub-principle, the chief issue concerns the meaning of the criterion of (in)compatibility. Little help in understanding this criterion is to be found on the face of the laws or in their preparatory works. A preliminary issue is whether phrasing of the criterion as a double negative ('not incompatible') denotes a slightly less stringent standard than that of straight compatibility. I am inclined to think it does.[56]

Arguably, the criterion could be read as merely requiring that the secondary purposes for which data is processed must not hinder realization of the primary purposes for which the data was collected. Yet such an argument reduces the criterion of compatibility/non-incompatibility to being simply a matter of promoting the efficiency of data processing largely for the data controller's benefit. It does not do justice to the broader rationale for the purpose limitation principle pointed to above; nor does it comport well with the fairness criterion outlined in section B.[57]

Accordingly, the phrase 'not incompatible' most likely connotes criteria additional to that just canvassed. One obvious criterion is that the secondary purposes are objectively similar to the primary purposes. Another relates to the context of the processing. Context breaks down into multiple sub-criteria, including the nature of the relationship between the controller and data subject, the nature of the data, and the nature of the impact that the further processing might have on the data subject in light of extant data privacy safeguards.[58] Further, in light of this context, the data subject ought reasonably to be able to read the secondary purposes into the primary purposes, such that the former purposes are objectively within the ambit of the data subject's reasonable expectations.[59]

A recent decision by the Norwegian Supreme Court affirms the latter criterion as a key element in assessing (in)compatibility.[60] This decision is

---

[54] For examples, see Bygrave (n 1) ch 18 (section 18.4.7).

[55] Section 33 of Norway's Personal Data Act, for instance, maintains the possibility for the Data Inspectorate to undertake a relatively open-ended assessment of licensing applications, albeit with respect to a narrower range of data-processing operations than was the case under the 1978 legislation. See further Bygrave (n 1) ch 18 (section 18.4.7).

[56] See too A29WP (n 41) 21; Waaben and Korfits Nielsen (n 41) 146. Cf my earlier doubts in Bygrave (n 1) 340.

[57] See too Bygrave (n 1) 340.     [58] See too A29WP (n 41) 25–26.

[59] A29WP (n 41) 24; Bygrave (n 1) 340; W Kotschy, 'Commentary to Directive 95/46/EC' in A Büllesbach, S Gijbrath, Y Poullet, and C Prins (eds), *Concise European IT Law* (2nd edn, Kluwer Law International 2010) 49, 52.

[60] Rt 2013, 143 [60]. Surprisingly, the Court indicated that determination of (in)compatibility also turns on an assessment of the necessity of the data re-purposing: Rt 2013, 143 [66]. With respect, it is difficult to see that criteria of necessity or proportionality are relevant here.

also noteworthy for affirming that the Norwegian provisions which transpose DPD Article 6(1)(b) (laying down the purpose specification principle) cannot be circumvented by reliance on provisions which transpose DPD Article 7(f) (permitting processing of personal data when necessary to pursue 'legitimate interests' that override those of the data subject). The Court of Appeal and (putatively) Data Inspectorate had taken a line permitting such circumvention, but the Supreme Court held that the former provisions must be respected in addition to the latter.[61]

In light of the latter decision, it is remarkable that Article 6(4) of the proposed GDPR permits circumvention of the (in)compatibility criterion in the purpose limitation principle if the processing has a legal basis in one of the grounds listed in points (a) to (e) of Article 6(1). The latter replicate the grounds in DPD Article 7(a) to (e). However, the proposal appears not to allow circumvention in respect of Article 6(1)(f), which replicates DPD Article 7(f).[62]

Finally, it is worthwhile dwelling a little on the principle of 'respect for context' in the Consumer Privacy Bill of Rights issued by the Obama Administration in 2012. The principle stipulates that '[c]onsumers have a right to expect that companies will collect, use, and disclose personal data in ways that are consistent with the context in which consumers provide the data'. This is the closest the Consumer Privacy Bill of Rights comes to embracing the principle of purpose limitation as elaborated above. The 'respect for context' principle is interesting as it is not far from a hitherto rarely expressed principle on respect for data subjects' reasonable expectations,[63] at the same time as it (along with the Consumer Privacy Bill of Rights generally) studiously steers clear of expressly mentioning notions of reasonable expectations or, indeed, (in)compatibility.

Context as a determinant of data privacy standards is increasingly highlighted in regulatory discourse.[64] However, it is far from being a new addition to the field. We see it already in, say, the OECD Guidelines.[65]

---

[61] Rt 2013, 143 [47].

[62] The A29WP is strongly opposed to Art. 6(4) and recommends its deletion: A29WP (n 41) 41.

[63] Cf the 'fairness principle' proposed by the US Information Infrastructure Taskforce established by the Clinton Administration. The principle reads: '[i]nformation users should not use personal information in ways that are incompatible with the individual's understanding of how it will be used, unless there is a compelling public interest for such use'. See US Information Infrastructure Task Force, 'Principles for Providing and Using Personal Information' (adopted 6 June 1995) II.D; available at: <http://aspe.hhs.gov/datacncl/niiprivp.htm>.

[64] See particularly the scholarship of Helen Nissenbaum on 'contextual integrity': H Nissenbaum, *Privacy in Context: Technology, Policy, and the Integrity of Social Life* (Stanford University Press 2010). See too eg, A29WP (n 41) 24ff.

[65] See Guidelines para. 3 ('These Guidelines should not be interpreted as preventing: (a) the application, to different categories of personal data, of different protective measures depending upon

# F. Data Subject Influence

A core principle of data privacy laws is that persons should be able to participate in, and have a measure of influence over, the processing of data on them by others. This principle embraces what the OECD Guidelines term the 'Individual Participation Principle' (paragraph 13), though rules giving effect to it embrace more than what is articulated in that particular paragraph.

Data privacy laws rarely contain one special rule expressing this principle in the manner formulated above. Rather, the principle manifests itself more obliquely through a combination of several categories of rules. First, there are rules aimed at making people aware of data-processing activities generally. Examples are rules requiring data controllers to provide basic details of their processing of personal data to DPAs, coupled with a requirement that the latter store this information in a publicly accessible register.[66]

Secondly, and arguably of greater importance, are rules aimed at making persons aware of basic details of the processing of data on themselves. This category of rules can be divided into three main sub-categories:

1) rules requiring data controllers to collect data directly from data subjects in certain circumstances;
2) rules requiring data controllers to orient data subjects directly about certain information on their data-processing operations; and
3) rules prohibiting the processing of personal data without the consent of the data subjects.

As noted in section B, rules falling under the first sub-category are found only in a minority of data privacy laws, though such rules could and should be read into the more common and general requirement that personal data be processed 'fairly'.

As for rules belonging to the second sub-category, influential examples of these are Articles 10–11 of the DPD which, in summary, require data controllers to directly supply data subjects with basic information about the parameters of their data-processing operations, independently of the data subjects' use of access rights. With the exception of the APEC Privacy Framework,

---

their nature and the *context* in which they are collected, stored, processed or disseminated'; emphasis added). See too Explanatory Memorandum para. 45 (stating that the Guidelines 'should not be applied in a mechanistic way irrespective of the kind of data and processing activities involved').

[66] See further Ch 6 (section C).

none of the other main international data privacy instruments lay down such requirements directly.[67] National laws have often instituted such require-ments only when data is collected directly from the data subject.[68] The cur-rent notification requirements pursuant to national laws of at least EU and EEA member states have been largely harmonized and expanded in accord-ance with the DPD. Some of these laws stipulate duties of information which go beyond the prima facie requirements of DPD Articles 10–11. These duties arise in connection with certain uses of personal profiles and video surveil-lance.[69] Also relevant are rules on mandatory notification of data security breaches. As noted in Chapters 2 and 3, such rules are found in the legislation of most American states, the E-Privacy Directive (Article 4(3)), the OECD Guidelines (paragraph 15(c)), and the proposed GDPR (Articles 31–32).

Thirdly, there are rules granting persons the right to gain access to data kept on them by other persons and organizations. For the sake of brevity, this right is described hereinafter as simply 'the right of access' or 'access right(s)'. Most, if not all, data privacy laws provide for such a right. An influential for-mulation of the right is given in DPD Article 12. This provides persons with a right of access not just to data relating directly to them but also to informa-tion about the way in which the data is used, including the purposes of the processing, the recipients and sources of the data, and 'the logic involved in any automated processing of data concerning [the data subject] . . . at least in the case of the automated decisions referred to in Article 15(1)'.[70] The right in Article 12 is similar to, but also more extensive than, the equivalent rights found in the other main international data privacy instruments. None of the latter, with the exception of the UN Guidelines, specifically mentions the right to be informed of the recipients of data. None of them specifically

---

[67] See the 'Notice' principle in para. 15 of the APEC Privacy Framework. The UN Guidelines' 'principle of purpose specification' (principle 3) stipulates that the purpose of a computerized per-sonal data file should 'receive a certain amount of publicity or be brought to the attention of the person concerned'. Cf the more generally formulated 'Openness Principle' in para. 12 of the OECD Guidelines: 'There should be a general policy of openness about developments, practices and policies with respect to personal data. Means should be readily available of establishing the existence and nature of personal data, and the main purposes of their use, as well as the identity and usual residence of the data controller'. Arts 10–11 of the Directive are supplemented by a requirement that member states 'take measures to ensure that processing operations are publicized' (Art. 21(1)) and to ensure that there is a register of processing operations open to public inspection (Art. 21(2)).

[68] See eg, US federal Privacy Act s 552a(e)(3); Switzerland's Data Protection Act Art.18(1) (only in relation to 'systematic' collection by federal government bodies).

[69] In relation to uses of personal profiles, see Norway's Personal Data Act s 21 and Iceland's Personal Data Act s 23. In relation to video surveillance, see s 40 of the Norwegian Act, s 24 of the Icelandic Act and s 6b(2) of the German Federal Data Protection Act. For analysis of s 21 of the Norwegian Act, see Bygrave (n 1) ch 18 (section 18.3.4).

[70] Article 15(1) is explained further on in this section.

mentions the right to be informed of the logic behind automated data processing. Outside Europe, it is rare to find national laws specifying the latter rights.

As an aside, very few data privacy laws specifically restrict so-called 'enforced access' whereby persons are pushed into utilizing their access rights in order to provide a body on which they are dependent (for example, employer, insurance company) with personal information normally unavailable to it. A lonely instance of such a restriction is the UK Data Protection Act (section 56). A similar restriction was also included in the 1992 amended proposal for the DPD (Article 13(2)). However, the Directive as it presently stands, fails to remedy the practice of enforced access clearly and directly.[71]

The third major category of rules are those allowing persons to object to others' processing of data on themselves and to demand that the data be rectified or erased insofar as it is invalid, irrelevant, illegally held, etc. The ability to object is linked primarily to rules prohibiting various types of data processing without the consent of the data subjects. Such rules are especially prominent in the DPD, relative to older codes. For instance, Convention 108 makes no express mention of a consent requirement, while the OECD Guidelines only requires consent as a precondition for disclosure of data to third parties (paragraph 10). The DPD stipulates consent both as one (albeit alternative) precondition for processing generally (Article 7(a)) and for processing of particular sensitive categories of personal data (Article 8(2)(a)).

The reference to 'consent' in DPD Articles 7(a) and 8(2)(a) must be read in light of Article 2(h), which defines 'the data subject's consent' as 'any freely given specific and informed indication of his wishes, by which the data subject signifies his agreement to personal data relating to him being processed'. From this definition, it appears that consent need not be in writing. However, the express registration of consent on paper or electronic medium will aid in fulfilling the requirement in Article 7(a) that consent be 'unambiguous' and, a fortiori, the requirement in Article 8(2)(a) that consent be 'explicit'.

The criterion 'unambiguous' means that the data subject's actions must leave no doubt that they have given consent. The data subject must accordingly have taken active steps to signal their consent; mere inaction will not be enough. The criterion 'explicit' in Article 8 is more stringent than 'unambiguous'.

---

[71] Article 12(a) stipulates that access rights are to be exercised 'without constraint', but it is uncertain if this phrase should be read only in the sense of 'without hindrance' or also in the sense of 'freely'/'without duress'. The French text uses the phrase 'sans contrainte' which arguably connotes both senses, whereas the German text uses the phrase 'frei und ungehindert'. The phrase used in the Danish text ('frit og uhindret') is similar to the German. Cf the Swedish text which only mentions 'utan hinder' ('without hindrance').

It means that the process of requesting and providing consent must occur as a formally separate process to the other transaction(s) to which the consent attaches. There must be a specific request by the controller for permission from the data subject to process the data in question, followed by a specific reply in the affirmative. Consent probably does not have to be in writing,[72] but there has to be at least some sort of record made of the request and reply, with measures in place to keep the record secure from unauthorized access and modification.

Consent is rarely laid down as the sole precondition for the particular type of processing in question; it tends to be one of several alternative prerequisites. This is also the case with the DPD. The alternative prerequisites are often broadly formulated, thereby reducing significantly the extent to which controllers are hostage to the consent requirement in practice. With regard to DPD Article 7, for example, most instances of processing will be able to be justified under the criteria in paragraphs (b)–(f) of the provision (set out in section C).

On their face, all of these alternative preconditions carry equal normative weight—that is, there appears to be no normative prioritization of consent relative to, say, proportionality as expressed in Article 7(f). The same can be said of the alternative preconditions for data processing specified in Article 8. However, in a small number of jurisdictions, the consent requirement has been given priority over the other preconditions such that a controller must ordinarily obtain the data subject's consent to the processing unless this would be impracticable.[73] It is doubtful that the Directive, as originally conceived, mandates such prioritization. However, the Directive does not disallow it. At the same time, case law of the ECtHR might provide a foundation for this prioritization and, indeed, may even require it for the processing of certain types of sensitive data, such as medical data—at least in situations

---

[72] See too Kotschy (n 59) 56.

[73] The case eg, in Estonia and, to a lesser extent, Belgium and Greece: see D Beyleveld, D Townend, S Rouillé-Mirza, and J Wright (eds), *Implementation of the Data Protection Directive in Relation to Medical Research in Europe* (Ashgate 2004) 155 and references cited therein. In Belgium, consent is apparently given priority only with respect to processing of *sensitive* personal data: see H Nys, 'Report on the Implementation of Directive 95/46/EC in Belgian Law' in Beyleveld and others (details earlier in this note) 29, 36. The Norwegian Data Privacy Tribunal previously held that controllers must ordinarily attempt to get consent unless there are reasons for waiver which are grounded in more than simply cost and convenience factors (decision in case 1/2004; followed in numerous cases up until 2012). However, the Tribunal reversed its line in 2012, claiming that this prioritization had insufficient legal basis: see decision in appeal case 1/2012; available at <www.personvernnemnda.no/vedtak/2012_01.htm>.

when the processing of such data cannot otherwise be justified under ECHR Article 8(2).[74]

It bears emphasis that, under the DPD, fairly comprehensive legislative limits are placed on the ability to contract around core data privacy rights and obligations.[75] Data subjects are largely prevented from disposing of their statutorily enumerated rights over use of the data, at their discretion or according to the dictates of the market. The statutory obligations placed on controllers are also largely insulated from contract-based modification. The consent mechanisms in DPD Articles 7(a) and 8(2)(a) do not permit a data subject to enter into an agreement that permits a controller from derogating fundamentally from their basic duties pursuant to, for example, the principles in Article 6 and the access rights in Article 12. Moreover, in the workplace context, European DPAs are generally sceptical to permitting employers to process data on their employees on the basis of putative consent by the latter. As noted above, consent must be freely given (Article 2(h)) and it is at the very least doubtful that an employee is normally able to agree freely to processing practices instigated by their employer.[76]

Some laws lay down specific rights to object to data processing or certain types of processing. The DPD contains important instances of such rights, namely in Article 14(a) (which provides a right to object to data processing generally), Article 14(b) (which sets out a right to object to direct marketing) and, most innovatively, Article 15(1), which grants a person the right

not to be subject to a decision which produces legal effects concerning him or significantly affects him and which is based solely on automated processing of data intended to evaluate certain personal aspects relating to him, such as his performance at work, creditworthiness, reliability, conduct, etc.[77]

The latter right could well be treated as the basis for a nascent data privacy principle—namely that fully automated assessments of a person's character should not form the sole basis of decisions that significantly impinge upon the person's interests.

---

[74] See eg, *Z v Finland* (1998) 25 EHRR 371 [95]–[96]; *MS v Sweden* (1999) 28 EHRR 313 [41].

[75] See further N Purtova, 'Private Law Solutions in European Data Protection: Relationship to Privacy, and Waiver of Data Protection Rights' (2010) 28 Netherlands Quarterly of Human Rights 179.

[76] A29WP, Opinion 8/2001 on the processing of personal data in the employment context (13 September 2001; WP 48).

[77] A right inspired by roughly similar provisions in French legislation: see Ch 2 (n 199). For further analysis of Art. 15, see Bygrave (n 1) ch 18 (sections 18.3.1 and 18.4.5). The right is not absolute; a person may be subjected to such decisions if they are, in summary, taken pursuant to a contract with the data subject or authorized by law, and provision is made for 'suitable measures' to safeguard the person's 'legitimate interests' (Art. 15(2)).

The above rights to object are not found in the other main international data privacy instruments.[78] They have rarely been found outside Europe, though this is changing under the influence of the DPD.[79]

With respect to rectification and erasure rights, most data privacy laws have provisions giving persons the right to demand that incorrect, misleading, or obsolescent data relating to them be rectified or deleted by those in control of the data, and require, with some qualifications, that controllers rectify or delete such data.[80]

## G. Data Quality

The principle of data quality stipulates that personal data should be valid with respect to what it is intended to describe, and relevant and complete with respect to the purposes for which it is intended to be processed. All data privacy laws contain rules directly embodying the principle, but they vary in their wording, scope, and stringency.

Regarding the first limb of the principle (concerning validity), laws use a variety of terms to describe the stipulated data quality. Convention 108 Article 5(d) and DPD Article 6(1)(d) state that personal data shall be 'accurate and, where necessary, kept up to date'. The equivalent provisions of some other codes refer only to a criterion of accuracy/correctness ('Richtigkeit'),[81] while others supplement the latter with other criteria, such as completeness.[82]

Regarding the principle's second limb, the DPD formulates this as a requirement that personal data be 'adequate, relevant and not excessive in relation to the purposes for which they are collected and/or further processed' (Article 6(1)(c)).[83] Some codes refer to the criteria of relevance, accuracy, and completeness but omit non-excessiveness.[84]

---

[78] Cf principles 5.5, 5.6, 6.10, and 6.11 of the International Labour Organisation's Code of Practice on Protection of Workers' Personal Data (1997) which seek to limit the use of automated decision-making procedures for assessing worker conduct: see further Bygrave (n 1) ch 18 (section 18.3.1).

[79] Recall eg, provision for such rights in the 2010 Supplementary Act on Personal Data Protection within ECOWAS, referenced Ch 2 (section H).

[80] See eg, DPD Art. 12(b), UN Guidelines principle 4, UK Act s 14, NZ Act IPP 7. Cf the relatively elaborate and controversial erasure requirements in the proposed GDPR Art. 17. For an overview of the discussion on these requirements (and one that takes account of equivalent US norms), see ML Ambrose and J Ausloos, 'The Right to Be Forgotten Across the Pond' (2013) 3 J of Info Policy 1.

[81] See eg, the Swiss Act Art. 5.     [82] See eg, OECD Guidelines para. 8.

[83] Similarly formulated requirements are found in many national laws, also outside Europe: see eg, US federal Privacy Act s 552a(e)(1), (5), and (6).

[84] See, eg, para. 8 of the OECD Guidelines and ss 4–8 of Canada's federal Privacy Act.

Finally, variation exists in terms of the stringency required of checks on the validity of personal data. The DPD's standard, for example, is in terms of 'every reasonable step must be taken' (Article 6(1)(d)). The reference to 'reasonable' probably implies that it is legitimate for controllers to take into account cost and resource factors when deciding upon measures to erase or rectify data. Less certain is the extent to which Article 6(1)(d) requires controllers to check regularly the accuracy of personal data in advance of evidence of data error.[85] By contrast, the UN Guidelines emphasize a duty to carry out 'regular checks' (principle 2).[86]

# H.  Data Security

The principle of data security holds that personal data should be protected against unauthorized attempts to disclose, delete, change, or exploit it. A representative provision to this effect is Article 7 of Convention 108:

Appropriate security measures shall be taken for the protection of personal data stored in automated data files against accidental or unauthorised destruction or accidental loss as well as against unauthorised access, alteration or dissemination.

The relevant provisions of the DPD are a little more detailed. Article 17(1) requires controllers to implement security measures for ensuring that personal data is protected from accidental and unlawful destruction, alteration, or disclosure. The measures taken are to be commensurate with the risks involved in the data processing 'having regard to the state of the Article and the cost of their implementation'. Controllers must also ensure—by way of contract or other legal act (Article 17(3))—that data processors engaged by them provide 'sufficient guarantees in respect of the technical security measures and organizational security measures governing the processing to be carried out' (Article 17(2)).[87] Further, the measures taken pursuant to Article 17(1) and (3) shall be documented (Article 17(4)).

The principle of data security occasionally manifests itself in relatively peculiar provisions. Section 41(4) of Denmark's Personal Data Act is a case in point. This states that for personal data which is processed for the public administration and is of particular interest to foreign powers, measures shall be taken to

---

[85]  For discussion, see Bygrave (n 1) 350.          [86]  See further Bygrave (n 1) ch 18 (section 18.4.4).

[87]  The latter requirements are supplemented in Art. 16 ('Any person acting under the authority of the controller or . . . processor, including the processor himself, who has access to personal data must not process them except on instructions from the controller, unless he is required to do so by law').

ensure that it can be disposed of and destroyed in the event of war or similar conditions.[88]

# I. Sensitivity

The principle of sensitivity holds that the processing of certain types of data that are regarded as especially sensitive for data subjects should be subject to more stringent controls than other personal data. We see some manifestation of this principle at work in ECtHR jurisprudence, particularly concerning health data.[89] Yet the principle is primarily manifest in statutory rules that place special limits on the processing of predefined categories of data. The most influential list of these data categories is provided in DPD Article 8(1): it embraces data on a person's 'racial or ethnic origin', 'political opinions', 'religious or philosophical beliefs', 'trade-union membership', 'health', and 'sexual life'.[90] Further, Article 8(5) makes special provision for data on criminal records and the like. Similar lists are found in numerous other data privacy codes at both international and national level, though these vary somewhat in scope. For instance, the list in Article 6 of Convention 108 omits data on trade-union membership and ethnic origin, while the list in the UN Guidelines includes data on membership of associations in general (not just trade unions). The lists in some national laws also include, or have previously included, data revealing a person to be in receipt of social welfare benefits.[91] The proposed GDPR includes 'genetic data' in its list (Article 9(1)) while the amendments to Convention 108 proposed by the T-PD add 'genetic data', 'biometric data uniquely identifying a person', and information on 'trade-union membership' (revised Article 6(1)).

Singling out relatively fixed sub-sets of personal data for special protection breaks with the otherwise common assumption in the field that the sensitivity of data is essentially context-dependent. Accordingly, attempts to single out particular categories of data for special protection independent of the context in which the data is processed, have not been without controversy.[92] Further,

---

[88] A similar rule was found in s 12(3) of the Danish Public Authorities' Registers Act 1978 (repealed) and s 29 of the Icelandic Protection of Personal Records Act 1989 (repealed).

[89] See eg, *Z v Finland* (1998) 25 EHRR 371 esp. [96].

[90] The preamble to the DPD describes these as 'data which are capable by their nature of infringing fundamental freedoms or privacy' (Recital 33).

[91] See s 6(6) of Finland's Personal Data Registers Act 1987 (repealed), s 4(2) of Sweden's Data Act 1973 (repealed), and Art. 3(c)(3) of the Swiss Act.

[92] For a forceful, highly persuasive critique of such attempts, see S Simitis, ' "Sensitive Daten"— Zur Geschichte und Wirkung einer Fiktion', in E Brem, JN Druey, EA Kramer, and I Schwander (eds), *Festschrift zum 65. Geburtstag von Mario M. Pedrazzini* (Verlag Stämpfli & Cie 1990) 469.

not all data privacy codes contain extra safeguards for designated categories of data. This is the case with the OECD Guidelines and many laws of the Pacific Rim countries.

In terms of the special protection given for these categories of data, the DPD stipulates that processing of them is prohibited (Article 8(1)) but then sets out exceptions to the prohibition (Article 8(2)). In summary, processing is permitted under the following, alternative conditions:

(a)  the data subject explicitly consents to the processing (except where national laws override this condition);

(b)  the processing is necessary for the data controller to meet obligations and rights pursuant to employment law, and is authorized by 'national law providing for adequate safeguards';

(c)  the processing is necessary for protecting the 'vital interests' of the data subject (or of another person where the data subject is incapable of consenting);

(d)  the processing is undertaken by a non-profit organization with a 'political, philosophical, religious or trade-union aim' and only concerns the organization's members or regular contacts, and the data are not disclosed to third parties without the data subject's consent;

(e)  the data in question 'are manifestly made public' by the data subject, or their processing is necessary for pursuit of legal claims.

Processing is also allowed if required for medical purposes and carried out by a 'health professional' or other person subject to an 'obligation of professional secrecy' (Article 8(3)). The exemptions may be supplemented by others that are laid down by national law or a decision of the national DPA (Article 8(4)). As for data on criminal convictions, processing of this sort of information, along with data on 'offences', 'security measures', 'administrative sanctions', and 'civil trials', are placed largely under control of official authority (Article 8(5)).

The inclusion of data on 'offences' and the like in a separate paragraph has been construed as evidence that the list of data categories in Article 8(1) is not exhaustive,[93] but the validity of this interpretation is doubtful.[94] The better view is that member states may specify data categories which elaborate on

---

[93]  D Bainbridge and G Pearce, 'The Data Protection Directive: A Legal Analysis' (1996) 12 CLSR 160, 163.

[94]  While para. 5 is described (in para. 6) as a derogation from para. 1, it seems prima facie to be quite independent of para. 1. Further, the wording of para. 1 (in conjunction with Recital 13) does not indicate that the data categories listed therein are instances of a broader data set.

the paragraph 1 categories but which do not constitute totally new categories. At the same time, the CJEU has held that the 'health' category of data 'must be given a wide interpretation so as to include information concerning all aspects, both physical and mental, of the health of an individual'.[95] Presumably, the other data categories specified in Article 8(1) must be construed broadly too.

[95] Case C-101/01 *Bodil Lindqvist* [2003] ECR I-12971 [55].

# 6

# Oversight and Enforcement of
# Data Privacy Law

## A. Data Privacy Agencies

### 1. Introduction

Almost every country with a fairly comprehensive statutory framework for data privacy has established a special data privacy agency (DPA) to oversee specifically the implementation of the framework. As elaborated in the following, DPAs are typically required to be functionally independent of the governments or legislatures which establish them. This means that they must have the capacity to arrive at their own decisions in concrete cases without being given case-specific instructions by other bodies. Insofar as such decisions are legally binding, however, they are usually subject to judicial review. Moreover, DPA decision-making must respect more general rules laid down in, say, administrative law.[1]

DPAs' oversight function typically encompasses the handling of complaints by members of the public over the processing of personal data. It can also involve the auditing of the legality of data-processing operations independent of complaints. Additionally, the agencies are frequently expected to orient and advise governments, parliaments, private organizations, and the general public about data privacy matters. Some DPAs are also responsible for oversight of FOI regimes.[2]

---

[1] A variety of other administrative, economic, and political mechanisms will also tend to challenge, if not undermine, their functional independence. For an instructive, detailed analysis of these mechanisms with respect to the early operations of the national DPAs of Sweden, France, the Federal Republic of Germany, and Canada, see DH Flaherty, *Protecting Privacy in Surveillance Societies* (University of North Carolina Press 1989).

[2] The case with, eg, the UK Information Commissioner's Office.

DPA powers are often broad and largely discretionary. In most cases, the agencies are empowered to issue legally binding (although appealable) orders. In some jurisdictions, however, the agencies do not have such competence,[3] or they have not had it in relation to certain sectors.[4]

Of the international data privacy codes, by far the most detailed and influential treatment of DPAs' competence and functions is found in the DPD. Thus, the DPD provides the point of departure for much of the following analysis.

## 2. Independence

Article 28(1) of the DPD requires each EU member state to establish one or more DPAs (termed 'supervisory authorities'). These are to 'act with complete independence in exercising the functions entrusted to them'. The reference to 'complete independence' means that great care must be taken in ensuring that the DPAs' inevitable *administrative* dependence on other bodies (for example, through budget and personnel allocations) does not undermine the functional independence they are otherwise supposed to have. It also means that administrative and legal frameworks which leave open even a small possibility of a DPA being instructed by another administrative body on how to exercise its functions, do not satisfy the criterion of Article 28(1).

The stringency of the independence criterion is underlined in CJEU jurisprudence. According to the Court, a supervisory authority must have 'complete independence' implying 'a decision-making power independent of any direct or indirect external influence'.[5] Moreover, 'the mere risk that the scrutinising authorities could exercise a political influence over the decisions of the supervisory authorities is enough to hinder the latter authorities' independent performance of their tasks'.[6] Applying these criteria, the Court found that DPAs in the German *Länder* were not completely independent as

---

[3] The case with, eg, Germany's Federal Data Protection Commissioner (Bundesdatenschutzbeauftragter): see the Federal Data Protection Act ss 24–26.

[4] A special case is Finland where primary responsibility for oversight and enforcement of national data privacy legislation is divided between two bodies: the Data Protection Ombudsman (Dataombudsmannen) and the Data Protection Board (Datasekretessnämden). Under the Personal Data Registers Act 1987 (repealed), the ombudsman had mainly advisory competence though extensive investigatory powers; by contrast, the board had power to issue legally binding orders, including competence to set aside provisions in the Act on a case-by-case basis. The latter competence was abolished by the current Personal Data Act, whilst the competence of the ombudsman to give legally binding orders was strengthened.

[5] Case C-581/07, *European Commission v Federal Republic of Germany* [2010] ECR I-1885 [19].

[6] [2010] ECR I-1885 [36].

they were subject to state scrutiny.[7] In a subsequent case, the Court found the independence criterion breached by organizational overlap between Austria's DPA (the Datenschutzkommission (DSK)) and the Federal Chancellery.[8] According to the Court, 'such an organisational overlap between the DSK and the Federal Chancellery prevents the DSK from being above all suspicion of partiality and is therefore incompatible with the requirement of "independence"'.[9] It held, though, that the DSK need not be given a separate budget to meet the independence criterion.[10]

This jurisprudence reflects the fact that the existence of an 'independent' DPA is an integral part of the right to data protection which is elevated to the level of constitutional right in the EU legal order.[11] Yet it reflects too ECtHR jurisprudence which emphasizes the need for independent monitoring and supervision of practices that interfere with the right(s) in ECHR Article 8(1).[12] An emphasis on independence is accordingly present in the Additional Protocol to Convention 108 which stipulates that supervisory authorities 'shall exercise their functions in complete independence' (Article 1(3)).[13]

We find such an emphasis also in the UN Guidelines (paragraph 8) and OECD Guidelines (paragraph 19(c)), although it is not as emphatically stated on the face of the latter Guidelines as in the European instruments. The OECD Guidelines stipulate simply that DPAs ('privacy enforcement authorities') should be invested with 'the governance, resources and

---

[7] Advocate General Mazák took a different view in the case. According to his Opinion, state oversight would not of itself rob a DPA of complete independence—indeed, it might even promote data privacy interests by ensuring that the DPA acts rationally, lawfully, and proportionally. State oversight would only breach the DPD if it involved abuse of state powers that hindered the ability of the DPA to exercise its functions with complete independence. As the Commission had failed to adduce evidence of such hindrance, he could find no breach of the DPD.

[8] Case C-614/10 *European Commission v Republic of Austria* [2012] ECR I-0000. The overlap consisted of: (i) integration of the DSK office with the Federal Chancellery departments; (ii) the fact that the senior manager of the DSK was a federal official subject to supervision; and (iii) the fact that the Federal Chancellor had an unconditional right to information covering all aspects of the DSK's work.

[9] [2012] ECR I-0000 [61].     [10] [2012] ECR I-0000 [58].

[11] See Ch 2 (section E(1)). Concomitantly, Art. 47 of the proposed GDPR elaborates on the independence criterion to a far greater extent than the DPD.

[12] See Ch 2 (section I(2)).

[13] The Additional Protocol's Explanatory Report states: 'A number of elements contribute to safeguarding the independence of the supervisory authority in the exercise of its functions. These could include the composition of the authority, the method for appointing its members, the duration of exercise and conditions of cessation of their functions, the allocation of sufficient resources to the authority or the adoption of decisions without being subject to external orders or injunctions' (para. 17).

technical expertise necessary... to make decisions on an objective, impartial and consistent basis' (paragraph 19(c)). The need for independence arises as a precondition for such decision making—a point made clear in the revised Guidelines' Explanatory Memorandum which states that paragraph 19(c) focuses on mechanisms to 'ensure that these authorities can take decisions free from influences that could compromise their professional judgment, objectivity or integrity'.

## 3. Duties and competence

According to DPD Article 28(2), DPAs must be consulted when administrative measures or regulations concerning data protection are drawn up. DPAs shall also be empowered to monitor, investigate, and intervene in data-processing operations, hear complaints, and take court action in the event of breach of national data privacy law (Article 28(3) and (4)). At the same time, they shall be required to maintain a publicly accessible register containing information about the data-processing activities of which they are notified (Article 21(2)).[14]

The Directive does not clearly specify whether or not DPAs shall be able to impose fines and order compensation for damages although such competence would clearly be compatible with the Directive. The Directive is also silent as to whether or not DPAs *must* be given competence to issue legally binding orders.[15] Article 28(3), read in conjunction with Recitals 9–11,[16] tends to suggest that such competence is required but the wording is not entirely conclusive:[17] authorities are to be given 'effective powers of intervention, such as, for example, that of delivering opinions..., ordering the blocking, erasure or destruction of data, of imposing a temporary or definitive ban on processing'. It could be argued that the various types of powers listed here are examples only of *options* that member states may choose between, not necessary constituents of the concept 'effective powers of intervention'; if they were intended to be regarded as necessary constituents, the term 'including' would

---

[14] Notification requirements are dealt with in section C, this chapter.

[15] Under the proposed GDPR, DPAs are clearly provided with competence to issue legally binding orders, and, indeed, must have such competence (Art. 53).

[16] Set out in Ch 2 (nn 105–7).

[17] The preparatory works are also not entirely conclusive on this point. See eg, COM(92) 422 final—SYN 287, 38 ('To enable the supervisory authority to carry out its duties it must also have effective powers of intervention, such as those enumerated by the Parliament in its opinion, and repeated in the amended proposal: power to order suppression, erasure of data, a ban on the processing operation, etc. Parliament referred to these measures as 'sanctions', but it does not appear necessary that the Directive should define their legal nature').

have been used instead of 'such as, for example'.[18] Moreover, the wording of the provision indicates that the notion of 'intervention' is to be read broadly, such that it covers mere delivery of opinion. As for the criterion 'effective', nothing in the Directive (or its preparatory works) conclusively indicates that this can *only* be satisfied through imposition of legally binding orders.[19]

Similar observations may be made of the Additional Protocol to Convention 108. This requires supervisory authorities to be vested with 'powers of investigation and intervention, as well as the power to engage in legal proceedings or bring to the attention of the competent judicial authorities violations of provisions of domestic law' (Article 1(2)(a)). The accompanying Explanatory Report indicates that '[p]arties have considerable discretion as to the powers which the authorities should be given for carrying out their task' (paragraph 11).[20] The OECD Guidelines also give OECD member countries considerable discretion in this respect, specifying that DPAs are to be provided with 'the governance, resources and technical expertise necessary to exercise their powers effectively' (paragraph 19(c)) but without elaborating on these powers. However, paragraph 19(c) must be read in light of the 2007 OECD Recommendation on Cross-Border Co-operation in the Enforcement of Laws Protecting Privacy. This urges member countries to empower DPAs with 'the necessary authority' to (a) 'deter and sanction' violations of data privacy law, (b) carry out 'effective investigations', and (c) 'permit corrective action to be taken against data controllers engaged in such violations' (paragraph 11).

---

[18] See also the statement of the Council's reasons regarding adoption of the common position for the Directive ('The supervisory authorities' powers of intervention are described in indicative fashion only, so as to allow Member States the requisite leeway in this area'): [1995] OJ C93/24.

[19] Indeed, there is evidence to suggest that the recommendations of an ombudsman can sometimes be as equally effective as such orders. On this point, see Flaherty's comprehensive study which found that, during the 1970s and early 1980s, the German Federal Data Protection Commissioner, despite having only advisory powers, had a more profound impact on the (federal) public sector in Germany than Sweden's Data Inspection Board had on the Swedish public sector: Flaherty (n 1) 26.

[20] Accordingly, the Report adds: 'The supervisory authority's power of intervention may take various forms in domestic law. For example, the authority *could* be empowered to oblige the controller of the file to rectify, delete or destroy inaccurate or illegally collected data on its own account or if the data subject is not able to exercise these rights himself/herself. The power to issue injunctions on controllers who are unwilling to communicate the required information within a reasonable time would be a *particularly effective* manifestation of the power of intervention. This power *could* also include the possibility to issue opinions prior to the implementation of data processing operations, or to refer cases to national parliaments or other state institutions' (paragraph 11; emphasis added).

## 4. Transnational cooperation

The Directive contains several provisions which enhance internationalization, at least within the EU, of supervisory and monitoring regimes in the field. Important in this regard is Article 28(6) which provides that member states' respective DPAs:

- may exercise their powers in relation to a particular instance of data processing even when the national law applicable to the processing is that of another member state;
- may be requested by another member state's authority to exercise their powers; and
- are to 'cooperate with one another to the extent necessary for the performance of their duties, in particular by exchanging all useful information'.

These provisions envisage high levels of cooperation between national DPAs. They should also entail increased knowledge and expertise within each of these authorities of other member states' laws.[21] Provisions with a similar thrust are contained in the Additional Protocol to Convention 108 (Article 1(5)) and in the OECD Guidelines (paragraph 20).

The practically most significant embodiment of regional DPA coordination is the A29WP. As noted in Chapter 2 (section E(1)), the 'Working Party on the Protection of Individuals with regard to the Processing of Personal Data' (A29WP) is mainly composed of representatives from each member state's DPA. It acts independently of the Commission and other EU organs but has advisory competence only. It aids the Commission by providing advice on: issues relating to the uniform application of national measures adopted pursuant to the Directive; data protection afforded by non-member states; possible changes to the Directive and other instruments affecting data protection; and codes of conduct drawn up at Community level (Article 30).

Despite having purely advisory competence, the Working Party has played an influential role in setting the Commission's agenda in data privacy matters.[22] Together with the European Data Protection Supervisor, the A29WP

---

[21] As stated in Ch 2 (section E(3)), the proposed GDPR pushes 'internationalisation' of DPA operations further: see Arts 55–56 on 'mutual assistance' and 'joint operations', plus Arts 57ff on the operation of the 'consistency mechanism'.

[22] See generally Y Poullet and S Gutwirth, 'The Contribution of the Article 29 Working Party to the Construction of a Harmonised European Data Protection System: An Illustration of "Reflexive Governance"?' in MV Pérez Asinari and P Palazzi (eds), *Défis du droit à la protection de la vie privée/ Challenges of privacy and data protection law* (Bruylant 2008) 569.

has been important for building up the EU's regulatory capacity in the field.[23] This is due not least to the sheer industry of both bodies. Since commencing operations in January 1996, the A29WP has generated a wealth of reports, recommendations, and opinions generally showing both insight and foresight. It has been fairly quick to grapple with 'cutting-edge' technological applications, such as biometrics and radio-frequency identification (RFID).[24] Yet as elaborated in section E(1), its influence has been most felt internationally in the application of the Directive's provisions on data flow to countries outside the EU.[25]

The A29WP is not the sole instance of transnational DPA cooperation. For example, systematic cooperation occurs between DPAs in the Asia–Pacific region, although not as intensively as in the EU. There is also regular contact between DPAs on a global basis. Previously this was formalized mainly in the annual International Data Protection and Privacy Commissioners' conference but we see increasing collaboration in investigative and enforcement efforts outside this conference framework, particularly against controllers that operate globally.[26]

# B. Other Regulatory Bodies

DPAs are not alone in monitoring or enforcing implementation of data privacy laws. A great number of other bodies are involved to varying degrees in one or more of the same tasks, even if their participation is not always formally provided for in data privacy instruments.

## 1. International level

On the international plane, notable examples of relevant bodies are the expert committees on data privacy and information policy formed under the

---

[23] See generally AL Newman, *Protectors of Privacy: Regulating Personal Data in the Global Economy* (Cornell University Press 2008). By 'regulatory capacity' is meant the formal resources (eg, statutory authority) and informal resources (eg, expertise) to draft, monitor, and enforce rules.

[24] See eg, Working Document on biometrics (1 August 2003; WP 80); Working Document on data protection issues related to RFID technology (19 January 2005, WP 105); Opinion 05/2012 on cloud computing (1 July 2012; WP 196); Opinion 02/2013 on apps on smart devices (27 February 2013; WP 202).

[25] As stated in Ch 2 (section E(3)), the proposed GDPR replaces the A29WP with an 'European Data Protection Board' which will also be composed of DPA representatives but have a broader, albeit still largely advisory, remit (Arts 64ff).

[26] A development partly spurred by the 2007 OECD Recommendation on Cross-Border Co-operation in the Enforcement of Laws Protecting Privacy.

umbrella of the CoE and OECD. Recall, for instance, the role of the T-PD in monitoring application of Convention 108 and in shaping its reform.[27]

As for EU bodies, the European Commission exercises pronounced influence on the development and practice of regulatory policy in the field. Its influence extends beyond the EU. It enjoys considerable powers in regulating transborder data flow to third countries (see DPD Articles 25(4)–25(6), 26(3)–26(4)). Principal in this respect is its power to determine whether a third country offers an adequate level of data protection for the purposes of Article 25.[28] However, the Commission exercises these powers with input from other EU bodies. The A29WP is one body. Another is a committee established under DPD Article 31 in furtherance of EU comitology requirements.[29] This 'Article 31 Committee' is composed of representatives from the member state governments. Unlike the A29WP, the committee has legal power over the Commission. If it disagrees with a Commission proposal, it can refer the proposal to the Council, which—acting by a qualified majority—may then determine the proposal's fate (Article 31(2)).

The Commission's influence in the field is set to grow significantly if the proposed GDPR is adopted. As noted in Chapter 2 (section E(3)), the proposed Regulation empowers the Commission to adopt delegated acts with respect to a broad range of processing operations (Chapter IX).[30] It also provides the Commission with veto powers over initiatives of national DPAs (Articles 60, 62). The strength of these powers is in tension with not only the general principle of subsidiarity in EU law[31] but also the 'independence' criterion for DPAs described in section A. Even so, the Commission will be subject to control by the European Parliament and the Council both of which will be able to block proposed delegated acts (Article 86(5)). Moreover, the Commission will only be able to adopt implementing acts (such as TBDF adequacy decisions pursuant to Article 41(3) and (5)) with the assistance of a committee similar to the current Article 31 Committee, in accordance with 'post-Lisbon' comitology procedures (Article 87).[32]

---

[27] See Ch 2 (section B).        [28] See further section E(1).

[29] Further on comitology, see HCH Hofmann, GC Rowe, and AH Türk, *Administrative Law and Policy of the European Union* (OUP 2011) 264–84; 386–404.

[30] The proposed Police and Criminal Justice Data Protection Directive also provides for such powers, though to a lesser degree.

[31] Further on subsidiarity, see Hofmann and others (n 29) 125–9.

[32] See Regulation (EU) No. 182/2011 laying down the rules and general principles concerning mechanisms for control by member states of the Commission's exercise of implementing powers [2011] OJ L55/13.

EU regulatory policy in the field is increasingly shaped by the European Parliament. This is principally due to its enhanced ability, under the Lisbon Treaty, to prevent Commission proposals taking effect. Thus, its deliberations on the proposed GDPR are decisive for the fate of the proposal. It has shown willingness to stop Commission initiatives with a detrimental impact on data privacy. In February 2010, for instance, it rejected by a large majority the transfer of financial records to the United States under a proposed interim 'SWIFT' agreement, holding that the proposed agreement lacked adequate privacy safeguards and was a disproportionate response to US concerns about terrorism.[33] It has also criticized earlier Commission initiatives in the field, such as the Safe Harbor agreement,[34] but lacked then the power to block them.

## 2. National level

At a national level, obvious examples of bodies that play an instrumental role in monitoring or enforcing data privacy law are parliamentary committees, ombudsmen, national auditing offices, and regulatory authorities with consumer protection as part of their remit. The role that the latter may play is demonstrated by the former UK Financial Services Authority (now Financial Conduct Authority) in respect of data security breaches.[35] It is further demonstrated by the US FTC in respect of regulating deceptive business practices involving processing of personal data, and in enforcing particular sets of data privacy rules.

Indeed, the FTC is now regarded as the de facto federal DPA for the USA. Although its field of competence is more restricted than is typical for European DPAs, its data privacy remit has expanded considerably over the past 15 years. In addition to its traditional power to enforce the prohibition

---

[33] 'SWIFT: European Parliament votes down agreement with the US', EP press release (11 February 2010). A few months later, though, the Parliament approved a revised agreement: European Parliament legislative resolution of 8 July 2010 on the draft Council decision on the conclusion of the Agreement between the European Union and the United States of America on the processing and transfer of Financial Messaging Data from the European Union to the United States for the purposes of the Terrorist Finance Tracking Program (11222/1/2010/REV 1 and COR 1—C7-0158/2010—2010/0178(NLE)).

[34] See EP Resolution on the Draft Commission Decision on the adequacy of the protection provided by the Safe Harbour Principles and related Frequently Asked Questions issued by the US Department of Commerce [2001] OJ C121/152.

[35] In 2007, the FSA fined the Nationwide Building Society £980,000 for losing a laptop containing customer data and for failing to have adequate data security procedures in place: 'FSA fines Nationwide £980,000 for information security lapses', FSA press release (14 February 2007); available at: <http://www.fsa.gov.uk/pages/Library/Communication/PR/2007/021.shtml>.

against deceptive business practices under section 5 of the Federal Trade Commission Act, the FTC has acquired enforcement powers with respect to the Fair Credit Reporting Act 1970, the Childrens' Online Privacy Protection Act 1998, the Financial Services Modernization Act ('Gramm-Leach-Bliley Act') 1999, and the Safe Harbor scheme.[36]

The FTC's pronounced role in the data privacy field is partly due to the absence of a specialized federal DPA in the USA. We see a similar pattern in Japan, which also has enacted data privacy legislation without initially establishing a specialized DPA. Yet rather than oversight being principally exercised by just one body, it has been exercised by Japan's various government ministries, under supervision of the Consumer Affairs Agency.[37]

In some countries, such as NZ and Germany,[38] data controllers are required to appoint internal officers to monitor their respective organizations' compliance with data privacy legislation and to function as contacts with the DPAs. As noted in Chapter 2 (section E(2)), most EU organs are also obliged to appoint internal data protection officers. If the proposed GDPR is adopted, a similar requirement will embrace a large number of private and public sector organizations in all EU member states.[39]

Some countries' laws make specific provision for industries, professions, etc., to draw up sectoral codes of conduct/practice on data privacy in cooperation with DPAs.[40] In certain cases, a code may even replace the relevant statutory rules as the standard to be observed by the organizations that subscribe to it.[41] The OECD Guidelines, DPD, and proposed GDPR encourage development of industry codes, although they fail to specify their exact legal status. In light of such encouragement, fewer codes have been established

---

[36] Further on this development and the resultant jurisprudence of the FTC on data privacy matters, see DJ Solove and W Hartzog, 'The FTC and the New Common Law of Privacy' (2014) 114 Columbia L Rev (forthcoming).

[37] See further H Miyashita, 'The Evolving Concept of Data Privacy in Japanese Law' (2011) 1 IDPL 229, 233. A specialized DPA is to be established from January 2014, but with its remit initially restricted to oversight of the identity number scheme set up under the 2013 Act on Use of Numbers to Identify Specific Individuals in Administrative Procedures ('My Number' Act). The scope of the agency's mandate is to be reconsidered within one year after the Act's entry into force (24 May 2016). See further H Miyashita, 'Japan's new ID Number Act' (2013) Privacy Laws & Business Intl Report, no. 124, 16.

[38] See s 23 of the NZ Privacy Act and ss 4f–4g of the German Federal Data Protection Act.

[39] More specifically, public authorities, private enterprises with more than 250 employees, and bodies engaged in 'regular and systematic monitoring of data subjects' (Art. 35).

[40] See eg, s 51(3)–(4) of the UK Data Protection Act, pt IIIAA of the Australia's federal Privacy Act, and Art. 25 of the Netherlands' Personal Data Protection Act.

[41] See eg, pt IIIAA of Australia's federal Privacy Act.

than might reasonably be expected. In Australia, for instance, where government has actively pushed 'co-regulation' for many years, only a handful of industry codes have been developed and approved pursuant to the Privacy Act. A major cause of this low level of industry uptake appears to be that code development is too costly and complex for most businesses.[42]

## 3. Judiciary

Last but not least, account must be taken of the judiciary. Courts are usually accorded a key role in interpreting and enforcing statutory norms. In some jurisdictions, particularly those with common law roots, courts also play a key role in developing norms outside statute. Yet a remarkable characteristic of the field of data privacy law is that many national courts' involvement in interpreting and enforcing statutory rules has been minor if not marginal, relative to the role played by DPAs.[43] The same may be said with respect to development of non-statutory rules. This has been offset to some degree by considerable growth in case law at the international level. As of 1 September 2013, the CJEU had handed down 19 decisions touching upon the DPD. There is no sign of the rate of growth of this case law tapering; rather it seems to be increasing. A similar pattern is evident with ECtHR case law on data privacy matters.

National courts are also increasingly generating data privacy jurisprudence but the development is slow in some jurisdictions. The Norwegian Supreme Court, for example, handed down its first decision dealing centrally with Norway's Personal Data Act in January 2013[44] —13 years after the legislation was enacted!

Nonetheless, one of the central judicial contributions to development of the field derives from a decision of a national court reached three decades ago. This is the 'Census Act' decision of December 1983 by the German Federal Constitutional Court.[45] In this case, the Court struck down parts of the Census Act (Volkzählungsgesetz) of 1983 for breaching Articles 1(1) and

---

[42] See further Office of Australian Federal Privacy Commissioner, *Getting in on the Act: The Review of the Private Sector Provisions of the Privacy Act 1988* (March 2005) 166ff.

[43] See further LA Bygrave, 'Where Have All the Judges Gone? Reflections on Judicial Involvement in Developing Data Protection Law' in P Wahlgren (ed), *IT och juristutbildning. Nordisk årsbok i rättsinformatik 2000* (Jure AB 2001) 113.

[44] Rt 2013 143; see further Ch 5 (n 60) and accompanying text.

[45] 65 BVerfGE 1. For an English translation of the Court's decision, see (1984) 5 Human Rights LJ 94ff. For detailed commentary, see eg, S Simitis, 'Die informationelle Selbstbestimmung— Grundbedingung einer verfassungs-konformen Informationsordnung' (1984) Neue juristische Wochenschrift 398.

2(1) of the Federal Republic's Basic Law.[46] The Court held that the two provisions give individuals a right to 'informational self-determination' ('informationelle Selbstbestimmung'); that is, a right for the individual 'to determine basically for himself whether his personal data shall be disclosed and utilised'.[47] The Court went on to hold that, although not absolute, the right will be infringed if personal data is not processed in accordance with basic data privacy principles.[48] Despite strong claims that the principles it stipulates have not been fully honoured in practice,[49] the judgment has had a galvanizing effect on data privacy regulation. Not only did it help stimulate efforts during the 1980s to revise and strengthen Germany's federal data protection legislation, it created an important benchmark for regulatory discourse in the field generally. Its transnational influence can be seen, for instance, in the judgment of April 1991 by the Hungarian Constitutional Court which struck down census legislation for violating the national Constitution. In reaching its decision, the Court expounded substantially the same line taken in the German judgment.[50]

Both of these decisions highlight the important role played by courts in elaborating the *constitutional* parameters of data privacy law in a given country. A court's preparedness to recognize data privacy rights in a national constitution, along with its conceptualization of the rationale and strength of such rights, go a long way to determining how they are implemented further 'down' the normative chain. A noteworthy feature of the Census Act decision is its recognition that the right to informational self-determination is beneficial not just for individuals *qua* individuals but also serves to secure the necessary conditions for active citizen participation in public life—in other words, to secure democracy.[51] This recognition has arguably helped to undermine the perception of data privacy as essentially in conflict with the needs of 'society', and, concomitantly, helped to embed fairly robust data privacy ideals in

---

[46] Article 1(1) provides: 'Human dignity is inviolable. To respect and protect it is the duty of all State authority'. Article 2(1) provides: 'Everyone has the right to the free development of his personality insofar as he does not violate the rights of others or offend against the constitutional order or against morality'.

[47] 65 BVerfGE 43 ('Das Grundrecht gewährleistet ... die Befugnis des Einzelnen, grundsätzlich selbst über die Preisgabe und Verwendung seiner persönlichen Daten zu bestimmen').

[48] 65 BVerfGE 46ff.

[49] S Simitis, 'Das Volkzählungsurteil oder der lange Weg zur Informationsaskese—(BVerfGE 65, 1)' (2000) 83 Kritische Vierteljahresschrift für Gesetzgebung und Rechtswissenschaft 359.

[50] See Hungary's Official Gazette (*Magyar Kozlony*), No. 30, 13 April 1991, 805. For commentary on the court's decision and its impact on Hungarian society, see I Székely, 'Hungary Outlaws Personal Number' (1991) 14 Transnational Data Report, no. 5, 25.

[51] 65 BVerfGE 1, 43.

German law and policy to a greater degree than had the Court simply viewed data privacy as important for individuals.

By contrast, the US Supreme Court has tended to underplay the broader societal benefits of data privacy,[52] and has only recognized, at best, a very stunted form of informational autonomy under the US Constitution—most notably, an 'individual interest in avoiding disclosure of personal matters' and an 'interest in independence in making certain kinds of important decisions'.[53] The Court has given fairly strong support to the latter interest but predominantly in contexts outside the data privacy sphere,[54] while its support for the former interest has been tepid.[55] This has contributed to the weak embedment of data privacy norms in the US legal system generally as compared to, say, the German system. To be sure, such norms are buttressed by other constitutional protections too, particularly the Fourth Amendment's 'right of the people to be secure in their persons, houses, papers, and effects, against unreasonable searches and seizures'. However, the bite of the Fourth Amendment has been both narrowed and blunted by the Court's conservative application of a 'reasonable expectations' test that limits protection to situations where an individual has 'an expectation of privacy that society is prepared to consider as reasonable'.[56] The test has been applied such as to leave untouched by the Fourth Amendment numerous instances of surveillance carried out in putatively public space.[57]

A somewhat similar test has been applied by the Canadian Supreme Court with respect to section 8 of the Canadian Charter of Rights and Freedoms, incorporated in Part I of the Constitution Act 1982. Section 8, akin to the Fourth Amendment, prohibits unreasonable searches and seizures. Although it does not mention privacy specifically, section 8 is acknowledged by the Supreme Court as aimed 'to protect individuals from unjustified state intrusions upon their privacy'.[58] The Court holds that section 8 only comes into play when an individual has a reasonable expectation of privacy.[59] While members of the Court have opined that section 8 'must be interpreted

---

[52] For the seminal analysis, see PM Schwartz, 'The Computer in German and American Constitutional Law: Towards an American Right of Informational Self-Determination' (1989) 37 American J of Comparative L 675.

[53] *Whalen v Roe* (1977) 429 US 589, 598ff.

[54] Most famously with respect to the right of a woman to decide for herself whether or not to have an abortion: *Roe v Wade* (1973) 410 US 113.

[55] Schwartz (n 52).     [56] *Katz v United States* (1967) 389 US 347, 361.

[57] See eg, R Gellman, 'A General Overview of Video Surveillance Law in the United States' in S Nouwt, BR de Vries, and C Prins (eds), *Reasonable Expectation of Privacy?* (T. M. C. Asser 2005) ch 2.

[58] *Lawson Hunter et al. v Southam Inc.* [1984] 2 SCR 148, 160.

[59] For elaboration of this test, see, eg, *R v Edwards* [1996] 1 SCR 128 esp. [45].

generously, and not in a narrow or legalistic fashion',[60] the application of the reasonable expectations test lessens its utility in promoting data privacy interests. For example, in *R v Plant*—a case with clear data privacy implications—the Court majority held that a police check of electricity consumption records relating to an individual's residence fell outside the scope of section 8 as the information 'cannot reasonably be said to reveal intimate details of the appellant's life since electricity consumption reveals very little about the personal lifestyle or private decision of the occupant of the residence'.[61] Moreover, the utility company 'prepared the records as part of an ongoing commercial relationship and there is not evidence that it was contractually bound to keep them confidential'.[62]

Outside constitutional law, courts occasionally develop data privacy norms and guarantees in legal fields other than what would normally be deemed 'data privacy'. In doing so, courts do not always consciously set out to develop data privacy standards; the latter can arise incidentally. A notable example is the development of a type of purpose limitation principle, together with a form for data subject influence principle, pursuant to Australian administrative law. In *Johns v Australian Securities Commission and Others*,[63] the High Court of Australia held that any personal information compulsorily collected pursuant to statute for a particular purpose may not be used for other purposes without the consent of the data subject. Further, it held that such information is kept as confidential information and, in the absence of data subject consent, may only be used or disclosed in accordance with express or implied statutory authority. Moreover, the Court found that the rules of natural justice required in this case (but not necessarily in all cases) that the plaintiff be given formal opportunity to object to the disclosure.[64] These limitations on repurposing and disclosure of compulsorily acquired information are arguably more stringent than the equivalent limitations under Australia's federal Privacy Act.

Evolution of the equitable action for breach of confidence might well provide another example. Over recent years, the courts in the UK have been

[60] *R v Dyment* [1988] 2 SCR 417 [15] *per* La Forest J.
[61] [1993] 3 SCR 281 [20].        [62] *Plant* (n 61) [21].        [63] (1993) 178 CLR 408.
[64] The primary issue at hand was whether the Australian Securities Commission had breached an obligation of confidence by disclosing to a Royal Commission the transcripts of compulsory examinations it had conducted of the plaintiff, under conditions facilitating dissemination of the transcripts to media representatives. The High Court found that a breach had occurred. See further G Greenleaf, 'High Court Confirms Privacy Right against Governments' (1994) 1 PLPR 1. English courts have taken a similar line: see esp. *Marcel v Commissioner of Police* [1992] Ch 225 and *Morris v Director of the Serious Fraud Office* [1993] 3 WLR 1; cf decision of the Hong Kong Court of Appeal in *Hall v Commissioner of ICAC* [1987] HKLR 210.

developing the law on breach of confidence so that it may apply to a greater range of situations than previously. This has been spurred partly by the enactment of the UK Human Rights Act 1998.[65] It is now clear that in the UK an action in equity for breach of confidence may lie where there is public disclosure of personal information about which the data subject has a reasonable expectation of privacy irrespective of whether the data subject has imparted the information in circumstances importing an obligation of confidence on the recipient.[66] This development helps to offset the continuing reluctance of English courts to recognize squarely a tort for breach of privacy at common law.[67] Yet it is also obviously of considerable significance as a supplement to, and reinforcement of, statutory data privacy rules limiting use and disclosure of personal information. It may also constrain collection of personal information because of the argument that any collection of such information involving a breach of confidence may (at least in some circumstances) constitute either unlawful or unfair collection.

## C. Notification and Licensing Schemes

Many data privacy laws lay down special rules to enhance DPAs' ability to monitor the practices of data controllers. These rules fall into two main categories: notification rules and licensing rules. The basic differences between them lie in the degree to which a DPA monitors data-processing activities *before* they begin, and the degree to which such monitoring involves formal authorization of these activities.

Notification rules require data controllers simply to notify DPAs of certain planned processing of personal information. Upon notification, processing

---

[65] See generally G Phillipson, 'Transforming Breach of Confidence? Towards a Common Law Right of Privacy under the Human Rights Act' (2003) 66 MLR 726.

[66] In the traditional cause of action for breach of confidence (outside contract), it has been necessary to satisfy three criteria: (1) the information must be confidential; (2) the information must have been imparted in circumstances 'importing an obligation of confidence'; and (3) there must be an unauthorized use or disclosure of that information to the detriment of the party imparting it. See *Coco v AN Clark (Engineers) Ltd* [1969] RPC 41, 47–48. Subsequent case law has, in effect, loosened both the first criterion (so that it may be satisfied where the information is private, not just confidential) and second criterion (so that it may be satisfied where the party obtaining the information knows or ought to know that the information is private). See generally Phillipson (n 65).

[67] A reluctance shared by most Australian courts, though not by those in the USA or NZ. While torts for breach of privacy have long been recognized in the USA (for the seminal analysis, see WL Prosser, 'Privacy' (1960) 48 California L Rev 338), the NZ Court of Appeal first recognized such an action in 2005 (see *Hosking v Runting* [2005] 1 NZLR 1). Also the Ontario Court of Appeal has recently found that Ontario law harbours a similar tort (see *Jones v Tsige* [2011] ONSC 1475).

is usually allowed to begin. Apart from the DPD, the main international data privacy codes refrain from specifically laying down such rules or, indeed, licensing rules.

The Directive requires, subject to several derogations, that controllers or their representatives notify the authority concerned of basic information about 'any wholly or partly automatic processing operation' they intend to undertake (Article 18(1)). With some exceptions, the types of information to be notified must include 'at least':

(a)  the identity of the controller and their representatives;
(b)  the purposes of the data processing;
(c)  the categories of data subject and data held on the latter;
(d)  the categories of recipients of the data;
(e)  proposed data transfers to third countries; and
(f)  a general description of adopted security measures for the processing (Article 19(1)).

The second category of rules require that controllers must apply for and receive specific authorization (that is, a license) from the relevant DPA prior to commencing a particular data-processing activity. Only a minority of countries operate, or have operated, with comprehensive licensing regimes.[68] It has been more common for countries to reserve licensing for, inter alia, putatively sensitive data,[69] or for certain sectors of business activity, such as credit reporting,[70] or for data matching.[71]

The DPD allows for a system of 'prior checking' by DPAs with respect to processing operations that 'are likely to present specific risks to the rights and freedoms of data subjects' (Article 20(1)). Elaborating on what might constitute such processing operations, Recital 53 refers to operations that are likely to pose specific risks 'by virtue of their nature, their scope or their purposes, such as that of excluding individuals from a right, benefit or contract, or by virtue of the specific use of new technologies'. It would appear from Article 28(3), together with Recitals 9, 10, and 54, that DPAs may stop planned data-processing operations pursuant to this system of 'prior

---

[68]  See eg, the regimes established pursuant to Latvia's Personal Data Protection Act 2000 Art. 22(2), Norway's Personal Data Registers Act (repealed), and Sweden's Data Act (repealed). For details on the old Norwegian licensing scheme, see further LA Bygrave, *Data Protection Law: Approaching Its Rationale, Logic and Limits* (Kluwer Law International 2002) ch 18 (section 18.4.7).

[69]  See eg, Art. 25 of France's Act on Information Technology, Data Files and Civil Liberties 1978, and s 33 of Norway's Personal Data Act 2000 (elaborated in the following).

[70]  See eg, s 15 of the Icelandic Act 1989 (repealed).

[71]  See eg ss 4(4) and 4(5) of Denmark's Private Registers Act (repealed).

checking'.[72] Recital 54 makes clear, though, that such a system is to apply only to a minor proportion of data-processing operations: 'with regard to all the processing undertaken in society, the amount posing such specific risks should be very limited'. This is confirmed by the CJEU.[73] In other words, regimes in which licensing is the rule rather than exception do not conform with the Directive.

At the same time, the fact that the Directive permits (though does not mandate) some licensing in addition to notification schemes, plus describes the preconditions for such licensing in a rather vague, open-ended way, provides (yet) another possibility for significant divergence in the regulatory regimes of EU and EEA member states. For example, Sweden's Personal Data Act dispenses with any licensing requirement, providing instead for mere notification (section 36).[74] By contrast, Norway's Personal Data Act operates with a qualified licensing requirement for processing sensitive data (section 33),[75] along with certain kinds of data processing by telecommunications service providers, insurance companies, and financial institutions.[76] The Data Inspectorate is also empowered to determine, on a case-by-case basis, that other data-processing operations require licensing when they 'clearly violate weighty interests concerning privacy protection' (section 33(2)).

Notification and licensing schemes exist not simply for the purposes of direct control on the part of DPAs; they can also be justified as learning or sensory mechanisms in the face of legislators' uncertainty about the appropriate regulatory response to data-processing activities. They put pressure on controllers to come in contact with DPAs, thereby allowing the latter (and, indirectly, data subjects and the public generally) to learn about controllers' practices and needs, and allowing DPAs to educate controllers about data privacy rules.[77]

---

[72] Article 28(3) provides that authorities generally are to have 'effective powers of intervention', including the ability to impose 'a temporary or definitive ban on processing'. Recital 54 specifies that an authority may 'give an opinion or an authorization' following a prior check.

[73] Joined Cases C-92/09 and C-03/09 *Volker und Markus Schecke GbR and Hartmut Eifert v Land Hessen* [2010] ECR I-11063 [104]–[105].

[74] The notification requirement does not apply if the data controller has appointed an internal data protection officer (s 37), though allowance is made for government regulations to override this exemption in cases involving 'particular risks for improper intrusion of personal integrity' (s 41).

[75] These are basically the data types described in DPD Art. 8 (see s 2(8) of the Personal Data Act). Licensing is not required if the data subject has voluntarily supplied the data or the processing is carried out by a government agency pursuant to statutory authorization (s 33(1)) or the processing consists of video surveillance for the purposes of crime control (s 37(2)).

[76] Personal Data Regulations 2000 Ch. 7.

[77] On this 'learning' aspect, see further CD Raab, 'Data Protection in Britain: Governance and Learning' (1993) 6 Governance 43, 53ff; CD Raab, 'Implementing Data Protection in Britain' (1996) 62 Intl Rev of Administrative Sciences 493, 507–8; H Burkert, 'Institutions of Data Protection—An

Nonetheless, they are bureaucratically burdensome for both controllers and DPAs—licensing rules especially so. Whether the 'educational' or other benefits they putatively deliver are sufficiently strong to outweigh this burden is questionable. Much depends on their scale and the resources available to the DPA. A comprehensive licensing regime administered by a DPA with few resources is definitely counterproductive, especially given the enormous scale of data processing that currently occurs. While not as patently counterproductive, a comprehensive notification scheme also runs a severe risk of engendering a great deal of 'red tape' with few concrete benefits for data privacy interests at the end of the day.

The European Commission appears to share this scepticism, though to a very limited degree. The proposed GDPR abolishes a general notification requirement, with a view to cutting compliance costs. These 'savings', however, are swallowed up by a variety of new obligations on controllers. Most notably, controllers must notify both DPAs and data subjects of data security breaches (Articles 31–32), document in detail all processing operations under their responsibility (Article 28), and undertake 'data protection assessments' (Article 33). Further, the proposed GDPR imposes licensing requirements that apply on the basis of the outcomes of the latter assessments—that is, for processing operations indicated by the assessments as 'likely to present a high degree of specific risks' (Article 34(2)(a)). Licensing requirements may also apply when deemed necessary by the DPA (Article 34(2)(b)). And they apply for certain types of data transfer to third countries lacking adequate data privacy regimes (Articles 34(1) and 42(2)(d)).

## D.  Sanctions and Remedies

Data privacy laws stipulate a variety of sanctions and remedies for breach of their provisions. Provision is usually made for a combination of penalties (fines, imprisonment), compensatory damages, and, where applicable, revocation of licences. Strict liability for harm is occasionally stipulated.[78] Sometimes allowance is made for the imposition of ongoing enforcement damages during the time in which a data controller fails to comply with DPA

---

Attempt at a Functional Explanation of European National Data Protection Laws' (1981–1982) 3 Computer/LJ 167, 180ff.

[78] See eg, s 49(2) of the Norwegian Personal Data Act in relation to harm caused by credit reporting agencies.

orders.[79] In many cases, compensation may be awarded for non-economic/ immaterial injury (emotional distress), as well as economic loss.[80] In a very few cases, allowance is made for class actions to be brought.[81]

Sanctions and remedies are dealt with in only very general terms by Convention 108, the OECD Guidelines, and UN Guidelines. Again, the DPD is more specific. It requires that data subjects be given the right to a 'judicial remedy' for 'any breach' of their 'rights' pursuant to the applicable national data privacy law (Article 22). It also stipulates that DPA decisions giving rise to complaints 'may be appealed against through the courts' (Article 28(3)).[82]

Article 22 does not require member states to permit individuals to go directly to the courts for breach of data privacy rights (effectively bypassing national DPAs) but leaves member states the possibility to allow direct access to the courts.[83] Less clear is whether the reference to 'rights' also embraces those provisions in the Directive which are formulated as duties or obligations on controllers. Given that breach of a duty or obligation is likely to result in infringement of a data subject's general right to privacy (a right that is indirectly, if not directly, guaranteed by the Directive),[84] and given that the Directive aims at ensuring a 'high' level of data protection,[85] an affirmative answer to the question seems most correct.

Ambiguity inheres also in Article 28(3): does it require member states to permit court appeals on both questions of law and questions of fact, or are states able to restrict appeals to questions of law only? As the term 'complaints' is not qualified in any way, the provision appears to encourage if not require a broad right of appeal. Yet EU legislators would probably be exceeding their legal competence if the provision were to require changes to

---

[79] See eg, s 47 of the Norwegian Personal Data Act and s 41 of the Icelandic Data Protection Act.

[80] See eg, s 48 of the Swedish Personal Data Act, s 47(1) of the Finnish Personal Data Act, and s 52(1A) of the Australian federal Privacy Act.

[81] See ss 36(2), 38, 38A–38C, and 39 of the Australian federal Privacy Act and s 37(2) of Hong Kong's Personal Data (Privacy) Ordinance.

[82] Article 28(3) also addresses the issue of standing with respect to DPAs: Each such authority is to be given 'the power to engage in legal proceedings where the national provisions adopted pursuant to this Directive have been violated or to bring these violations to the attention of the judicial authorities'.

[83] Cf Art. 22 of the 1992 Amended Proposal for the Directive (COM(92) 422 final—SYN 287) which makes no mention of administrative remedies prior to court referral: 'Member States shall provide for the right of every person to a judicial remedy for any breach of the rights guaranteed by this Directive'. Had this provision been adopted, data subjects would have found it easier to go straight to the courts with their complaints, bypassing national data protection authorities and any other administrative complaints-resolution bodies.

[84] See esp. Art. 1(1).     [85] Recital 10 in the Directive's preamble.

present domestic rules limiting judicial review of administrative decisions to questions of law.

Turning to the issue of compensation, the Directive stipulates that in the event of suffering damage from a breach of national provisions adopted pursuant to it, data subjects must be able to receive compensation from the controller responsible for the damage (Article 23(1)). However, Article 23(2) allows for the complete or partial exemption of controllers from liability if they are able to prove that they are 'not responsible for the event giving rise to the damage'. The provisions in Articles 22 and 23 are backed up by Article 24, which requires member states to adopt 'suitable measures' (notably sanctions) for ensuring 'full implementation' of the Directive's provisions.

The Directive fails to specify clearly whether or not the term 'damage' in Article 23 covers both economic and non-economic (for example, emotional) loss. Recitals 9 and 10 weigh in favour of a broad interpretration of the term.[86] Further, the Commission's intention with respect to the equivalent provisions in its 1990 Directive proposal was that '[t]he concept of damage covers both physical and non-physical damage'.[87] Nothing indicates that this intention changed in the subsequent drafting process leading to adoption of the Directive,[88] and nothing indicates that this intention has not been shared by either the European Parliament or Council.[89]

The provisions on remedies and sanctions in Chapter VIII of the proposed GDPR follow closely the above provisions of the DPD and suffer from the same ambiguities. However, they go further than the DPD in significant respects. They extend liability to data processors (in addition to controllers) (Articles 75 and 77). They give interest groups (not just DPAs) legal standing

---

[86] See Ch 2 (n 95 and n 97). Cf Recital 55 which states that 'any damage which a person may suffer as a result of unlawful processing must be compensated for by the controller'. However, one cannot place much weight on the presence of 'any' in the English text of the recital since other texts, such as the French, German, Danish, and Swedish, omit the adjective altogether.

[87] COM(90) 314 final—SYN 287, 40. Again, both terms are somewhat diffuse, but the reference to 'non-physical damage' (the German text uses the term 'immateriell Schaden'; the French text 'le préjudice moral') seems sufficiently broad to embrace emotional distress.

[88] See eg, COM(92) 422 final—SYN 287, 33 ('Article 23(1), like Article 21(1) in the initial proposal, places a liability on the controller to compensate *any* damage caused to any person': emphasis added). The German text is similar ('Schadenersatz für jeden Schaden einer Person zu leisten'), though not the French text ('une obligation de réparer le préjudice causé à toute personne').

[89] The A29WP claims that the notion of damages in the Directive 'includes not only physical and financial loss, but also any psychological or moral harm caused (known as "distress" under UK or US law)': see A29WP, 'Transfers of personal data to third countries: Applying Articles 25 and 26 of the EU data protection directive', Working Document (24 July 1998; WP 12) 13.

before courts (Article 76(1)). They provide for cross-jurisdictional coordination of parallel court proceedings (Article 76(3)–(4)). And they provide for a scaling up of monetary fines in line with the increasing severity of offences (Article 79).

This proposed strengthening of formal sanctions reflects concern over fairly extensive evidence of weak levels of enforcement, compliance, and awareness with respect to many of the European national laws in the field. This is particularly disturbing given that European regimes are often held up as providing strong levels of data privacy in the global context. Some of this evidence came to light during the European Commission's first study on the implementation of the DPD, undertaken a decade ago.[90] Shortly after release of that study, the A29WP declared it would give greater priority to formal enforcement actions.[91] Nonetheless, more recent studies have backed up the findings of the Commission's study.[92] Taken together, the studies show that the low levels of compliance are due not so much to lack of formal enforcement powers but rather to the fact that DPAs have not been given sufficient funding and other resources to expand their enforcement efforts.

At the same time, my impression is that the paucity of formal enforcement actions is partly rooted in the preference of many DPAs to resolve conflict in a relatively quiet way involving 'back-room' negotiation rather than publicly striking out with threatened use of punitive sanctions.[93] While this approach has its strengths, it also has problems. Not only can it obscure the positive achievements of the agencies,[94] it can hinder the transparency of their decision-making and hence their ability to provide prescriptive guidance to other data controllers.

As intimated earlier, there is no necessary link between tougher enforcement powers and better compliance. Compliance levels are a function of

---

[90] European Commission, *First Report on the Implementation of the Data Protection Directive (95/46/EC)* (COM(2003) 265).

[91] Declaration of the Article 29 Working Party on enforcement (24 November 2004; WP 101).

[92] See eg, EU Agency for Fundamental Rights, Data Protection in the European Union: the Role of National Data Protection Authorities (Publications Office of the EU 2010); LRDP KANTOR Ltd and Centre for Public Reform, 'Comparative Study on Different Approaches to New Privacy Challenges, in Particular in the Light of Technological Developments: Final Report', Report for European Commission (20 January 2010); available at: <http://ec.europa.eu/justice/policies/privacy/docs/studies/new_privacy_challenges/final_report_en.pdf>; I-A Ravlum, *Behandling av personopplysninger i norske virksomheter* (Transportøkonomisk Institutt 2006).

[93] My impressions here are based on perusal of the annual reports issued by the DPAs of Australia, Denmark, Norway, Switzerland, and the UK, together with Flaherty's description (n 1) of enforcement practices in Sweden, France, Canada, and the Federal Republic of Germany.

[94] Agencies are often equally, if not more, concerned about curbing an *unrealized potential* for privacy-invasive activity as about providing a remedy after such activity occurs. Measuring the impact of anticipatory forms of control can be more difficult than for reactive, *ex post facto* control forms.

numerous factors of which enforcement powers and the ability to use such powers are just two. Other factors include the seriousness with which a given community generally takes data privacy matters, the extent to which the administrative and corporate cultures of a given jurisdiction are imbued with respect for data privacy ideals, and the talents of the DPAs. In some jurisdictions, social mores are particularly important. For example, Miyashita observes that while the formal sanctions for breaches of data privacy rules in Japan are weaker than those in Europe,

> it is crucially important to understand that a data breach in Japan means the disruption of social trust and the intimate relationship with customers. In Japan, the risk of loss of social trust and business reputation is regarded as much more significant than paying a fine.[95]

Similarly, it cannot be assumed that a DPA with strong formal powers will necessarily have greater success in fulfilling its objectives than an agency with weaker formal powers. Experience from Germany, for instance, indicates that, given a particular constellation of the sorts of factors listed above, a significant degree of compliance can be achieved without a DPA having the power to issue legally binding orders (for example, prohibiting certain forms of data processing).[96]

## E. Inter-legal Aspects of Data Privacy Law

This section deals with two aspects of data privacy law that may involve the overlap and, in some cases, collision of laws in different jurisdictions. The first aspect concerns regulation of transborder data flow (dealt with in section E((1)); the second concerns the determination of when a country's data privacy law applies to a given data-processing operation (section E(2)). As shown in the following, both aspects continue to be the subject of considerable controversy.

## 1. Transborder data flow

All European data privacy laws contain rules restricting the flow of personal data to countries without sufficient levels of data protection. The chief aim of these rules is to hinder data controllers from avoiding the requirements of data privacy laws by shifting their data-processing operations to countries with more lenient

---

[95] Miyashita (n 37) 233.        [96] Flaherty (n 1).

requirements (so-called 'data havens').[97] This concern has rarely been shared to the same degree by legislators in non-European countries; accordingly, many of these laws have not contained rules specifically allowing for restrictions on transborder flows of personal data. Such rules, though, are increasingly being incorporated in non-European legislation, largely under the influence of the DPD.

As elaborated in Chapter 2, all of the main international data privacy instruments contain rules specifically addressing the matter of transborder data flows, though they differ in terminology, stringency, and scope. The rules with the greatest international impact are contained in the DPD. They are accordingly the focus of this section.

Regarding flows of personal data between EU/EEA member states, the basic rule in the Directive is that such flows cannot be restricted for reasons concerned with protection of the 'fundamental rights and freedoms of natural persons, and in particular their right to privacy with respect to the processing of personal data' (Article 1(2)). This prohibition is premised on the assumption—expressed in Recitals 8 and 9 in the Directive's preamble, and necessitated by Article 12(3)(a) of Convention 108—that implementation of the Directive will result in equivalent levels of data protection across the EU/EEA.

As for transfer of personal data to countries outside the EU/EEA ('third countries'), this is regulated in Articles 25–26. The point of departure is that 'transfer... may take place only if... the third country in question ensures an adequate level of protection' (Article 25(1)).

A preliminary question concerns the precise meaning of 'transfer', which is not defined in the Directive. The CJEU addressed aspects of the question in *Lindqvist*, holding that the website publishing in dispute did not constitute a data 'transfer' for the purposes of Article 25.[98] The Court gave three grounds. First, it held that the uploading of the data to the webpage did not lead to a direct transfer of the data to a person who might access the data from a third country; the transfer would instead occur 'through the computer infrastructure of the hosting provider where the page is stored'.[99] Secondly, the Court could not presume a legislative intention that the TBDF provisions should embrace website publishing, in light of the state of technological development at the time the Directive was drafted.[100]

---

[97] See generally R. Ellger, *Der Datenschutz im grenzüberschreitende Datenverkehr: eine rechtsvergleichende und kollisionsrechtliche Untersuchung* (Nomos 1990) 87ff and references cited therein. For discussion of claims that these rules are partly intended to protect economic and 'sovereignty' interests as well, see Ch 4 (section B(3)).

[98] Case C-101/01 *Bodil Lindqvist* [2003] ECR I-12971. For the case facts, see Ch 4 (n 111).

[99] *Lindqvist* [61].

[100] *Lindqvist* [68]. For critique of this and the first-mentioned justification, see DJB Svantesson, 'Privacy, Internet and Transborder Data Flows: An Australian Perspective' (2010) 4 Masaryk

A third (and more convincing) justification was based on the consequence of concluding otherwise:

If Article 25 of Directive 95/46 were interpreted to mean that there is 'transfer [of data] to a third country' every time that personal data are loaded onto an internet page, that transfer would necessarily be a transfer to all the third countries where there are the technical means needed to access the internet. The special regime provided for by Chapter IV of the directive would thus necessarily become a regime of general application, as regards operations on the internet. Thus, if the Commission found, pursuant to Article 25(4) of Directive 95/46, that even one third country did not ensure adequate protection, the Member States would be obliged to prevent any personal data being placed on the internet.[101]

However, the Court left unclear the status, under the TBDF rules, of several parameters by which data is actually disseminated via the World Wide Web and related platforms. One such parameter is the location of the server(s) of the hosting provider—does that location matter? Another is the kind of access to hosted data that persons in third countries are given—for example, may we properly speak of a transborder transfer of such data when the access is intentionally provided by the uploader and restricted to predefined persons or organizations? Scholars disagree over the legal significance of various permutations of these parameters.[102] These uncertainties are unfortunate given the immense development of online social networks and cloud-computing services in the decade since the Lindqvist decision was handed down.[103]

Turning to the issue of adequacy of protection offered by a third country, this 'shall be assessed in the light of all the circumstances surrounding a data transfer or set of data transfer operations' (Article 25(2)). Assessment of adequacy will in many cases lie firstly with the data exporters and secondly with national DPAs. However, the European Commission has the power to make determinations of adequacy which are binding on EU (and EEA) member states (Article 25(6)). It does so with input from the A29WP,[104] Article 31 Committee,[105] and the

---

University J of Law and Technology 1, 15–16; LA Bygrave, 'Data Privacy Law and the Internet: Policy Challenges' in N Witzleb, D Lindsay, M Paterson, and S Rodrick (eds), *Emerging Challenges in Privacy Law: Comparative Perspectives* (CUP, forthcoming 2014) ch 12.

[101] *Lindqvist* [69].

[102] See eg, SY Esayas, 'A Walk in the Cloud and Cloudy it Remains: The Challenges and Prospects of "Processing" and "Transferring" Personal Data' (2012) 28 CLSR 662, 668–9, and references cited therein.

[103] In light of that development it is especially unfortunate that the proposed GDPR—which regulates TBDF along much the same lines as the DPD—also does not define 'transfer'.

[104] Which may deliver a non-binding opinion on the proposed decision (Art. 30(1)(a) & (b)).

[105] Which may object to the proposed decision and, if necessary, refer the matter to the Council for final determination (Art. 31(2)).

European Parliament.[106] The main methodological criteria for assessing adequacy are set out by the A29WP in a Working Document from 1998.[107] Although not in themselves legally binding on the Commission, these criteria form an important point of departure for Commission decisions on adequacy. At the same time, these criteria are neither precisely formulated nor always rigidly applied. We can discern recent evidence of both the A29WP and Commission taking a pragmatic approach that places weight on the probability of Europeans being adversely affected by any shortcomings in a third country's regime, in light of the likely amount of trade between that country and Europe.[108] Such a factor is not addressed explicitly in the A29WP's criteria.

The Commission has so far decided that the following jurisdictions satisfy the adequacy test:[109] Andorra, Argentina, Canada, Faroe Islands, Guernsey, Israel, Isle of Man, Jersey, NZ, and Uruguay. Adequacy determinations have additionally been made for the US Safe Harbor scheme (described further on in this section) and schemes for transfer of PNR data to US and Australian authorities. Doubts about the adequacy of the Australian regime more generally have been expressed by the A29WP,[110] but the Commission has yet to make a final decision on the matter.

The impact of the adequacy rule is significantly mitigated by a set of derogations in Article 26. These derogations permit transfer of personal data to a third country lacking adequate protection if, in summary, the proposed transfer:

(1) occurs with the consent of the data subject; or
(2) is necessary for performing a contract between the data subject and the controller, or a contract concluded in the data subject's interest between the controller and a third party; or
(3) is required on important public interest grounds, or for defending 'legal claims'; or

---

[106] Which is able to check whether the Commission has properly used its powers.

[107] 'Working Document on transfers of personal data to third countries: Applying Articles 25 and 26 of the EU data protection directive' (24 July 1998; WP12).

[108] See A29WP, Opinion 11/2011 on the level of protection of personal data in New Zealand (4 April 2011; WP 182) (finding the NZ regime as adequate on the basis of, inter alia, the limited amount of trade between NZ and Europe). Commenting on this Opinion, Greenleaf and Bygrave go so far as to suggest that '[a]dequacy is in inverse proportion to proximity including economic and social proximity, not just geographical': G Greenleaf and LA Bygrave, 'Not Entirely Adequate but far away: Lessons from How Europe Sees New Zealand Data Protection' (2011) Privacy Laws & Business Intl Report, no. 111, 8, 9.

[109] The decisions are available at: <http://ec.europa.eu/justice/data-protection/document/international-transfers/adequacy/index_en.htm>.

[110] Opinion 3/2001 on the level of protection of the Australian Privacy Amendment (Private Sector) Act 2000 (26 January 2001; WP 40).

(4) is necessary for protecting the data subject's 'vital interests'; or

(5) is made from a register of publicly available information (Article 26(1)).

A further derogation is permitted if the proposed transfer is accompanied by 'adequate safeguards' instigated by the controller for protecting the privacy and other fundamental rights of the data subject (Article 26(2)). The latter provision also states that 'such safeguards may... result from appropriate contractual clauses'. In the same way as under Article 25, the Commission is empowered to make binding determinations of what constitute 'adequate safeguards' for the purposes of Article 26(2) (see Article 26(4)). It has exercised this power by stipulating standard contractual clauses that may be used to govern data transfers.[111]

Another form of 'adequate safeguard' is 'Binding Corporate Rules' (BCRs). The idea of BCRs is that a group of companies draft their own set of data privacy rules which are enforceable against each entity in the group regardless of location. Once approved by an appropriate DPA, the BCRs permit cross-border data transfers within the company group.[112] While ostensibly attractive, the practicalities of this co-regulatory strategy are still being thrashed out. A major problem has been the dearth of a single, pan-European approval system for BCRs. The Commission has yet to set up such a system. However, the A29WP has lessened, though not eliminated, the problem by developing a coordinated fast-track procedure for BCR approval by all of the relevant national DPAs.[113]

Articles 25–26 have occasioned considerable controversy in some 'third countries', especially the USA which has feared the provisions' potentially detrimental impact on US business interests. Shortly after the DPD entered into force, US federal government officials estimated that its TBDF restrictions threatened up to US$120 billion in trade—an amount far higher than had supposedly been at stake in previous transatlantic trade conflicts.[114]

---

[111] Decision 2001/497/EC on standard contractual clauses for the transfer of personal data to third countries, under Directive 95/46/EC [2001] OJ L181/19; Decision 2004/915/EC amending Decision 2001/497/EC as regards the introduction of an alternative set of standard contractual clauses for the transfer of personal data to third countries [2004] OJ L385/74; Decision on standard contractual clauses for the transfer of personal data to processors established in third countries under Directive 95/46/EC of the European Parliament and of the Council [2010] OJ L39/5.

[112] See further C Kuner, *European Data Protection Law: Corporate Compliance and Regulation* (2nd edn, OUP 2007) 218–32.

[113] Working Document establishing a model checklist application for approval of Binding Corporate Rules (14 April 2005; WP 108). See too Working Document setting up a framework for the structure of Binding Corporate Rules (28 June 2008; WP 154).

[114] D Heisenberg, *Negotiating Privacy: The European Union, The United States, and Personal Data Protection* (Lynne Rienner Publishers 2005) 2, 84.

The initial tensions between the USA and EU over these restrictions ended up being patched over, at least temporarily, in the form of a 'Safe Harbor' scheme brokered by the European Commission and US Department of Commerce.[115] This allows for the flow of personal data from the EU to US organizations that voluntarily agree to abide by a set of data privacy principles based loosely on the DPD. The principles, set out in Annex I to the Commission's Safe Harbor decision, are considerably watered down in their scope and stringency relative to the Directive's requirements. Yet adherence to them is regarded by the Commission as satisfying the adequacy requirement under Article 25.[116] As such, they signal that the scheme's brokers were ultimately concerned not so much with protection of privacy but protection of TBDF. Heisenberg states:

[B]oth the EU Commission and the US Department of Commerce wanted to give the appearance of protecting Europeans' privacy, but whether or not it was actually protected was relatively unimportant to both. The chief goal of the Safe Harbor Agreement was to keep data flowing between the two economic regions, and that purpose was achieved.[117]

Despite slow corporate take-up in its early days, the Safe Harbor scheme now has close to 2,500 corporations (including major businesses) formally certifying adherence to it.[118] It has been heralded as a 'resounding success, both in terms of raising the level of privacy compliance in the USA, and in facilitating the recognition by US business that privacy is a critical factor to success in the global marketplace'.[119] Nonetheless, considerable doubts attach to its efficacy in terms of privacy protection. These doubts were present during its earlier years,[120] and they have recently resurfaced in the aftermath of the revelations over the so-called 'PRISM' electronic surveillance program run by the US National Security Agency (NSA).[121] According to these revelations, a number

[115] Decision 2000/520/EC on the adequacy of the protection provided by the safe harbor privacy principles and related frequently asked questions issued by the US Department of Commerce [2000] OJ L215/7.

[116] The adequacy of the Safe Harbor scheme is also recognized for EEA purposes: see EEA Joint Committee decision No. 108/2000 of 30 November 2000 [2001] OJ L45/47.

[117] Heisenberg (n 114) 160.

[118] See 'US-EU Safe Harbor List', available at: <https://safeharbor.export.gov/list.aspx>.

[119] D Greer, 'Safe Harbor—a Framework That Works' (2011) 1 IDPL 143, 145.

[120] See eg, the findings in J Dhont, MV Pérez Asinari, Y Poullet, JR Reidenberg, and LA Bygrave, 'Safe Harbour Decision Implementation Study', Report for European Commission (April 2004); available at: <http://ec.europa.eu/justice/policies/privacy/docs/studies/safe-harbour-2004_en.pdf>.

[121] See eg, C Connolly, 'EU/US Safe Harbor—Effectiveness of the Framework in relation to National Security Surveillance', Speaking/background notes for an appearance before the European Parliament's Committee on Civil Liberties, Justice and Home Affairs, 7 October 2013; available at: <http://www.europarl.europa.eu/document/activities/cont/201310/20131008ATT72504/201310 08ATT72504EN.pdf>.

of major US-based corporations—many of which formally adhere to the Safe Harbor scheme—have been collaborating in the program and related surveillance efforts of the NSA, enabling the latter to gain ready access to personal data kept on, or transmitted between, the corporations' servers, and that this collaboration has been allegedly over and above what has been legally required of the corporations.[122] However, at the time of writing, there remains considerable uncertainty (at least for the general public) over the precise nature of not just these interactions but of many other aspects of the PRISM program. Moreover, the corporations have denied that their involvement goes beyond what is legally required of them. With respect to Safe Harbor, questions have arisen as to whether or not the corporations are breaching the Safe Harbor privacy principles or are exempted, under the Safe Harbor scheme, from having to comply with those principles in the context of PRISM, and whether the entire Safe Harbor scheme ought to be suspended.

These are difficult questions to answer conclusively from a European standpoint. The difficulty is exacerbated not just by lack of clarity over the 'facts' of PRISM but by a paucity of authoritative guidance on how the Safe Harbor rules are to be applied and enforced. The rules' reach and application are elaborated on by a set of Frequently Asked Questions (FAQs) set out in Annex II to the European Commission's Safe Harbor decision, along with other documentation in Annexes III and IV, but the guidance is superficial in many respects. Complicating the picture is that Annex I spells out that 'U.S. law will apply to questions of interpretation and compliance with the Safe Harbor Principles (including the Frequently Asked Questions) and relevant privacy policies by safe harbor organizations, except where organizations have committed to cooperate with European Data Protection Authorities'. It cannot be assumed that US law operates with the same principles for interpreting legal instruments as EU law.

There is also considerable disagreement between European DPAs as to the import of key exemptions from liability under the scheme. The fourth paragraph of Annex I states, inter alia, that '[a]dherence to these Principles may be limited: (a) to the extent necessary to meet national security, public interest, or law enforcement requirements'. The Irish Data Protection Commissioner's office seems to take the view that PRISM-related activity is covered by this exemption,[123] whereas the A29WP along with German DPAs are doubtful

---

[122] See generally the documentation compiled by the Guardian at <http://www.theguardian.com/world/prism> and the documentation on Wikipedia at <http://en.wikipedia.org/wiki/PRISM_(surveillance_program)>.
[123] Letter of 23 July 2013 to Mr Maximilian Schrems; available in redacted version at <http://www.europe-v-facebook.org/Response_23_7_2013.pdf>.

that it does.[124] In any case, there is growing disquiet over the Safe Harbor agreement on the part of EU institutions. The European Parliament has recently issued a resolution calling for a 'full review' of the agreement in light of the PRISM revelations.[125] Viviane Reding (Vice President of the European Commission and in charge of the Commission's 'Justice, Fundamental Rights and Citizenship' portfolio) has stated that 'the Safe Harbor Agreement might not be so safe after all', adding that the Commission is working on 'a full assessment' of the scheme which will be presented before the end of 2013.[126]

The Safe Harbor agreement makes provision for a suspension of data flows to 'harborites' in particular circumstances. European DPAs may suspend data flows when

there is a substantial likelihood that the Principles are being violated; there is a reasonable basis for believing that the enforcement mechanism concerned is not taking or will not take adequate and timely steps to settle the case at issue; the continuing transfer would create an imminent risk of grave harm to data subjects; and the competent authorities in the Member State have made reasonable efforts under the circumstances to provide the organisation with notice and an opportunity to respond (Article 3(1)(b)).

Four *cumulative* criteria must therefore be satisfied before suspension may occur. At this point in time, it is not possible to invoke the provision—we are still at the information-gathering stage.

Transatlantic tensions over TBDF have flared not just in relation to the Safe Harbor scheme but also in the direct aftermath of the '9/11' terrorist attacks when US border control agencies demanded advance disclosure of PNR data on persons flying from Europe to the USA. These tensions were also temporarily quelled through a series of negotiations between the European Commission and US government.[127] However, they are flaring up again as the EU deliberates over the TBDF restrictions in the proposed

---

[124] Letter of 13 August 2013 to Viviane Reding; available at <http://ec.europa.eu/justice/data-protection/article-29/documentation/other-document/files/2013/20130813_letter_to_vp_reding_final_en.pdf>; Press release ('Conference of data protection commissioners says that intelligence services constitute a massive threat to data traffic between Germany and countries outside Europe') of 24 July 2013; available at <http://www.bfdi.bund.de/EN/Home/homepage_Kurzmeldungen/PMDSK_SafeHarbor.html?nn=408870>.

[125] European Parliament Resolution of 4 July 2013 on the US National Security Agency surveillance programme, surveillance bodies in various Member States and their impact on EU citizens' privacy (P7_TA(2013)0322).

[126] N Nielsen, 'EU questions decade-old US data agreement', EU Observer, 22 July 2013; available at <http://euobserver.com/justice/120919>.

[127] See further LA Bygrave, 'International Agreements to Protect Personal Data' in JB Rule and G Greenleaf (eds), *Global Privacy Protection: The First Generation* (Edward Elgar 2008) 15.

GDPR. While those restrictions are intended to introduce more flexibility into the TBDF regime—for example, the proposed Regulation specifically provides for a BCR-based transfer scheme (Article 43), and permits adequacy assessments on a sectoral as opposed to countrywide basis (Article 41)—they do not deviate significantly from the current approach: restrictions are still to be imposed using an adequacy test as point of departure (Article 41).[128] Moreover, they operate with broadly similar derogations from this test as under the DPD (see Article 44).

Debate over the EU's restrictions on TBDF has occasionally centred on their legality under international trade law, most notably the 1994 General Agreement on Trade in Services (GATS) which, in effect, restricts signatory states from limiting TBDF in ways that involve arbitrary or unjustified discrimination against other such states.[129] At the same time, GATS allows restrictions on transborder data flow when necessary to secure compliance with rules relating to 'protection of the privacy of individuals in relation to the processing and dissemination of personal data and the protection of confidentiality of individual records and accounts' (Article XIV(c)(ii)). However, such restrictions are also subject to a basic prohibition against 'arbitrary or unjustifiable discrimination between countries where like conditions prevail', and against 'disguised restriction on trade in services' (chapeau of Article XIV).

A fairly cogent argument can be made that the EU has breached the chapeau criteria by entering into the Safe Harbor agreement with the USA but without, it would seem, offering other third countries (for example, Australia) the same opportunity to negotiate such an agreement. Yet it is difficult to reach a firm conclusion as to the validity of this argument—and, indeed, on the more general issue of whether Articles 25 and 26 of the Directive have been or are being applied in breach of the chapeau—because of the unpredictability of WTO jurisprudence on such matters. The WTO Appellate Body has yet to establish firm, generally applicable standards for interpreting the chapeau, insisting instead on case-by-case analysis.[130]

---

[128] And it extends application of the test to international organizations.

[129] See Agreement Establishing the World Trade Organization, adopted 15 April 1994, Annex 1B, especially Arts II(1), VI(1), XIV(c)(ii), and XVII. For prominent instances of the US discussion, see PP Swire and RE Litan, *None of Your Business: World Data Flows, Electronic Commerce, and the European Privacy Directive* (Brookings Institution Press 1998) and G Shaffer, 'Globalization and Social Protection: The Impact of EU and International Rules in Ratcheting Up of U.S. Privacy Standards' (2000) 25 Yale J of Intl L 1, 46ff. For non-US perspectives, see eg, CL Reyes, 'WTO-Compliant Protection of Fundamental Rights: Lessons from the EU Privacy Directive' (2011) 12 Melbourne J of Intl Law 141; RH Weber, 'Regulatory Autonomy and Privacy Standards under the GATS' (2012) 7 Asian J of WTO and Intl Health L and Policy 25.

[130] See further Reyes (n 129) esp. 174–6.

## 2. Applicable law

The issue as to which national data privacy law is to apply to a given data-processing operation is one of the most vexed in the field. It stumped the Expert Group responsible for drafting the original OECD Guidelines. According to the Explanatory Memorandum to the Guidelines, the Expert Group 'devoted considerable attention to issues of conflicts of laws', but their discussion

confirmed the view that at the present stage, with the advent of such rapid changes in technology, and given the non-binding nature of the Guidelines, no attempt should be made to put forward specific, detailed solutions. Difficulties are bound to arise with respect to both the choice of a theoretically sound regulatory model and the need for additional experience about the implications of solutions which in themselves are possible (paragraph 74).

Further, the Group found that technological developments made it difficult to identify one or more appropriate connecting factors to indicate one applicable law (paragraph 75). And the appropriateness of a solution, they remarked, 'seems to depend upon the existence of both similar legal concepts and rule structures, and binding commitments of nations to observe certain standards of personal data protection' (paragraph 75).

The same problems appear to have afflicted the Expert Group responsible for the 2013 revision of the OECD Guidelines, the drafters of Convention 108, as well as The Hague Conference on Private International Law.[131] The UN Commission on International Trade Law (UNCITRAL) has also broached the issue of conflict of laws in the field of data privacy, characterizing it as a 'potentially serious problem'.[132]

Bearing these difficulties in mind, EU legislators could plausibly be regarded as foolhardy when daring to lay down rules on the issue of applicable law in the DPD. Not surprisingly, the Directive is the first and only of the main international data privacy instruments to deal specifically with the determination of applicable law. And not surprisingly, the rules on point are arguably the most controversial, misunderstood, and mysterious of the Directive's provisions. Nonetheless, they are to be credited for introducing a little more uniformity to the rather disparate and divergent sets of rules on point that existed at the national level prior to the Directive's adoption.[133]

---

[131] Regarding the latter, see MV Pérez Asinari, 'International Aspects of Data Protection: *Quo Vadis* EU?' in MV Pérez Asinari and P Palazzi (eds), *Défis du droit à la protection de la vie privée/ Challenges of privacy and data protection law* (Bruylant 2008) 381, 403, and references cited therein.

[132] Pérez Asinari (n 131) 404.

[133] For an overview of these rules, see LA Bygrave, 'Determining Applicable Law Pursuant to European Data Protection Legislation' (2000) 16 CLSR 252.

The rules on applicable law laid down by the Directive are found in Article 4, which reads:

1. Each Member State shall apply the national provisions it adopts pursuant to this Directive to the processing of personal data where:
   (a) the processing is carried out in the context of the activities of an establishment of the controller on the territory of the Member State; when the same controller is established on the territory of several Member States, he must take the necessary measures to ensure that each of these establishments complies with the obligations laid down by the national law applicable;
   (b) the controller is not established on the Member State's territory, but in a place where its national law applies by virtue of international public law;
   (c) the controller is not established on Community territory and, for purposes of processing personal data makes use of equipment, automated or otherwise, situated on the territory of the said Member State, unless such equipment is used only for purposes of transit through the territory of the Community.
2. In the circumstances referred to in paragraph 1(c), the controller must designate a representative established in the territory of that Member State, without prejudice to legal actions which could be initiated against the controller himself.

It will be readily seen that the principal criterion for determining applicable law is the data controller's place of establishment, largely irrespective of where the data processing occurs. It will also be readily seen that the provisions permit the data privacy laws of European states to apply to controllers established outside the EU. This 'extra-territorial' effect has been the internationally most controversial aspect of the rules.

Such effects, though, are far from unique to the EU legislation in the field. For example, the provisions of Australia's federal Privacy Act may have extra-territorial application,[134] as may the US Children's Online Privacy Protection Act 1998.[135] And we find non-European countries including rules in their data privacy legislation which are modelled on DPD Article 4.

---

[134] This is due to the broad construction given to the term 'in Australia' in s 5B of the Act. See especially Explanatory Memorandum to the federal Privacy Amendment (Enhancing Privacy Protection) Act 2012, 218 ('The collection of personal information "in Australia" under paragraph 5B(3)(c) includes the collection of personal information from an individual who is physically within the borders of Australia... by an overseas entity').

[135] The Act applies to 'operators' which are broadly defined as 'any person who operates a website located on the Internet or an online service and who collects or maintains personal information from or about the users of or visitors to such website or online service, or on whose behalf such information is collected or maintained, where such website or online service is operated for commercial purposes, including any person offering products or services for sale through that website or online service, involving commerce [among various constellations of states]' (s 1302(2)).

Malaysia is a case in point.[136] Further, the rationale for the rules in DPD Article 4, as elaborated in the preparatory works, is eminently defensible. The rationale is twofold: (i) to prevent a data subject being deprived of protection due to a controller moving operations to a third country with a view to circumventing the local law; (ii) to avoid the same processing operation being governed by the laws of more than one country.[137]

Several criteria in Article 4 demand clarification: these are 'establishment', 'in the context of the activities', and 'equipment'. None of these are directly defined in the legislation, although the Recitals provide some help. Recital 19 states that the criterion of establishment 'implies the effective and real exercise of activity through stable arrangements'. Moreover, Recital 19 continues, 'the legal form of such an establishment, whether simply branch or a subsidiary with a legal personality, is not the determining factor in this respect'.

As for 'equipment', the impression it gives of something materially substantial and solid is misleading. Recital 20 uses the term 'means used' instead of 'equipment'. Other language versions of the Directive tend to refer simply to 'means' (French 'moyens'; German 'Mittel'). In other words, the term is to be construed broadly and somewhat loosely.

Turning to the phrase 'in the context of the activities', neither the Recitals nor the preparatory works provide guidance on its meaning, and it has been occasionally overlooked in national transpositions of Article 4.[138] Indeed, it could be treated as superfluous for the operation of Article 4(1)(a). The more approriate view, however, is that it has been intended to have a meaningful function. That function arguably comes to light in the context of controllers that are established in multiple member states. While each such establishment shall, as a point of departure, apply the law of the state in which it is established, the phrase 'in the context of the activities' suggests that the law of a state of establishment shall only be applied to data-processing operations that have some sort of connection to the activities of the locally established enterprise.[139] Taking this line helps to minimize the potential for one

---

[136] Personal Data Protection Act 2010 s 2.  [137] See COM (92) 422 final—SYN 287, 13.

[138] The case, eg, in Norway.

[139] The line is expressly embraced in, inter alia, Austria's Data Protection Act § 3(2) ('Abweichend von Abs. 1 ist das Recht des Sitzstaates des Auftraggebers auf eine Datenverarbeitung im Inland anzuwenden, wenn ein Auftraggeber des privaten Bereichs (§ 5 Abs. 3) mit Sitz in einem anderen Mitgliedstaat der Europäischen Union personenbezogene Daten in Österreich zu einem Zweck verwendet, der keiner in Österreich gelegenen Niederlassung dieses Auftraggebers zuzurechnen ist') and in the preparatory works to the Danish Personal Data Act: see *Behandling af personoplysninger*, Betænkning nr 1345 (1997) 221.

data-processing operation being governed by the laws of two or more states due to the fact that there are two or more controllers for that operation, each established in different states. In this respect, it bears emphasis that the definition of 'controller' in Article 2(d) envisages control to be shared—that is, a controller is a body 'which alone or *jointly with others* determines the purposes and means of the processing of personal data' (emphasis added).

The most problematic aspect of Article 4 is its potential for regulatory overreaching, particularly in the online environment. The routine use of cookies mechanisms by website operators in third countries may involve utilization of 'equipment' (browser programs on the devices used by the visitors to access the web) in an EU state (assuming that the cookies are properly classified as personal data).[140] It has been argued, though, that the 'equipment' being utilized must be under the control of the controller and that this control does not pertain when an EU-based data subject accesses a website using his/her own computer.[141] Nonetheless, control of a computer will often be shared; a website operator can induce the 'visiting' computer to carry out certain processing operations beyond the knowledge or preferences of the computer owner. And, as noted above, the 'controller' role is defined in terms of exercising partial rather than absolute control.

The extraterritorial reach of the proposed GDPR is also potentially expansive in the online context. The Commission Proposal stipulates that the Regulation shall apply to controllers outside the EU when they process personal data on data subjects 'residing in the Union' and the 'processing activities are related to (a) the offering of goods or services to…data subjects in the Union; or (b) the monitoring of their behaviour' (Article 3(2)). These are very liberal criteria for extraterritorial reach, particularly in the online world. They ache for clarification and justification yet, remarkably, the Proposal provides neither![142] As Svantesson observes:

whichever version is finally entering into force, this provision seems likely to bring all providers of Internet services such as websites, social networking services and app

---

[140] See further, eg, Bygrave (n 133).

[141] See eg, U Dammann and S Simitis, *EG-Datenschutzrichtlinie* (Nomos Verlagsgesellschaft 1997) 129; L Moerel, 'The Long Arm of EU Data Protection Law: Does the Data Protection Directive Apply to Processing of Personal Data of EU Citizens by Websites Worldwide?' (2011) 1 IDPL 23, 33.

[142] One glaring issue is whether the requirement that the data subject be 'in the Union'—present in Art. 3(2)(a)—is also to be read into the monitoring criterion in Art. 3(2)(b). For discussion, see DJB Svantesson, 'The Extraterritoriality of EU Data Privacy Law—Its Theoretical Justification and its Practical Effect on US Businesses' (Working paper, 2013); available at: <http://works.bepress.com/dan_svantesson/55/>, 41.

providers under the scope of the EU Regulation as soon as they interact with data subjects residing in the European Union. While this can be said to be the case already under the current EU approach to extraterritoriality, it is submitted that the new approach, as found in the proposed Regulation, goes even further, or at a minimum, more clearly emphasizes the significant extraterritorial dimension of the data privacy law.[143]

[143] Svantesson (n 142) 40.

# 7

# Prospects for Global Consensus

The preceding chapters demonstrate concern across many countries to protect privacy and related interests in the face of technological developments. In many cases, this concern has been translated into the enactment of data privacy laws. While the most far-reaching of these laws are still predominantly European, readiness to establish at least rudimentary regulatory equivalents is increasingly global. Moreover, data privacy laws in the various countries expound, for the most part, broadly similar core principles and share a great deal of common ground in enforcement patterns. This notwithstanding, the preceding chapters also highlight numerous points of difference between the various data privacy regimes. It is pertinent, therefore, to conclude with some brief comments about the chances of achieving greater harmonization of regimes across the globe.

To be blunt, the short-term chances of extensive harmonization are slim.[1] This is partly because of the strength of ingrained ideological and cultural differences around the world. These differences arise even between members of the Western, liberal democratic sphere and will not disappear quickly. Recall the ongoing tensions in the EU–US relationship. Future international policy-making in the field will have to engage seriously with nations and cultures outside that sphere; bridging differences there will be even more daunting.

Nonetheless, calls continue to be made for the adoption of a UN framework convention on data privacy or of an additional protocol to ICCPR Article 17 which would set out globally applicable data privacy standards.[2]

---

[1] See too eg, C Kuner, 'An International Legal Framework for Data Protection: Issues and Prospects' (2009) 25 CLSR 307; JR Reidenberg, 'Resolving Conflicting International Data Privacy Rules in Cyberspace' (2000) 52 Stanford L Rev 1315.

[2] See eg, comments by the then NZ Privacy Commissioner, Marie Shroff, cited in T Pullar Strecker, 'UN treaty on privacy possible', *The Dominion Post*, 5 April 2010; available at: <http://www.stuff.co.nz/technology/3546868/UN-treaty-on-privacy-possible>; Resolution of the 35th Conference of Data Protection and Privacy Commissioners on 'anchoring data protection and the protection of privacy in international law' (adopted 24 September 2013); available at: <https://privacyconference2013.org/web/pageFiles/kcfinder/files/5.%20International%20law%20resolution%20EN%281%29.pdf>.

The vision behind such calls is commendable, but it is well-nigh impossible to identify a sufficiently strong, dynamic, and representative body to broker such instruments efficiently, especially if they are to have real bite. Further, there is no guarantee that, once adopted, such instruments will be signed and ratified by all major states.

In any field, proposals for international conventions generally—especially multilateral initiatives—face particularly serious obstacles. One obstacle is the sheer clutter of the ideological landscape in which conventions must now be brokered. The horizons for regulatory policy are filled by cross-cutting sets of norms and interests—human rights, trade, national security, law enforcement, etc.—about which it is increasingly difficult to reach global consensus. Commitment to 'multi-stakeholderism' adds to these problems. The outcomes of the World Summit on the Information Society are testimony to this.[3]

The OECD is sometimes touted as a body through which a global agreement on data privacy could be brokered, yet it seeks generally to produce guidelines and other instruments of 'soft law' rather than 'hard law'. Its ability to broker a broadly acceptable agreement might also be hampered by its pro-trade agenda and limited membership.

The CoE is another candidate, and it is not averse to creating international 'hard law', yet its ability to foster global consensus will be handicapped by its regional status and bias. This handicap notwithstanding, Convention 108 is sailing up as a 'second-best' alternative to brokering a fresh multilateral treaty in the field, particularly with the CoE's recent encouragement of non-member states to seek accession. The success of this effort will depend on the outcomes of the current reform of the Convention. As Greenleaf memorably puts it:

the success of globalisation depends largely on the perceptions of non-European states, and whether they wish to apply to accede to the Convention. The 'modernised' Convention will have to pass the Goldilocks Test. Its standards cannot be too 'hot': they must not impose data protection standards so high that domestic political opinion will not accept them. But the standards must not be too 'cold': they cannot be so low that they will require free flow of personal information to other Parties to the Convention who provide a much lower standard of data protection than they do (but sufficient to allow them to accede); and nor can they allow those parties to re-export personal data to other countries with standards that are too low. The Convention's standards of data protection must be 'just right' to ensure eventual global adoption. At present, we cannot say whether it will be 'just right'.[4]

[3] See further A Hubbard and LA Bygrave, 'Internet Governance Goes Global' in LA Bygrave and J Bing (eds), *Internet Governance: Infrastructure and Institutions* (OUP 2009) ch 6.
[4] G Greenleaf, 'A World Data Privacy Treaty? "Globalisation" and "Modernisation" of Council of Europe Convention 108' in N Witzleb, D Lindsay, M Paterson, and S Rodrick (eds), *Emerging Challenges in Privacy Law: Comparative Perspectives* (CUP, forthcoming 2014) ch 6.

As for harmonization efforts at the regional level, the track records of APEC, the African Union, and ASEAN are yet to be firmly established. Within the EU—home to the hitherto most ambitious efforts—harmonization remains incomplete but will be given a strong 'shot in the arm' if the proposed GDPR is adopted. It would not be surprising, though, if the harmonization objectives originally envisaged by the Commission end up being considerably watered down. In 1995, Simitis made some telling observations of member states' attitudes during the DPD's lengthy gestation:

Experience has shown that the primary interest of the Member States is not to achieve new, union-wide principles, but rather to preserve their own, familiar rules. A harmonization of the regulatory regimes is, therefore, perfectly tolerable to a Member State as long as it amounts to a reproduction of the State's specific national approach.[5]

The outcome of the deliberations over the proposed GDPR will also depend on the influence of actors from outside Europe. US government officials as well as US businesses are paying close attention to the progress of the proposed Regulation and making extensive efforts to blunt its bite—as happened during the drafting of the DPD. A US diplomat has been cited as warning of a new trade war in the event that certain rights in the proposed Regulation, such as the right to be forgotten, are not watered down.[6] Yet efforts are also being made to dampen open conflict. At a conference arranged in Brussels shortly after the Commission issued its legislative proposal, Viviane Reding (European Commission Vice President) and John Bryson (US Secretary of Commerce) issued a joint statement stressing collaboration and conciliation at the intergovernmental level.[7] Moreover, the recent revelations over the PRISM program seem to have reduced, at least temporarily, openly aggressive lobbying by US bodies for weakening the stringency of the proposed Regulation. At the same time, the revelations have increased the resolve of European legislators to adopt a relatively strong set of new data privacy rules within the next year or so.[8]

---

[5] S Simitis, 'From the Market to the Polis: The EU Directive on the Protection of Personal Data' (1995) 80 Iowa L Rev 445, 449.

[6] Pinsent Masons, 'US Diplomat Warns of "Trade War" if "Right to Be Forgotten" Proposals Are Followed Through', *Out-Law.com*, 4 February 2013; available at: <http://www.out-law.com/en/articles/2013/february/us-diplomat-warns-of-trade-war-if-right-to-be-forgotten-proposals-are-followed-through/>.

[7] V Reding and J Bryson, 'EU–U.S. Joint Statement on Data Protection by European Commission Vice-President Viviane Reding and U.S. Secretary of Commerce John Bryson', Speech delivered at High Level Conference on Privacy and Protection of Personal Data, Brussels, 19 March 2012; available at: <http://europa.eu/rapid/press-release_MEMO-12-192_en.htm>.

[8] See esp. Conclusions of the European Council 24/25 October 2013 (EUCO 169/13; 25 October 2013) para. 8; available at: <http://consilium.europa.eu/uedocs/cms_data/docs/pressdata/en/ec/139197.pdf>.

Yet open conflict persists. Particularly salient is the ongoing struggle between large US corporations like Google and Facebook with European DPAs over the setting of data privacy standards for Internet-based services. The outcome of this struggle is difficult to predict. Facebook and Google have conceded some ground, but reluctantly.[9]

Although this struggle is still being played out, it is possible in one sense to identify a victor already. If the criterion for victory is set in terms of which party to the struggle has been most successful in setting global legislative standards in the field, Europe is the winner. The overwhelming bulk of countries that have enacted data privacy laws have followed, to a considerable degree, the EU model as manifest in the DPD. An extensive and fairly up-to-date analysis on point states: 'something reasonably described as "European standard" data protection laws are becoming the norm in most parts of the world with data privacy laws'.[10] The USA, in contrast, is an increasingly solitary outlier in the field. This marginalization is all the more remarkable given the extensive international purchase of US regulatory preferences in other areas of information policy, such as telecommunications regulation, protection of intellectual property, and governance of the Internet naming and numbering system.

As Newman ably shows, the predominance of European policy preferences in setting data privacy standards across large parts of the globe is fundamentally a reflection of the fact that the EU has greater regulatory capacity in the field than does the USA. Enhanced regulatory capacity within the EU has enhanced the ability to shape international markets.[11] In this process, the considerable size of the EU market is a necessary but not sufficient condition for influencing other markets.[12] Of particular importance has been the network of European DPAs which have been able, collectively, to punch well beyond their individual weight. Their advocacy of data privacy interests has been crucial at particular junctures in the development of EU policy. The

---

[9] See eg, A29WP, 'Google: The Beginnings of a Dialogue', Press Release (16 September 2008); available at: <http://ec.europa.eu/justice/policies/privacy/news/docs/pr_16_09_08_en.pdf>; L Essers, 'Facebook to Delete All European Facial Identification Data', *Computerworld*, 21 September 2012; available at: <http://www.computerworld.com/s/article/9231566/Facebook_to_delete_all_European_facial_recognition_data>.

[10] G Greenleaf, 'The Influence of European Data Privacy Standards outside Europe: Implications for Globalization of Convention 108' (2012) 2 IDPL 68, 77.

[11] AL Newman, *Protectors of Privacy: Regulating Personal Data in the Global Economy* (Cornell University Press 2008) 121.

[12] Newman (n 10) 100.

USA has lacked an equivalent set of authorities despite providing an early model for them.[13]

Talk of winners and losers should not blind us, though, to the considerable degree of transatlantic co-production of regulatory outcomes in the field. As highlighted in the preceding chapters, it is far from the case that the EU has been able to impose unilaterally its regulatory vision on the USA and other countries. Many facets of the transatlantic data privacy equation are the product of a cross-fertilization of regulatory traditions.[14] The Safe Harbor scheme is an obvious case in point; the PNR agreements another. In some cases, US law has inspired EU legislative developments. Security breach notification rules are an example in this respect, while interest in BCRs has undoubtedly been nourished by the US Sarbanes–Oxley Act with its pronounced emphasis on corporate accountability.[15]

Finally, focus on the EU–US relationship should not blind us to the actions of other countries. My hunch is that, in the long term, the transatlantic dialogue on data privacy is unlikely to persist as the internationally most important driver of standards in the field. Other major players are likely to muscle their way onto the data privacy stage. In this respect, the role of the Peoples' Republic of China will be intriguing to follow. China will increasingly have a voice on data privacy issues, although the import of its message remains to be deciphered, let alone clearly heard.

---

[13] Newman (n 10) 53.

[14] PM Schwartz, 'The E.U.–U.S. Privacy Collision: A Turn to Institutions and Procedures' (2013) 126 Harvard L Rev 1966.

[15] Public Company Accounting Reform and Investor Protection Act (Sarbanes–Oxley Act) 2002.

# Bibliography

## A. BOOKS AND JOURNAL ARTICLES

Alston, P, 'The Historical Origins of the Concept of "General Comments" in Human Rights Law' in Boisson de Chazournes, L, and Gowland Debbas, V (eds), *The International Legal System in Quest of Equity and Universality: Liber Amicorum Georges Abi-Saab* (Martinus Nijhoff 2001) 763–76.

Ambrose, ML, and Ausloos, J, 'The Right to Be Forgotten across the Pond' (2013) 3 J of Info Policy 1–23.

Avgerou, C, and Cornford, T, *Developing Information Systems: Concepts, Issues and Practice* (2nd edn, Macmillan 1998).

Bagger Tranberg, C, *Nødvendig behandling af personoplysninger* (Thomson 2007).

—— 'Proportionality and Data Protection in the Case Law of the European Court of Justice' (2011) 1 IDPL 239–48.

Bainbridge, DI, *EC Data Protection Directive* (Butterworths 1996).

—— and Pearce, G, 'The Data Protection Directive: A Legal Analysis' (1996) 12 CLSR 160–8.

Barron, JH, 'Warren and Brandeis, "The Right to Privacy", 4 Harv L Rev 193 (1890): 'Demystifying a Landmark Citation' (1979) 13 Suffolk University L Rev 875–922.

Beck, U, *Risk Society: Towards a New Modernity* (Sage 1992).

Bennett, CJ, *Regulating Privacy. Data Protection and Public Policy in Europe and the United States* (Cornell University Press 1992).

—— *The Privacy Advocates: Resisting the Spread of Surveillance* (MIT Press 2008).

—— and Raab, CD, *The Governance of Privacy. Policy Instruments in Global Perspective* (2nd edn, MIT Press 2006).

Beyleveld, D, Townend, D, Rouillé-Mirza, S, and Wright, J (eds), *Implementation of the Data Protection Directive in Relation to Medical Research in Europe* (Ashgate 2004).

Bing, J, 'Information Law?' (1981) 2 J of Media Law and Practice 219–39.

—— 'The Council of Europe Convention and the OECD Guidelines on Data Protection' in *Regulation of Transnational Communication: Michigan Yearbook of International Legal Studies* (Clark Boardman Company 1984) 271–303.

—— *Data Protection in Practice—International Service Bureaux and Transnational Data Flows*, CompLex 1/85 (Universitetsforlaget 1985).

Blanck, LJ, 'Personvern—nytt navn på "gamle" rettsspørsmål?' (1979) Lov og Rett 117, 122–3.

Blume, P, *Personregistrering* (3rd edn, Akademisk forlag 1996).

—— *Personoplysningsloven* (Greens§Jura 2000).

—— 'Controller and Processor: Is There a Risk of Confusion?' (2013) 3 IDPL 140–5.

Boehm, F, *Information Sharing and Data Protection in the Area of Freedom, Security and Justice* (Springer 2012).

Breyer, P, 'Telecommunications Data Retention and Human Rights: The Compatibility of Blanket Traffic Data Retention with the ECHR' (2005) 11 European LJ 365–75.

Brown, I, and Marsden, C, *Regulating Code: Good Governance and Better Regulation in the Information Age* (MIT Press 2013).

Bull, HP, *Datenschutz oder Die Angst vor dem Computer* (Piper 1984).

Burkert, H, 'Institutions of Data Protection—An Attempt at a Functional Explanation of European National Data Protection Laws' (1981–1982) 3 Computer/LJ 167–88.

—— 'The Law of Information Technology—Basic Concepts' (1988) Datenschutz und Datensicherung [later 'Datenschutz und Datensicherheit'], no. 8, 383–7.

—— 'Data Protection and Access to Data' in Seipel, P (ed), *From Data Protection to Knowledge Machines* (Kluwer Law and Taxation 1990) 49–69.

—— 'Systemvertrauen: Ein Versuch über einige Zusammenhänge zwischen Karte und Datenschutz' (1991) á la Card Euro-Journal, no. 1, 52–66.

—— 'Access to Information and Data Protection Considerations' in Terwangne de, C, Burkert, H, and Poullet, Y (eds), *Towards a Legal Framework for a Diffusion Policy for Data Held by the Public Sector* (Kluwer Law and Taxation 1995) 23–54.

Burnett, M, and Leonard, P, 'The APEC Cross-Border Privacy Rules System: an Australian Perspective' (2013) 9 Privacy Law Bulletin 128–30.

Burnham, D, *The Rise of the Computer State* (Weidenfeld and Nicholson 1981).

Burton, C, Kuner, C, and Pateraki, A, 'The Proposed EU Data Protection Regulation One Year Later: The Albrecht Report', *Bloomberg BNA Privacy and Security Law Report* (21 January 2013) 1–7.

Busser de, E, 'Purpose Limitation in EU-US Data Exchange in Criminal Matters: The Remains of the Day' in Cools, M, and others (eds), *Readings on Criminal Justice, Criminal Law & Policing* (Maklu 2009) 163–201.

Bygrave, LA, 'The Privacy Act 1988 (Cth): A Study in the Protection of Privacy and the Protection of Political Power' (1990) 19 Federal L Rev 128–53.

—— 'Data Protection Pursuant to the Right to Privacy in Human Rights Treaties' (1998) 6 Intl J of Law and Information Technology 247–84.

—— 'Where Have All the Judges Gone? Reflections on Judicial Involvement in Developing Data Protection Law' in Wahlgren, P (ed), *IT och juristutbildning. Nordisk årsbok i rättsinformatik 2000* (Jure AB 2001) 113–25 (also published in (2000) 7 PLPR 11–14, 33–6).

—— 'Determining Applicable Law Pursuant to European Data Protection Legislation' (2000) 16 CLSR 252–7.

—— 'Balancing Data Protection and Freedom of Expression in the Context of Website Publishing—Recent Swedish Case Law' (2002) 18 CLSR 56–8.

—— *Data Protection Law: Approaching Its Rationale, Logic and Limits* (Kluwer Law International 2002).

—— 'International Agreements to Protect Personal Data' in Rule, JB, and Greenleaf, G (eds), *Global Privacy Protection: The First Generation* (Edward Elgar 2008) 15–49.

—— 'The Body as Data? Biobank Regulation via the "Back Door" of Data Protection Law' (2010) 2 Law, Innovation and Technology 1–25.

—— 'Data Protection versus Copyright' in Svantesson, DJB, and Greenstein, S (eds), *Internationalisation of Law in the Digital Information Society: Nordic Yearbook of Law and Informatics 2010–2012* (Ex Tuto Publishing 2013) 55–75.

—— 'Data Privacy Law and the Internet: Policy Challenges' in Witzleb, N, Lindsay, D, Paterson, M, and Rodrick, S (eds), *Emerging Challenges in Privacy Law: Comparative Perspectives* (CUP, forthcoming 2014) ch 12.

—— and Schartum, DW, 'Consent, Proportionality and Collective Power' in Gutwirth, S, Poullet, Y, De Hert, P, de Terwangne, C, and Nouwt, S (eds), *Reinventing Data Protection?* (Springer 2009) 157–73.

Cate, FH, 'The Failure of Fair Information Practice Principles' in Winn, JK (ed), *Consumer Protection in the Age of the 'Information Economy'* (Ashgate 2006) 341–77.

Charlesworth, A, 'Clash of the Data Titans? US and EU Data Privacy Regulation' (2000) 6 European Public Law 253–74.

Cole, PE, 'New Challenges to the US Multinational Corporation in the European Economic Community: Data Protection Laws' (1985) 17 New York University J of Intl Law and Politics 893–947.

Collins, FS, *The Language of Life: DNA and the Revolution in Personalized Medicine* (HarperCollins 2010).

Connolly, C, 'EU/US Safe Harbor—Effectiveness of the Framework in relation to National Security Surveillance', Speaking/background notes for an appearance before the European Parliament's Committee on Civil Liberties, Justice and Home Affairs, 7 October 2013; available at: <http://www.europarl.europa.eu/document/activities/cont/201310/20131008ATT72504/20131008ATT7250 4EN.pdf>.

Craig, P, and de Búrca, G, *EU Law* (5th edn, OUP 2011).

Cretella, J Jr, *Comentários à Constituição Brasileira de 1988* (3rd edn, Forense Universitária 1994).

Currie, I, and Klaaren, J, *The Promotion of Access to Information Act Commentary* (Siber Ink 2002).

Dammann, U, '§ 3 Weitere Begriffsbestimmungen' in Simitis, S (ed), *Bundesdatenschutzgesetz* (7th edn, Nomos 2011) 297–377.

—— and Simitis, S, *EG-Datenschutzrichtlinie: Kommentar* (Nomos 1997).

Date, CJ, *An Introduction to Database Systems* (6th edn, Addison-Wesley 1995).

DeCew, JW, *In Pursuit of Privacy: Law, Ethics, and the Rise of Technology* (Cornell University Press 1997).

Dresner, S, 'India Gives Commitment on New Privacy Initiative' (2004) Privacy Laws & Business Intl Report, no. 72, 1, 3, 17.

Dutton, WH, and Meadow, RG, 'A Tolerance for Surveillance: American Public Opinion Concerning Privacy and Civil Liberties' in Levitan, KB (ed), *Government Infostructures* (Greenwood Press 1987) 147–70.

Eberle, EJ, *Dignity and Liberty: Constitutional Visions in Germany and the United States* (Praeger 2002).

Eger, JM, 'Emerging Restrictions on Transborder Data Flow: Privacy Protection or Non-Tariff Trade Barriers' (1978) 10 Law and Policy in International Business 1055–103.

Elgesem, D, 'Remarks on the Right of Data Protection' in Bing, J, and Torvund, O (eds), *25 Years Anniversary Anthology in Computers and Law* (TANO 1995) 83–104.

Ellger, R, *Der Datenschutz im grenzüberschreitende Datenverkehr: eine rechtsvergleichende und kollisionsrechtliche Untersuchung* (Nomos 1990).

Esayas, SY, 'A Walk in the Cloud and Cloudy It Remains: The Challenges and Prospects of "Processing" and "Transferring" Personal Data' (2012) 28 CLSR 662–78.

Eskeland, S, *Fangerett* (2nd edn, TANO 1989).

Essers, L, 'Facebook to Delete All European Facial Identification Data', *Computerworld* (21 September 2012); available at: <http://www.computerworld.com/s/article/9231566/Facebook_to_delete_all_European_facial_recognition_data>.

Farnsworth, DP, 'Data Privacy: An American's View of European Legislation' (1983) 6 Transnational Data Report, no. 5, 285–90.

Flaherty, DH, *Protecting Privacy in Surveillance Societies* (University of North Carolina Press, 1989).

Floridi, L, *Information: A Very Short Introduction* (OUP 2010).

Freund, PA, 'Privacy: One Concept or Many' in Pennock, JR, and Chapman, JW (eds), *Privacy: Nomos XIII* (Atherton Press 1971) 182–93.

Frowein, JA and Peukert, W, *Europäische MenschenRechtsKonvention: EMRK-Kommentar* (2nd edn, NP Engel 1996).

Gavison, R, 'Privacy and the Limits of Law' (1980) 89 Yale LJ 421–71.

Geiger, H, 'Europäischer Informationsmarkt und Datenschutz' (1989) 5 Recht der Datenverarbeitung, no. 5/6, 203–10.

Gellman, RM, 'Fragmented, Incomplete, and Discontinuous: The Failure of Federal Privacy Regulatory Proposals and Institutions' (1993) 4 Software LJ 199–238.

—— 'A General Overview of Video Surveillance Law in the United States' in Nouwt, S, de Vries, BR, and Prins, C (eds), *Reasonable Expectation of Privacy?* (TMC Asser 2005) ch 2.

Greenleaf, G, 'High Court Confirms Privacy Right against Governments' (1994) 1 PLPR 1–3.

—— 'Australia's APEC Privacy Initiative: The Pros and Cons of "OECD Lite"' (2003) 10 PLPR 1–6.

—— 'APEC's Privacy Framework Sets a New Low Standard for the Asia–Pacific' in Kenyon, AT, and Richardson, M (eds), *New Dimensions in Privacy Law: International and Comparative Perspectives* (CUP 2005) 91–120.

—— 'Australia' in Rule, JB, and Greenleaf, G (eds), *Global Privacy Protection: The First Generation* (Edward Elgar 2008) 141–73.

—— 'Data Surveillance in India: Multiple Accelerating Paths' (2010) Privacy Laws & Business Intl Report, no. 105, 15–17.

—— 'The Influence of European Data Privacy Standards outside Europe: Implications for Globalization of Convention 108' (2012) 2 IDPL 68–92.

—— ' "Modernising" Data Protection Convention 108: A Safe Basis for a Global Privacy Treaty?' (2013) 29 CLSR 430–6.

—— 'A World Data Privacy Treaty?: "Globalisation" and "Modernisation" of Council of Europe Convention 108' in Witzleb, N, Lindsay, D, Paterson, M, and Rodrick, S (eds), *Emerging Challenges in Privacy Law: Comparative Perspectives* (CUP forthcoming 2014) ch 6.

—— and Bygrave, LA, 'Not Entirely Adequate but far away: Lessons from How Europe sees New Zealand Data Protection' (2011) Privacy Laws & Business Intl Report, no. 111, 8–9.

—— and Waters, N, 'Obama's Privacy Framework: An Offer to Be Left on the Table?' (2012) Privacy Laws & Business Intl Report, no. 119, 6–9.

—— and Tian, GY, 'China Expands Data Protection through New 2013 Guidelines' (2013) Privacy Laws & Business Intl Report, no. 122, 1, 4–6.

Greer, D, 'Safe Harbor—a Framework That Works' (2011) 1 IDPL 143–8.

Grossman, GS, 'Transborder Data Flow: Separating the Privacy Interests of Individuals and Corporations' (1982) 4 Northwestern J of Intl Law and Business 1–36.

Guadamuz, A, 'Habeas Data: The Latin American Response to Data Protection' (2000) JILT, no. 2; available at: <http://www2.warwick.ac.uk/fac/soc/law/elj/jilt/2000_2/guadamuz/>.

—— 'Habeas Data vs the European Data Protection Directive' (2001) JILT, no. 3; available at: <http://www2.warwick.ac.uk/fac/soc/law/elj/jilt/2001_3/guadamuz>.

Harris, DJ, O'Boyle, M, Warbrick, C, and Bates, E, *Harris, O'Boyle & Warbrick: Law of the European Convention on Human Rights* (2nd edn, OUP 2009).

Hartlev, M, 'The Implementation of Data Protection Directive 95/46/EC in Denmark' in Beyleveld, D, Townend, D, Rouillé-Mirza, S, and Wright, J (eds), *Implementation of the Data Protection Directive in Relation to Medical Research in Europe* (Ashgate 2004) 57–71.

Heisenberg, D, *Negotiating Privacy: The European Union, The United States, and Personal Data Protection* (Lynne Rienner Publishers 2005).

Henke, F, *Die Datenschutzkonvention des Europarates* (Peter Lang 1986).

Hert de, P, 'Balancing Security and Liberty within the European Human Rights Framework: A Critical Reading of the Court's Case Law in the Light of Surveillance and Criminal Law Enforcement Strategies after 9/11' (2005) 1 Utrecht L Rev 68–92.

—— and Papakonstantinou, V, 'The Data Protection Framework Decision of November 27, 2008 Regarding Police and Judicial Cooperation in Criminal Matters—A Modest Achievement, However Not the Improvement Some Have Hoped for' (2009) 25 CLSR 403–14.

—— and Gutwirth, S, 'Data Protection in the Case Law of Strasbourg and Luxemburg: Constitutionalisation in Action' in Gutwirth, S, Poullet, Y, De Hert, P, de Terwangne, C and Nouwt, S (eds), *Reinventing Data Protection?* (Springer 2009) 14–29.

Hijmans, H, 'The European Data Protection Supervisor: The Institutions of the EC Controlled by an Independent Authority' (2006) 43 CML Rev 1313–42.

Hofmann, HCH, Rowe, GC, and Türk, AH, *Administrative Law and Policy of the European Union* (OUP 2011).

Hondius, FW, *Emerging Data Protection in Europe* (North Holland 1975).

Howe, DW, 'Victorian Culture in America' in Howe, DW (ed), *Victorian America* (University of Pennsylvania Press 1976) 3–28.

Hubbard, A and Bygrave, LA, 'Internet Governance goes Global' in Bygrave, LA, and Bing, J (eds), *Internet Governance: Infrastructure and Institutions* (OUP 2009) 213–35.

Hughes, GL, and Jackson, M, *Hughes on Data Protection in Australia* (2nd edn, Law Book Company 2001).

Inness, JC, *Privacy, Intimacy, and Isolation* (OUP 1992).

Karanja, SK, *Transparency and Proportionality in the Schengen Information System and Border Control Co-Operation* (Martinus Nijhoff 2008).

Keller, H, and Grover, L, 'General Comments of the Human Rights Committee and Their Legitimacy' in Keller, H, and Ulfstein, G (eds), *UN Human Rights Treaty Bodies: Law and Legitimacy* (CUP 2012) 116–98.

Kirby, MD, 'Legal Aspects of Transborder Data Flows' (1991) 5 Intl Computer Law Adviser, no. 5, 4–10.

—— 'Privacy Protection, a New Beginning: OECD Principles 20 Years On' (1999) 6 PLPR 25–9, 44.

Kirsch, WJ, 'The Protection of Privacy and Transborder Flows of Personal Data: The Work of the Council of Europe, the Organization for Economic Co-operation and Development and the European Economic Community' (1982) Legal Issues of European Integration, no. 2, 21–50.

Korff, D, *Study on the Protection of the Rights and Interests of Legal Persons with regard to the Processing of Personal Data relating to such Persons*, final report to European Commission (October 1998); available at: <http://papers.ssrn.com/sol3/papers.cfm?abstract_id=1288583>.

—— *Data Protection Law in the European Union* (Direct Marketing Association/ Federation of European Direct and Interactive Marketing 2005).

Kotschy, W, 'Commentary to Directive 95/46/EC' in Büllesbach, A, Gijbrath, S, Poullet, Y, and Prins, C (eds), *Concise European IT Law* (2nd edn, Kluwer Law International 2010) 49–64.

Kuner, C, *European Data Privacy Law and Online Business* (OUP 2003).

—— *European Data Protection Law: Corporate Compliance and Regulation* (2nd edn, OUP 2007).

—— 'An International Legal Framework for Data Protection: Issues and Prospects' (2009) 25 CLSR 307–17.

—— *Transborder Data Flows and Data Privacy Law* (OUP 2013).

—— and Cate, FH, Millard, C, and Svantesson, DJB, 'The End of the Beginning' (2012) 2 IDPL 115–16.

Laudon, KC, 'Markets and Privacy' (1996) 39 Communications of the Association for Computing Machinery 92–104.

Lenhart, A, and Madden, M, 'Teens, Privacy, and Online Social Networks' (Pew Research Center 2007); available at: <www.pewinternet.org/Reports/2007/Teens-Privacy-and-Online-Social-Networks.aspx>.

Lessig, L, *Code, and Other Laws of Cyberspace* (Basic Books 1999).

Lindsay, D, 'An Exploration of the Conceptual Basis of Privacy and the Implications for the Future of Australian Privacy Law' (2005) 29 Melbourne University L Rev 131–78.

Litman, J, 'Information Privacy/Information Property' (2000) 52 Stanford L Rev 1283–313.

Liu, N, *Bio-Privacy: Privacy Regulations and the Challenge of Biometrics* (Routledge 2011).

Lukes, S, *Individualism* (Blackwell 1973).

Lyon, D, *The Electronic Eye: The Rise of Surveillance Society* (Polity Press 1994).

Madden, M, Lenhart, A, Cortesi, S, Gasser, U, Duggan, M, Smith, A, and Beaton, M, 'Teens, Social Media, and Privacy' (Pew Research Center 2013); available at: <http://www.pewinternet.org/Reports/2013/Teens-Social-Media-And-Privacy.aspx>.

Mallmann, O, *Zielfunktionen des Datenschutzes: Schutz der Privatsphäre, korrekte Information; mit einer Studie zum Datenschutz im Bereich von Kreditinformationssystemen* (Metzner 1977).

Mahler, T, Ranheim, MR, and Cojocarasu, DI, 'Hvordan vurderer nasjonale domstoler datalagringsdirektivet opp mot grunn- og menneskerettigheter?' in Schartum, DW (ed), *Overvåking i en rettsstat* (Fagbokforlaget 2010) 147–64.

Makulilo, AB, 'Data Protection Regimes in Africa: Too far from the European "Adequacy" Standard?' (2013) 3 IDPL 42–50.

McGuire, RP, 'The Information Age: An Introduction to Transborder Data Flow' (1979–80) 20 Jurimetrics J 1–7.

Mell, P, 'Seeking Shade in a Land of Perpetual Sunlight: Privacy as Property in the Electronic Wilderness' (1996) 11 Berkeley Technology LJ 1–92.

Messadie, G, *La fin de la vie privée* (Calmann-Levy 1974).

Michael, J, *Privacy and Human Rights. An International and Comparative Study, with Special Reference to Developments in Information Technology* (UNESCO/Dartmouth 1994).

Miller, A, *The Assault on Privacy: Computers, Data Banks and Dossiers* (University of Michigan Press 1971).

Miyashita, H, 'The Evolving Concept of Data Privacy in Japanese Law' (2011) 1 IDPL 229–38.

—— 'Japan's New ID Number Act' (2013) Privacy Laws & Business Intl Report no. 124, 16.

Moerel, L, 'The Long Arm of EU Data Protection Law: Does the Data Protection Directive Apply to Processing of Personal Data of EU Citizens by Websites Worldwide?' (2011) 1 IDPL 28–46.

Moiny, J-P, 'Are Internet Protocol Addresses Personal? The Fight Against Online Copyright Infringement' (2011) 27 CLSR 348–61.

Napier, BW, 'International Data Protection Standards and British Experience' (1992) Informatica e diritto, no. 1–2, 83–100.

Newman, AL, *Protectors of Privacy: Regulating Personal Data in the Global Economy* (Cornell University Press 2008).

Niblett, GBF, *Digital Information and the Privacy Problem*, OECD Informatics Studies No. 2 (OECD 1971).

Nielsen, N, 'EU questions decade-old US data agreement', (EU Observer, 22 July 2013; <http://euobserver.com/justice/120919>.

Nissenbaum, H, *Privacy in Context: Technology, Policy, and the Integrity of Social Life* (Stanford University Press 2010).

Nugter, ACM, *Transborder Flow of Personal Data within the EC* (Kluwer Law and Taxation 1990).

Nys, H, 'Report on the Implementation of Directive 95/46/EC in Belgian Law' in Beyleveld, D, Townend, D, Rouillé-Mirza, S, and Wright, J (eds), *Implementation of the Data Protection Directive in Relation to Medical Research in Europe* (Ashgate 2004) 29–41.

Office of the US Special Trade Representative, 'Trade Barriers to Telecommunications, Data and Information Services' (1981) 4 Transnational Data Report, no. 5, 53.

Ong, R, 'Recognition of the Right to Privacy on the Internet in China' (2011) 1 IDPL 172–9.

Öman, S, 'Implementing Data Protection in Law' (2004) 47 Scandinavian Studies in Law 389–403.

Paine, C, Reips, U-D, Stieger, S, Joinson, A, and Buchanan, T, 'Internet Users' Perceptions of "Privacy Concerns" and "Privacy Actions"' (2007) 65 Intl J of Human-Computer Studies 526–36.

Passi, S, and Wyatt, S (eds), *Overview of Online Privacy, Reputation, Trust, and Identity Mechanisms* (EINS Consortium 2013); available at: <www.internet-science.eu/sites/internet-science.eu/files/biblio/EINS_D5_1_1_final_0.pdf>, ch 3.

Patton, MQ, *Qualitative Evaluation and Research Methods* (3rd edn, Sage 2002).

Pérez Asinari, MV, 'International Aspects of Data Protection: *Quo Vadis* EU?' in Pérez Asinari, MV and Palazzi, P (eds), *Défis du droit à la protection de la vie privée/ Challenges of privacy and data protection law* (Bruylant 2008) 381–413.

Phillipson, G, 'Transforming Breach of Confidence? Towards a Common Law Right of Privacy under the Human Rights Act' (2003) 66 MLR 726–58.

Pinegar, KR, 'Privacy Protection Acts: Privacy Protectionism or Economic Protectionism?' (1984) 12 Intl Business Lawyer 183–8.

Pinsent Masons, 'US Diplomat Warns of "Trade War" if "Right to Be Forgotten" Proposals Are Followed Through', *Out-Law.com*, 4 February 2013; <http://www.out-law.com/en/articles/2013/february/us-diplomat-warns-of-trade-war-if-right-to-be-forgotten-proposals-are-followed-through/>.

Poullet, Y, 'Data Protection between Property and Liberties—A Civil Law Approach' in Kaspersen, HWK, and Oskamp, A (eds), *Amongst Friends in Computers and Law: A Collection of Essays in Remembrance of Guy Vandenberghe* (Kluwer Law and Taxation Publishers 1990) 161–81.

—— and Gutwirth, S, 'The Contribution of the Article 29 Working Party to the Construction of a Harmonised European Data Protection System: An Illustration of "Reflexive Governance"'? in Pérez Asinari, MV, and Palazzi, P (eds), *Défis du droit à la protection de la vie privée/Challenges of privacy and data protection law* (Bruylant 2008) 569–609.

Prosser, WL, 'Privacy' (1960) 48 California L Rev 338–423.

Purtova, N, 'Private Law Solutions in European Data Protection: Relationship to Privacy, and Waiver of Data Protection Rights' (2010) 28 Netherlands Quarterly of Human Rights 179–98.

—— *Property Rights in Personal Data: A European Perspective* (Kluwer Law International 2012).

Raab, CD, 'Data Protection in Britain: Governance and Learning' (1993) 6 Governance 43–66.

—— 'Police Cooperation: The Prospects for Privacy' in Andersen, M, and Boer den, M (eds), *Policing Across National Boundaries* (Pinter 1994) 121–36.

—— 'Implementing Data Protection in Britain' (1996) 62 Intl Rev of Administrative Sciences 493–511.

—— and Bennett, CJ, 'Taking the Measure of Privacy: Can Data Protection Be Evaluated?' (1996) 62 Intl Rev of Administrative Sciences 535–56.

Ravlum, I-A, *Behandling av personopplysninger i norske virksomheter* (Transportøkonomisk Institutt 2006).

Rawls, J, *A Theory of Justice* (OUP 1972).

Regan, PM, 'Protecting Privacy and Controlling Bureaucracies: Constraints of British Constitutional Principles' (1990) 3 Governance 33–54.

—— *Legislating Privacy: Technology, Social Values, and Public Policy* (University of North Carolina Press 1995).

—— 'American Business and the European Data Protection Directive: Lobbying Strategies and Tactics' in Bennett, CJ and Grant, R (eds), *Visions of Privacy: Policy Choices for the Digital Age* (University of Toronto Press 1999) 199–216.

—— 'The United States' in Rule, JB, and Greenleaf, G (eds), *Global Privacy Protection. The First Generation* (Edward Elgar 2008) 50–80.

Reidenberg, JR, 'Resolving Conflicting International Data Privacy Rules in Cyberspace' (2000) 52 Stanford L Rev 1315–71.

Reyes, CL, 'WTO-Compliant Protection of Fundamental Rights: Lessons from the EU Privacy Directive' (2011) 12 Melbourne J of Intl L 141–76.

Rob, P, and Coronel, C, *Database Systems: Design, Implementation, and Management* (8th edn, Thomson 2009).

Rule, J, *Privacy in Peril* (OUP 2007).

—— and McAdam, D, Stearns, L, and Uglow, D, *The Politics of Privacy: Planning for Personal Data Systems as Powerful Technologies* (Elsevier 1980).

—— and Hunter, L, 'Towards Property Rights in Personal Data' in Bennett, CJ, and Grant, R (eds), *Visions of Privacy: Policy Choices for the Digital Age* (University of Toronto Press 1999) 168–81.

Saarenpää, A, 'Data Protection: In Pursuit of Information. Some Background to, and Implementations of, Data Protection in Finland' (1997) 11 Intl Rev of Law Computers and Technology 47–64.

Samuelsen, E, *Statlige databanker og personlighetsvern* (Universitetsforlaget 1972).

Schartum, DW, *Rettssikkerhet og systemutvikling i offentlig forvaltning* (Universitetsforlaget 1993).

Schwartz, PM, 'The Computer in German and American Constitutional Law: Towards an American Right of Informational Self-Determination' (1989) 37 American J of Comparative L 675–701.

—— 'European Data Protection Law and Restrictions on International Data Flows' (1995) 80 Iowa L Rev 471–96.

—— 'Property, Privacy, and Personal Data' (2004) 117 Harvard L Rev 2056–128.

—— 'The E.U.–U.S. Privacy Collision: A Turn to Institutions and Procedures' (2013) 126 Harvard L Rev 1966–2013.

—— and Reidenberg, JR, *Data Privacy Law: A Study of United States Data Protection* (Michie Law Publishers 1996).

Schweizer, RJ, 'Europäisches Datenschutzrecht—Was zu tun bleibt' (1989) Datenschutz und Datensicherung [later 'Datenschutz und Datensicherheit'], no. 11, 542–6.

Schwerdtner, P, *Das Persönlichkeitsrecht in der deutschen Zivilordnung* (J Schweitzer Verlag 1977).

Seip, H, 'Data Protection, Privacy and National Borders' in Bing, J and Torvund, O (eds), *25 Years Anniversary Anthology in Computers and Law* (TANO 1995) 67–82.

Seipel, P, 'Transborder Flows of Personal Data: Reflections on the OECD Guidelines' (1981) 4 Transnational Data Report, no. 1, 32–44.

Selmer, KS, 'Realising Data Protection' in Bing, J, and Torvund, O (eds), *25 Years Anniversary Anthology in Computers and Law* (TANO 1995) 41–65.

Shaffer, G, 'Globalization and Social Protection: The Impact of EU and International Rules in Ratcheting Up of U.S. Privacy Standards' (2000) 25 Yale J of Intl L 1–88.

Sieghart, P, *Privacy and Computers* (Latimer 1976).

Simitis, S, 'Die informationelle Selbstbestimmung—Grundbedingung einer verfassungs-konformen Informationsordnung' (1984) Neue juristische Wochenschrift 398–405.

—— 'Reviewing Privacy in an Information Society' (1987) 135 University of Pennsylvania L Rev 707–46.

—— 'Datenschutz und Europäische Gemeinschaft' (1990) 6 Recht der Datenverarbeitung, no. 1, 3–23.

—— ' "Sensitive Daten"—Zur Geschichte und Wirkung einer Fiktion' in Brem, E, Druey, JN, Kramer, EA, and Schwander, I (eds), *Festschrift zum 65. Geburtstag von Mario M. Pedrazzini* (Verlag Stämpfli & Cie 1990) 469–93.

—— 'From the Market to the Polis: The EU Directive on the Protection of Personal Data' (1995) 80 Iowa L Rev 445–69.

—— 'Das Volkzählungsurteil oder der lange Weg zur Informationsaskese— (BVerfGE 65, 1)' (2000) 83 Kritische Vierteljahresschrift für Gesetzgebung und Rechtswissenschaft 359–75.

—— (ed), *Bundesdatenschutzgesetz* (7th edn, Nomos 2011).

—— and Dammann, U, Mallmann, O, and Reh, HJ, *Kommentar zum Bundesdatenschutz-gesetz* (3rd edn, Nomos 1981).

Solove, DJ, *Understanding Privacy* (Harvard University Press 2008).

—— Rotenberg, M, and Schwartz, PM, *Information Privacy Law* (4th edn, Aspen Publishers 2011).

—— and Hartzog, W, 'The FTC and the New Common Law of Privacy' (2014) 114 Columbia L Rev (forthcoming).

Svantesson, DJB, 'Privacy, Internet and Transborder Data Flows: An Australian Perspective' (2010) 4 Masaryk University Journal of Law and Technology 1–20.

—— 'The Extraterritoriality of EU Data Privacy Law—Its Theoretical Justification and Its Practical Effect on US Businesses' (Working paper, 2013); available at: <http://works.bepress.com/dan_svantesson/55/>.

Swire, PP, and Litan, RE, *None of Your Business: World Data Flows, Electronic Commerce, and the European Privacy Directive* (Brookings Institution Press 1998).

Székely, I, 'Hungary Outlaws Personal Number' (1991) 14 Transnational Data Report, no. 5, 25–7.

—— 'New Rights and Old Concerns: Information Privacy in Public Opinion and in the Press in Hungary' (1994) 3 Informatization and the Public Sector 99–113.

—— 'Hungary' in Rule, JB, and Greenleaf, G (eds), *Global Privacy Protection: The First Generation* (Edward Elgar 2008) 174–206.

Tan, JG, 'A Comparative Study of the APEC Privacy Framework—A New Voice in the Data Protection Dialogue?' (2008) 3 Asian J of Comparative Law, issue 1, article 7; available at: <http://www.bepress.com/asjcl/vol3/iss1/art7/>.

Tapper, C, 'New European Directions in Data Protection' (1992) 3 J of Law and Information Systems 9–24.

Thomson, JJ, 'The Right to Privacy' (1975) 4 Philosophy and Public Affairs 295–314.

Torgersen, H, 'Forskning og personvern' in Blekeli, RD, and Selmer, KS (eds), *Data og personvern* (Universitetsforlaget 1977) 223–37.

Traça, JL, and Embry, B, 'An Overview of the Legal Regime for Data Protection in Cape Verde' (2011) 1 IDPL 249–55.

—— 'The Angolan Data Protection Act: First Impressions' (2012) 2 IDPL 40–5.

Vitalis, A, 'France' in Rule, JB, and Greenleaf, G (eds), *Global Privacy Protection: The First Generation* (Edward Elgar 2008) 107–40.

Wacks, R, *Personal Information: Privacy and the Law* (Clarendon Press, 1989).

Wang, H, *Protecting Privacy in China: A Research on China's Privacy Standards and the Possibility of Establishing the Right to Privacy and the Information Privacy Protection Legislation in Modern China* (Springer 2011).

Ware, WH, 'A Historical Note' in US Department of Health and Human Services, Task Force on Privacy, *Health Records: Social Needs and Personal Privacy* (Conference Proceedings) (US Government Printing Office 1993) Addendum A.

Warner, M, and Stone, M, *The Data Bank Society: Organizations, Computers and Social Freedom* (Allen & Unwin 1970).

Warren, S, and Brandeis, L, 'The Right to Privacy' (1890) 4 Harvard L Rev 193–220.

Waters, N, 'The APEC Asia-Pacific Privacy Initiative—a New Route to Effective Data Protection or a Trojan Horse for Self-regulation?' (2009) 6 SCRIPTed 75; available at: <http://www.law.ed.ac.uk/ahrc/script-ed/vol6-1/waters.asp>.

Weber, RH, 'Regulatory Autonomy and Privacy Standards under the GATS' (2012) 7 Asian J of WTO and Intl Health Law and Policy 25–48.

Westin, AF, *Privacy and Freedom* (Atheneum 1970).

—'Civil Liberties and Computerized Data Systems' in Greenberger, M (ed), *Computers, Communications, and the Public Interest* (The Johns Hopkins Press 1971) 151–68.

Whitman, JQ, 'The Two Western Cultures of Privacy: Dignity versus Liberty' (2004) 113 Yale LJ 1151–221.

Wiik Johansen, M, Kaspersen, K-B, and Bergseng Skullerud, ÅM, *Personopplysningsloven. Kommentarutgave* (Universitetsforlaget 2001).

Wilson, KG, *Technologies of Control: The New Interactive Media for the Home* (University of Wisconsin Press 1988).

Yourow, HC, *The Margin of Appreciation Doctrine in the Dynamics of the European Court of Human Rights Jurisprudence* (Martinus Nijhoff 1996).

## B. REPORTS AND OTHER DOCUMENTS

### Australia

Australian Law Reform Commission, *Privacy*, Report No. 22 (AGPS 1983).

—— *For Your Information: Australian Privacy Law and Practice*, Report No. 108 (ALRC 2008).

Morison, WL, Report on the Law of Privacy to the Standing Committee of Commonwealth and State Attorneys-General, Report no. 170/1973 (AGPS 1973).

Office of Australian Federal Privacy Commissioner, *Community Attitudes to Privacy*, Information Paper 3 (AGPS 1995).

—— *Getting in on the Act: The Review of the Private Sector Provisions of the Privacy Act 1988* (AGPS 2005).

**Council of Europe**

*(i) Resolutions*

Resolution (73) 22 on the Protection of the Privacy of Individuals vis-à-vis Electronic Data Banks in the Private Sector (adopted 26 September 1973).

Resolution (74) 29 on the Protection of the Privacy of Individuals vis-à-vis Electronic Data Banks in the Public Sector (adopted 24 September 1974).

*(ii) Recommendations*

Recommendation R (80) 2 on exercise of discretionary powers by administrative authorities (adopted 11 March 1980).

Recommendation R (81) 19 on access to information held by public authorities (adopted 25 November 1981).

Recommendation R (83) 10 on the protection of personal data used for scientific research and statistics (adopted 23 September 1983).

Recommendation R (87) 15 regulating the use of personal data in the police sector (adopted 17 September 1987).

Recommendation R (89) 2 on the protection of personal data used for employment purposes (adopted 18 January 1989).

Recommendation R(90) 13 on prenatal genetic screening, prenatal genetic diagnosis and associated genetic counselling (adopted 21 June 1990).

Recommendation R (91) 10 on the communication to third parties of personal data held by public bodies (adopted 9 September 1991).

Recommendation R (92) 1 on use of analysis of deoxyribonucleic acid (DNA) within the framework of the criminal justice system (adopted 10 February 1992).

Recommendation R (92) 3 on genetic testing and screening for health care purposes (adopted 10 February 1992).

Recommendation R (95) 4 on the protection of personal data in the area of telecommunications services, with particular reference to telephone services (adopted 7 February 1995).

Recommendation R (97) 5 on the protection of medical data (adopted 13 February 1997).

Recommendation R (97) 18 on the protection of personal data collected and processed for statistical purposes (adopted 30 September 1997).

Recommendation R (99) 5 for the protection of privacy on the internet (adopted 23 February 1999).

Recommendation R (2002) 9 on the protection of personal data collected and processed for insurance purposes (adopted 18 September 2002).

Recommendation Rec (2006) 4 on research on biological materials of human origin (adopted 15 March 2006).

Recommendation CM/Rec (2010) 13 on the protection of individuals with regard to automatic processing of personal data in the context of profiling (adopted 23 November 2010).

Recommendation CM/Rec (2012) 3 on the protection of human rights with regard to search engines (adopted 4 April 2012)

Recommendation CM/Rec (2012) 4 on the protection of human rights with regard to social networking services (adopted 4 April 2012).

*(iii) Reports and opinions*

Consultative Committee of the Convention for the Protection of Individuals with regard to Automatic Processing of Personal Data, 'Modernisation of Convention 108' (T-PD(2012)4Rev3_en, 29 November 2012).

—— 'Opinion on Uruguay's request to be invited to accede to Convention 108 and its additional Protocol' (T-PD (2011) 08 rev en, 26 May 2011).

—— 'Kingdom of Morocco—request to be invited to accede to Convention 108' (T-PD (2012) 09 rev, 18 October 2012).

**Denmark**

*Delbetænkning om private registre*, Bet 687 (Statens trykningskontor 1973).

**European Union**

*(i) Commission*

Communication: Safeguarding Privacy in a Connected World: A European Data Protection Framework for the 21st Century (COM(2012) 9 final).

Decision 2000/520/EC on the adequacy of the protection provided by the safe harbor privacy principles and related frequently asked questions issued by the US Department of Commerce [2000] OJ L215/7.

Decision 2001/497/EC on standard contractual clauses for the transfer of personal data to third countries, under Directive 95/46/EC [2001] OJ L181/19.

Decision 2004/915/EC amending Decision 2001/497/EC as regards the introduction of an alternative set of standard contractual clauses for the transfer of personal data to third countries [2004] OJ L385/74.

Decision on standard contractual clauses for the transfer of personal data to processors established in third countries under Directive 95/46/EC of the European Parliament and of the Council [2010] OJ L39/5.

Evaluation report on the Data Retention Directive (Directive 2006/24/EC) (COM (2011) 225 final).

First Report on the Implementation of the Data Protection Directive (95/46/EC) (COM(2003) 265 final).

Proposal for a Directive on the protection of individuals with regard to the processing of personal data by competent authorities for the purposes of prevention, investigation, detection or prosecution of criminal offences or the execution of criminal penalties, and the free movement of such data (COM(2012) 10 final).

Proposal for a Regulation on the protection of individuals with regard to the processing of personal data and on the free movement of such data (General Data Protection Regulation) (COM(2012) 11 final).

Recommendation 81/679/EEC relating to the Council of Europe convention for the protection of individuals with regard to automatic processing of personal data [1981] OJ L246/31.

*(ii) European Parliament*

Legal Affairs Committee, Subcommittee on Data Processing and Individual Rights, *Verbatim record of the public hearing on data processing and the rights of the individual* (PE 52.496, 6 February 1978).

—— *Report on the Protection of the Rights of the Individual in the Face of Technical Developments in Data Processing* (the 'Bayerl Report') (EP Doc 100/79, PE 56.386 final, 4 May 1979).

—— *Second Report on the Protection of the Rights of the Individual in the Face of Technical Developments in Data Processing* (the 'Sieglerschmidt Report') (EP Doc 1-548/81, PE 70.166 final, 12 October 1981).

Resolution on the protection of the rights of the individual in the face of developing technical progress in the field of automatic data processing [1975] OJ C60/48.

Resolution on the protection of the rights of the individual in the face of developing technical progress in the field of automatic data processing [1976] OJ C100/27.

Resolution on the protection of the rights of the individual in the face of technical developments in data processing [1979] OJ C140/34.

Resolution on the protection of the rights of the individual in the face of technical developments in data processing [1982] OJ C87/39.

Resolution on the Draft Commission Decision on the adequacy of the protection provided by the Safe Harbour Principles and related Frequently Asked Questions issued by the US Department of Commerce [2001] OJ C121/152.

Resolution on the US National Security Agency surveillance programme, surveillance bodies in various Member States and their impact on EU citizens' privacy (P7_TA(2013)0322, 4 July 2013).

*(iii) Council*

Conclusions of the European Council 24/25 October 2013 (EUCO 169/13; 25 October 2013); <http://www.consilium.europa.eu/uedocs/cms_data/docs/pressdata/en/ec/139197.pdf>.

*(iv) Article 29 Working Party*

Declaration of the Article 29 Working Party on enforcement (24 November 2004; WP 101).

Joint Opinion on the Proposal for a Council Framework Decision on the Use of Passenger Name Records (PNR) for Law Enforcement Purposes, Presented by the Commission on 6 November (5 December 2007; WP145).

Opinion 3/2001 on the level of protection of the Australian Privacy Amendment (Private Sector) Act 2000 (26 January 2001; WP 40).

Opinion 8/2001 on the processing of personal data in the employment context (13 September 2001; WP 48).

Opinion 4/2007 on the concept of personal data (20 June 2007; WP 136).
Opinion 11/2011 on the level of protection of personal data in New Zealand (4 April 2011; WP 182).
Opinion 5/2012 on cloud computing (1 July 2012; WP 196).
Opinion 2/2013 on apps on smart devices (27 February 2013; WP 202).
Opinion 3/2013 on purpose limitation (2 April 2013; WP 203).
Press release: 'Google: The Beginnings of a Dialog' (16 September 2008).
Recommendation 1/2007 on the standard application for approval of binding corporate rules for the transfer of personal data (10 January 2007; WP133).
Working Document on notification (3 December 1997; WP8).
Working Document on transfers of personal data to third countries: Applying Articles 25 and 26 of the EU data protection directive (24 July 1998; WP12).
Working Document on biometrics (1 August 2003; WP 80).
Working Document on data protection issues related to RFID technology (19 January 2005, WP 105).
Working Document establishing a model checklist application for approval of Binding Corporate Rules (14 April 2005; WP 108).
Working Document setting up a framework for the structure of Binding Corporate Rules (28 June 2008; WP 154).

*(v) EU Agency for Fundamental Rights*

*Data Protection in the European Union: the Role of National Data Protection Authorities* (Publications Office of the EU 2010).

### Norway

*(i) Parliamentary papers*

Odelsinnstilling no. 47 (1977–78), *Om lov om personregistre mm.*
Odelstingsproposisjon no. 2 (1977–78), *Om lov om personregistre mm.*
Odelstingsproposisjon no. 92 (1998–99), *Om lov om behandling av personopplysninger (personopplysningsloven).*

*(ii) NOU Reports*

*Persondata og personvern*, NOU 1974:22.
*Offentlige persondatasytem og personvern*, NOU 1975:10.

### OECD

*(i) Guidelines, recommendations, and declarations*

Declaration for the Future of the Internet Economy (Seoul Declaration) (18 June 2008; C(2008)99).
Guidelines on the Protection of Privacy and Transborder Flows of Personal Data (1980).
Guidelines for the Security of Information Systems (1992).
Guidelines for Cryptography Policy (1997).
Guidelines for Consumer Protection in the Context of Electronic Commerce (1999).

Guidelines for the Security of Information Systems and Networks (2002).
Guidelines on Human Biobanks and Genetic Research Databases (2009).
Recommendation of the Council concerning Guidelines governing the Protection of Privacy and Transborder Flows of Personal Data (23 September 1980; (C(80)58/FINAL).
Recommendation of the Council on Cross-Border Co-operation in the Enforcement of Laws Protecting Privacy (12 June 2007; C(2007)67).
Recommendation of the Council concerning Guidelines governing the Protection of Privacy and Transborder Flows of Personal Data (11 July 2013; (C(2013)79).

*(ii) Reports*
*Policy Issues in Data Protection and Privacy* (1976).

**Sweden**
*Data och integritet*, SOU 1972:47.
*En ny datalag*, SOU 1993:10.

**United Kingdom**
Committee on Privacy (the Younger Committee), *Report of the Committee on Privacy*, Cmnd 5012 (HMSO 1972).

**United Nations**
General Assembly, *Guidelines Concerning Computerized Personal Data Files* (Doc E/CN.4/1990/72).
Human Rights Committee, *General Comment 16* (UN Doc A/43/40, 181–183; UN Doc CCPR/C/21/Add.6; UN Doc HRI/GEN/1/Rev 1, 21–23).

**United States of America**
Clinton, W, and Gore, A Jr, *A Framework for Global Electronic Commerce* (US Government Printing Office 1997).
Department of Health, Education and Welfare (DHEW), Secretary's Advisory Committee on Automated Personal Data Systems: *Records, Computers, and the Rights of Citizens* (US Government Printing Office 1973).
Federal Trade Commission, *Protecting Consumer Privacy in an Era of Rapid Change: Recommendations for Businesses and Policymakers* (March 2012); available at: <http://ftc.gov/os/2012/03/120326privacyreport-pdf>.
Information Infrastructure Task Force, *Privacy and the National Information Infrastructure: Principles for Providing and Using Personal Information* (June 1995); available at: <http://aspe.hhs.gov/datacncl/niiprivp.htm>.
National Conference of State Legislatures, 'State Security Breach Notification Laws' (20 August 2012); available at: <http://www.ncsl.org/issues-research/telecom/security-breach-notification-laws.aspx>.
Privacy Protection Study Commission, *Personal Privacy in an Information Society* (US Government Printing Office 1977).

The White House, *Consumer Data Privacy in a Networked World: A Framework for Protecting Privacy and Promoting Innovation in the Global Digital Economy* (US Government Printing Office 2012).

**Miscellaneous**

Association of South East Asian Nations (ASEAN), *ASEAN Economic Community Blueprint* (January 2008); available at: <http://www.asean.org/archive/5187-10.pdf>.

Dhont, J, Asinari, MVP, Poullet, Y, Reidenberg, JR, and Bygrave, LA, 'Safe Harbour Decision Implementation Study', Report for European Commission (April 2004); available at: <http://ec.europa.eu/justice/policies/privacy/docs/studies/safe-harbour-2004_en.pdf>.

International Labour Office (ILO), *Protection of Workers' Personal Data* (ILO 1997).

LRDP KANTOR Ltd and Centre for Public Reform for the European Commission, 'Comparative Study on Different Approaches to New Privacy Challenges, in Particular in the Light of Technological Developments: Final Report', Report for the European Commission (20 January 2010); available at: <http://ec.europa.eu/justice/policies/privacy/docs/studies/new_privacy_challenges/final_report_en.pdf>.

Nordic Council of Ministers, *Information Security in Nordic Countries*, Nordiske Seminar- og Arbejdsrapporter 1993: 613 (Nordic Council of Ministers 1993).

Reding, V, and Bryson, J, 'EU–U.S. joint statement on data protection by European Commission Vice-President Viviane Reding and U.S. Secretary of Commerce John Bryson', Brussels, 19 March 2012; available at: <http://europa.eu/rapid/press-release_MEMO-12-192_en.htm>.

# Index

access
  illegal 132–3
  rights of 52, 91, 96–7, 159–60
accountability 47–8, 77, 78, 209
accuracy 36, 52, 163
adequate protection 39n, 63, 81, 100, 123, 191–5
administrative law 11–12, 149, 182
African regulatory initiatives 80–2, 83, 105–6
Air Passenger Name Records 69, 197
Angola 105
APEC (Asia-Pacific Economic Cooperation) 19, 50, 207
  regulatory initiatives 75–9, 83
applicable law 39–40, 63, 199–203
Area of Freedom, Security and Justice (AFSJ) xxvii, 69–71
Argentina 103
ASEAN (Association of South East Asian Nations) 79, 83, 207
Australia 6, 15, 50, 79, 103, 117–18, 140, 182
  national identity card 20–1, 122
Austria 139, 142, 171, 201n
authoritarian repression 10, 113

Belgium 15, 118n
Benin 105, 106
Bennett, CJ 6n, 7, 20, 25, 109
biobanks 16–17, 128
biological material 126–9
biometric data 126, 165
Blume, P 73
Brazil 102–3, 124
Bryson, John 207
Burkina Faso 105, 106
Burnett, M 79

Canada 15, 50, 102, 181–2
Cape Verde 105
case law 3, 13
CCTV 89
celebrities 90
China 104, 209
choice of law 39–40, 63, 199–203
choice principle 76
civil society groups 19

collective entities 139–40
collection limitation 45
collision of laws 39–40, 190, 199
Colombia 103
comparative law xxvi
compensation 187–8
competition law 15
compliance burdens 71, 73, 186
compliance levels 189–90
computerization 23–4
conceptualization 23–9
conflicts of laws 39–40, 190, 199
consensus 205–9
consent 91, 160–1
consequentialist ideology 112, 113
context, respect for 115, 156–7
controllers 17
  accountability 48
  communication to data subjects 47
  compliance burdens 71, 73, 186
  Convention 108 31–6, 101–2, 206–7
    basic principles 36–8, 119
    gaps in 38–41
    harmonization of data privacy regions 34
    incorporation into domestic legislation 35–6
    non-member signatories 32–3
    sectoral recommendations 41–3
convergence of policy 109
co-regulation 178–9
core principles 1–2
  data quality 12, 52, 163–4
  data security 2, 164
  data subject influence 158–63
  definition and role of principles 145–6
  fair and lawful processing 146–7
  minimality 151–2
  proportionality 2, 59, 95, 147–50
  purpose limitation 153–7
  sensitivity 165–7
  see also sensitive data
Costa Rica 103
Council of Europe (CoE) 12, 17, 18, 206
  Convention 108 31–6, 101–2, 206–7
    basic principles 36–8, 119
    gaps in 38–41
    harmonization of data privacy regimes 34, 41

Council of Europe (CoE) (*cont.*):
  Convention (*cont.*):
    incorporation into domestic legislation 35–6
    non-member signatories 32–3
    sectoral recommendations 41–3
Court of Justice of the EU (CJEU) 58, 60–1,
  70, 149, 150, 170, 179, 185, 191–2
courts 18, 179–83
cross-jurisdictional variations xxvii–xxviii
  choice of law 39–40, 63, 199–203
  conflicts of laws 39–40, 190, 199
customer lists 5

Dammann, U 136
data controllers *see* controllers
data privacy agencies (DPAs) 3–4, 18, 19, 52,
  64, 73, 74, 169–70
  duties and competence 172–3
  independence 170–2
  privacy enforcement authorities 49–50
  transnational cooperation 174–5
data privacy law
  actors in the field 17
    legislative field 18–20
    operative sphere 17–18
  aims 117
    economic protectionism 123–5
    formal aims 118–21
    less formal aims 121–5
    obscurity of 117–18
  catalysts and origins 8
    fears 10–11
    legal factors 11–15
    technological and organizational
      developments 9–10
  core principles *see* core principles
  definition of field 1–4
  implementation *see* oversight and enforcement
  nomenclature and conceptualization 23–9
  regulatory cross-fertilization and
    colonization 15–17
  scope 126
    collective entities 139–40
    definition of data and information 126–9
    personal data *see* personal data
    type of data 129
    type of data processing 140–2
    type of sector 142–4
  significance of field 4–8
data processing 140–2
data processors *see* processors
data protection 26, 28
  relationship to privacy 28–9
Data Protection Directive (DPD) 53–4, 122,
  125, 134

content 63–4
data protection as fundamental right 58–9
field of application 62
gestation 54–6
harmonization efforts 59–61
interpretation and policy thrust 56–8
rules on applicable law 199–202
data quality 12, 52, 163–4
Data Retention Directive 66–8, 114
data security 2, 164
data subjects 9, 12, 17
  access rights 91, 96–7, 159–60
  communication by data controllers 47
  consent 160–1
  influence over data processing 158–63
defamation 11
De Hert, P 93
Denmark 16, 139
'digital natives' 22–3
DNA profiles 128
domestic purposes 143–4
Dubai 106

Economic Community of West African States
  (ECOWAS) 19, 80
economic protectionism 35, 123–5
electronic communications 64–8
employee surveillance 8
enforcement *see* oversight and enforcement
E-Privacy Directive (EPD) 64–6, 114, 139
equivalent protection 38, 48
EU legislation xxv, 6–7, 101
  Data Protection Directive (DPD) 53–4,
    122, 125, 134
    content 63–4
    data protection as fundamental
      right 58–9
    field of application 62
    gestation 54–6
    harmonization efforts 59–61
    interpretation and policy thrust 56–8
    rules on applicable law 199–202
  Data Retention Directive 66–8, 114
  E-Privacy Directive (EPD) 64–6, 114, 139
  global standard setting 208
  proportionality principle 2, 59, 95, 147–50
  proposed General Data Protection
    Regulation 71, 72–5, 159, 165, 176,
    178, 186, 202, 207
  right to private life 6, 58
  Social Charter 8
Eurojust 69
European Commission 54–6, 176–7, 186, 189
European Convention on Human Rights
  Article 8 34, 38, 40, 86, 111

access and rectification rights 96–7
  interference 90–2
  justification for interference 92–6
  object and ambit 87–90
  Article 13 97–8
European Court of Human Rights 86–98,
  128–9, 148, 150, 154, 171, 179
European Data Protection Supervisor
  (EDPS) 68–9
European Direct Marketing Association 19
European Economic Area (EEA) 54
European Union 18
  Area of Freedom, Security and Justice (AFSJ)
    xxvii, 69–71
  Court of Justice (CJEU) 58, 60–1, 70, 149,
    150, 170, 179, 185, 191–2
  institutions 68–9
  internal market 55, 57
  legislation *see* EU legislation
  Safe Harbor Agreement 76, 133, 177, 178,
    195, 196, 197, 198, 209
Europol 69

Facebook 114, 208
fair and lawful processing 146–7
fair information practice 27, 29, 33–4,
  115–16, 148
fears 10–11
Federal Trade Commission (FTC) 110–11,
  114–15, 177–8
Finland 6, 7, 95, 120, 135
framework laws 3
France 15, 119, 139
freedom of expression 11, 111
freedom of information (FOI) 2, 11, 12, 15
Freund, PA 119
fundamental rights 58–9, 82–98

General Data Protection Regulation
  (proposed) 71, 72–5, 159, 165, 176, 178,
  186, 202, 207
genetic information 42, 165
  biobanks 16–17
Germany 6, 15, 21, 26, 28, 99, 120–1, 135–6,
  150, 152, 170–1, 179–81
global consensus 205–9
Google 114, 115, 208
Greenleaf, G 206–7

habeas data 26, 102–3
harmonization 34, 59–61, 74, 205, 207
harms-focused ideology 77, 112
Hofmann, HCH 69
Hondius, FW 24, 54
human rights xxvi, 12–13, 57, 58, 82–98

human rights treaties 82–3
  ECHR Article 8 34, 38, 40, 86, 111
    access and rectification rights 96–7
    interference 90–2
    justification for interference 92–6
    object and ambit 87–90
  ECHR Article 13 97–8
  ICCPR Article 17 85–6
Hungary 15, 21n, 180
Hustinx, Peter 20

Iceland 139
identification/identifiability 130
  accuracy of link between data and
    individual 133–4
  ease of 130–2
  IP addresses 137–8
  legally relevant agent of 132–3
  requirement of individuation 135
  restricting expansive potential 135–7
  use of auxiliary information 134–5
ideological positions 7, 25, 112
illegal access 132–3
India 104–5
industry groups 19, 116
information and communication technology
  (ICT) 9, 24
information control 27, 28
'information society' 5
intellectual property rights (IPR) 13
inter-governmental organizations 19
International Chamber of Commerce 19
international codes xxv, 31
  African initiatives 80–2, 83
  APEC initiatives 75–9, 83
  ASEAN initiatives 79
  Council of Europe *see* Council of Europe
  EU initiatives *see* EU legislation
  harmonization 34, 59–61, 74,
    205–6, 207
  human rights *see* human rights treaties *and*
    fundamental rights
  OECD initiatives 43–51
  sectoral instruments
    Area of Freedom, Security and Justice
      (AFSJ) 69–71
    current reform 71–5
    electronic communications 64–8
    EU institutions 68–9
  UN initiatives 51–3
international commerce 11
International Labour Organisation 19
International Telecommunications Union 19
Internet 5, 64, 143–4, 149, 191–2,
  202, 208

interoperability 49, 78
intimate information 27, 36–7
  *see also* sensitive data
IP (Internet Protocol) addresses 137–8
Ireland 138
ISPs (Internet Service Providers) 138n, 149
Israel 106
Italy 139

Japan 103, 178, 190
journalistic purposes 143
judiciary 18, 179–83

Kirby, Michael 20, 44, 110
Korff, D 117
Kuner, C 125

labour law 13
lawful processing 146–7
legislation 3, 11–15
  actors in the field 18–20
  *see also* EU legislation; international codes;
    national legislation
Leonard, P 79
liberal democracies 7, 25
licensing 183–6
Lindsay, D 112, 113, 117
location data 65n

McNealy, Scott 22
mass mobilization 20–1
Mauritius 105, 106
medical data 95–6
Mexico 103
minimality 151–2
monitoring regimes 63, 169–86
  *see also* oversight and enforcement
Morocco 33, 105, 106
'multi-stakeholderism' 206

Napier, BW 117
national legislation 99–100
  Africa and Middle East 105–6
  Americas 102–3
    *see also* USA
  Asia and Oceania 103–5
  Europe 100–2
national security 62, 143
necessity 94–6, 148, 150
Netherlands 6, 101
Newman, AL 113, 208
New Zealand 50, 103, 122
nomenclature 23–9
non-governmental organizations 19, 77

Norway 12, 26, 120, 124, 127, 134, 139, 141,
    144n, 153, 156–7, 179, 185
notification schemes 183–6

OECD (Organisation for Economic
    Cooperation and Development) 17, 18,
    206
  Guidelines 43–51, 75, 76, 109, 199
organizational developments 9–10
oversight and enforcement
  data privacy agencies (DPAs) 3–4, 18, 19,
      52, 64, 73, 74, 169–70
    duties and competence 172–3
    independence 170–2
    transnational cooperation 174–5
  inter-legal aspects 190
    applicable law 199–203
    transborder data flow 190–8
  international level 175–7
  judiciary 179–83
  national level 177–9
  notification and licensing schemes 183–6
  sanctions and remedies 186–90

personal data 4–5, 22, 24, 46, 48, 55, 57, 63,
    64, 74, 78, 181
  biological material 126–9
  commercial use 114–15
  definition 129–30
  ICCPR Article 17 84–5
  identification/identifiability 130
    accuracy of link between data and
        individual 133–4
    ease of 130–2
    IP addresses 137–8
    legally relevant agent of 132–3
    requirement of individuation 135
    restricting expansive potential 135–7
    use of auxiliary information 134–5
  medical data 95–6
  re-purposing 91
Personal Identification Numbers (PINs) 10
personal integrity 26, 118
personal purposes 143–4
political ideologies 7, 25
population databases 10
Portugal 118
principles of data privacy law *see* core
    principles
PRISM 5n, 125, 195, 196, 197, 207
privacy concerns 3, 5, 6, 23, 28–9,
    118–19
privacy definitions 27–8
Privacy International 19

privacy paradigm 25, 108
private life, right to 5–6, 58, 87, 88
private sector 142–3
procedural fairness 12
procedural principles *see* core principles
processors 18
property rights 14
proportionality principle 2, 59, 95, 147–50
protectionism 35, 123–5
public concern 20–3
public figures 90
public sector 142–3
purpose limitation 46–7, 91, 153–7
purpose specification 52

Raab, CD 25
reasonableness 132
rectification rights 96, 163
Reding, Viviane 20, 197, 207
Regan, PM 110
regulatory bodies
    international level 175–7
    national level 177–9
    *see also* data privacy agencies
regulatory colonization 16–17
regulatory cross-fertilization 15–17
remedies 186–90
re-purposing 9, 91
risk assessment 37n, 48, 186
Rowe, GC 69
Russian Federation 101–2

Safe Harbor Agreement 76, 133, 177, 178,
    195, 196, 197, 198, 209
sanctions 186–90
Schengen Information System (SIS) 69
Schwartz, PM 110
sectoral differentiation 142–4
sectoral instruments
    Area of Freedom, Security and Justice
        (AFSJ) 69–71
    current reform 71–5
    electronic communications 64–8
    EU institutions 68–9
security breach notification 48, 114, 186
self-regulation 50
semantics 24
sensitive data 27, 36–7, 46, 52–3, 165–7
Seychelles 105, 106
Simitis, Spiros 20, 121, 207
soft law 3, 53
South Africa 105, 106, 139
South America 26, 102–3
state security 62
    agencies 90, 92, 93

statutory law *see* legislation
supervisory regimes 63
    *see also* oversight and enforcement
surveillance 89, 90–1, 94
    telephone tapping 92, 93
    *see also* PRISM
Svantesson, DJB 202
Sweden 11, 26, 28, 99, 101, 124–5, 154, 185
SWIFT 177
Switzerland 26, 138, 139

technological developments 9–10
telephone tapping 92, 93
totalitarianism 113
trade-union membership 37n, 165
traffic data 65n, 66, 114
transborder data flows (TBDF) 10, 34,
    43, 45, 48, 49, 53, 63, 77, 78, 100,
    110, 123–5
    adequate protection 191, 192, 193, 194,
        195
    Safe Harbor Agreement 76, 133, 177, 178,
        195, 196, 197, 198, 209
transnational cooperation 45, 174–5
Trinidad and Tobago 103
Tunisia 105, 106

UK 6, 7, 15, 136–7, 154, 177, 182–3
United Nations (UN) 18, 51–3
Uruguay 33, 103
USA 13, 21, 24, 27, 33–4, 99–100
    Federal Trade Commission (FTC) 110–11,
        114–15, 177–8
    marginalization 208
    PRISM 5n, 125, 195, 196, 197, 207
    Safe Harbor Agreement 76, 133, 177, 178,
        195, 196, 197, 198, 209
    Supreme Court 111, 181
    transatlantic data privacy divide 107, 208–9
        commonality 108–9
        difference 109–11
        explanations for 112–16
utilitarian ideology 112

'war on terror' 5
    *see also* PRISM
Westin, Alan 20, 21
Whitman, JQ 112
worker co-determination 13
workplace surveillance 8
World Intellectual Property Organisation
    (WIPO) 18
World Trade Organisation (WTO) 19, 198
World Wide Web Consortium 19